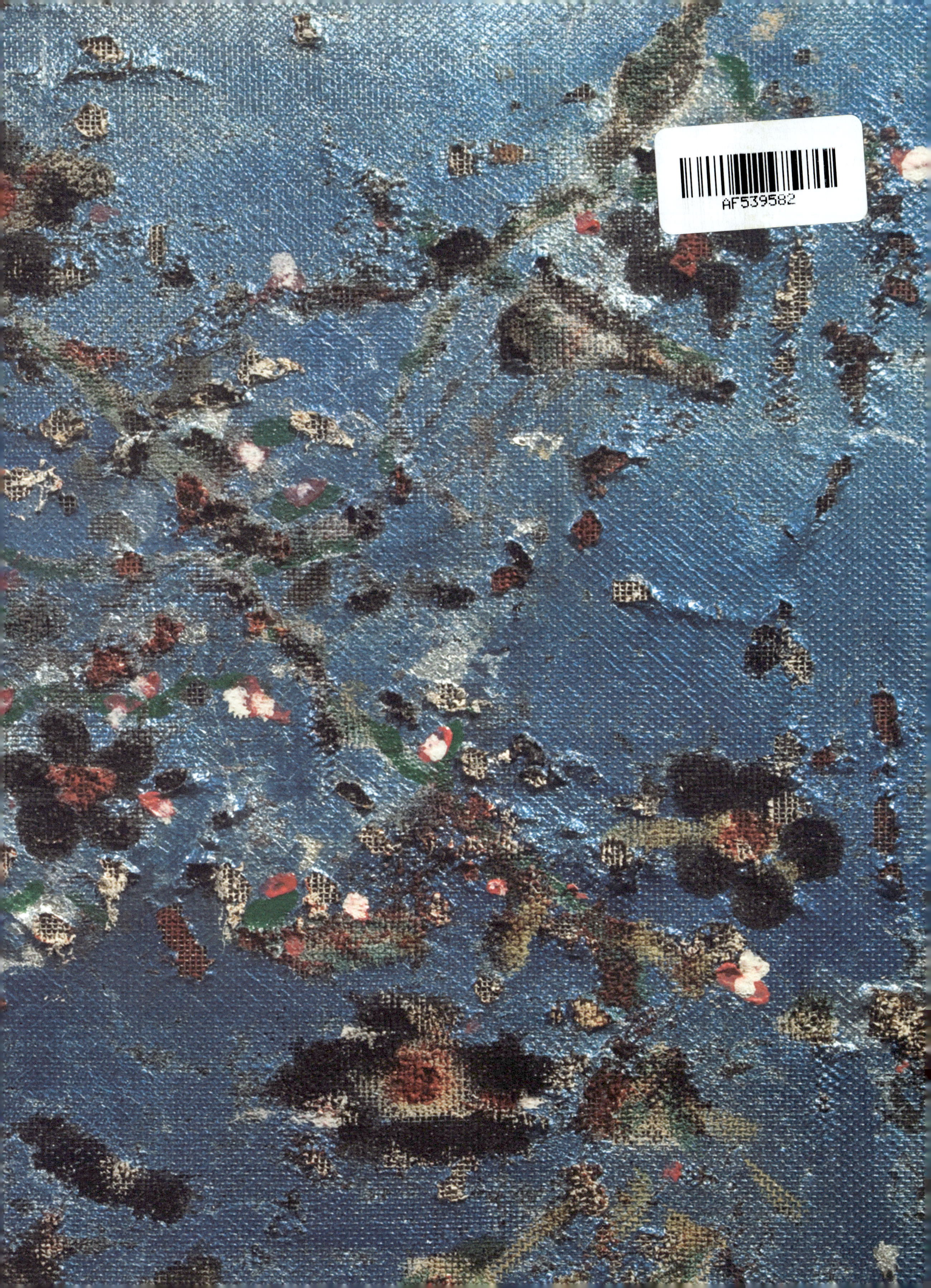

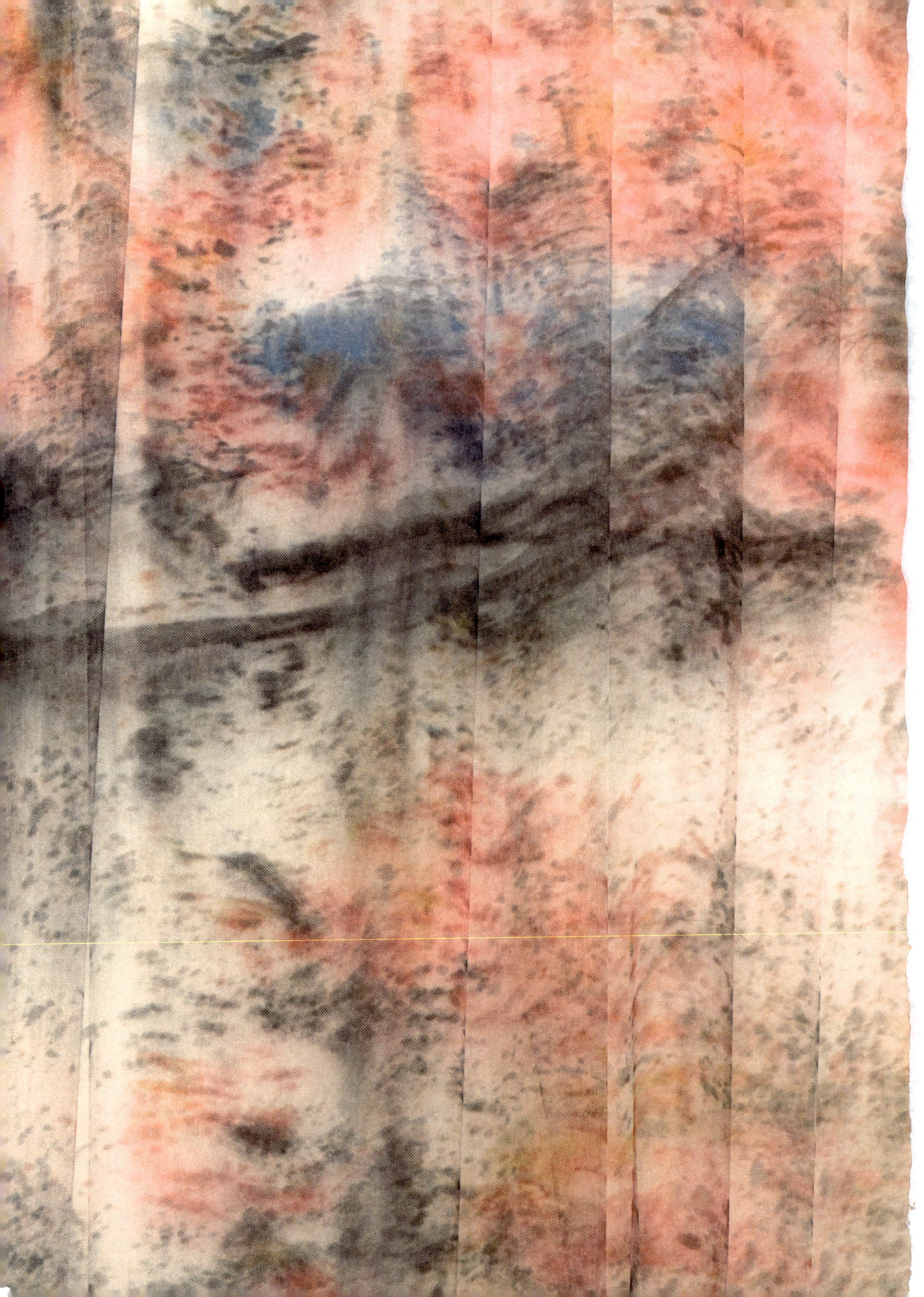

THE WANDERING VEIL

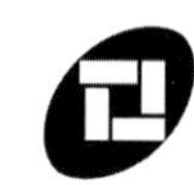

TEL AVIV MUSEUM OF ART, ISRAEL

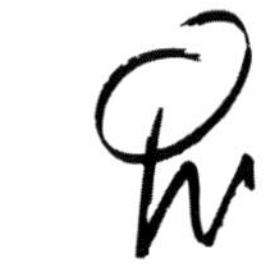

THE OPEN MUSEUM, TEFEN, ISRAEL

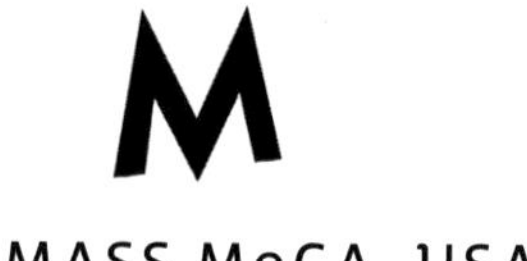

MASS MoCA, USA

THE WANDERING VEIL

IZHAR PATKIN

This catalog is published on the occasion of the traveling exhibition **Izhar Patkin: The Wandering Veil**.

Tel Aviv Museum of Art, Joseph and Rebecca Meyerhoff Pavilion, June 2012
Acting Director: Shuli Kislev
Curator: Ellen Ginton
Associate Curator: Anat Danon-Sivan
Registrars: Shraga Edelsburg, Alisa Friedman-Padovano, Shoshana Frankel
Conservators: Dr. Doron J. Lurie, Maya Dresner, Hasia Rimon, Noga Schusterman, Klara Karlova
Lighting: Naor Agayan, Lior Gabai, Asaf Menachem, Haim Beracha
Installation Production: Tucan Ltd.

The Open Museum, Tefen Industrial Park, June 2012
Curator: Ruthi Ofek
Assistants to the Curator: Dana Gross, Yasimin Kunz
Registrar: Rachel Lazar
Installation: Sami Sisso, Issac Elmakias
Public Relations & Communication: Yael Shavit

Massachusetts Museum of Contemporary Art, 2013
Director: Joseph Thompson
Assistant to the Director: Paulette Wein
Director of Exhibition Planning: Dante Birch
Director of Information Technology: John McAlister
Director of Fabrication and Art Installation: Richard Criddle
Operations Manager: Art McConnell

Catalog
Design: Kristin Johnson
Production: Kfir Malka
Photography: Mary Bachmann, Paula Court, D. James Dee, Avraham Hay, David Heald, David Horowitz, Yasimin Kunz, Robert McKeever, Helaine Messer, Michael James O'Brien, Gene Ogami, Phillips / Schwab, Adam Reich, Ringling Museum of Art, Sèvres—Cité de la céramique / Gérard Jonca, Christian Schwager, Jan Silberstein, Stedelijk Museum, Fernando Torre, Peter Christiansen Valli, Whitney Museum of American Art, Ellen Page Wilson
Hebrew text editing: Orna Yehudaioff
Translation: Einat Adi
English editing: Kristin Jones, Ariana Reines
Printing: A. R. Printing Ltd.

The exhibition and catalog have been made possible thanks to the generous support of:
ARTIS, BFAMI / British Friends of the Art Museums of Israel, Wendy Fisher, Jacob Lee, Anne Marie MacDonald, Suzy and Elihu Rose, David Ross, Rivka Saker and Uzi Zucker, Ellen and Harvey Sanders, Dafna Schmerin, Irit Strauss, Marie-Claude Stobart, Blancpain Art Contemporain, the Centre International de Recherche sur le Verre et les Arts Plastiques (CIRVA), the Manufacture nationale de Sèvres, and to all the individuals and institutions that lent works to the exhibition.

Measurements are given in inches and centimeters, height precedes width precedes depth.

On the covers: *Madonna and Child* (detail), 2007–12, Sèvres porcelain, pâte nouvelle, 89 3/8 x 31 1/5 x 31 1/5" (227 x 80 x 80 cm)

2012, Tel Aviv Museum of Art, cat. 5/12.
ISBN 978-965-539-048-3

Printed in Israel

Contents

To the living and to the dead,
with apologies to anyone I may have left out

Foreword

Working on "Izhar Patkin: The Wandering Veil" has been a genuine pleasure for us, and we are delighted that it will be seen in three museums and on two continents.

More than two decades ago, Ellen Ginton suggested mounting a comprehensive survey of Patkin's work for the Tel Aviv Museum of Art. The late Mordechai (Moti) Omer nurtured the idea, bringing it to its current ambitious scale. Ruthi Ofek proposed that the exhibition be further expanded to include The Open Museum, Tefen Industrial Park, in northern Israel. Joseph Thompson, at the Massachusetts Museum of Contemporary Art in the United States, has turned the collaboration into an international one.

This survey is organized thematically rather than chronologically, focusing on the last decade but also including groundbreaking earlier works. Patkin was born in Israel in 1955, and he lives and works in New York City. Key to his vision is the confluence of themes from his homeland with narratives of global cultural migration. "The Wandering Veil" encompasses his life as well as the mercurial nature of his objects. Patkin's unique visual vocabulary defies categorization: in his work, theme invents technique and vice versa, casting the objects he creates in a continuous theater of becoming.

Since his 1981 debut show of "invented" reproductions at the Kitchen in New York, Patkin has continued to challenge himself and us with his conundrums. These have included the marriage of metaphor and identity in his "Meta Bride" exhibition at the Holly Solomon Gallery in 1983; his presentation of a Genet play as a painting on black rubber curtains at the 1987 Whitney Biennial; and *Don Quijote Segunda Parte*, in which fiction gazes at reality, shown at the 1990 Venice Biennale. In the 1990 Stedelijk Museum survey show "Four-Piece Suit," his inventive "reverse" paintings were exhibited alongside *Presidential Wax*, a series of large-scale photocollages that Patkin perforated to achieve an illusive veil-like presence.

Patkin's work has been collected in depth by the Solomon R. Guggenheim Museum; the Museum of Modern Art; the Whitney Museum of American Art; the Tel Aviv Museum of Art; The Open Museum, Tefen; the Los Angeles County Museum of Art; The Museum of Contemporary Art, Los Angeles; and many other prominent institutions. An essential supplement to "Izhar Patkin: The Wandering Veil," the essays, conversations, and poetry included in this book—by scholars, curators, writers, and poets—reflect his work's scope and complexity, as well as its absorbing and original vision.

Ellen Ginton Tel Aviv Museum of Art
Ruthi Ofek The Open Museum, Tefen
Joseph Thompson Massachusetts Museum of Contemporary Art

The Name and the Father

The Wandering Veil

IZHAR PATKIN AND DAVID ROSS IN CONVERSATION, FEBRUARY 2012, NEW YORK CITY

DAVID ROSS: Let's begin with the early works in the exhibition. In looking at *My Promise Can't Be Broken* (1981; page 28), it becomes clear that your concern with notions of the performative is not necessarily with performance, but with the implications of narrative and storytelling. It seems to me that the performative lies beneath these early works and continues throughout your career.

IZHAR PATKIN: Cinema and Duchamp changed everything in painting. They both threw the canvas into a state of anxiety (see Ellen Ginton's essay on theatricality in Patkin's work on page 226). When I went to school, Super-8 films, performance art, and the documentation of performance were a door out of the canvas ghetto. That door was very seductive. Today it's video, but I'm still in love with the promise of painting, and its object.

DR: In *My Promise Can't Be Broken,* the curtain opens up to reveal no painting—just the wall, just the stretcher.

IP: I painted it for my first solo show at the Holly Solomon Gallery, and I was questioning the promise of painting itself. In the context of that show, which was titled "The Meta Bride," this declaration was seen as both a wedding promise and an audacious statement by a young painter. *My Promise Can't Be Broken* is a rubber curtain framed under Plexiglas, but the viewer can physically draw the curtain open with a set of magnets.

DR: So you made the canvas accessible. The painting can be opened and closed through the glass, and you see the wall. But that is sort of a letdown. Or are you saying that there is no painting?

IP: This framed curtain/canvas may be on the verge of disappearance, but it is a painting. However, the promise of my veil paintings is neither the metaphor of the window nor that of the wall. Modernism tried to do away with the promise of the narrative window. All you were left with was the image *of* the wall, a white on white.

DR: Or the ghost, which is prevalent as metaphor and motif throughout the body of work in this exhibition.

IP: The first painting I remember seeing when I was growing up was a posthumous portrait of my uncle Izhar Patkin, whom I am named after. My grandmother commissioned this portrait after he was killed in the military. It was a painting of a ghost, and it was my namesake.

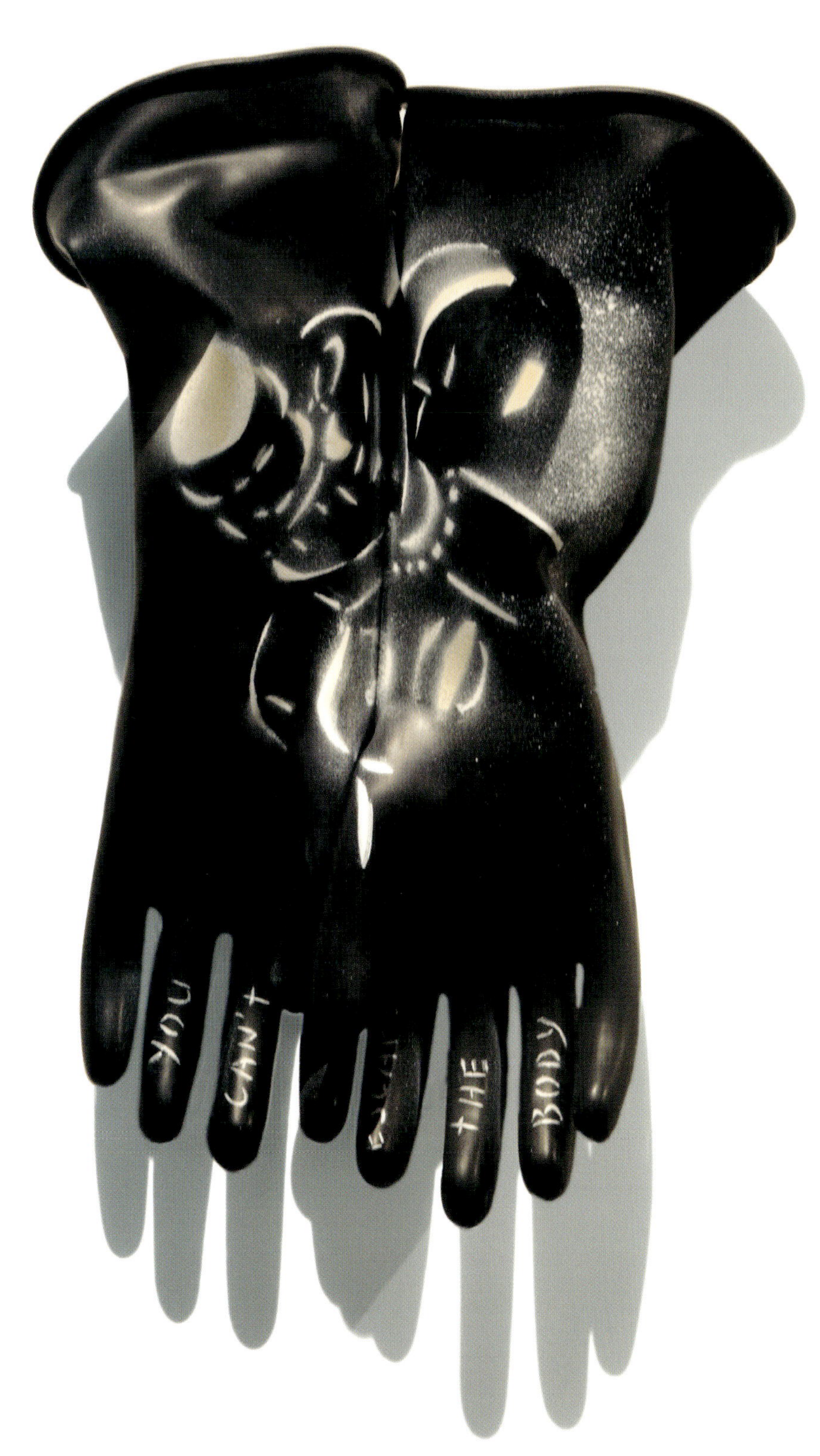
YOU
CAN'T
THE
BODY

DR: Naming is the first act of creation.

IP: Your name is your first ghost, a profound encounter. I was born soon after my eighteen-year-old uncle was killed. The family's pain was so deep they could not even utter his/my name. I was de facto nameless until the age of three.

DR: You have made a ghost painting of that picture.

IP: Yes, and I am planning to open this survey show with it.

DR: Is that a sentimental gesture, or are you announcing an aspect of your relationship to the past?

IP: It announces history, and it announces the first wound. But not only mine. Think of all those who die on both sides of any conflict. How many generations later will their heirs still carry those ghosts? A ghost is essentially an unresolved or suspended emotion. It is not an abstraction or a representation of an emotion. It is a manifestation that questions its own presence. Later in life, I understood that the role of the artist as a narrator is to suspend ghosts.

DR: An artist once told me that all work is self-portraiture. You started out with a number of literal self-portraits, such as *Ghost Chair* (1978; page 31), with you in the chair.

IP: Yes, that work is from my last year of art school, and I know it's a little silly to put that in a show as an adult. But there is an important seed in this drawing. It's a photograph of me dressed in black, sitting on a white chair. I drew the chair over my body with a white pencil, turning both the chair and me into ghosts. This was a harbinger of things to come with the translucencies. The chair looks a bit like a veil.

DR: Do you believe that everything you do reveals your intentions?

IP: You are simultaneously unveiling yourself and weaving your veil, the tissue of your text, as Barthes would say.

DR: Tell me about the *Samaritana* (1980–81; page 33) curtain. Was this self-portrait your first painting on pleated curtains?

IP: Yes. It is painted in a preposterous utopian Russian Constructivist posture, complete with the red satin banner on the side! I sprayed my portrait with stencils on black rubber. A blurred line that cuts through the top of my head could be both a landscape and a vision. On the bottom it says "Samaritana," as in one responsible Good Samaritan.

DR: But you have now re-created an exhibition copy without the text of thirty years ago. Why did you delete the subtitle of the original painting, with its idealistic description? Is diminished idealism what happens to all of us?

IP: The process of "un-indoctrinating" oneself is never-ending. It's essential for anyone who wants to be a serious originator of ideas.

DR: I have always thought that artists should create self-portraits periodically, throughout their lives, so that they can measure their sense of self, of self-worth or self-loathing.

IP: One of my favorite lines of Borges is from *Dreamtigers:* "A man sets himself the task of portraying the world. Through the years he peoples a space with images of provinces . . . rooms . . . instruments, stars, and people. Shortly before his death, he discovers that that patient labyrinth of lines traces the image of his face."[1]

DR: But in all good stories, the hero goes on a journey of self-discovery.

IP: Yes. Character development is the most complex aspect of any narrative.

DR: Do you feel that you have become less idealistic?

IP: Not at all. When I paint, I am just as innocent as ever. I am not letting go of that. What's the point of making art without it? I have faith in mystery.

DR: The themes and ideas of any serious artist are born early and become more refined throughout their careers. In your early perforated-photographic works, you invented collages of continuous morphing visual images. They were also organized as an architectural construct, which eventually became your veil rooms.

IP: What everyone does with Photoshop today, which is morph one image into another, I did back then in handmade physical collage (*Untitled,* 1980–81; pages 34–35). There was no digital morphing. Those early collage works were a harbinger on many fronts.

DR: There is more to your interest in using morphing technology, which of course you use in the creation of the images for the veil rooms. You invented an architecture for your circular narratives, one that can be entered into and walked through, where there is no beginning and no end.

IP: When does any story start? 1948? 1967? 0? There is a narrative of a god who started it all, but even he molded it out of preexisting chaos. For the artist, one story flows into another in a constant performance of creation. My glass sculpture of Shiva, the dancer and the seducer, is about this state of endless creation. Any statue of Shiva is Shiva. In other words, it is a manifestation, not a mere representation. This was a departure from my Judeo-Christian culture, closing the distance between the artist and the object and its meaning. I combined my Shiva with two other legendary creative dancers, Carmen Miranda and Josephine Baker, both famous exiles. And I made him leap out of a circle of roses, a Garden of Eden I suppose, as a self-exile. That sculpture is called *Where Each Is Both* (1994; pages 200–201). In exile, the story of one culture merges into another.

DR: Can you talk about the idea of exile in your work? You chose to move to New York, and you are hardly a political exile or refugee.

IP: The exilic voice is the dissenting voice. You don't even have to travel. As the Kashmiri-American poet Agha Shahid Ali put it: "When I write in English I am in exile in my own language." The perspective of comparative religion, culture, and literature is intrinsic to the exilic state of mind.

DR: But you are not sentimental when you talk about exile.

IP: Not in the banal sense. Shahid always said that what we call sentimental in the West is called "loss" in the East.

DR: You're not being nostalgic?

IP: *Nostalgia* derives from Greek words meaning homecoming plus pain. In that sense, one can also be nostalgic for a new home, not just the return of the familiar. Home can be a new painting. I really don't like the monopoly that Jewish culture thinks it has over the notion of homecoming and the diaspora. In today's global reality, every motherland has a great diaspora, often in America. The relationship between all motherlands and their diasporas is one of the most fantastic and progressive gifts any country could wish for. It's the internal-eye's view, but from the outside.

DR: Your work moves freely between the extremely personal and private to the global, as in the marvelous portrait of your late father. You painted him on the tulle veil from a tourist snapshot taken in front of the World Trade Center years before 9/11 (pages 38–41). It's a magical picture, not only because you are remembering your father, but also because something else is happening.

IP: This is a painting of two ghosts, my personal one and the public one. And although I am always reluctant to get too personal in terms of biography, it surfaces one way or another. But the introduction of an autobiographical element is also a device. It's a lure that turns the passive viewer into a hunter. Or as the Indian author Gita Mehta told me, "into a stalker, which is even better!" After all, we are in the business of visual seduction.

DR: On a metaphorical level, what does your father's portrait represent? Your show deals with such large themes of life and death, transformation, and the ghost of the absent or the present.

IP: It's not up to me to assign to any painting a particular reductive meaning. I am the author, not the destination. Does the viewer really need to know that my father passed away soon after the World Trade Center fell?

DR: But it's not meaningless for the viewer to see this man sitting on a bench, which seems to be floating in the air in front of a building that only exists in our memory. That has broader implications.

IP: I want the tulle veils to physically take you into another world of memories, to question the how and the extent to which things exist. I have always believed that even the most abstract thought needs an object to exist. Words are objects. Even the nameless god needed the word. For example, there is an early piece called *You Can't Escape the Body* (1981; page 11). One of the things I always ask myself is how much body a work of art really needs to exist and to convey its plot. I think the tulle veil paintings are the climax of that dilemma. Not only are they translucent and ephemeral, but the netting physically resists the registration of the image. The images and metaphors aren't passive; they are active. There is a game of hide and seek on the tulle pleats. The viewer has to be very active to hunt down the phantom images. They are there and not there at the same time. The images are always fleeting, like thoughts looking for their bodies, in search of their manifestations.

DR: The images on the veil paintings are fugitive, floating somewhere between printmaking, photography, and painting.

IP: The painted veils may seem unorthodox, but they are unwaveringly paintings because they have the logic, intention, and concerns of a painter. I employ digital printing just as Johns and Warhol used the stencil and the silkscreen. In my "reverse" screen paintings with the carpet motifs, *Gardens for the Global City* (1991–present; pages 142–49), I don't use a brush either. Yet there is so much hand in those paintings, as I physically push the oil paint from the backside of the wire-mesh canvas to the front, that they are practically finger paintings. Their paint has real meat.

DR: I like how the crude finger work takes on such an elegant presence because of the way you express the raw oil paint through the mesh of the screens. I am not questioning the painterliness of the veil paintings, but whether or not they also function as sculpture because of their volume and the way that people experience them in space.

IP: The question of how much body a work needs to actually exist is inherent in both my sculptures and my paintings. Everything I do is narrative-driven. The narrative determines the body, and vice versa. As Wittgenstein said, "We cannot express through language what expresses itself in language." The material and the narrative are equal actors in the construction of the plot. You can escape neither.

DR: You create new connections between media that were previously seen as distinct, almost like an act of translation. In the poems of the legendary Kashmiri American Agha Shahid Ali, one can't help feeling the tension between the forms and the spaces that your work and your life occupy.

IP: With one word, the emperor's translator could bring down the empire.

DR: The main project of this exhibition is your collaboration with Agha Shahid Ali, who like many poets, was also a great translator. One of the early works in the project is *Violins* (2006; pages 52–63), based on the poem "Violins," which Ali translated, at the behest of Edward Said, from the renowned Palestinian poet Mahmoud Darwish.

IP: Let's use the word *adapted.*

DR: How do you define the difference between an adaptation and a translation?

IP: Well, in an adaptation you're not translating verbatim—you're reinventing the medium, and you don't pretend to be an invisible creator.

DR: Then would you say that your work in relationship to Ali's work is an adaptation? Almost like a stage director reinterpreting a Shakespearean play?

IP: Absolutely. In fact, if we detour for a moment to literature, when you have to translate a text from a classical language to English, you must adapt to a very different metaphorical dial. English doesn't tolerate the density of metaphors that classical languages thrive on. Shahid dreamed in Indian classical languages and wrote in English. His "wandering" poems became the text that I had to put into a third language—the painterly—without using words at all. Each of the veil rooms is an adaptation of a different Shahid poem. I had to invent a different time and place for each one, a stage on which to evoke and visualize each poem. In Shahid's adaptation of Darwish's "Violins," the *sound* of the word *violins* morphs into *violence*. In my *Violins* room, I transformed the image of a cello recital in the White House into a "theater of war." I worked from a photograph of Pablo Casals's 1961 performance in the East Room, where he is bowing to the audience. But I painted him with his back to the president, the first lady, and their guests. They all face scenes of war—armies, death, and fleeing refugees—an image that doesn't appear in Darwish's poem or in Shahid's adaptation. For me, the paradox of theater and war was a perfect way to visualize the drama of two great poems.

DR: Digging deeper, one would recall Casals's famous declaration, "My cello is my weapon." And then you painted pigeons on the White House ballroom floor to remind us of Casals's "Song of the Birds," a traditional Catalan song that he routinely played to protest the Franco dictatorship.

IP: Using images, like Casals, that are developed characters in themselves is a device that helps me widen the scope of the narrative.

DR: It is quite a challenge to create a visual adaptation that's not a literal translation or illustration of a text, but, rather, a setting-off point for another level of metaphoric interpretation. Great painters always do this. The way Masaccio used the Bible for his painting of the exile made you look back at that text in a new way.

IP: I began working this way early on with *The Black Paintings* (1985–86; pages 212–17), based on Jean Genet's play *The Blacks*. It's a play about race that I adapted into a room of white images stenciled on black rubber curtains. Each wall became an act. I painted an underworld palace in a nocturnal domain, complete with a lunar eclipse. The metaphors I used for *black* were almost encyclopedic in scope.

DR: Why did you paint a white ghost among the blacks?

IP: The play presented me with a visual impossibility. The plot has a murder that never happened. Genet asks the blacks to pretend to kill a white prostitute. Imagine, if I had painted a murder that never happened, it would have instantly become evidence of its having happened. So how do you paint something that hasn't happened or won't happen? My solution was to use a ghost as the murdered figure. You can't kill a ghost, and it had to be recognizable, so I had the black characters murder a white ghost in the guise of Manet's famous courtesan, Olympia. Like Casals, she functions as a meta-device.

DR: You were dealing with racial politics in an indirect way.

IP: But the metaphorical way is no less political. In *The Meta Bride* (1982; page 225), I painted a black bride on a white tulle veil—a Snow White complex. We are all born into metaphors that don't fit us. The role of the artist is to reinvent them. Metaphor is the artist's arena, my theater of war.

DR: The collaboration with Agha Shahid Ali, who uses metaphor so richly, must have been very appealing to you.

IP: The publisher Anne Marie MacDonald wanted us to do a book together. I was deeply moved by Shahid and his writing, and we both decided that the Jew and the Muslim should meet on the veil. I suggested that the veil be the meeting place, not something that veils. We recognized that the exilic condition was a recurring motif in our vocabulary, since we both lived away from our troubled birth cultures. Whatever was to come out of the collaboration, we decided to call our project "Veiled Threats." It was Ishmael and Isaac from the get-go. Tragically, two years after we started working, he was diagnosed with brain cancer, and he died very young. We were the best of friends.

DR: It's a shame that he never lived to see any of your veil paintings completed. Did he understand what you were going to do?

IP: He wrote the last poem expressly for our collaboration. It was his requiem and the summation of his rich vocabulary. For months he called it "The Veil Suite," evoking an object, a place. But a few days before he died, he changed it to "The Veiled Suite."

DR: "Veil" versus "veiled."

IP: It was very perplexing for me, because as close friends, collaborators, and artists, we never believed in anything that was veiled. I kept *The Veil Suite* as the title for my painting. *"Make me* *now your veil, then see if you can veil yourself from me"*—this line from the poem frames it all.

DR: The form of that last poem is very complex, especially for a man suffering the final stages of brain cancer.

IP: He wrote it as a canzone. Dante was one of the inventors of the canzone in its classical form, which is so structurally complex that nobody has ever written more than two. This was Shahid's third. He wrote it without any short-term memory, his vision so ravaged by the cancer—it brings to mind Milton's blindness. He wrote as beautifully as his beloved Emily Dickinson. Both possessed an effervescent genius.

DR: This talk about the effervescent and the void brings me back to a motif that appears throughout your work. It is the notion of the emptied center, the missing parts, the holes in the mesh.

IP: In 1980 I started the *Tatting* series (pages 208–9) with the image of an empty armchair set in a starry celestial landscape. An orphaned cupid, perched on the arm of the chair, refers to the Modernist secular myth of the vacant seat of God. Was it ever occupied? Where does meaning reside? What is the promise of a painting? Is it in the painting or is it in you? Is the painting a manifestation of your desires, or is it a representation of something else? Why is there a distance between the painting and the painter?

DR: Is this part of the Modernist concern with the death of the author?

IP: The death of God was one thing. But how the art world took the writings of Mallarmé, Barthes, and Foucault about the death of the author to a cynical conclusion was tragic! Art became a masquerade of appropriation and pastiche at the price of originality.

Shimon Adaf brilliantly proposes "the ghost story" (page 44) as an ideal "genre" model for my work. He argues that if one sees Modernism's dominant genre as the detective story, which always starts with the corpse or missing body, and if one skips the cynical era of picaresque post-Modernism, "the ghost story offers itself [for Patkin's work] as the best genre."

For me, as a painter the real corpse in art after Modernism is neither God's nor the author's. It is not the phantoms of extinct birds in my Sèvres plates and the eggcups that I made as their tombstones, nor is it the hole I left in the Sèvres porcelain clock. It is the body of painting itself. My childless porcelain *Madonna and Child* (2007-12; pages 88-91) is a provocation, perhaps, though not in her grasping a shroud of a missing god, but, rather, her holding out a fresh start for the blank canvas, or at least what could be a new dress.

But you asked about the death of the author. The voided center of authority is a wonderfully complex narrative that was at the heart of Western Enlightenment. In *Motl, Son of Pesye the Cantor,* a book I love by the great Yiddish writer Sholem Aleichem, there is a chapter that starts with "Hallelujah, I'm an orphan." Motl, the orphan who journeys from the old world to America, is too young to have been indoctrinated when his father dies. He dreams of becoming a secular musician, but ends up as a cartoonist and a painter of graven images. You could say that I took his story a step further when I made the Shiva, a god, a dancer, a seducer.

DR: So the notion of the *lack* is not an issue of something negative or missing, but something liberating?

IP: It's the notion of potentiality. Shlomzion Kenan writes about it brilliantly in her essay on the Madonna and Child (page 80).

DR: For you, potentiality goes beyond metaphor. It is more about the concept of manifestation.

IP: I wander among cultures. The chasm between abstraction, representation, and manifestation is embodied in my story. I was born into a world with a Jewish abstract god. I live in the iconic economy of Western Christian representation. And I acknowledge the great gods of manifestation in the pagan religions of the East. Unfortunately or not, our secular language is still anchored in religious vocabulary. This is true not just in art and literature, but also in science. Even quantum physics names subatomic particles after mysterious gods. Freud demystified hysteria and named his theories after pagan phenomena. Gershom Scholem said, "The secularization of language[2] is only a *façon de parler,* a phrase! It is impossible to empty out words that are filled to the breaking point with specific meanings lest it be done at the sacrifice of the language itself!"[3] We can't escape that language. But do we really need to? He also said that the death of the name of God is the death of language.[4] The Jewish ban on graven images that necessitated abstraction and repressed the mimetic drive is deep in my cultural background. But the dilemma for me is: Why draw the line at images when words have a body, too? That's monotheism for you, the idolatry of language. No wonder Ezekiel eats the scroll . . .

DR: And representation?

IP: Representation is essentially Catholic. The icon was supposed to solve the problem of idolatry because it's only a representation, a substitution. But the paradox was that the Veil of Veronica, in which God was made visible, even when multiplied as representations, is nothing but the one Vera-Icona.

DR: The only true image. The control of information as the birth of capitalism.

IP: As if this super-branding were not enough, the icon also offers salvation. What is a painting supposed to offer? And which model is it supposed to follow? Where does the meaning reside? Is it in the object? Is it the painting itself? Outside? Shimon Adaf elaborates on this dilemma and the notion of "the veil principle" in his "Ghost Essay."

DR: When did you start to negotiate this crisis?

IP: I remember going to Europe for the first time as a young boy. Visiting the big museums with all the great religious paintings, I was perplexed. Were these museums or churches? Later on, in art school, I was indoctrinated into the narrative of western art history and was trained to see the universal value of those wonderful paintings.

DR: Now you are thinking, "universal values, not so fast"! You see how everything is still anchored in religious ideologies.

IP: I was also indoctrinated into American popular culture. Secular capitalism holds the same false promise of redemption as the icon. It's not an invitation to a process of catharsis. Today, globalism offers the redemption of the free market. But some cultures might see it as an invasion of an iconic economy of false gods. And we know that the icon is indeed the economy of the Christian church. This is how images in today's global culture become veiled threats. An artist in the age of globalism has to be in a constant process of un-indoctrination. Western art is no less an invasion than McDonald's or Starbucks.

DR: And what would be a manifestation of hamburger?

IP: I hope more than a clown with a Quarter Pounder at the Golden Arches. I can always offer you a word on a scroll . . . manifestation is something that comes from paganism, where the gods are phenomena. Let's say you were a follower of classical Greek religion and you just displayed your little tchotchkes on the mantelpiece. Today, you would be described as having good taste and a good design sense; the Greeks would say Zeus was at work, because he is the god of good order.

DR: That's interesting because it leads to how we imbue notions of character in things. For instance, developing a character in a painting is very different than doing it in a play. How do you evoke character without talk, sound, or subtitles?

IP: When I look at a great Ingres portrait, I know what he thought about the women he painted. He makes me think that I know who they were in their time. You can call them figures of speech.

DR: So they function both metaphorically and metonymically? They make you feel that you have possibly reached beyond representation.

IP: Every time I see his portraits, I say I never want to see another photograph in my life.

DR: Do you link the process of catharsis, perhaps as it was in classical Greek drama, to character development?

IP: Yes, but not as an act of moral purification, and obviously it's a different kind of dialogue. However, in painting, as in literature and drama, character can be evoked by something as simple as color, or the subversion of the expected. For example, there is an image of a dress in my painting *The Perfect Existence in the Rose Garden: Confirmation* (1988; page 92). It's a red dress in the middle of a *hortus conclusus* with red roses, a medieval enclosed garden. Traditionally, the virgin would be sitting inside protected by the thorns. In my painting there is a red dress without the wearer. In another painting called *Madonna and Child* (1998; page 93) I did some years later, she is wearing a red dress and the child is not there.

DR: And so the red dress itself is a character.

IP: The red dress and the color red are actors in the plots of both paintings. Every element in the painting is a character in the narrative. I don't have canvases that are meaninglessly hidden under paint. If it's painted on a screen, then the screen is a player. Gold leaf could be a character just like the image of a dress. The redness itself is a character. Characters develop between and within each painting. This happens in the tension between the material and the image, the elements of surprise and discovery that change the course of the narrative. The tension makes the metaphor active rather than descriptive. Everything in my work, like in a dream, is a manifestation. I have a dream ensemble cast of characters!

DR: What about the significance of Felix Mendelssohn, or the Mendelssohns in general, actual characters that appear in your *Judenporzellan* (1998–2002; pages 95–99)?

IP: I came upon a historical anecdote of ridiculous bureaucratic anti-Semitism, the story of *Judenporzellan.* It was 1769 and the Jews of Berlin were forced to buy inferior-grade porcelain from the king's failing factory. One man humiliated by this scam was Moses

Mendelssohn. He was a father of the Jewish enlightenment and the Enlightenment in general, yet this great philosopher was forced to buy cheap porcelain monkeys. I cast him and his family as an allegory for our time. Moses Mendelssohn was open-minded, he was scholarly, he was liberal, and his thinking went beyond ghettoized doctrines. Importantly, he was not messianic. I wanted to celebrate a hero who would stand in stark contrast to the dangerous messianic tendencies that I see in Israel and around the world.

DR: But you chose to depict Felix Mendelssohn holding a *Judenporzellan* teapot, instead of the top hat that he wore in real life when he met Queen Victoria.

IP: Felix inherited the porcelain from his legendary grandfather. The porcelain was his ghost, the skeleton in the family closet passed down from one generation to the next. As I have woven this story into my collages, the porcelain is neither an heirloom of shame nor a badge of honor. A silly teapot survived to tell the story of an anti-Semitic bureaucratic farce. But what truly endured was the Mendelssohns' extraordinary works. The *Judenporzellan* was not only the ghost in the Mendelssohn family closet, but also the shame of King Frederick.

DR: We talked about the exilic, but what about the notion of the refugee?

IP: I grew up hearing stories of refugees and pioneers. My mother came from a very old Jerusalemite family who became refugees in 1948 when they had to flee their home. My father's people chose to come to Palestine in the 1920s to build a new life away from the shadow of Russian pogroms. I have a lot of empathy for all things that have to do with exodus, refugees, and exile. I remember one distinct moment after my father passed away when my mother and sister were organizing the family album. I asked my mother why there was only one photo of her childhood. She explained that they had all been lost when the family fled their burning home. Her story made an indelible impression, because it was about things disappearing, and it was about the world of images.

DR: In your work, you explore the relationship between contemporary Israel and the plight of the Palestinians.

IP: Yes, I have empathy for both. This is not a competition for who suffers most. It's the complex landscape I come from (see Ruthi Ofek essay on page 128).

DR: For the last two decades, you have been working on your extraordinary screen paintings of carpets, *Gardens for the Global City*. What do you mean by "the global city" and how do these paintings represent that concept?

IP: The title came out of my friendship and conversations with Herbert Muschamp, who is also the character in my sculpture *Don Quijote Segunda Parte* (1987; pages 186–89), a character who becomes the reality of his own fiction, and for whom the distinction between reality and illusion is an illusion to itself (see interview with Muschamp on page 204). Borges says that "defeated by reality... he [Don Quixote] was survived only briefly by Miguel de Cervantes. . . ."[5]

DR: I recall that you were great friends even before he became the legendary *New York Times* architecture critic.

IP: During our formative years, I made *The Black Paintings* and he was working on a book called *Narrative Architecture*, which was never published (see Muschamp's text on *The Black Paintings* on page 210). We had many conversations about the meaning of narrative. I talked about meta-narrative and how it was anchored in religious vocabulary. He was looking for the vernacular in architectural theory. Once we were talking about the International Style, and I told him that as a kid I thought International Style was a big world's fair where every country was represented and how years later I realized that International Style meant that all modern cities around the world look the same. Herbert gave me the title *Gardens for the Global City*. That series uses Asian Oriental carpet compositions to tell the story of Modernist painting such as the New York School. There is no history of oil painting in the East as we know it in the West. Their painting is in carpets and miniatures, and it was very interesting for me to find a way to mix the two. Not unlike when I worked with Shahid.

DR: For me, the veil rooms stand out because of how you use metaphor and how you take the viewer not to different places, but beyond.

IP: It was wonderful to learn from Shahid how his metaphors were not only magical but verged on witchcraft: Love is not like fire. Love is fire. It will burn you. The frog becomes the prince. There is a total transformation. In "Evening" (page 174), there is actually a magician in the poem!

> *Some terrible magician, hidden behind curtains,*
> *has hypnotized Time*
> *so this evening is a net*
> *in which the twilight is caught.*
> *Now darkness will never come—*
> *and there will never be morning.*

In my painting (2008; pages 176–85) I chose Venice as the arena of frozen time. A magician on a gondola releases a black cloud of birds to usher in the night, to restart the cycle of time. What could be a negative becomes optimistic.

DR: In *The Dead Are Here* (2009; pages 154–65), you go into an even more inventive direction.

IP: This painting is based on the lost love story of Laila and Majnoon, the Romeo and Juliet of the East. They couldn't marry because Majnoon didn't come from the right family and the loss sent him mad. Majnoon in Arabic means "crazy." Traditional miniatures depict Majnoon as only being able to communicate with animals. Laila is shown sitting under a tree reading his letters. In my painting, the white pages of his letters morph into tombstones, the arena for this unrequited love story. I took the model of Fragonard's *Progress of Love,* in which there is a garden where love progresses. I turned it into a cemetery with cherry blossoms in full bloom, but where love does not progress.

DR: There is another kind of love and death in *The Veil Suite* (2007; pages 68–75).

IP: In Shahid's last masterpiece, his requiem, "The Veiled Suite," he depicts God as the common lover who betrays you. God makes himself absent. He abandons you like all lovers do. If there is one promise he keeps, it's that he will kill you. But Shahid, the poet, has the last word. He is dying, but he has not lost his spirit. Loss is the source of all great poetry.

DR: That's what Lewis Hyde would call the gift.

IP: The gift he gave himself. In the end he prevails. Of course, leave it to Shahid to make the connection between "veil" and "prevail."

DR: Finally, one of the most interesting things in this exhibition is the way in which all the painterly adaptations of poems and stories fit into a broader narrative. It's like a group of songs with a libretto. And all of a sudden there is an opera.

IP: I constructed the show in a thematic rather than chronological way. One work leads into another emotionally. For example, in *The Veil Suite,* there is the image of the dead poet with a black veil over his head and his black shadow below, rising on clouds of snow that evoke the ascending Virgin. The poet is the only full-bodied character in the painting. All the other characters are depicted as mere shadows, as if they are in the room with the viewer, casting their shadows on the veil painting. Behind this veil, the next work is my white porcelain Madonna holding the empty shroud or the vacant canvas. Who will be whose veil? Maybe the viewer becomes a veil blocking the scenery, maybe the ghost in it, maybe the shadow?

DR: And that relationship becomes a meta-narrative of its own.

IP: Yes. The wandering veil.

NOTES

1
Jorge Luis Borges, *Dreamtigers*, trans. Mildred Boyer and Harold Morland (Austin: University of Texas Press, 1964), 93.

2
For generations Hebrew was mostly a sacred language used for prayer or study, until modern Hebrew was secularized by the Zionist enterprise and actualized as the daily spoken language of Israelis.—Ed.

3
Gershom Scholem, "Pledge to Our Language, letter to Franz Rosenzweig," in Udi Aloni, *What Does a Jew Want?* (New York: Columbia University Press, 2011), 247.

4
"Language is Name. In the name rests the power of Language, its abyss is sealed with the name. We have no right to conjure up the old names day after day without calling forth their hidden power. They will appear, since we have called upon them, and undoubtedly they will appear with vehemence!" Scholem, "Pledge to Our Language, letter to Franz Rosenzweig," in Aloni, *What Does a Jew Want?*, 248.

5
Borges, *Dreamtigers*, 42.

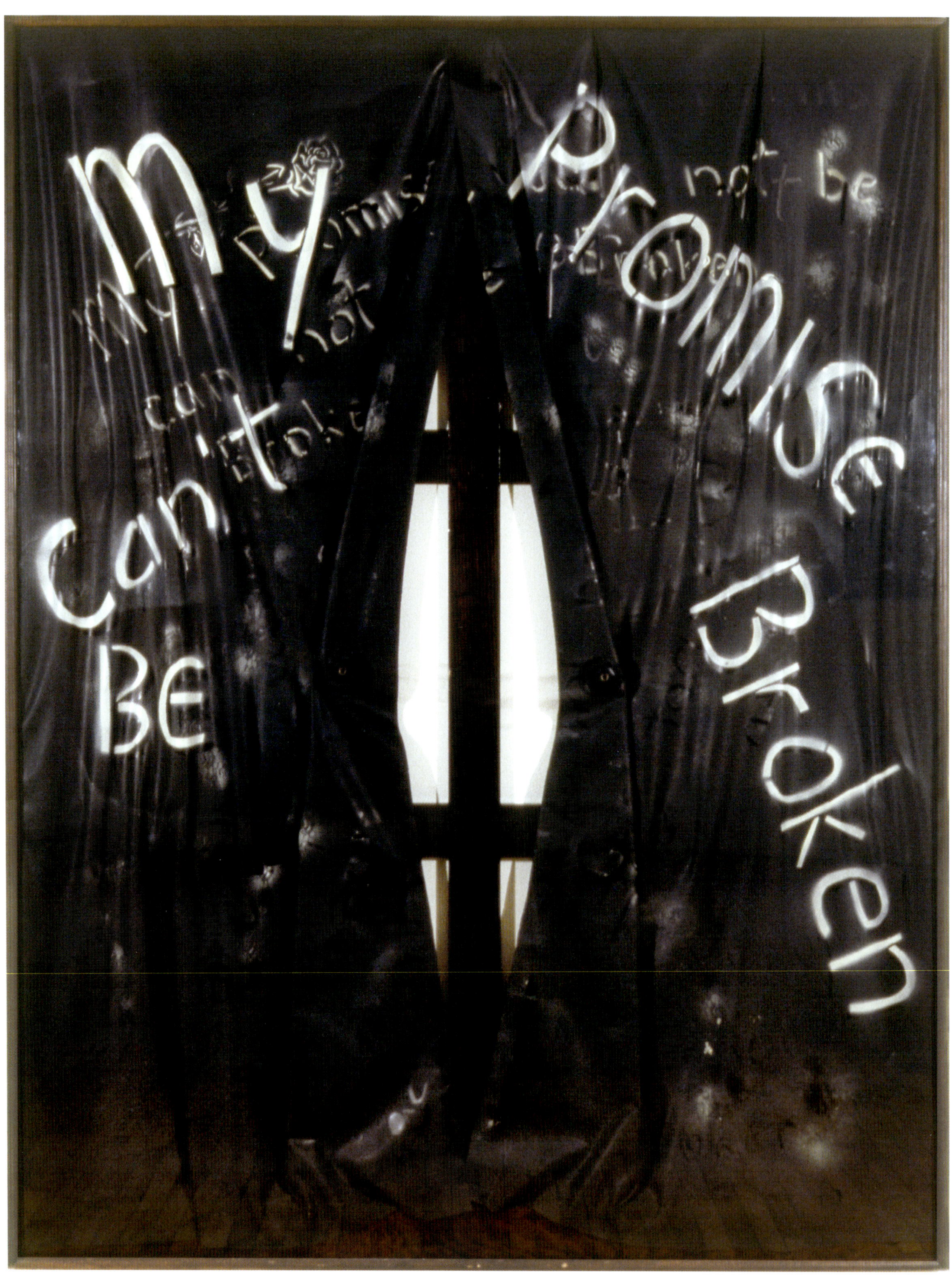
My Promise
Can
Be
Broken
not be

Cinema and Duchamp changed everything in painting. When I went to school, Super-8 films, performance art, and the documentation of performance were a door out of the canvas ghetto. That door was very seductive. Today it's video, but I'm still in love with the promise of painting, and its object.

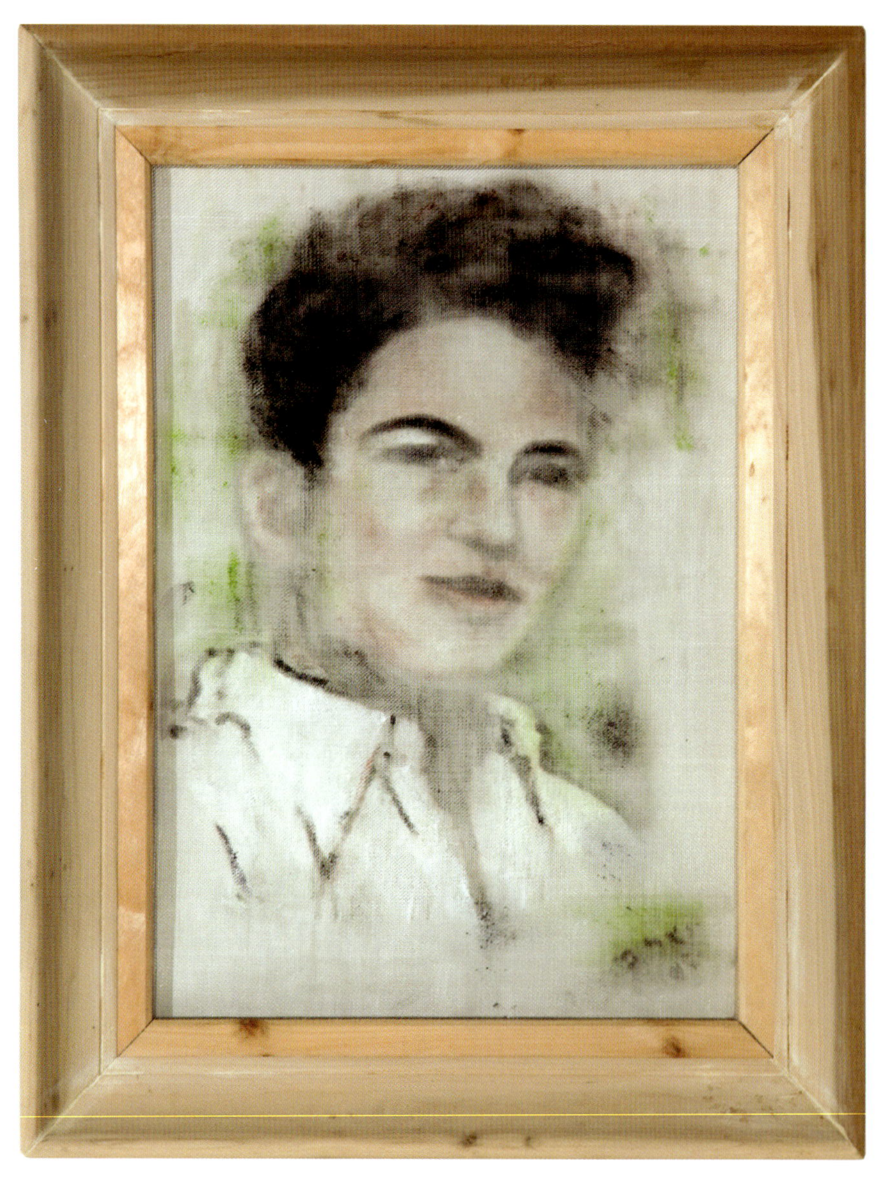

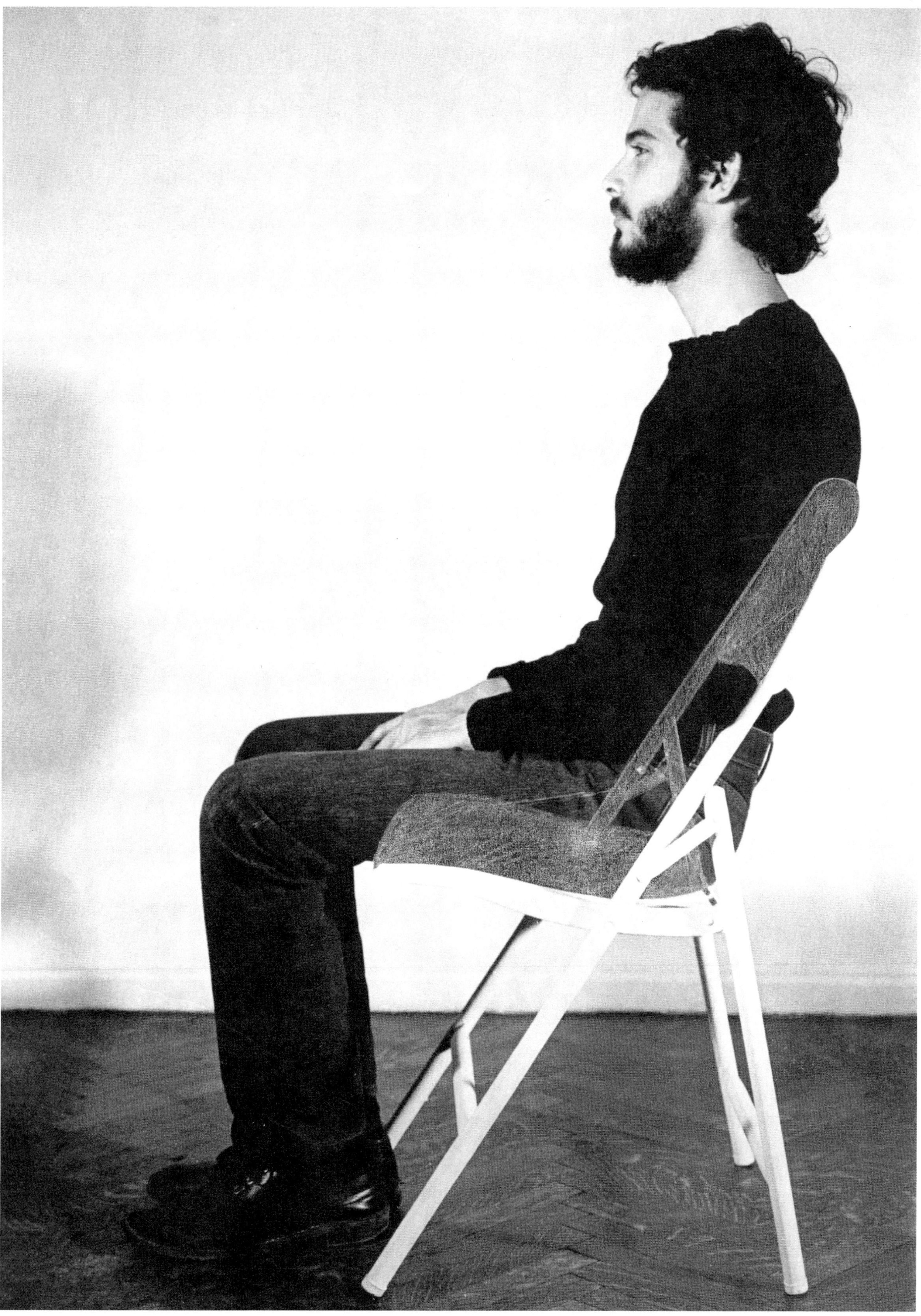

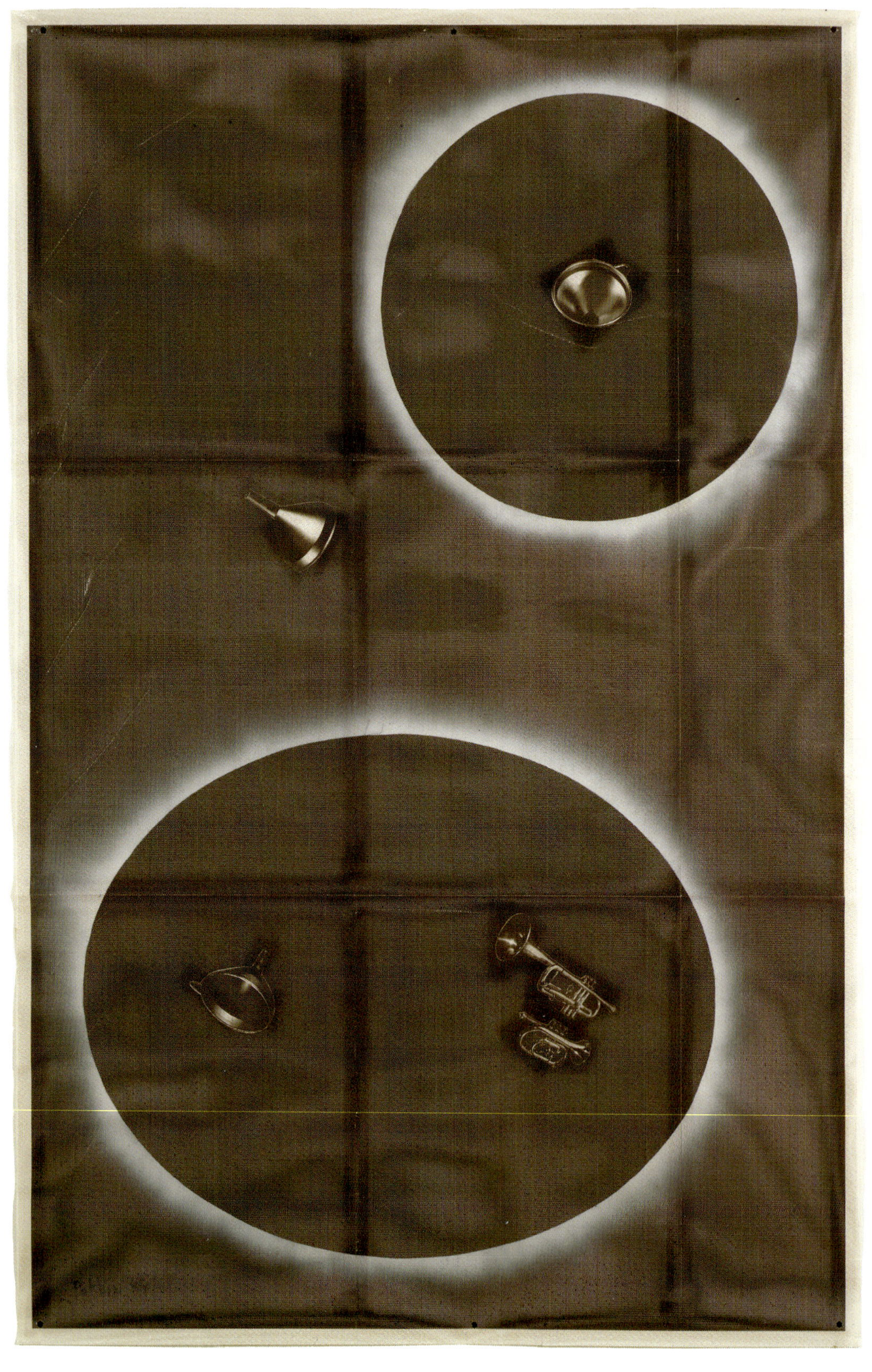

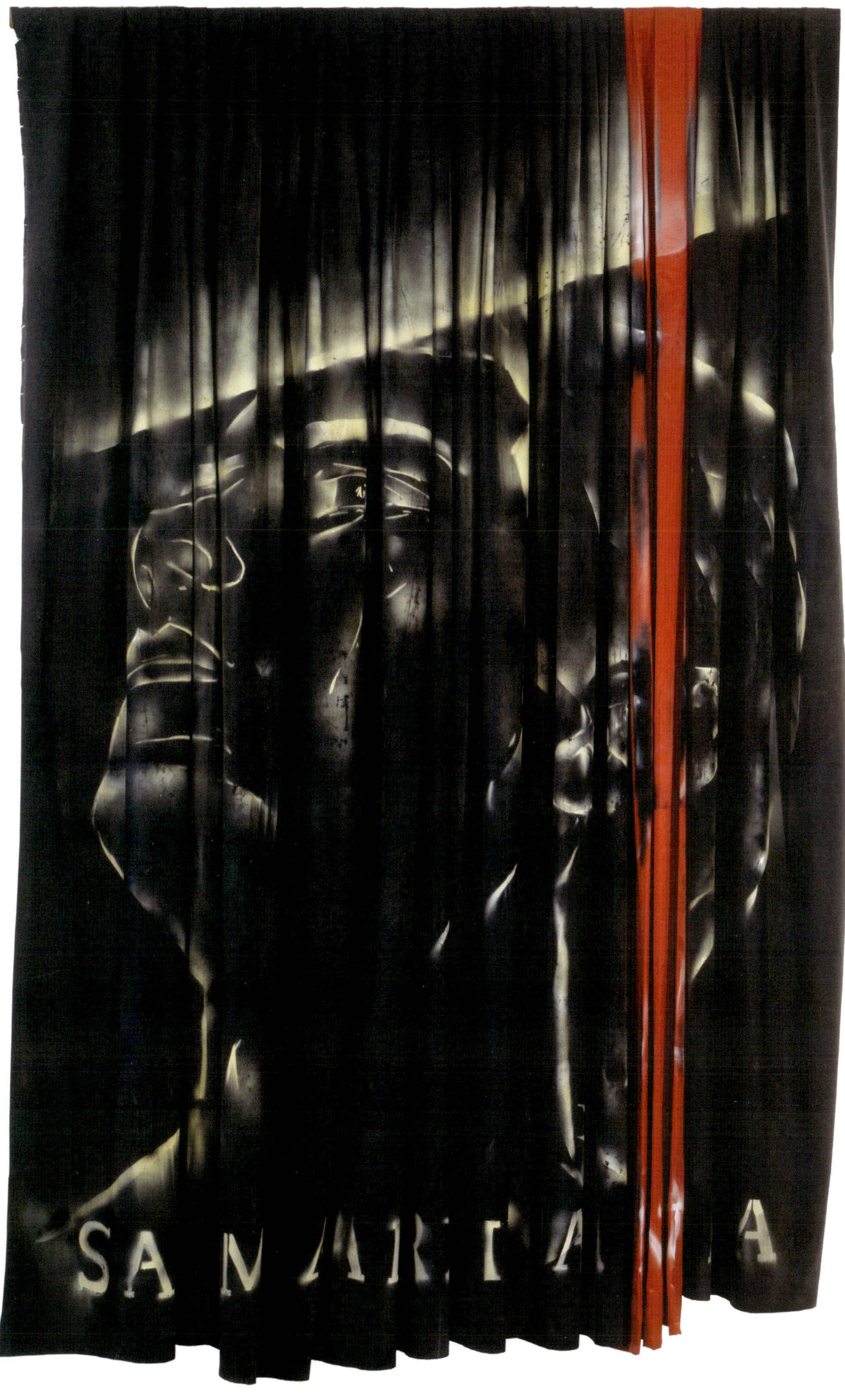

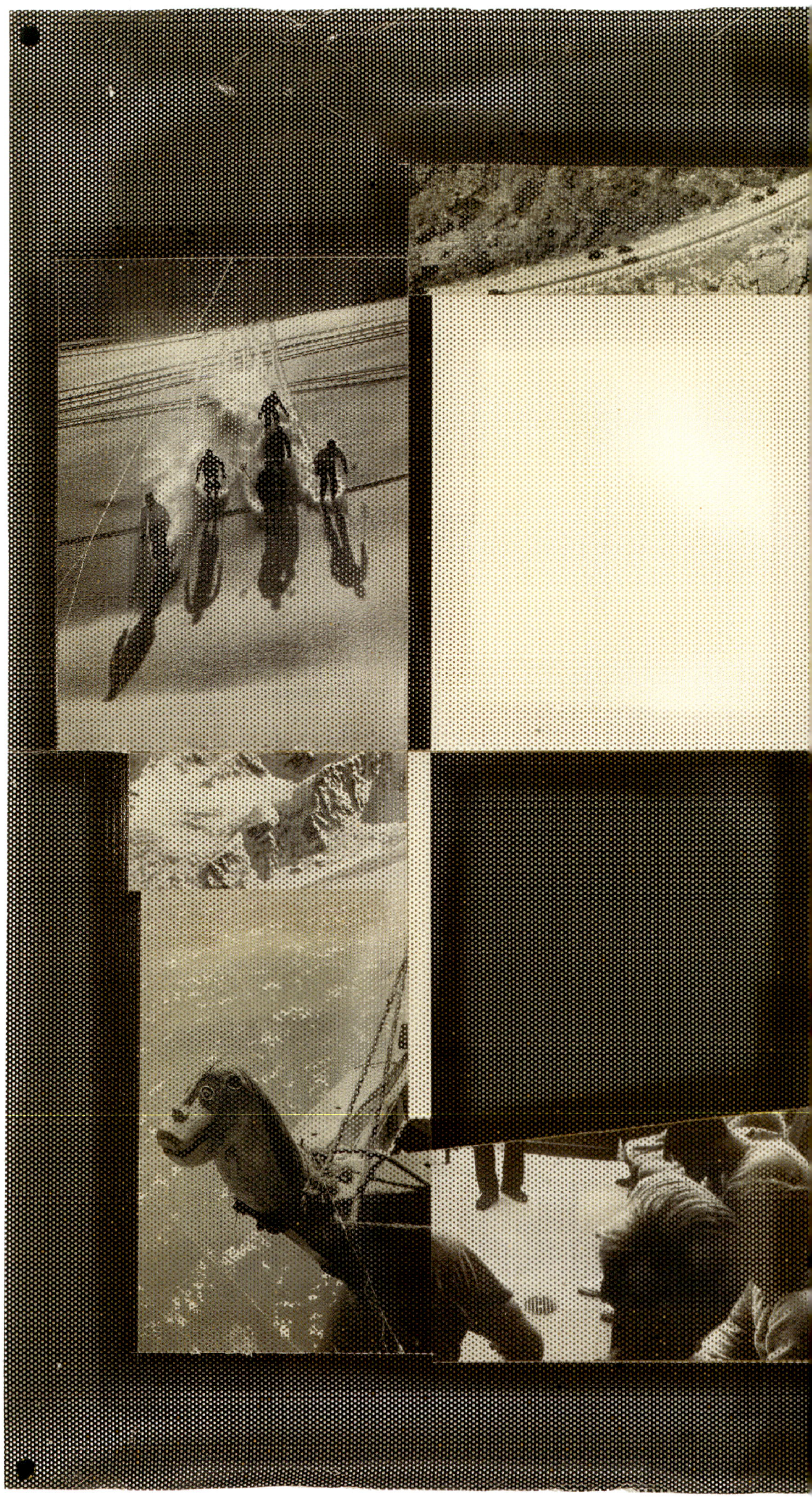

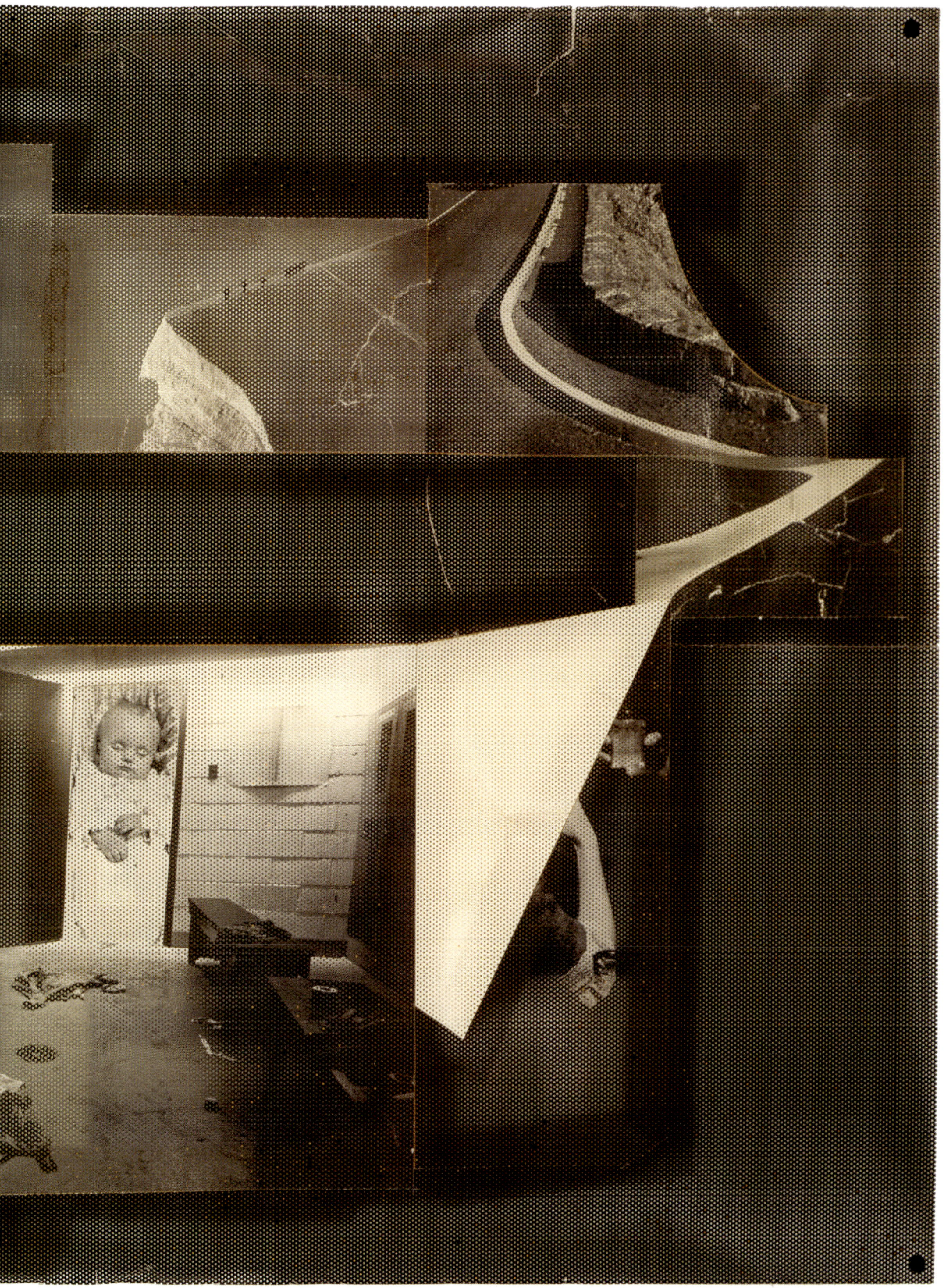

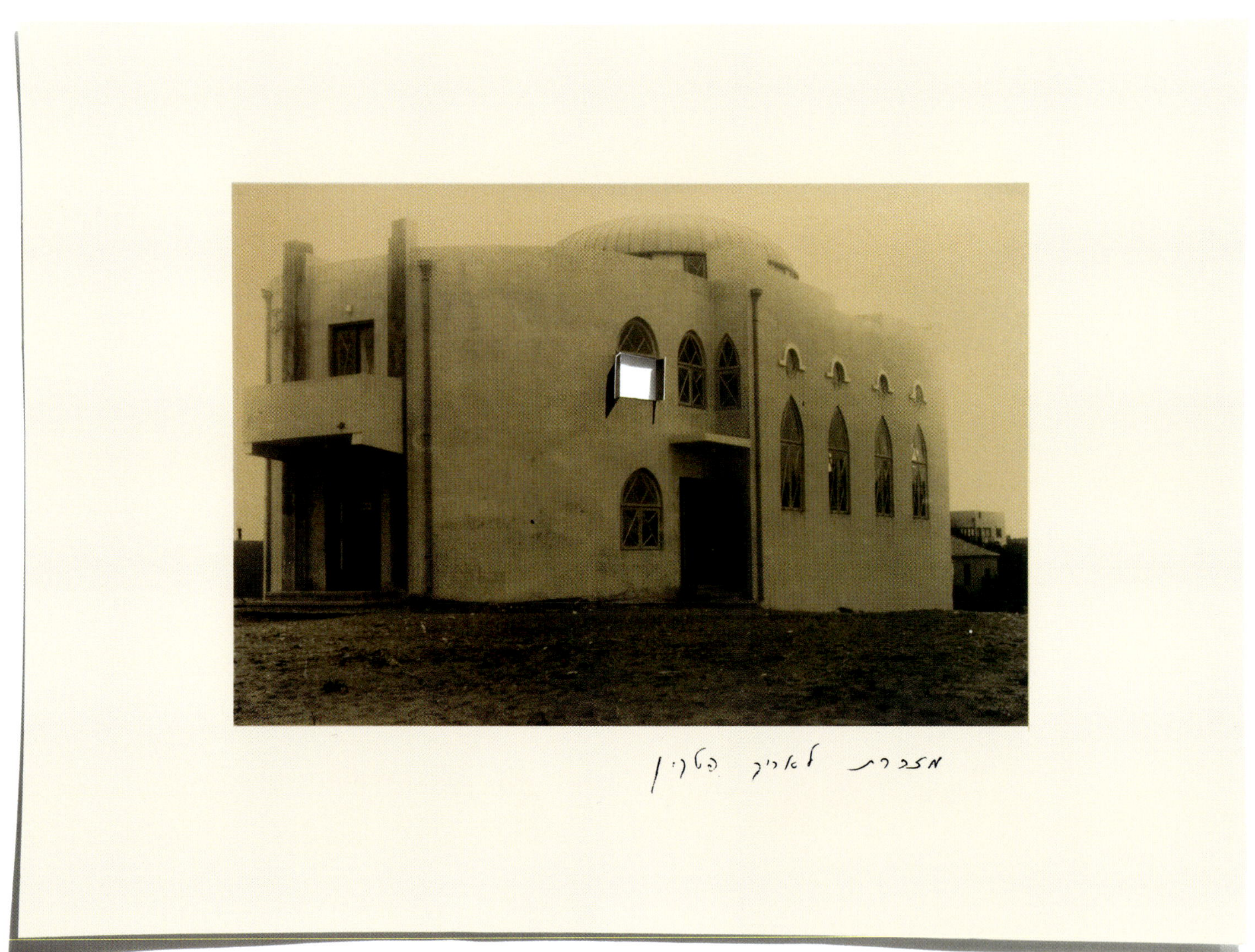
מזכרת לאריך הטרין

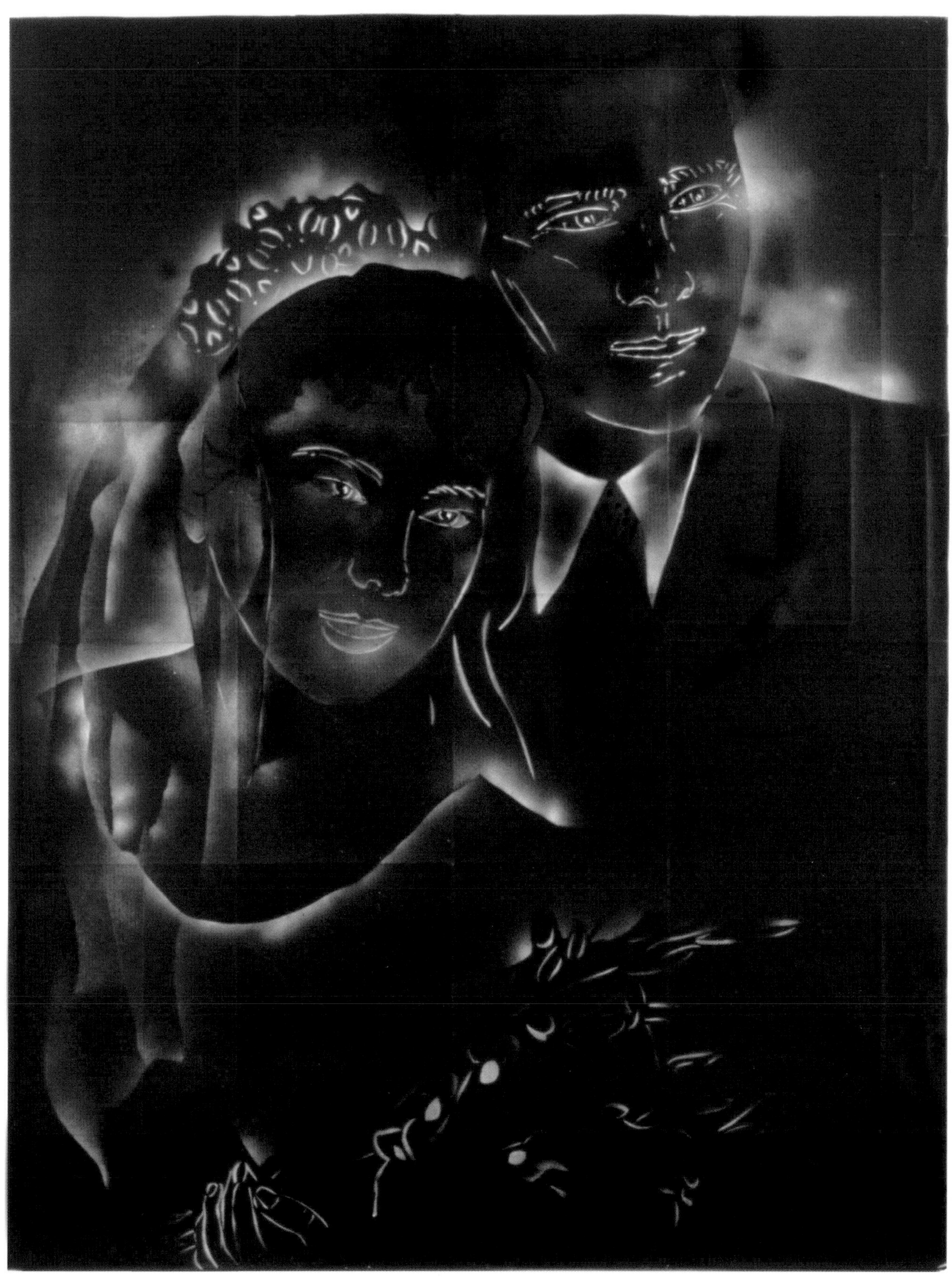

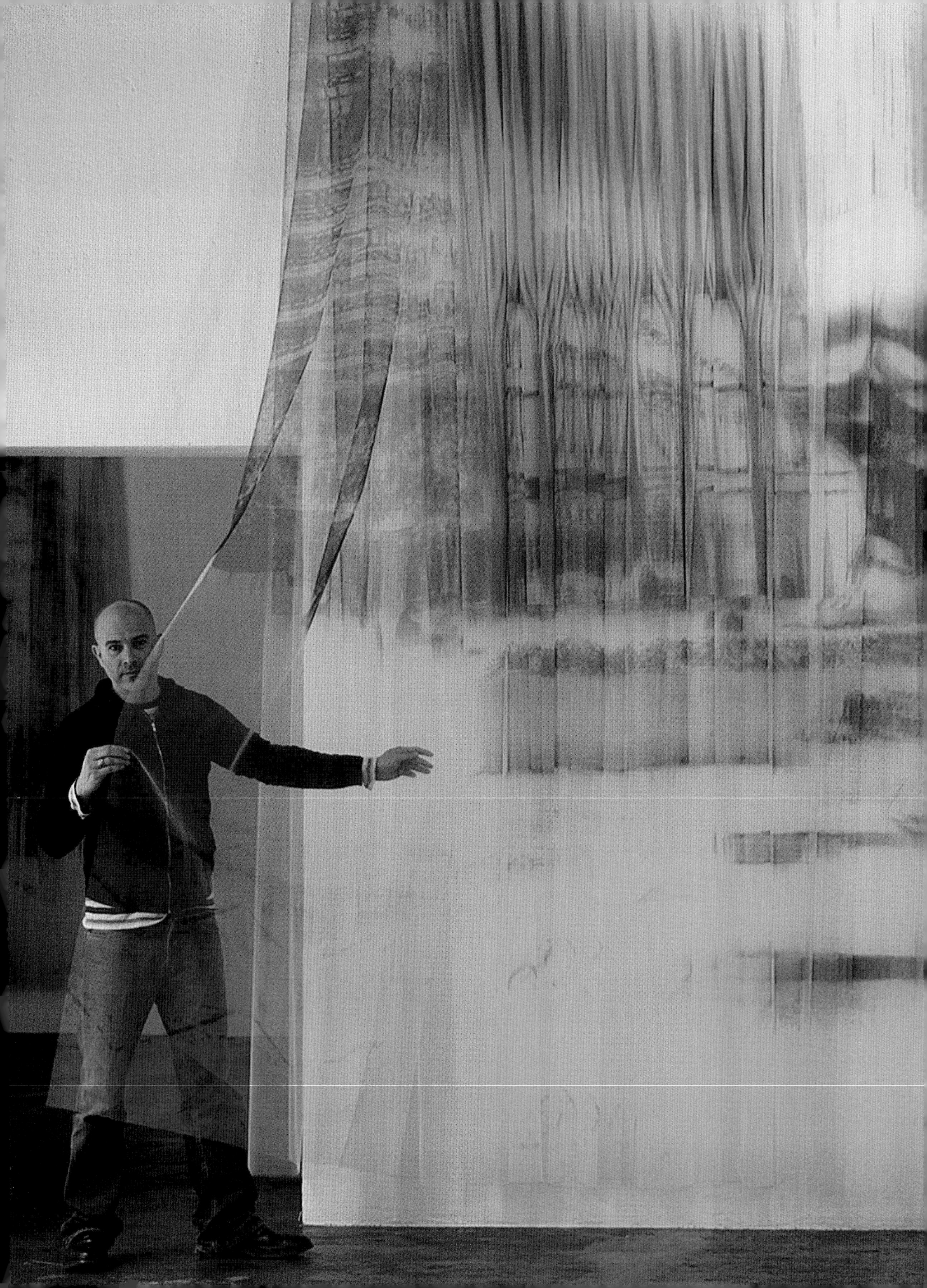

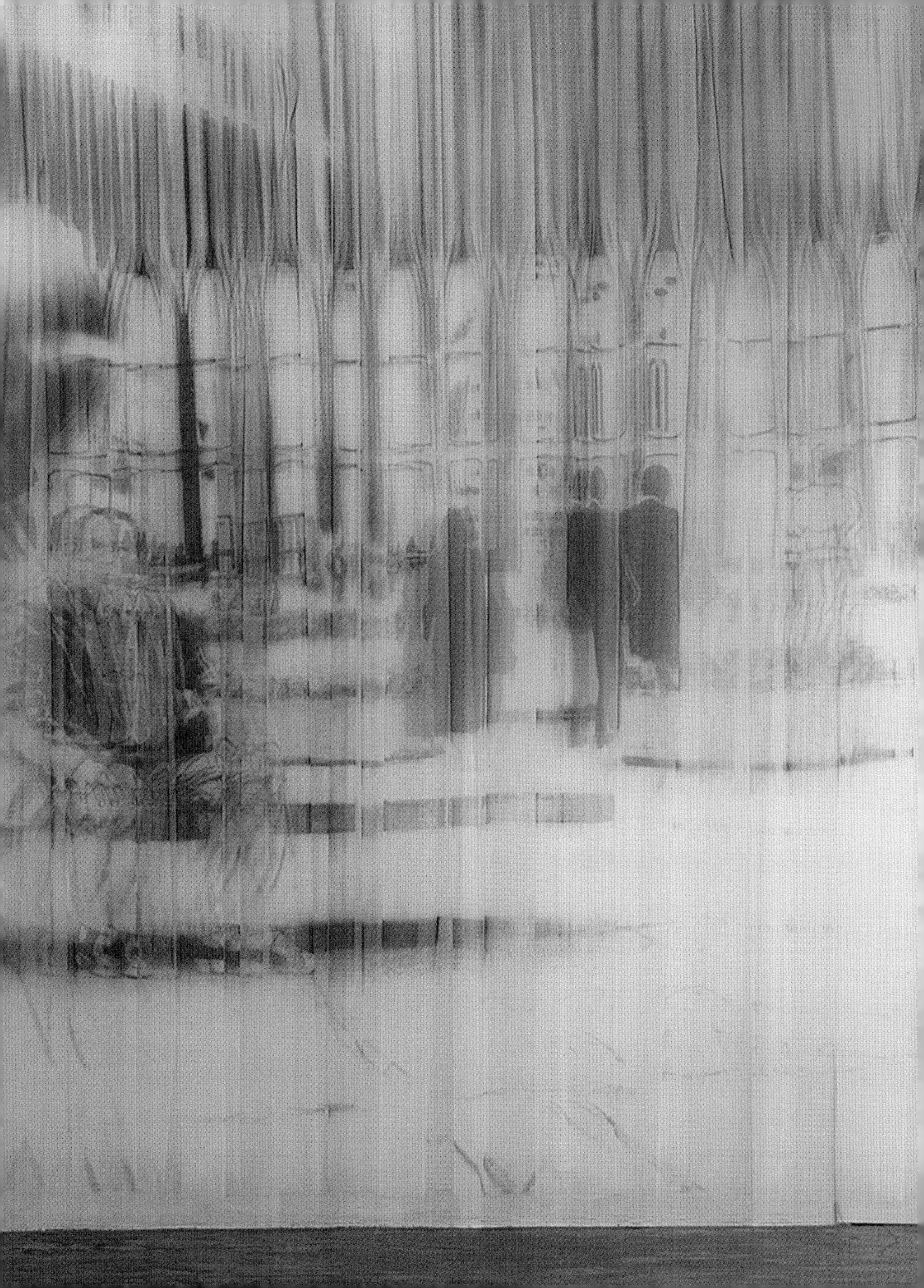

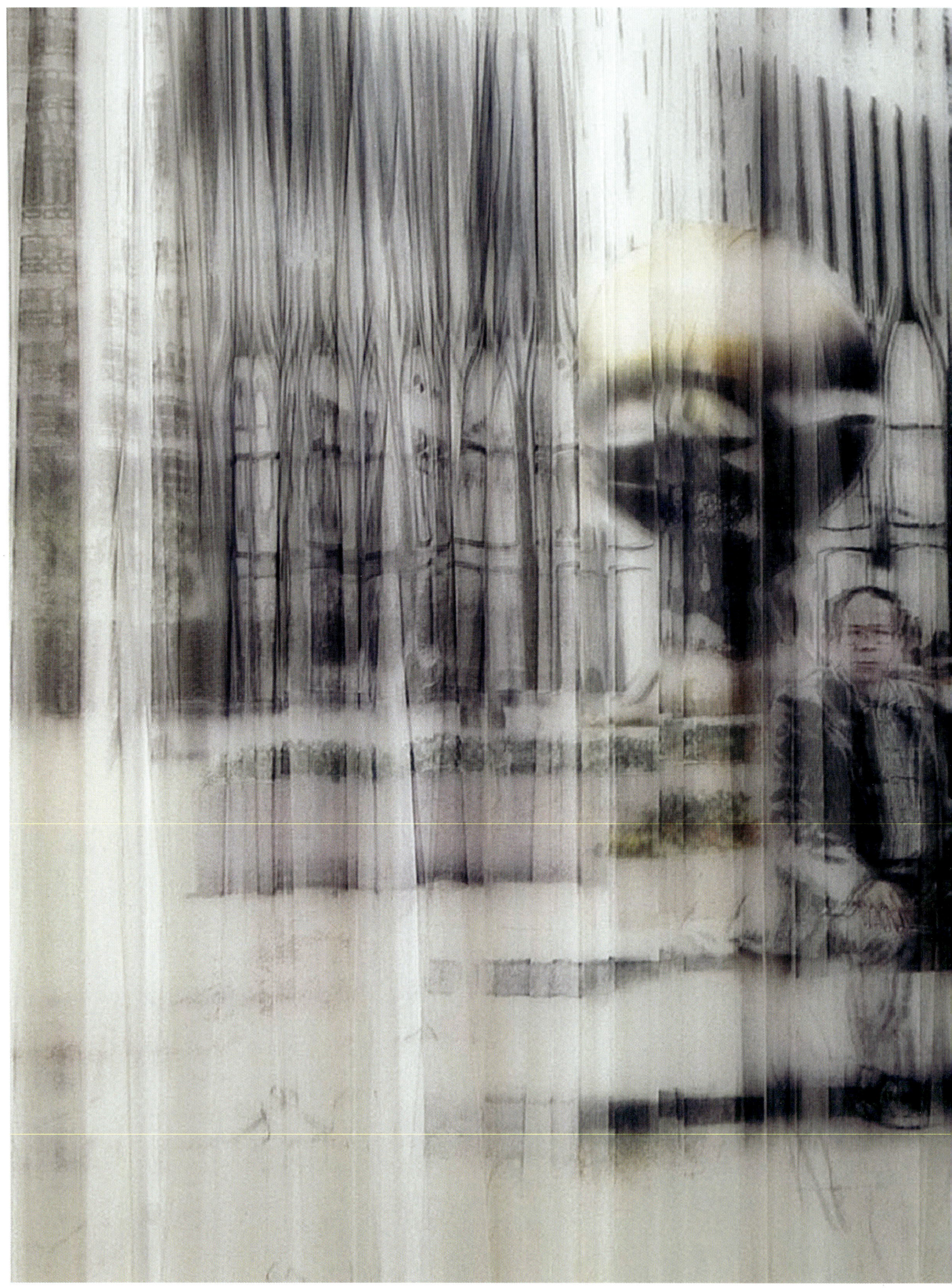

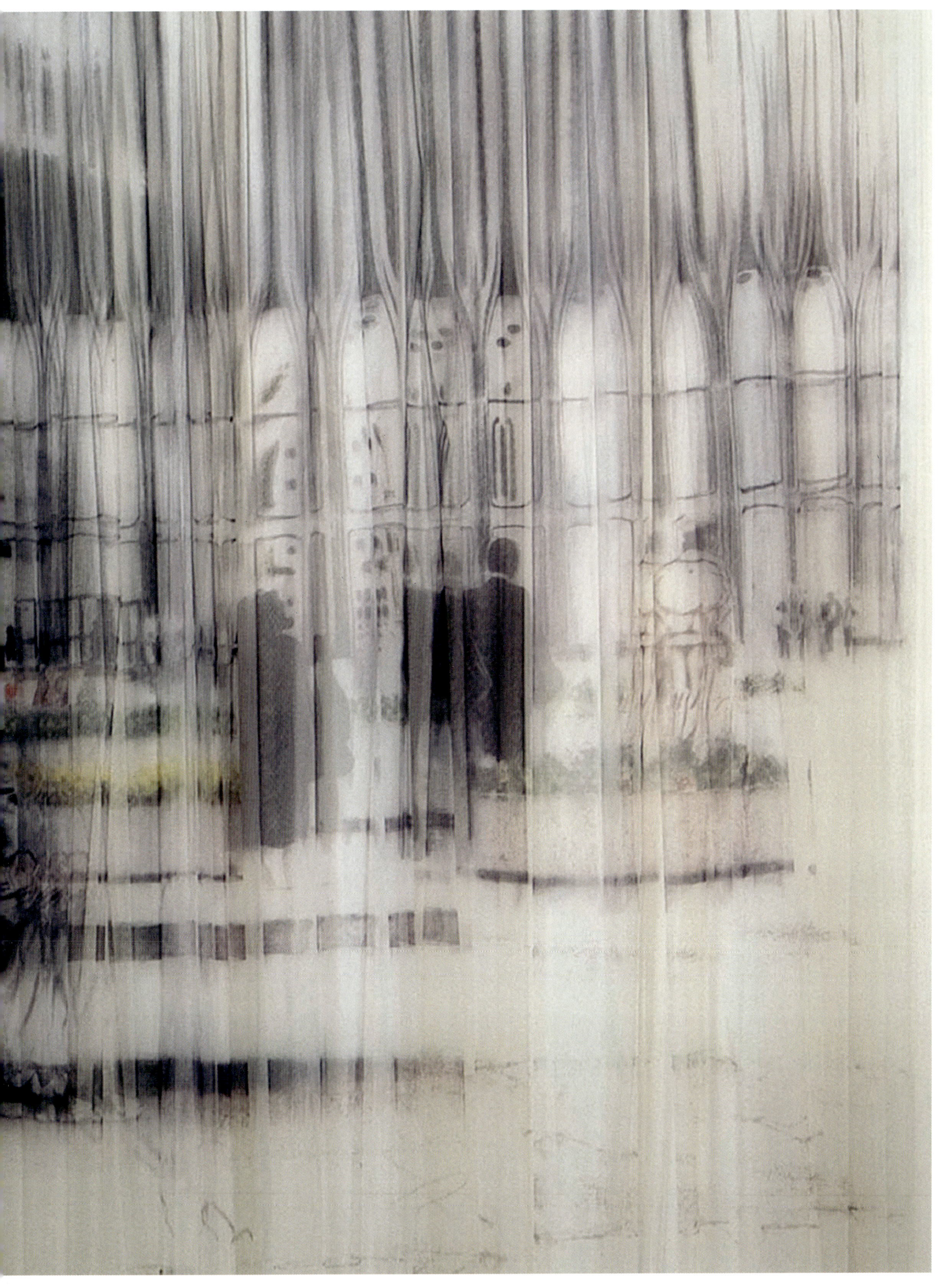

Pictures Are Nets

The Ghost Essay

Rashi[1] *(Rabbi Shlomoh Itzhaki) seems to draw a connection between the notion of the Veil and the notion of the Body, since each is described, separately and in different contexts, either as loaded with souls or as loaded with all the actions of humankind.*

Haviva Pedaya, *Vision and Speech*[2]

STORY/VEIL

I watch Izhar Patkin's dead—as I have conjured them throughout my life—gradually drawn on a misty film of lace, observing the living with their wisdom, which is nothing but a frozen kingdom and waiting, waiting, waiting, immeasurable waiting.

*

It is eerie for me to admit, but I saw the ghostly images as they came into being and took shape in Patkin's veil chambers. I watched as they materialized into an ethereal, gauzy interior, steadily unfurling into their silent, painterly occupancy. Even in a final state—gathering from one another, veil from image and image from veil—they still grasped at being, as if only my gaze were required for them to exist. But a hand could suddenly draw the veils aside, and the paintings would vanish.

*

The moment they become scaffolding for the narrative, the veils are endowed with a meaning other than themselves. Yet these painted veils serve as their own purpose. How can something become a purpose in itself when something outside itself endows it with meaning?

STORY

It is not the particular story that I seek to follow, but the underlying principles of the narrative.

*

One may propose the reductive generalization that each epoch has a literary genre that best captures its essence for its living contemporaries, or for the spirits it invokes.

*

Let's take Modernism, with its belief that a classical Logos[3] or eternity underlies all phenomena. Or its inner conviction that these essentials may materialize through the transient; or its chronic mourning over a world irrevocably lost—all the while delivering a universe made of signs. Then its ideal genre was unmistakably the detective story, a curtain raiser with the shock of the crime, the corpse, and the mobilization of the agents of truth.

*

Lets take post-Modernism, which relinquished the Logos and its essentials for the frivolous convenience of living in a landscape whose raw materials are already processed products. On the run from metaphysical classifications and alienated from them, its supreme genre was the picaresque story, with its haughty transitions between episodes and adventures, whose claims are bound to the confines of adventure.

*

The present, for instance . . .

*

The present?

*

Now, let's take the present, that in which only the present exists. It is the offspring of monstrous historical consciousness overflowing with data, an increasingly elaborate capacity for reconstruction and resurrection of memory that has no duration, not even the duration of occurrence. It is a series of displays and associations, a *self* that had just been convinced it is a mere tangle of randomness, in order to substantiate the multitude of its appearance.

*

In our present, the ghost story offers itself as the best genre, for its underlying premise is the weaving of a phenomenon from one unresolved moment into another. And because of the emotions that wind up suspended in the tension between the two: guilt, repression, age-old rage, and a need for reparation, striving for justice, refusing solace.

*

For the ghost story model is often perceived as "the return of the repressed," whether the ghost is a fragment of refuted content of repressed truth or the burden of morals pertaining to a formative stage of the Self.

*

But in the age of the *now,* in which everything tries to push its way into the present with the same degree of urgency and with the same existential anxiety, the gaps between time collapse. The duration necessary for the return of the repressed slowly evaporates. Nevertheless, that which we seek to cover up or avert our gaze from, whether it be in the realm of politics, ethics, or aesthetics, responds to the same laws of nature and still haunts us.

*

If we could articulate the ceaseless presence of the repressed, then, what ghost show would materialize? How would it manifest? We must extricate ourselves from literature—which is, at its best, an art of chronology—and leap into a medium capable of capturing temporal relations in space and matter.

VEIL

In the Book of Exodus 6:12, Moses, commanded to speak with the Pharaoh, says: "How then will Pharaoh hearken to me, seeing that I am of closed lips?" (עֲרַל שְׂפָתָיִים—*are'l sfa-ta-yeem*). Rashi's commentary is: "Literally, of 'closed' lips.[4] Similarly, I say, every expression of

עָרְלָה (*are'la*) denotes a closure . . . the foreskin of the flesh, by which the male membrum is closed up and covered."

*

The transposition of the Hebrew letters between *are'la* (ערלה—foreskin) and *re'ala* (רעלה—veil) occurs in both post-Mishnaic [5] Hebrew and Maimonides' writings. It is indicative, as is evident in Rashi's commentary, of the way biblical, Mishnaic, and Rabbinic Judaism regarded the screen, the curtain, or the veil: as a deadening device.[6]

*

First was the *Parochet*[7] (the sacred curtain) in the Tent of the Tabernacle, meant to segregate the Holy from the Holy of Holies. Then there was the screen that partitioned the Mishkan's courts;[8] the sacred court versus the profane court, God's lair versus the years of wandering in the desert.

*

But even before that, the underlying logic: Hebraic roots and Judaism in their wake are a way of thinking, an outlook on life that is never unequivocal. Concepts of limitations, delineations, restrictions, and exceptions are at its foundation, but the most significant is the line that must not be crossed between the pure and the contaminated, and between genera of holiness.

*

The veil, as metaphor, is one of the most tactile images for scrutinizing the perceivable. One could maintain that the entire Jewish Halacha—the collective body of Jewish law according to the Mishnah—consists of a way of life that was expanded to the point of becoming a metaphysical order. One could also maintain that from the very beginning this way of life was in accordance with a hidden metaphysical order. Be that as it may, Tractate Ohalot[9] assigns the veil a role as a material partition that either transmits something or impedes its passage between one realm and another. In the context of what is defined as pure or impure, a tent, a fabric, a treetop, or a ship are merely renditions of boundaries, never things in their own right.

*

It is for good reason that Rashi does not waver on the foreskin (*are'la*). Removing that which closes up and covers the flesh—that is the covenant with God—is also emasculation. Drawing closer to His presence is contingent on sanctification (*Hitkadshut*), and an awakening. This blossoming is always accompanied by a renunciation, a blemishing of Eros—an immolation. The relationship between God and the believer is akin to the relationship between man and woman. Accordingly, the Mishnah specifies that only virgins wear the bridal veil. The groom who draws it aside becomes master of the bride's pleasures of the flesh, master of her hymen.

*

A complex web ties aniconism to the Jewish notion of the veil. Giving God explicit eyes confines Him; an image without eyes means an inevitability permeated by His gaze. To withstand the revelation of His glory, a mortal's gaze must be sheathed or emasculated. His very existence seems to hold a potential for calamity. God bridles it with diverse veils, inhibits His very manifestation for man's sake.

*

Even in the upper chambers, we have learned, there are screens, and the sages, who descend to the chariot[10] to debate commandments and circumstances, hear God's heavenly voice (*bat kol*) proclaiming His will or judgment from behind the Veil.[11]

VEIL /STORY

This is what I was taught as a child: In the Jewish universe, there is always a plughole. For every citation, there is a countercitation. And in extreme cases, one infraction annuls another. A mitzvah overcomes a prohibition, or the other way around.

*

When Moses first proclaims himself "of closed lips," his complaint is ignored. When he is introduced to his mission (Exodus 4), Moses protests, "For I am slow of speech and slow of tongue." Yet the Midrash[12] (Shmot Rabba 3:20) tells us that this was God's intention when he created Moses. Had He wished to make Moses coherent or whole, He would have made his speech unslurred.

*

Maimonides, probably the most eloquent advocate the Jewish world has known for negating God's appellations and refusing to behold Him in any configuration of image, also produced the most elaborate theory of prophecy. According to him, Moses alone was allowed to encounter God face to face. Everyone else was on lesser standing, and thus God appeared to them only through a facet of his providence: speech, a distant image, or a parable.

*

Between Moses and God there is a game of deliberate concealments, which can only take place in the narrow gap between the protective hiding of God's face (*Hester Panim*)[13] and the command to remove the foreskin. Moses pleads with God to allow him to see; Moses turns his eyes down; God reveals Himself to Moses in all his glory; God shelters Moses with his hand. Between God and his chosen, the deep familiarity with the Veil principle and when to apply it is a tenet underlying the treatise of revelation.

*

The same tenet takes material form in Patkin's ghost story. The painted veils, which are spatial entities, not sculptures, refuse their ordained role of transmitting and impeding. They use the narrative as a counterweight to the material object. The "closed lips"/ערלה/veil/canvas is an illusion of both transparency and representation.

In the ghost story, the repressed return in filmy appearance, as an image on the brink of evaporation. Look them in the eye or avoid them.

*

Thus, the spectator and I stand in the veil chambers at the epicenter of paralyzed time. On one veil, Patkin's father sits with the gothic pillars of New York's former World Trade Center looming over him (pages 38–41). There, in another veil room, a magician hypnotizes time, bringing it to a standstill. Elsewhere, Jewish refugees from one era and Palestinians from another carry their salvaged possessions (pages 112–17), their future emotional baggage. The picture will keep haunting us. It is a timeless image of exile, without denying any of the suffering or absolving blame.

*

Beyond the misty lace and the ink brushstrokes, our dead amass substance and stare back at our time with wisdom. Perhaps it is because they are stripped of circumstance and consequence. Perhaps it is because we see their souls laid bare. Or maybe it is because of the triumph of their love while they were still alive.

*

I need (duration) to make sense (of these sentences).

*

We are at the dawn of a new age when *time* will pass without duration.

*

Between this age and myself are Patkin's veil chambers.

Shimon Adaf

NOTES

1

RASHI is an acronym for "Rabbi Shlomo ben Yitzchak" (1040–1105). Born in Troyes, France, and educated in Germany, he was without doubt the greatest commentator on the Written Law as well as on the Oral Law.

2

Haviva Pedaya, *Vision and Speech: Models of Prophecy in Jewish Mysticism* [in Hebrew] (Los Angeles: Cherub Publishers, 2002).

3

Aristotle's three main forms of rhetoric: Ethos, Logos, and Pathos.

4

Closed lips: Heb. עֲרַל שְׂפָתַיִם, Literally, of "closed" lips. Similarly, every expression of (עָרְלָה) I say, denotes a closure: e.g., "their ear is clogged (עֲרֵלָה)" (Jer. 6:10), [meaning] clogged to prevent hearing; "of uncircumcised (עַרְלֵי) hearts" (Jer. 9:25), [meaning] clogged to prevent understanding ... the foreskin of the flesh, by which the male membrum is closed up and covered; "and you shall treat its fruit as forbidden (וַעֲרַלְתֶּם עָרְלָתוֹ)" (Lev. 19:23), [i.e.,] make for it a closure and a covering of prohibition, which will create a barrier that will prevent you from eating it. "For three years, it shall be closed up [forbidden] (עֲרֵלִים) for you" (Lev. 19:23), [i.e.,] closed up, covered, and separated from eating it.

5
The Mishnah consists of six orders (*sedarim*; singular is *seder*), each containing seven to twelve tractates (*masechtot*; singular is *masechet*, literally, "web"), sixty-three in total, and further subdivided into chapters and paragraphs or verses.—Trans.

6
It refers to the relationship between veil, foreskin, and "closed lips."

7
The *Parochet* is also the Torah Ark Curtain.

8
In Hebrew, the Tent of the Tabernacle is called the *Mishkan*. The *Mishkan* was divided into two sections: a large court called the Holy Place and a small section called the Holy of Holies. The curtain that separates the Holy of Holies from the Holy Place is called the Veil. This veil was made of blue, purple, and scarlet, and fine twined linen, with the figures of cherubim. The *Mishkan* had to be portable and easily set up and easily taken down (Exod. 26: 31-33).

9
Seder Taharot, Tractate Ohalot, chapter 8, addresses questions of corpse uncleanliness. It is an abstract reading of "the tent," defined as a contained space of certain cubic handbreadth, which serves to permit the passage of impure corpse-matter or to prevent its entry.—Trans.

10
In the Hekhalot and Mercava literature (a large corpus of Jewish mystical writings), descending to the chariot or ascending to it means visiting God's heavenly throne-chariot and compelling the angels to grant revelations. The concept of the chariot is associated with Ezekiel's vision (Ezek. 1:4-26).—Trans.

11
E.g., Talmud Bavli, Tractate Chagigah 15a.—Trans.

12
Midrash is a form of rabbinic literature for interpreting biblical stories beyond the simple distillation of religious, legal, or moral teachings. There are two types of Midrash: *Midrash Aggada* and *Midrash Halakha*.

13
Hester Panim (literally, "hiding face") refers to concealed divine providence.—Trans.

VIOLINS

Violins weep with gypsies going to Andalusia
Violins weep for Arabs leaving Andalusia

Violins weep for a time that does not return
Violins weep for a homeland that might return

Violins set fire to the woods of that deep deep darkness
Violins tear the horizon and smell my blood in the vein

Violins weep with gypsies going to Andalusia
Violins weep for Arabs leaving Andalusia

Violins are horses on a phantom string of moaning water
Violins are the ebb and flow of a field of wild lilacs

Violins are monsters touched by the nail of a woman now distant
Violins are an army, building and filling a tomb made of marble and *Nahawund**

Violins are the anarchy of hearts driven mad by the wind in a dancer's foot
Violins are flocks of birds fleeing a torn banner

Violins are complaints of silk creased in the lover's night
Violins are the distant sound of wine falling on a previous desire

Violins follow me everywhere in vengeance
Violins seek me out to kill me wherever they find me

Violins weep for Arabs leaving Andalusia
Violins weep with gypsies going to Andalusia

Poem by Mahmoud Darwish
Version by Agha Shahid Ali (with Ahmad Dallal)

* *Nahawund: One of the classical Arabic musical modes.*

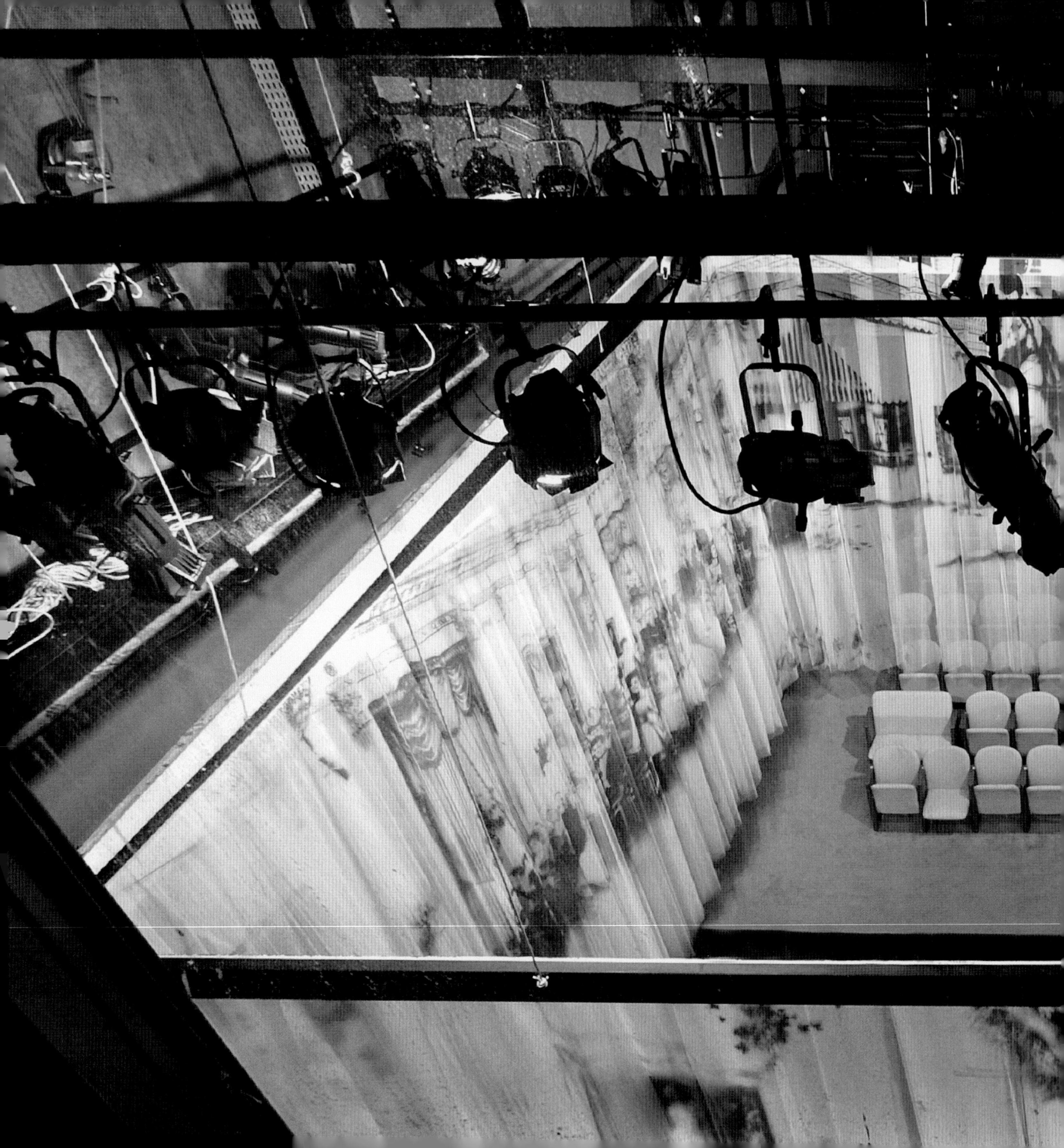

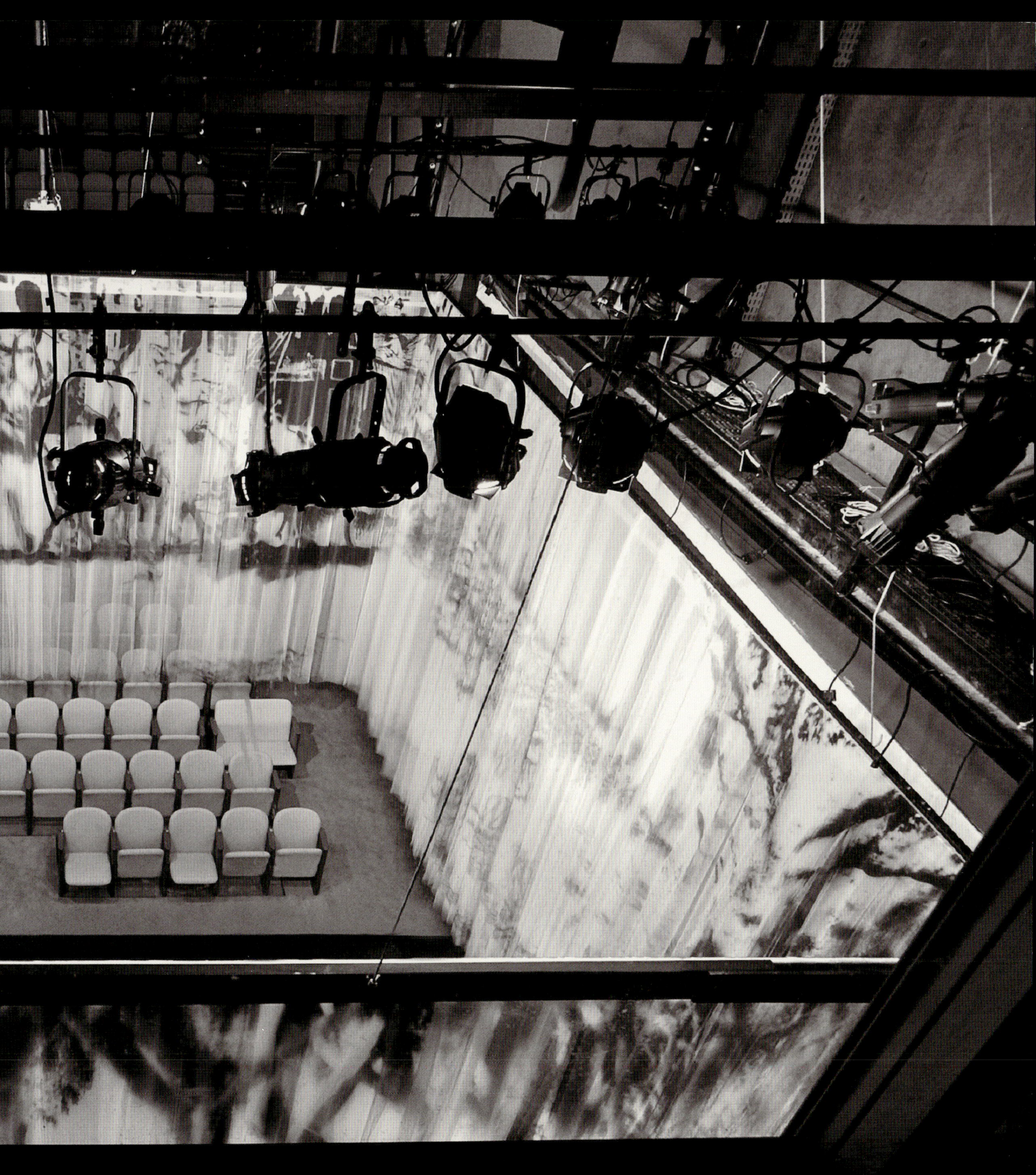

For me, the curtain is a canvas. It's not meant to be a curtain over a window. It's meant to occupy the space of painting.

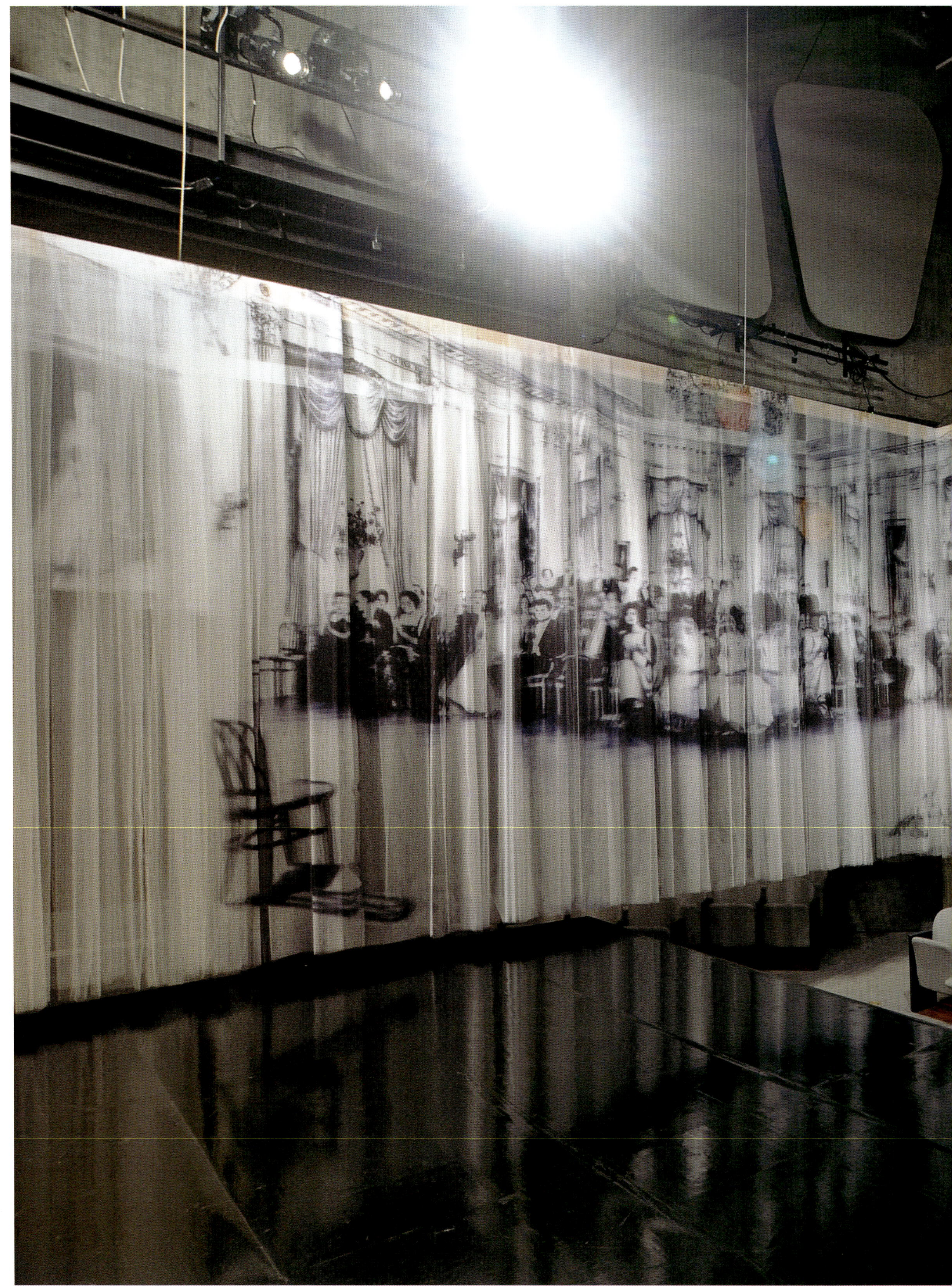

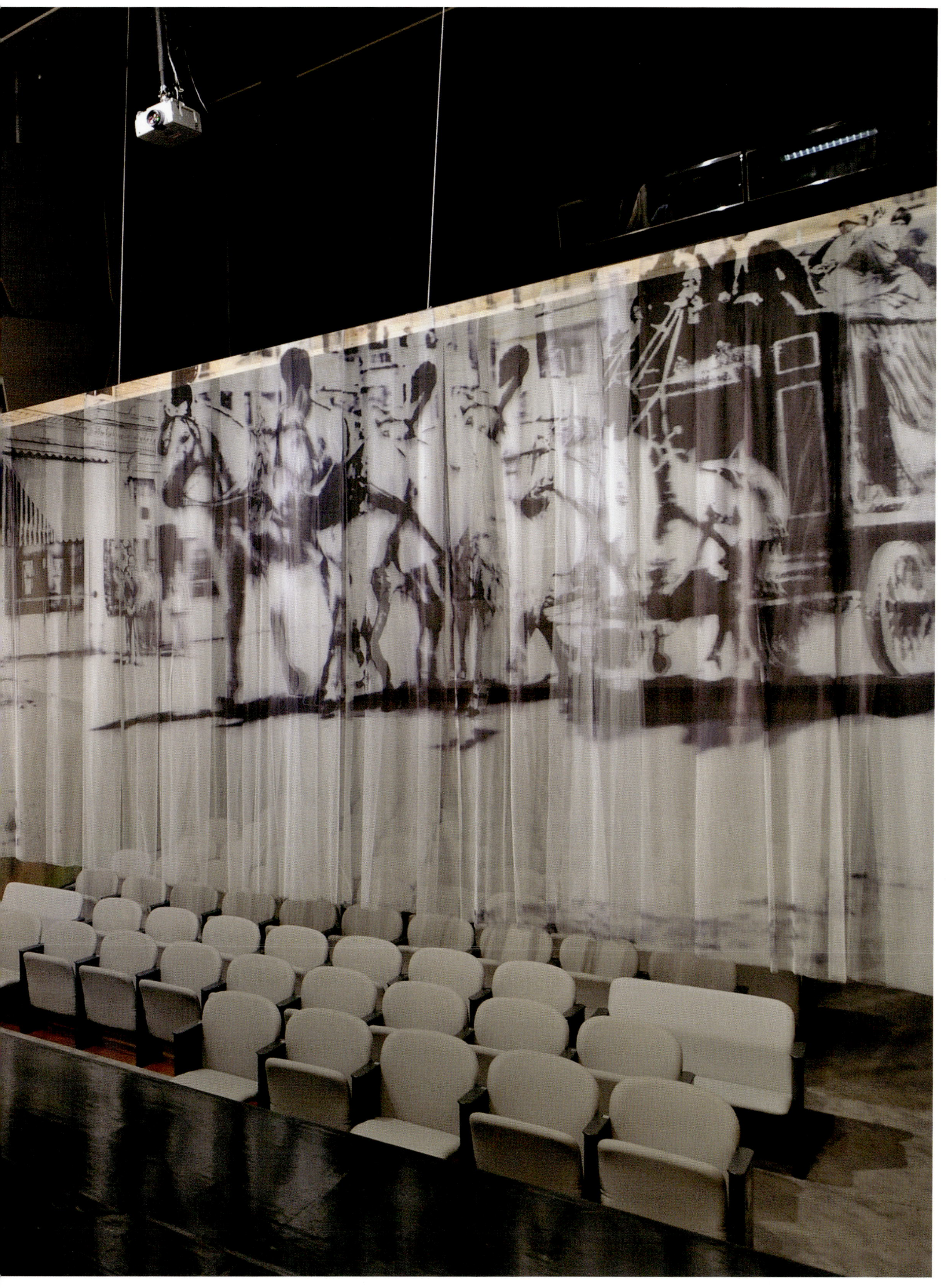

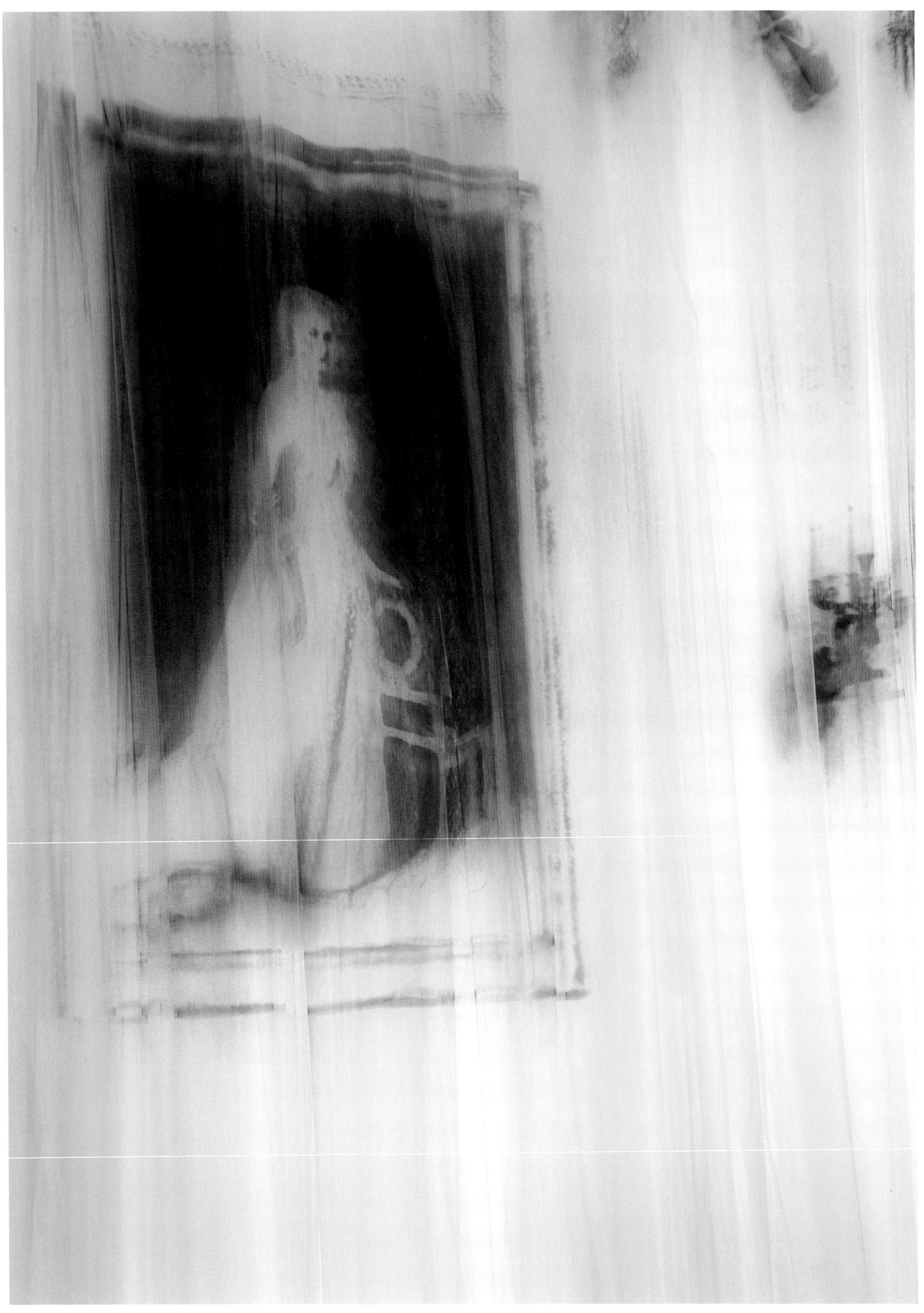

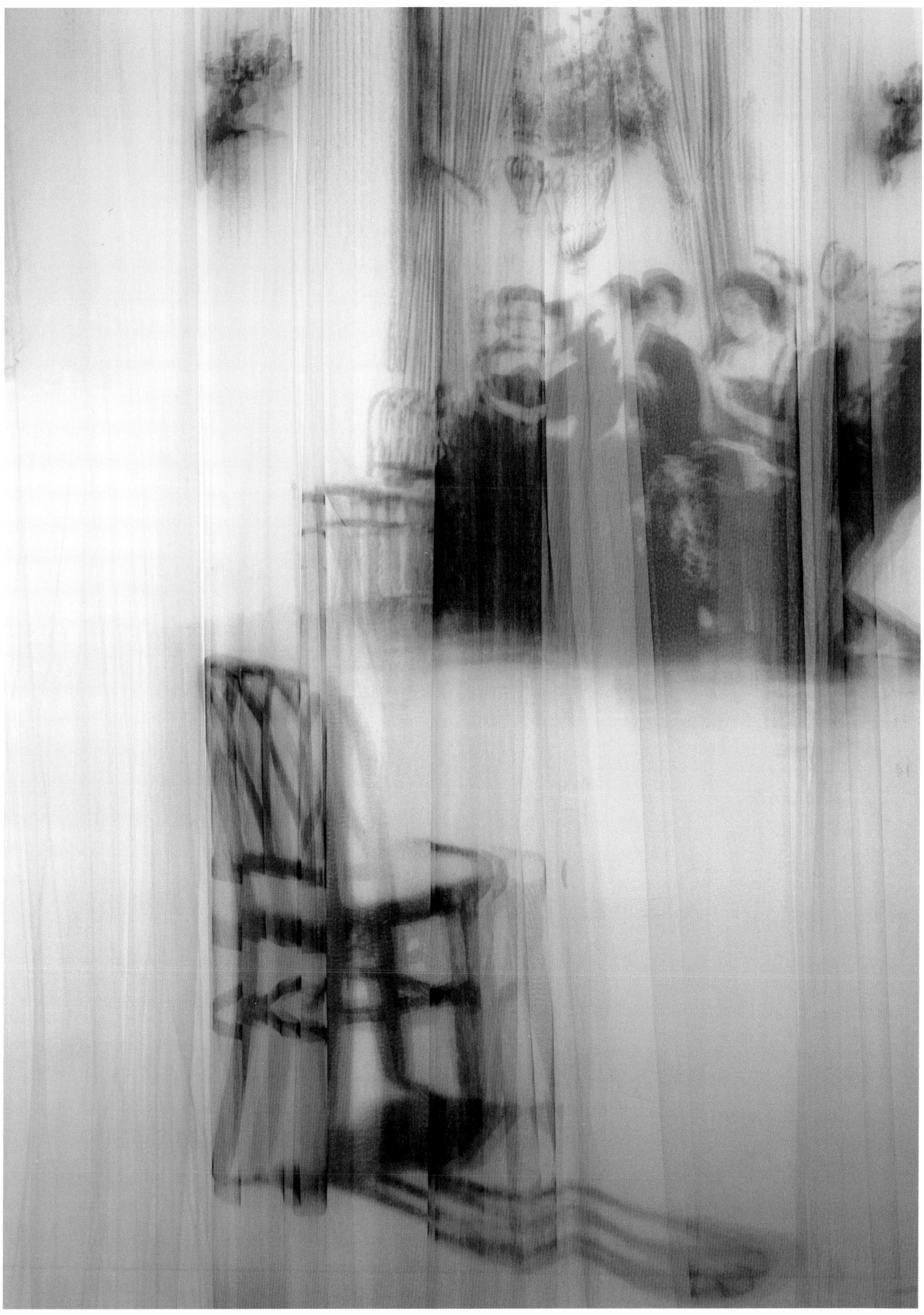

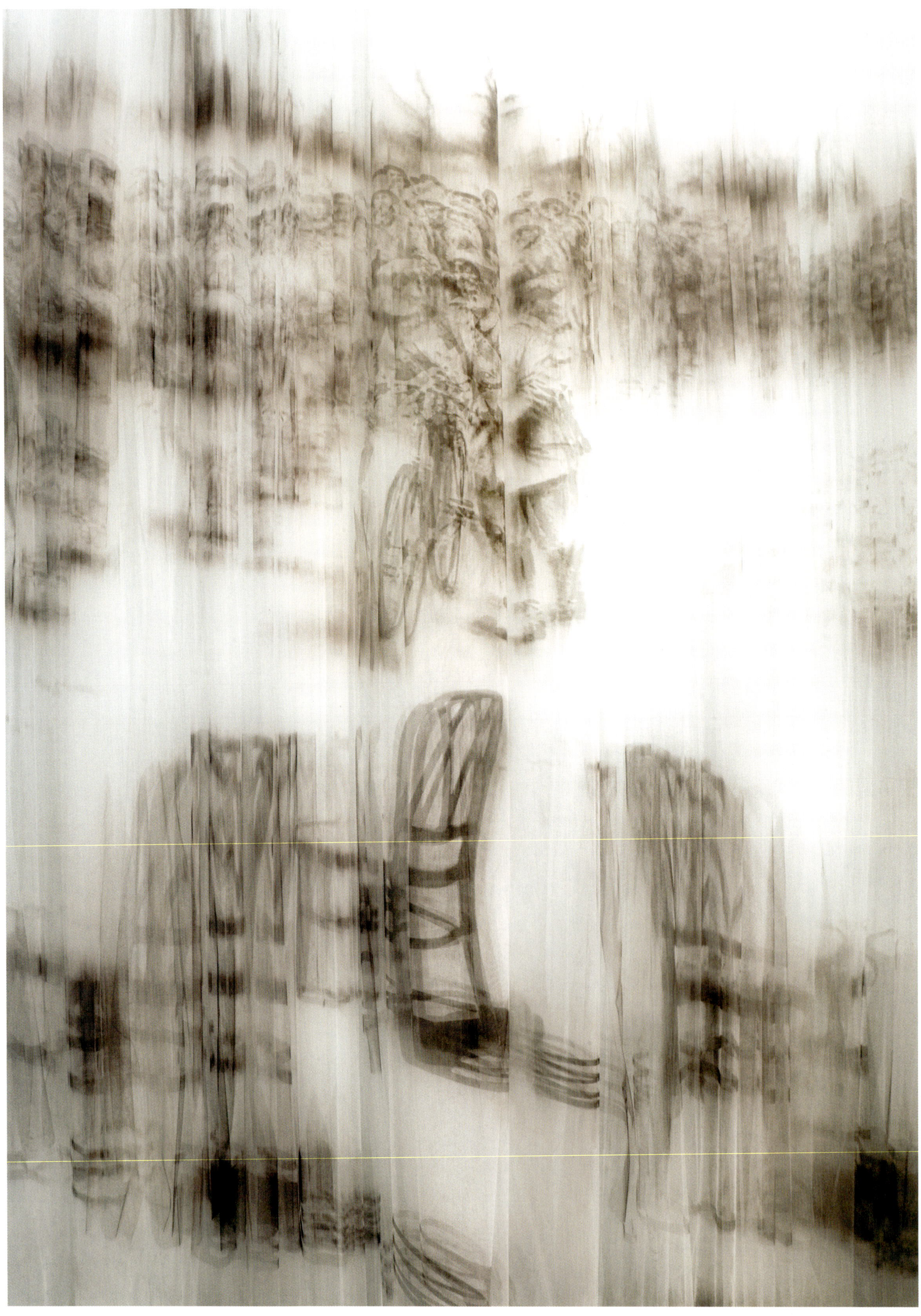

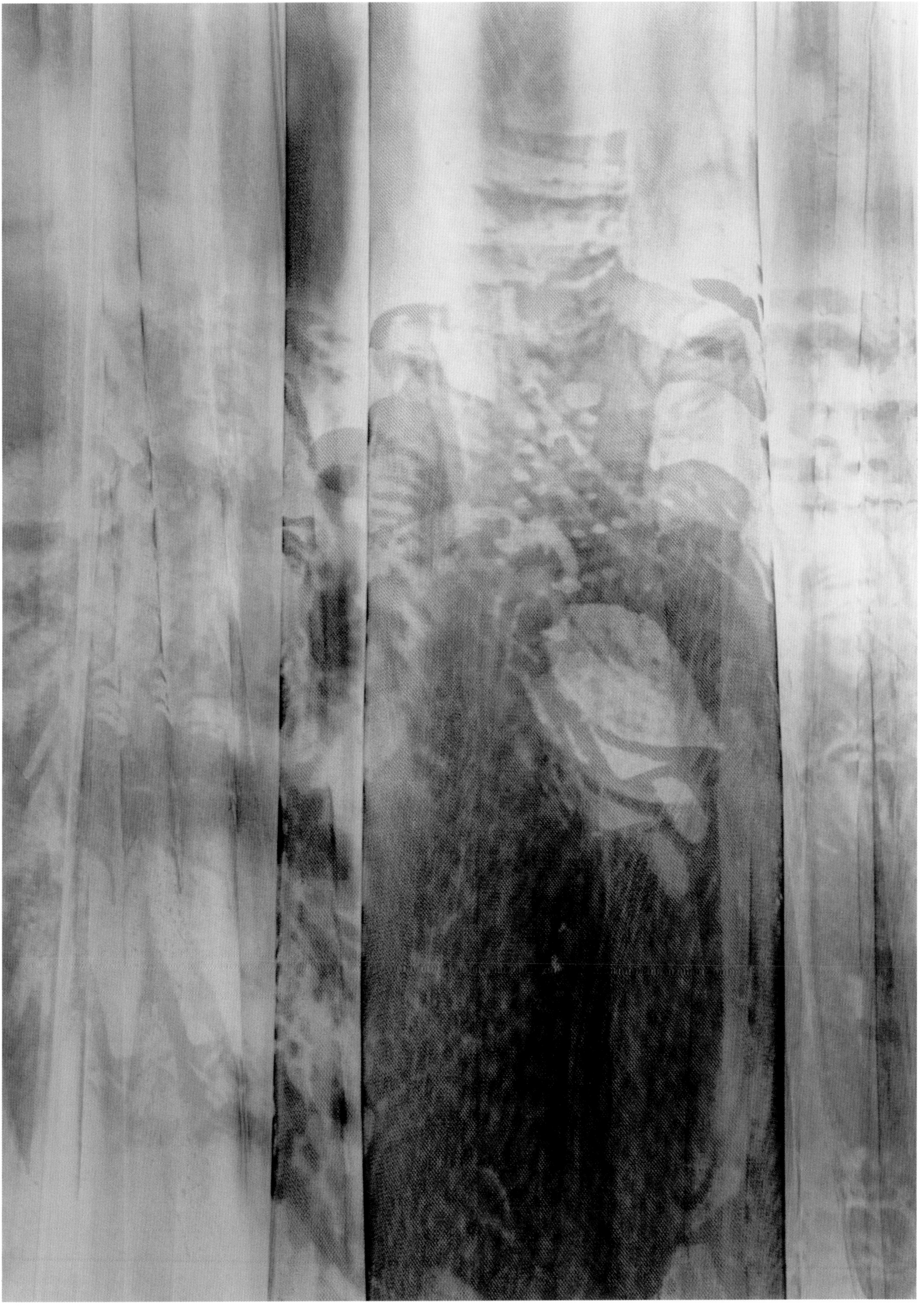

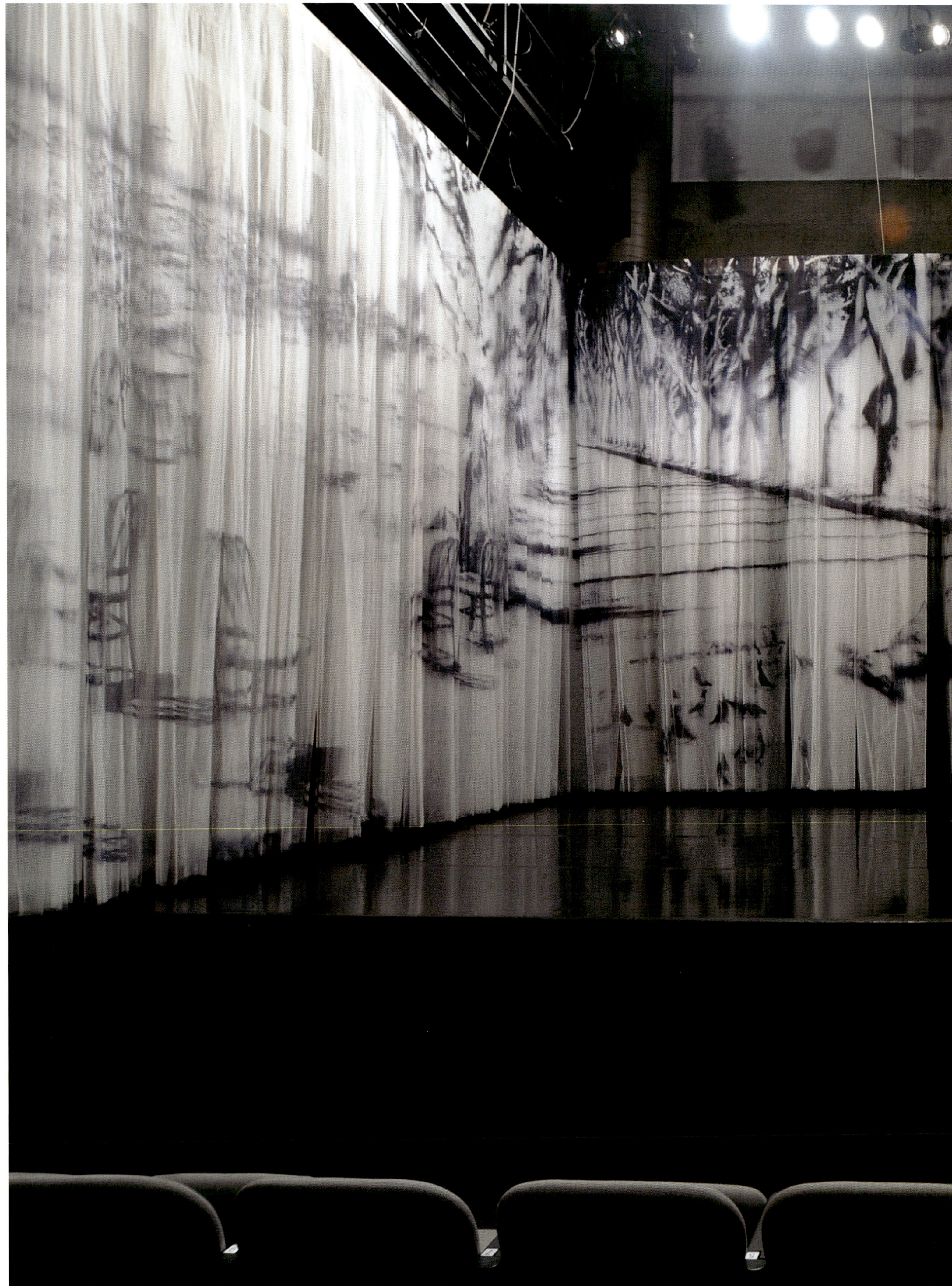

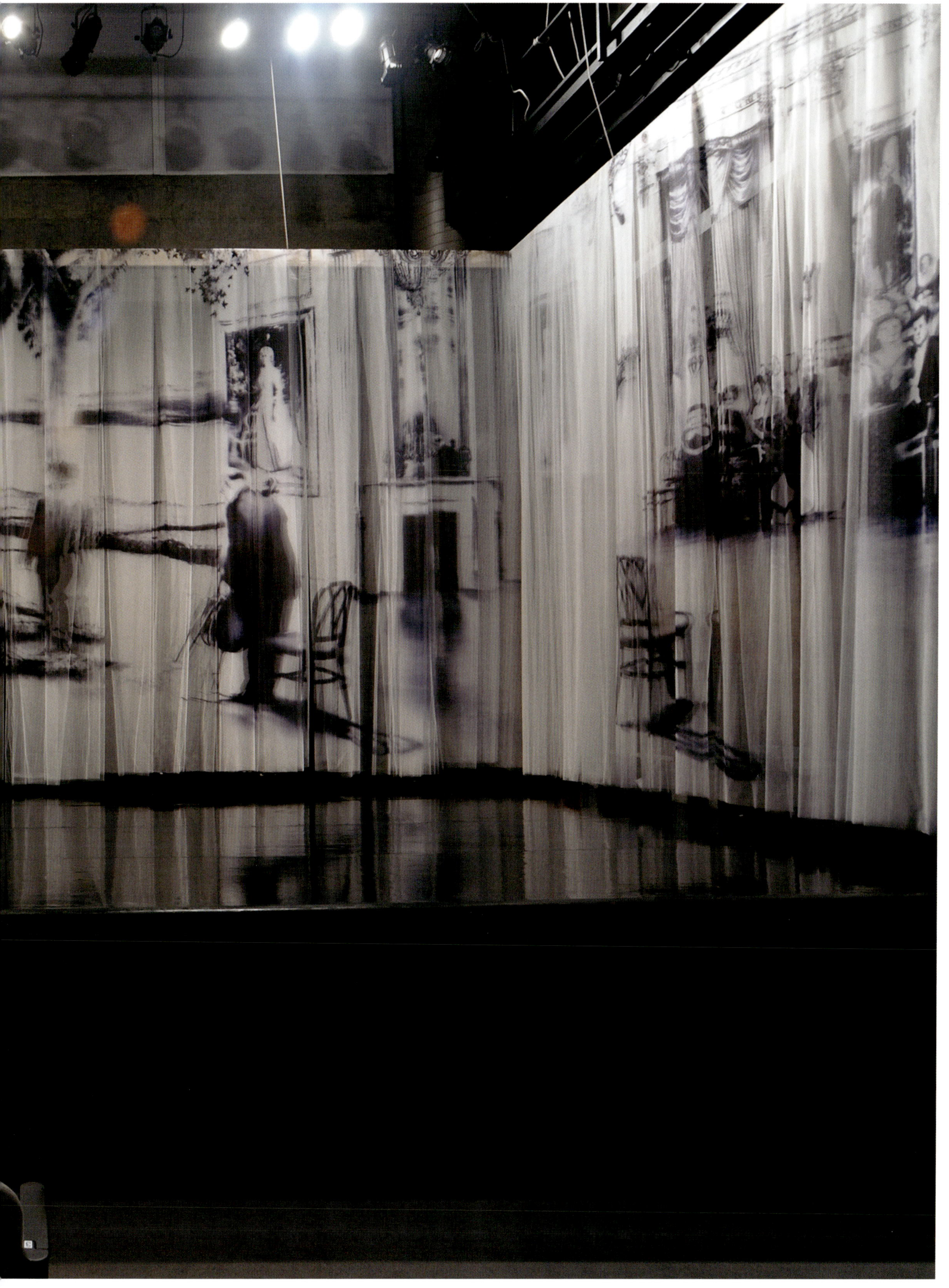

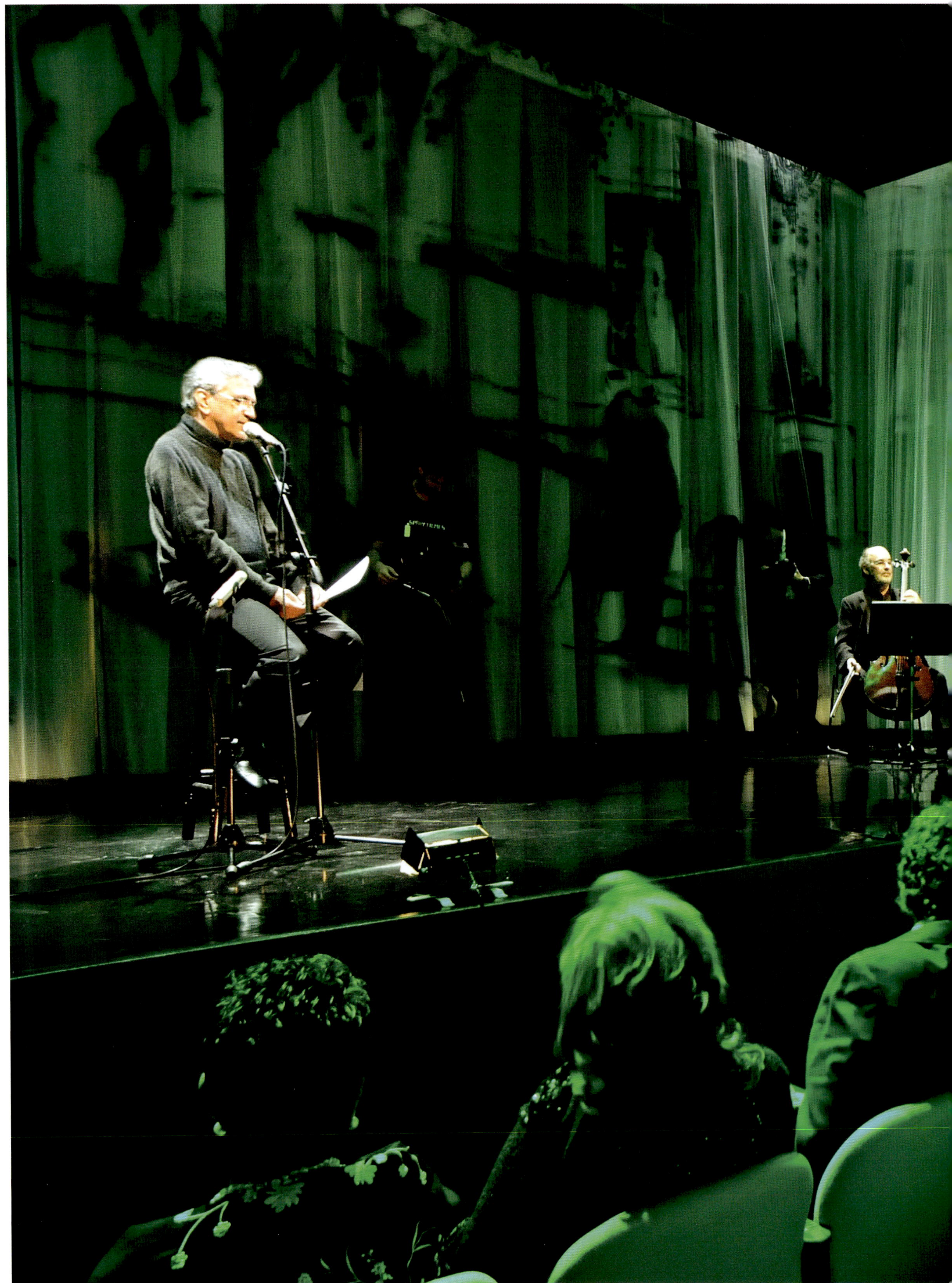

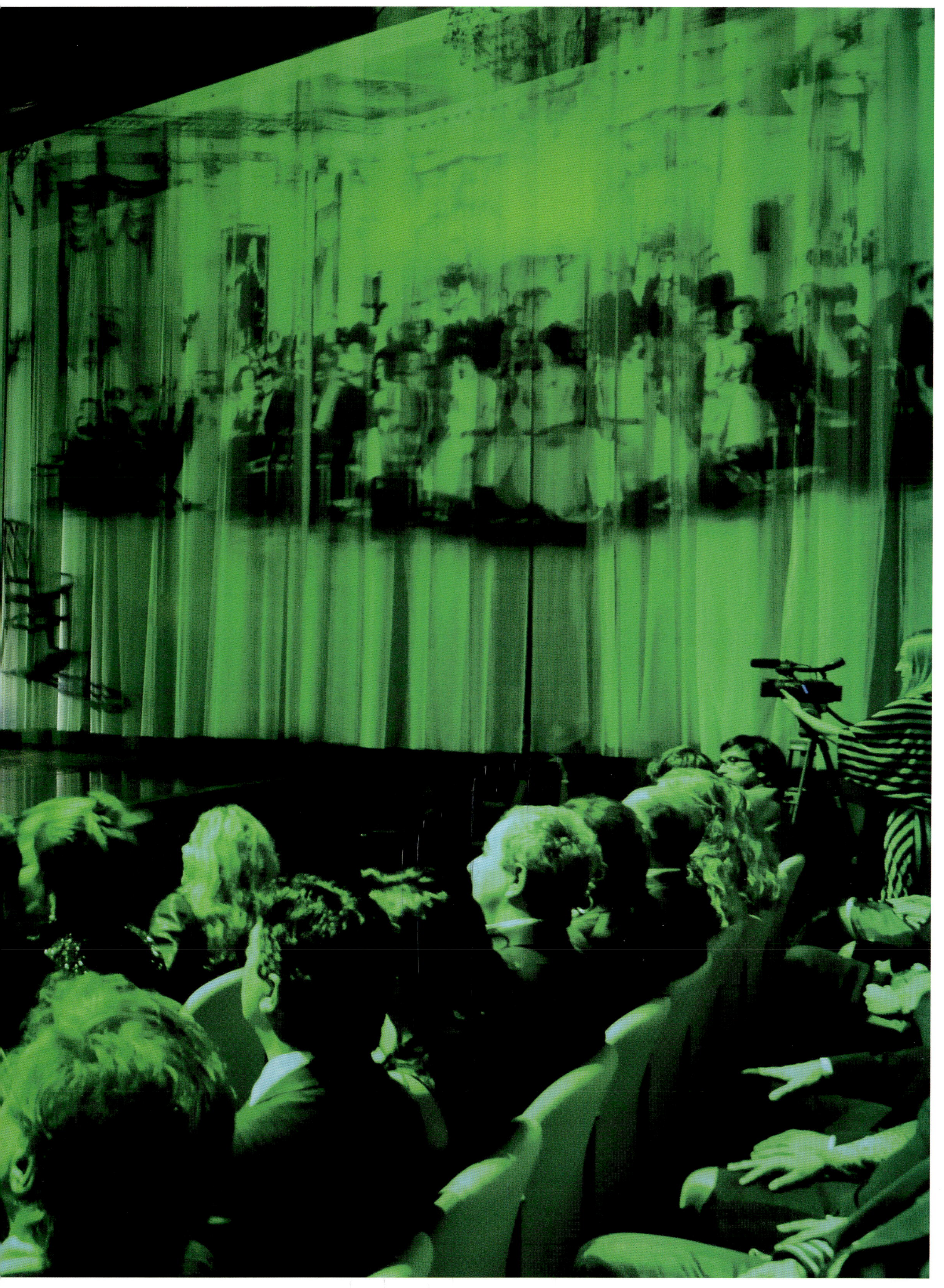

THE VEILED SUITE

Faceless, he could represent only two alternatives:
that he was either a conscious agent of harm,
*or that he would unknowingly harm me anyway.**

"No mortal has or will ever lift my veil,"
he says. Strokes my arm. What poison is his eyes?
Make me now your veil, then see if you can veil
yourself from me. Where is he not from? Which vale
of tears? Am I awake? There is little sense
of whether I am his—or he is my—veil.
For, after the night is fog, who'll unveil
whom? Either he knows he is one with the night
or is unaware he's an agent of night—
nothing else is possible (who is whose veil?)
when he, random assassin sent by the sea
is putting, and with no sense of urgency,

the final touches on—whose last fantasy?
Where isn't he from? He's brought the sky from Vail,
Colorado, and the Ganges from Varanasi
in a clay urn (his heart measures like the sea).
He's brought the desert too. It's deep in his eyes
when he says: "I want you to be mine alone, see."
What hasn't he planned? For music Debussy,
then a song from New Orleans in the *Crescent*'s
time nearing Penn Station. What's of the essence?
Not time, not time, no, not time. I can foresee
he will lead each night from night into night.
I ask, "Can you promise me this much tonight:

that when you divide what remains of this night
it will be like a prophet once parted the sea.
But no one must die! For however this night
has been summoned, I, your mortal every night,
must become your veil . . . and I must lift your veil
when just one thing's left to consider: the night."
There's just one thing left to consider, the night
in which we will be left to realize
when the ice begins to break down in his eyes.
And the prophecies filming his gaze tonight?
What will be revealed? What stunning color sense
kept hidden so long in his eyes, what essence

of longing? He can kill me without a license.
The moon for its ivory scours the night.
Sent by the fog, he nearly empties in me all sense
of his gaze, till either he or I have lost all sense;
midnight polishes the remains of a galaxy.
What is left to polish now? What fluorescence?
Is there some hope of making a world of sense?
When I meet his gaze, there is again the veil.
On the farthest side of prophecy, I still need a veil.
Perhaps our only chance will be to ignite
the doom he sometimes veils in his eyes,
and the universe lost, like I am, in his eyes.

I wait for him to look straight into my eyes.
This is our only chance for magnificence.
If he, carefully, upon this hour of ice,
will let us almost completely crystallize,
tell me, who but I could chill his dreaming night.
Where he turns, what will not appear but my eyes?
Wherever he looks, the sky is only eyes.
Whatever news he has, it is of the sea.
But now is the time when I am to realize
our night cannot end completely with his eyes.
Something has happened now for me to prevail,
no matter what remains of this final night.

What arrangements haven't you made for tonight!
I am to hand you a knife from behind the veil
now rising quickly from your just-lit incense.
I'm still alive, alive to learn from your eyes
that I am become your veil and I am all you see.

(for Patricia O'Neill)

Poem by Agha Shahid Ali

* *From a dream in which I said this to myself (Spring 2000).*

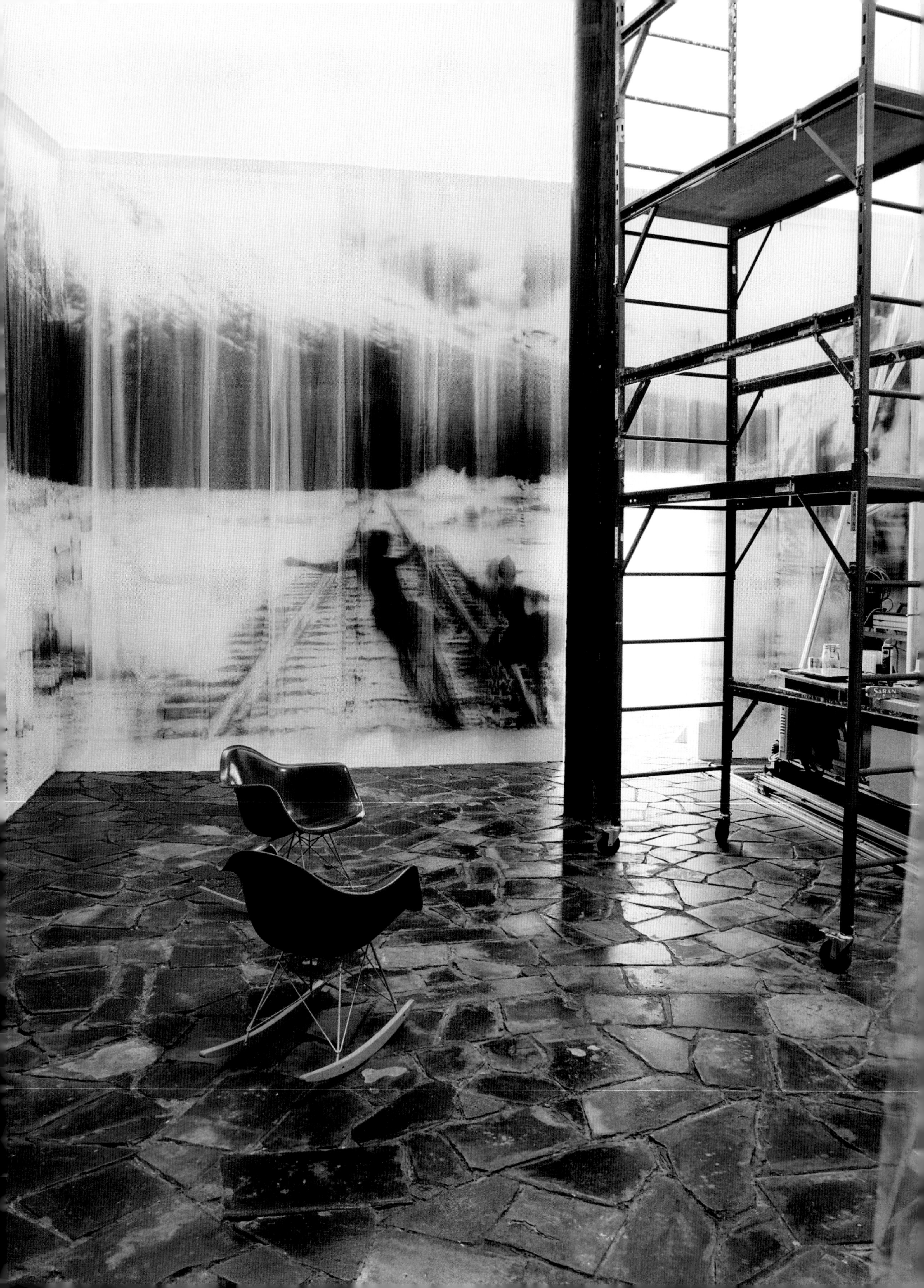
SARAN

Shahid's "wandering" poems became the text that I had to put into another language—the painterly—without using words at all. Each veil room is an adaptation of a different poem. I had to invent a different time and place for each one, a stage on which to evoke and visualize each poem.

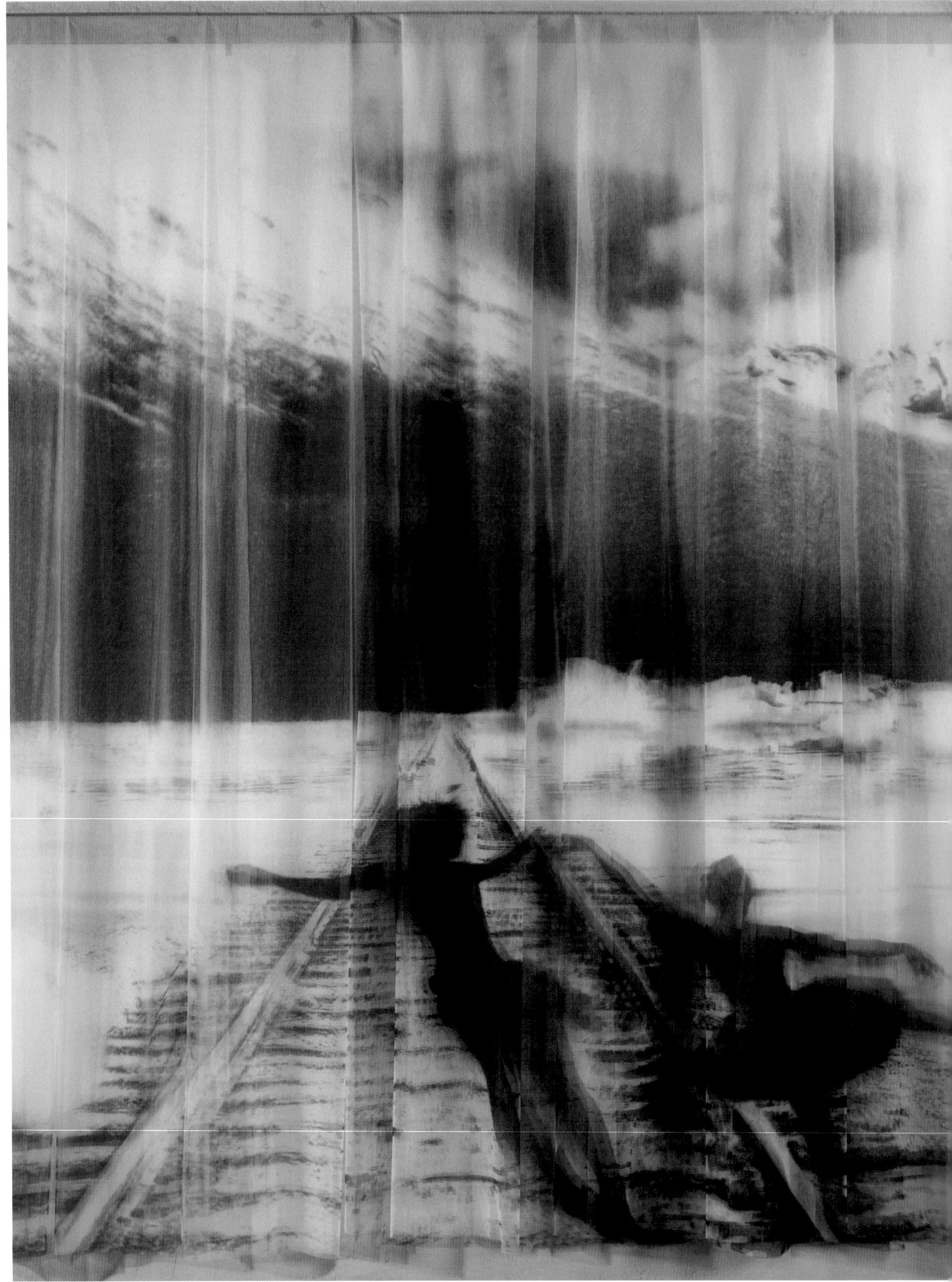

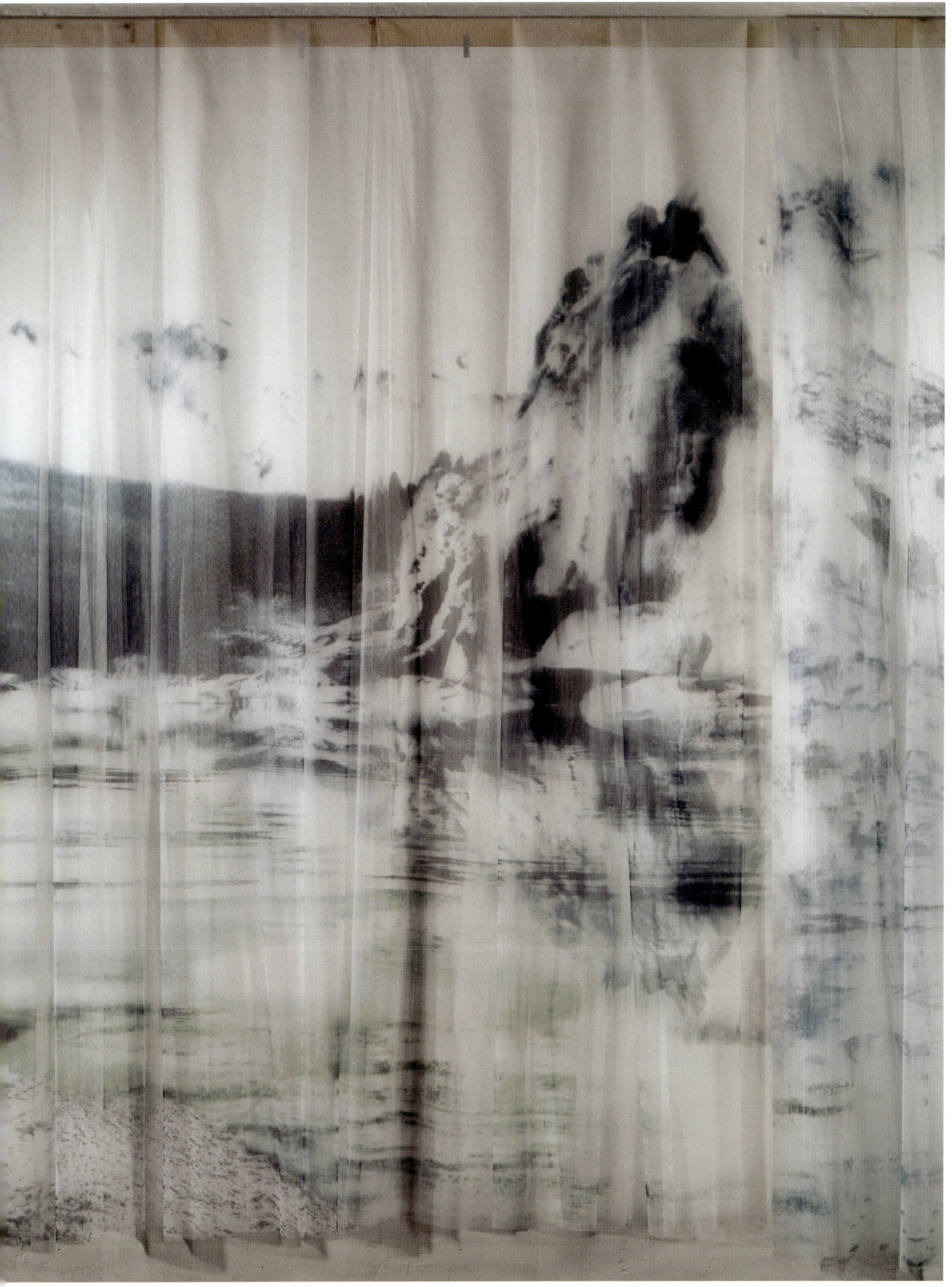

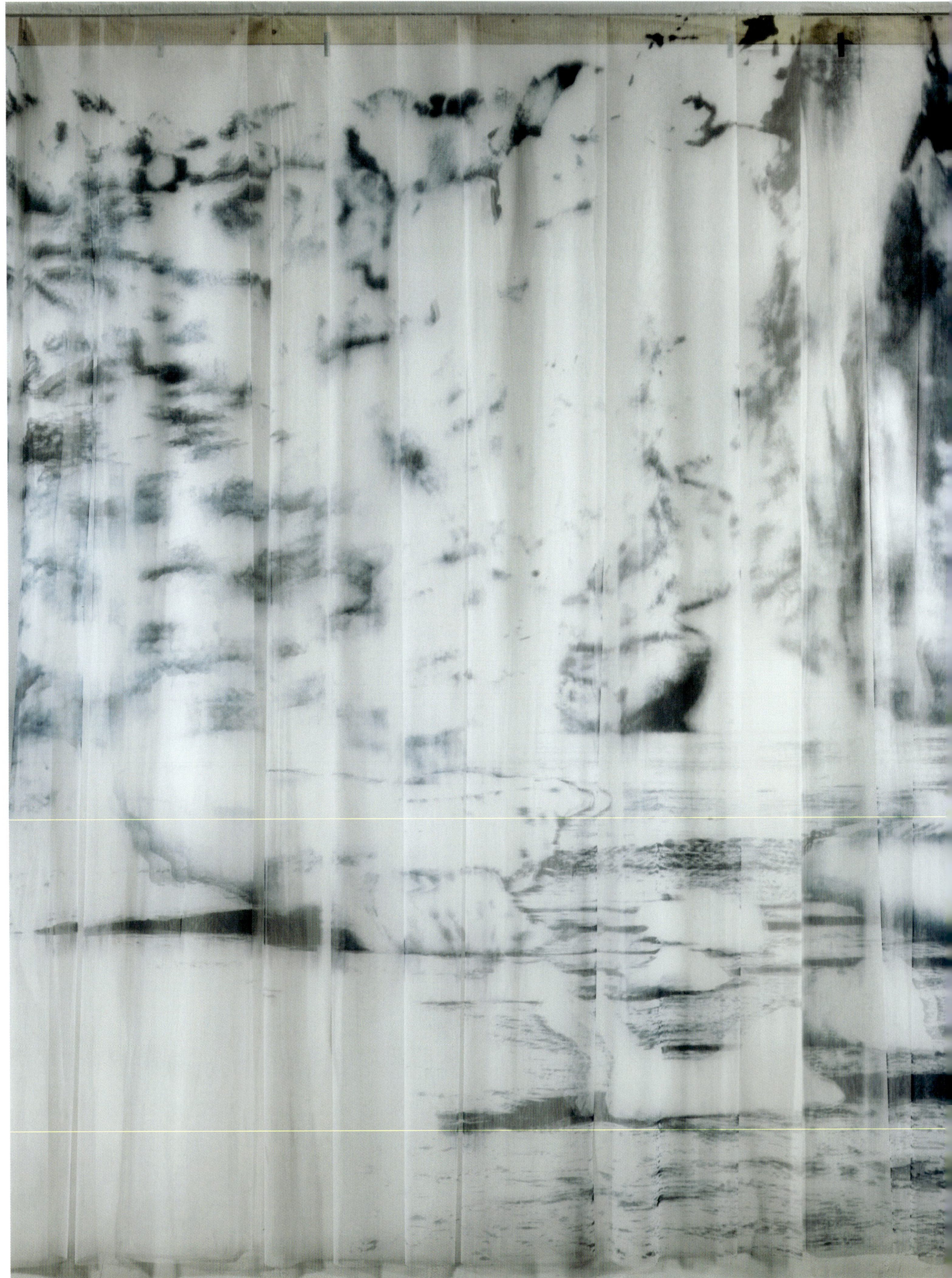

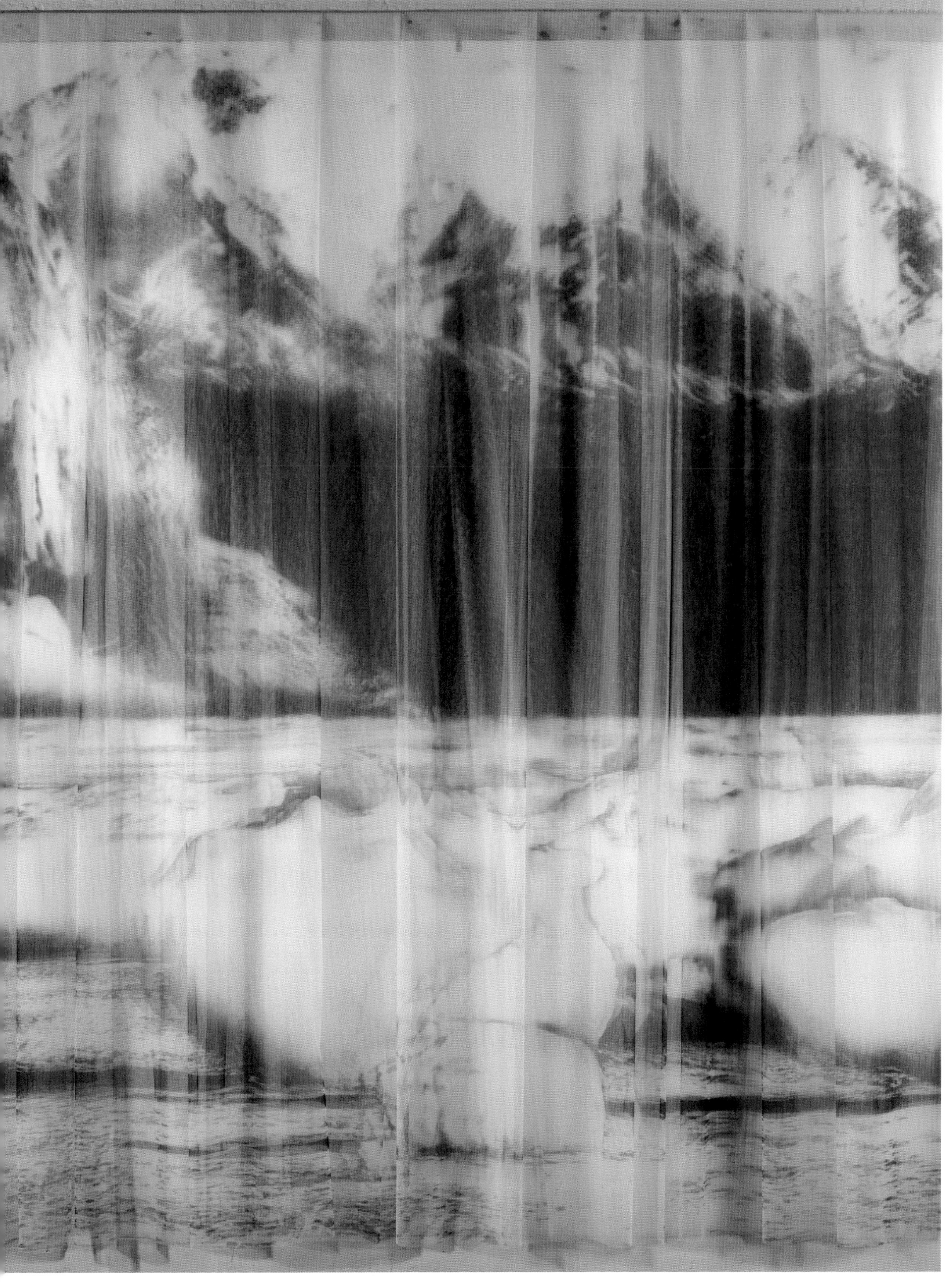

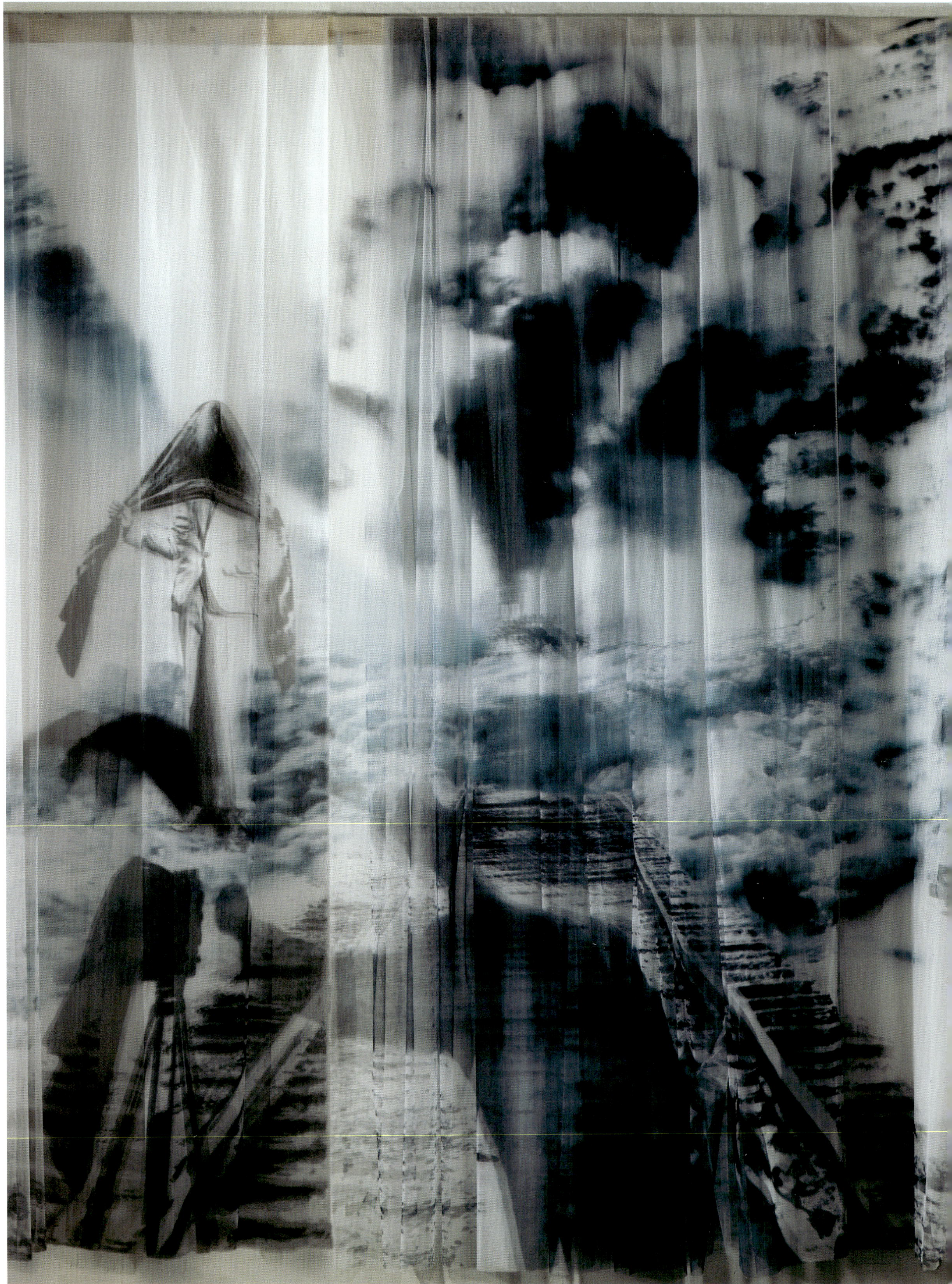

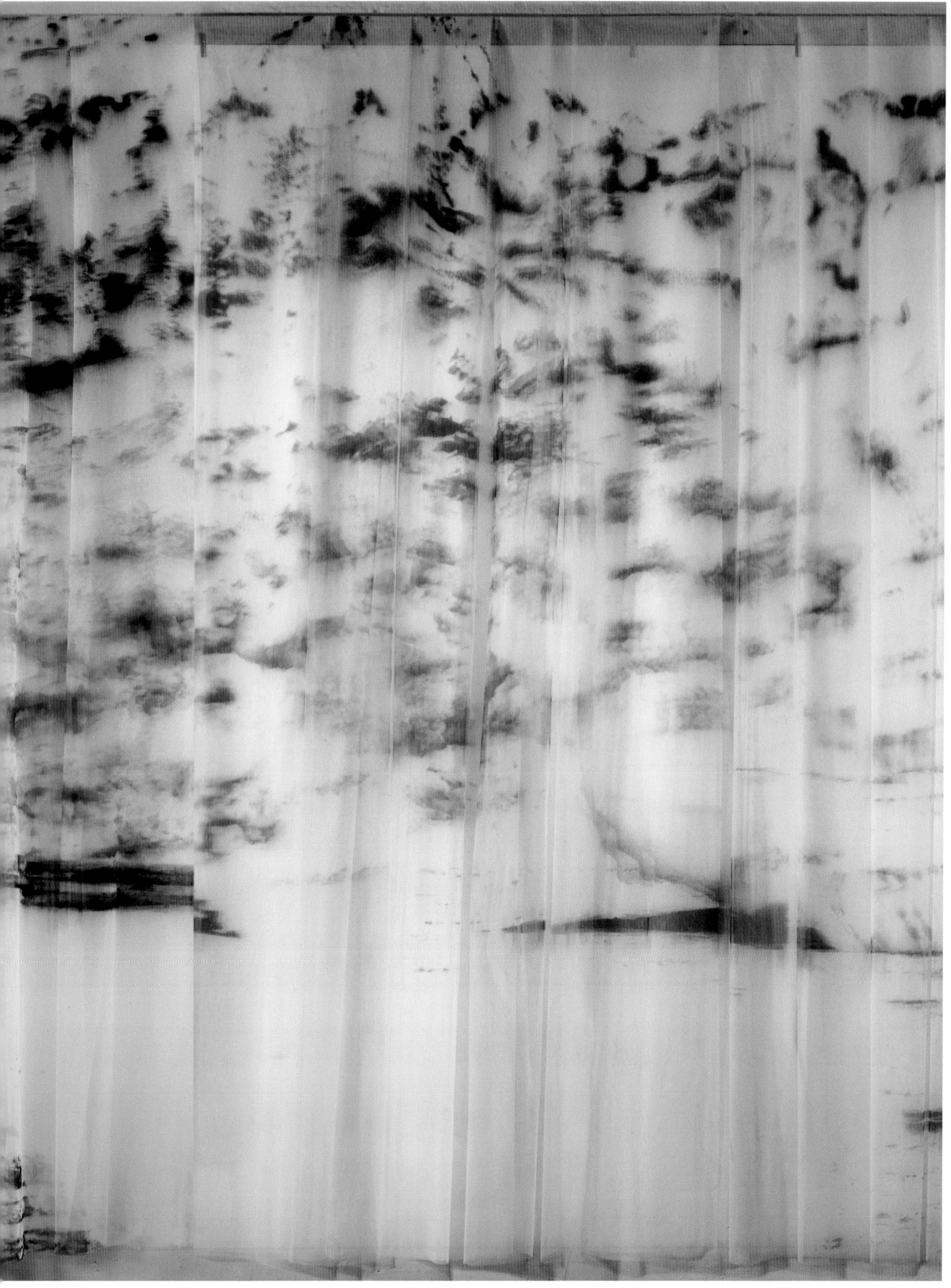

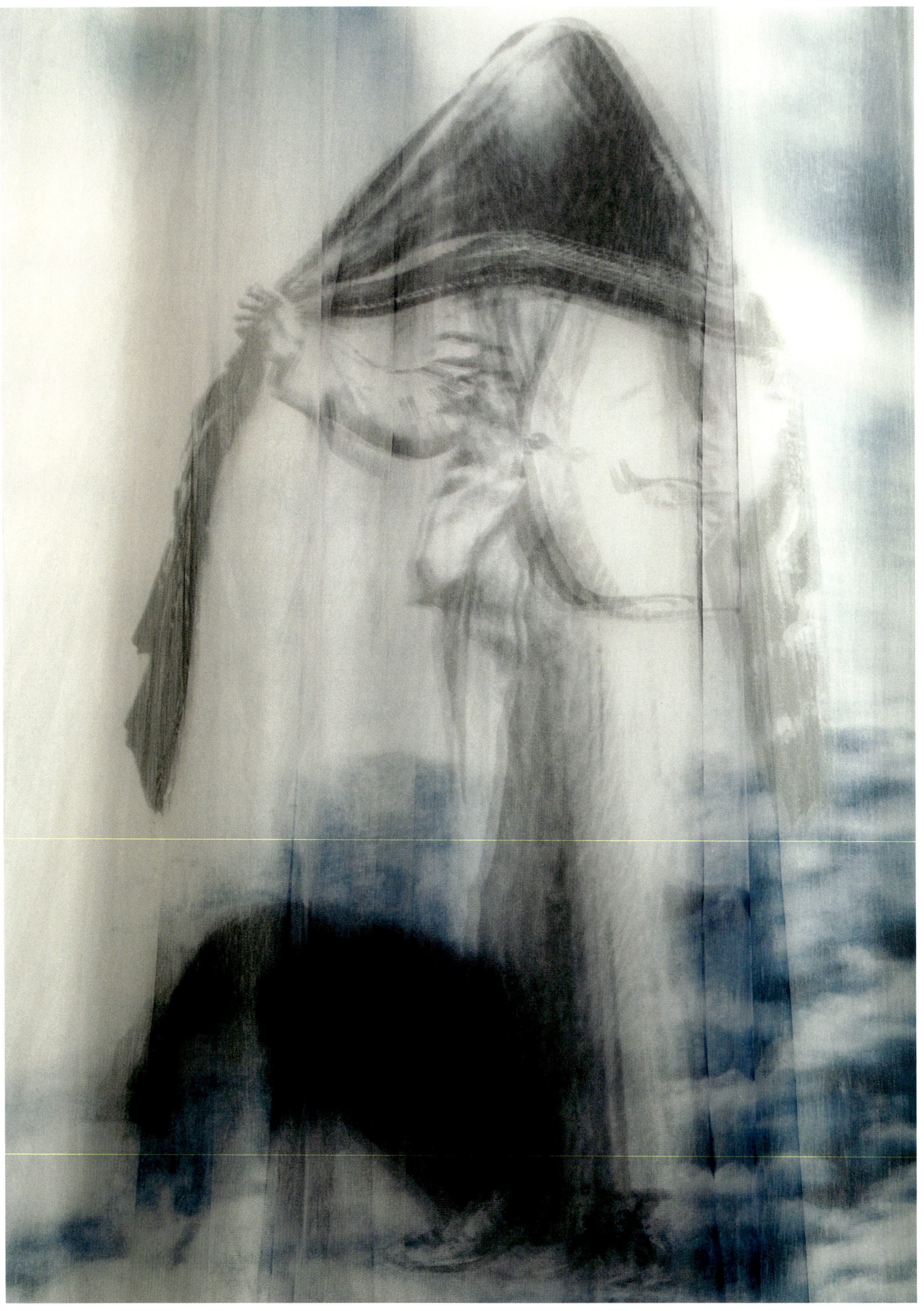

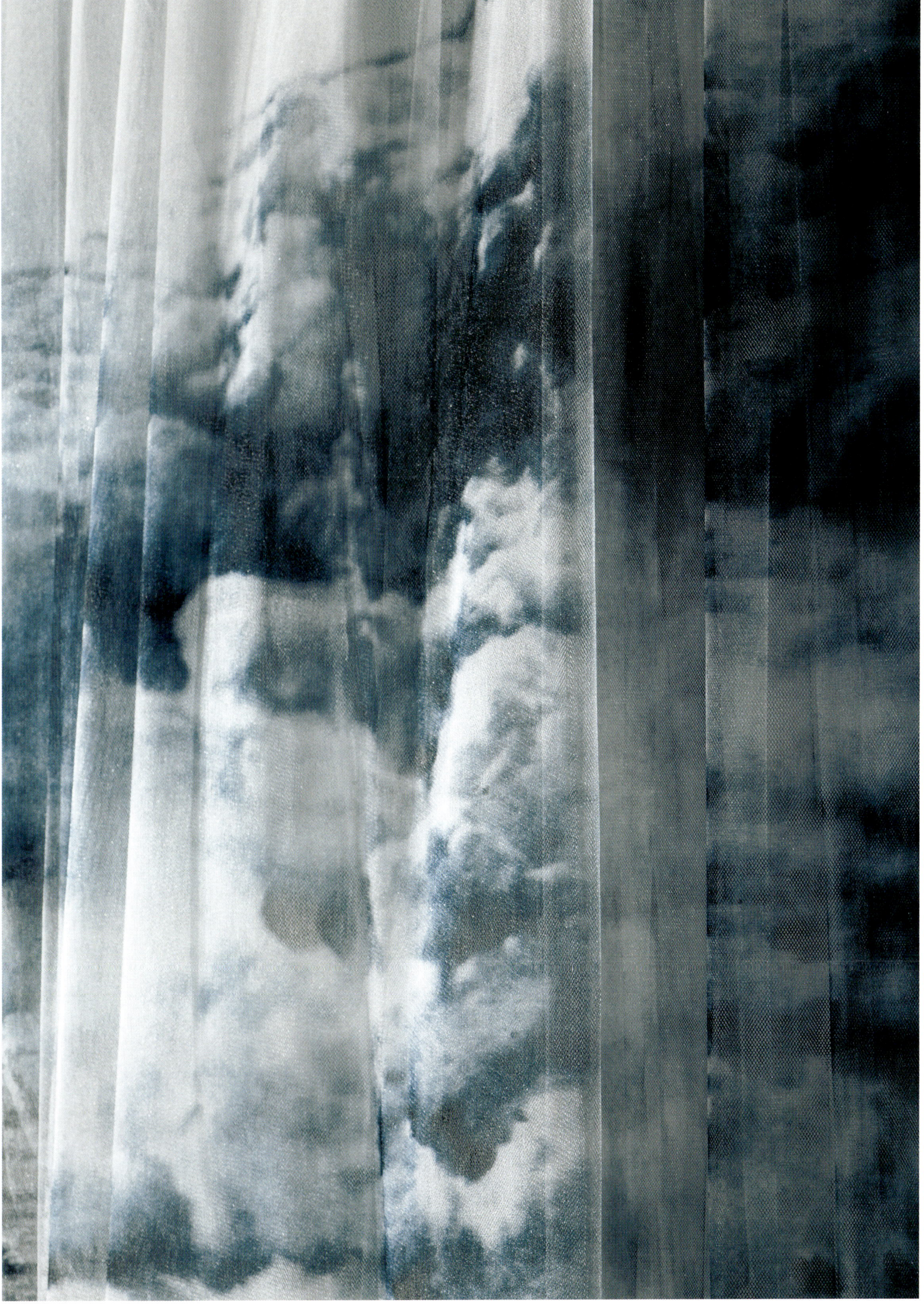

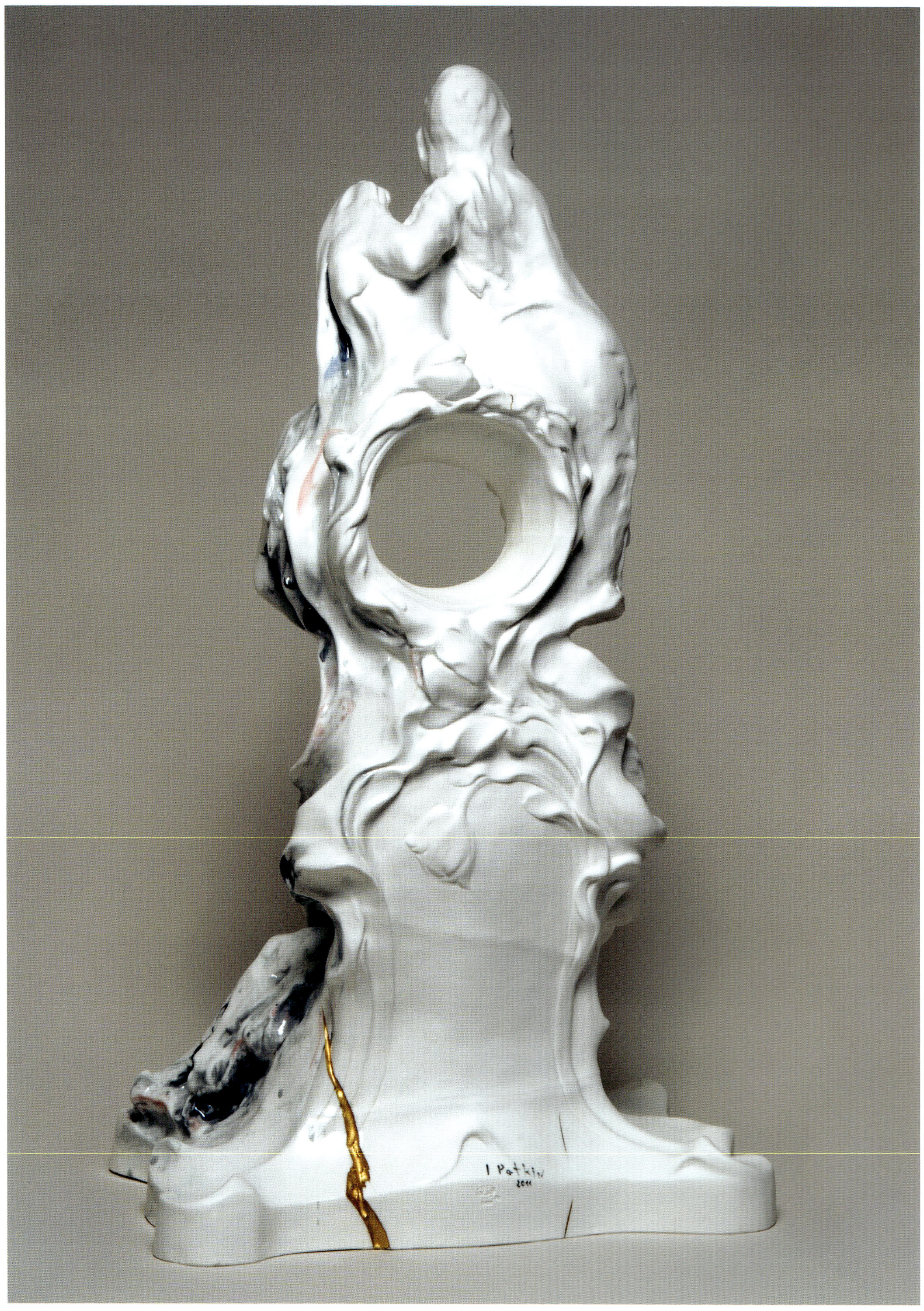
I Potkin
2011

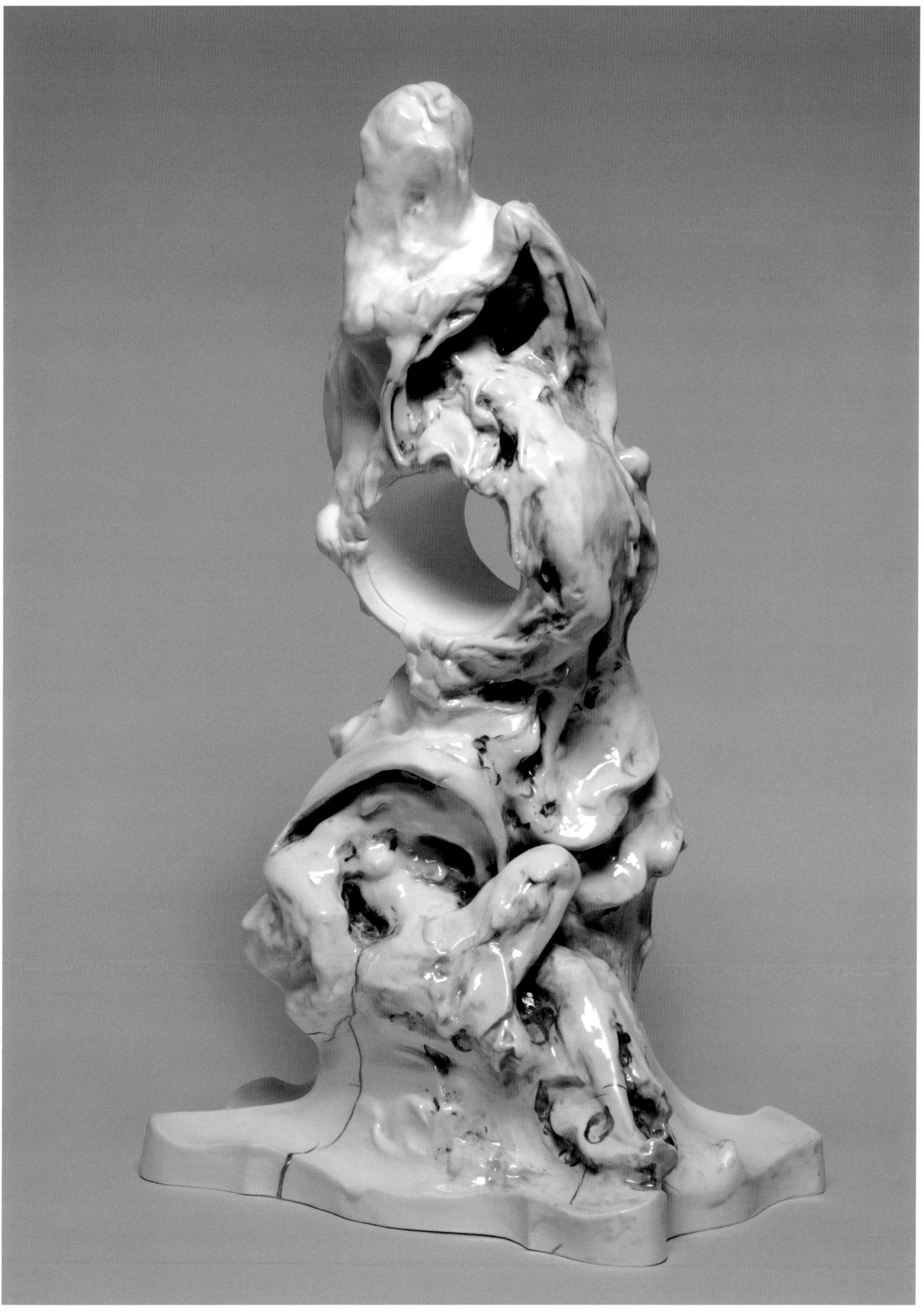

Endangered Species

Madonna and Child in Seven Veils

Earth, isn't this what you want? To arise in us, invisible?

Rainer Maria Rilke, *Ninth Duino Elegy*

THIS IS YOUR MADONNA?

One early spring morning not long ago, I drove with Izhar Patkin to Sèvres, the Parisian suburb renowned for its porcelain manufactory, where he was about to cast his *Madonna and Child.*

"So, this is your Madonna?" asked Bruno, the master mold-maker.

"Her?" (pointing at me) asked his pale apprentice, who showed me into an atelier filled with winged, fragile, hard-paste gods, where I was asked to undress. Pollen whirled in a pool of light. Fir trees shimmered outside as daylight waned, while Bruno and his apprentice draped strips of cloth soaked in white plaster over me, onto me. Lithe flesh, crude plaster, soft cloth, brittle porcelain. Matter coming together to make a matrix—a negative of a missing body.

Which second skin would tell the story of the absent body? Of its second coming?

THIS IS YOUR MADONNA!

Here she is (I am) your Madonna, Izhar. Neck stretched forth, crown tilted toward the light, back taut as an unplucked string about to resonate the most exquisite of sounds, harrowingly suspended between the "about to" and the "no longer" of its promise. Indefinitely calm between two terrors, her gaze is turned inward. Her thighs are heavy, sturdy as the Himalayan rock that gave birth to Kali, goddess of time, change, and paramount reality. Something of Kali's terrifying dance atop the inert body of her consort, Lord Shiva, is evoked by this Madonna's silent dance over the body of her vanquished Cupid. Frail as a girl, impregnable as the wheels of time, she holds out a firm arm to cradle an empty blanket. A natural evolution, perhaps, of a gesture made by the Theotokos of Vladimir, the twelfth-century birth-giver of God, the Byzantine icon who with one hand supported her puppyish infant and with the other pointed to her baby, Jesus, as the incarnation of the logos. Word turns to flesh, image to icon.

Reflective and stalwart, the Madonna cradles a void, *presents* an absence. In her lap the sturdy porcelain softens, caves in, and yields to the diaphanous swaddling cloth that swaddles nothing. Her gaze traces the missing infant.

The blanket is not the only empty space. Her porcelain body is itself a void, the negative of my body. A hollow where I once was. And yet her *being*-in-the-world is indisputable. Her body grounds itself in place, as a body must if it is to stand in for a being that is, as yet, placeless. She is stable in space, but subtly moves in time to where she is her own lack, her own mother, *Mater*, matter, the fullness of an empty moon. She is silent. So is her child, of whom for a moment, we lost sight—but there he is beneath her! Vanquished, perhaps sacrificed. She gazes inward and sees time spiraling forth, solid as a mountain. Placid as a mirror lake. Only her right toe frolics in a secret dance, allowing itself to unhinge into one final tremor, a memento of love. No wonder her newborn, brought quite unnaturally into life beneath her, is named *Amour Menaçant* (menacing love). She must crush him to ensure his silence, must keep his finger against his lips, lest he let a word slip about her act of love with God.

ABILITY AND THE ABILITY NOT-TO-BE

In his essay "On Potentiality," Giorgio Agamben examines Anna Akhmatova's account of what gave birth to her poems. It was late in 1930 and for months she had been standing with dozens of other mothers outside the Leningrad prison where her son, and their sons, were being held. One day one of the mothers recognized Akhmatova as the famous poet and asked her, "Can you speak of this?" Akhmatova was silent for a moment and then, without knowing how or why, found an answer to the question. "Yes, I can,"[1] she said. Not because, being a great poet, she possessed the gift to skillfully describe atrocities, Agamben explains, but, rather, because she fell into what is "for most of us perhaps the hardest and bitterest experience possible: the moment of potentiality."[2]

In Agamben's chilling reading of Aristotle, potentiality isn't only the ability to do something, but the ability *not* to do it: it is not a moment of mere lack of action or lack of being, but, rather, it is the pregnant, present lack of action or of being that presents the potentiality, precisely, for nonbeing. The empty cloth in the Madonna's lap carries the burden of this potentiality.

Man, says Agamben, has forgotten how *not to be able*. For Agamben, to "be able not to" would shatter the binary of potentiality/actuality and enable the moment of potentiality to subside within the actuality. This Madonna had achieved something like this: she is pregnant with the potentiality not to have a child. And yet she searches for him with Akhmatova, wandering from one room to the next, peering into the empty cradle, until she accepts that the angels have taken him:

> *Where is your gypsy boy, tall one,*
> *That over black kerchief did weep,*
> *Where is your small first child*
> *What memory of him do you keep?*[3]

ICON AND ECONOMY

On another sunny day, in another spring, Izhar and I went for a walk through Venice, from the Bridge of Sighs (where long ago the condemned would glimpse their city for the last time), through San Marco, to the late Peggy Guggenheim's palace. I was under the spell of Mrs. Guggenheim's list of deceased pups when Izhar handed me a book: *Image, Icon, Economy: The Byzantine Origins of the Contemporary Imaginary* by Marie-José Mondzain. "It's all in here," he said. "Our entire economic system of images started with the Byzantine solution to the prohibition on idolatry!"

Throughout his career, Patkin has been searching for some iconophilic expression of Jewish aniconism—some juncture where the visible, shocked by its own obscenity, might take cover and find form at the same time.

During the Byzantine iconoclastic crises of the eighth and ninth centuries, icon became to image what symbol would (as of the seventeenth century) become to sign in semantic systems. When the church fathers decreed that the image should henceforth remain hidden while the icon remained visible, they redeemed the image from the charge of idolatry and wove the mysterious affinity between icon and *oikonomia*. In translations, the word *economy* is "rendered by different terms such as *incarnation, plan, design, administration, providence, responsibility, duties, compromise, lie or guile . . .*"[4] These inform early discussions of divine representations in icons as a primarily economical question.

From that point onward, and in fact to this day, a magical furnace of divine economy aimed at redeeming humanity has been at work within us. Like the Freudian object of desire that is forever missing or partial, the icon is structured around layers of absence and is negotiated through a series of disappearances that culminate in Jesus's incarnation in flesh.

In a series of economic transactions, God has need of a son, the son of a church, the church of power, and so on. Thus, a face-to-face encounter between God and man in the manner of the Old Testament is no longer possible. From here on, the economy, which Mondzain identifies as an "empty concept" or a "negative image," will be the vehicle through which the plurality of God's names will be made visible by substitution.

Trying on a commedia dell'arte mask in a tourist stall, I hazarded, "So the Madonna's missing baby is something like the departure of God from his icon?" "Even better," Izhar said, "if her womb is an icon factory, why give birth to any baby at all?" I later found this in Mondzain's book: "The Icon contemplates us. In its turn, it becomes God's gaze at the contemplator's flesh, which gets caught in an informational and transformational circuit of relationships . . . it is the effective and efficient form of the lack that the divine model of each and every economy assumed in the 'kenosis' of its annihilation."[5]

The emerald waters below us grew deep, palazzos reflected in their murk. We'd reached Santa-Maria Della Salute, the Baroque church whose every ornament references the Black Death. Too bad for the iconoclasts who lost the war with the iconophiles, I thought. The bastards lost twice; smashing and getting smashed. Very little of them, other than parodies and lies, remain. When I got back home, I lost the book, but managed to buy another.

SALOME

That femininity had been since time immemorial thought of in terms of absence has famously given rise to the Eves, Medusas, Medeas, and Sophias of the world. But Izhar's Madonna's affair with absence is not quite the same as your average castratrix's role as a stand-in for death, or a meeting point of womb and tomb. She is in the business of revealing the invisible and of being laid bare by it. In this way she is perhaps closest to Kali: dark daughter of the Himalayas and consort of Shiva, who, with her skull necklace, stands for both doom and salvation, destruction and ultimate truth.

But as I sat encased in plaster-soaked cloth at the porcelain factory, another daughter—this one a Jewish princess—came to mind: my namesake, Salome. I was named after Shlomzion: Salome Alexandra, Queen of Judea, who lived in Jerusalem a mere hundred years before the infamous daughter of Herodias. But it was the hysterical, lusty princess who was truer to the Hebrew root from which the name is derived: *shalem*, which denotes both peace and wholeness. For Flaubert and Mallarmé she was the virgin-whore; for Wilde and Strauss, she was a femme fatale. But for all of them, she was the fin-de-siècle decadent fantasy, and as Wilde put it, "Decadence is the subordination of the whole to the parts."

In Oscar Wilde's *Salome: A Tragedy in One Act*, the main trope for arguing virgin/whore, object/subject, seeing/being-seen, empty/whole relations is the moon. Every character in Wilde's play, down to the last slave, likens Salome to the moon. And for Salome, the moon is a virgin: "She is cold and chaste. I am sure she is a virgin. She has the beauty of a virgin. Yes, she is a virgin. She has never defiled herself. She has never abandoned herself to men, like the other goddesses."

But for Herodias, the moon is a mad whore:

"The moon has a strange look to-night. Has she not a strange look? She is like a mad woman, a mad woman who is seeking everywhere for lovers. She is naked too. She is quite naked. The clouds are seeking to clothe her nakedness, but she will not let them. She shows herself naked in the sky. She reels through the clouds like a drunken woman . . . I am sure she is looking for lovers. Does she not reel like a drunken woman? She is like a mad woman, is she not?"[6]

Two classical points of view are about to converge here on moon and sun, spectator and object of desire, castrated woman and decapitated prophet, but also the very dualism out of which they are forged. In the circus of desire Herod looks at Salome, Salome looks at Iokanaan, all look at the moon which in turn reflects light—and, true to the decadent tradition, the moon is replaced with artifice, with the mirror, the silver charger, as light-reflecting and light-deflecting devices multiply until a myriad of viewpoints and seen objects erupt and we're in a crazy hall of mirrors, where virgin and whore are no longer antinomies, no longer just two. And as Salome vanquishes the gaze, traditional moon metaphors are exchanged for sun metaphors; the absent, the obscure, and the gazed-upon are once again presented—made present—and revealed. The reflection is an optical illusion because the reflector is (herself) transparent, infinite, absent. The moonlight, the desire of the flesh for the holy man, the virgin's yearning for the divine—these are all fluid tropes, forever shifting in a symbolic economy, balanced against primordial nothingness. Like Salome, the Madonna asks for plurality instead of duality. No longer is she reduced to being either a mother or a child, barren or pregnant, looking or being looked at. She has become a faint crescent at dawn, with only a fickle contour encircling her like "the shadow of a white rose in a mirror of silver."

THE VIRGIN CANVAS

First there was a body, then a mold that negated it, then body again, hollow, over another hollow body, an angel this time, then an empty cloth. How many layers of negation are required to rule out solitude? Her gaze is turned inward. Made of supple but solid material, she is full although she contains nothing. So much for the emptiness that Modern art has been so keen to attain. That piece of fabric that was born as Venus's washcloth and reaches its apotheosis as Jesus's empty swaddling cloth.

This is the blank page the writer yearns to write. Barthes's author, who demands to die, Blanchot's writer, who asks to be erased, in order to lose literature to the night, to reach *the vacuum* which opens the work "altogether to itself, rendering it absolutely present . . . the work's very coming to be is revealed by the flash of its disappearance."[7] And in the words of Avital Ronell, it "all comes down to the way literature dresses up the wound of its non-being when it goes out into the world."[8] What with? A diaper. A blanket. A piece of cloth. A canvas. "All great art is kenotic," Mondzain says. "The line, the void, and the Virgin's body."[9]

THE SMILE

I am the one who has been subtracted from the sculpture. The memory of my shadow doubles and deepens in the folds of the empty cloth of Izhar's *Madonna and Child*. Still, I rejoice in her trinity of absences: body, child, a divine lover. They give this Madonna her grandeur gained by loss. Out of her silence—which in turn silences Cupid's pressed lips—comes a steady vertigo, the kind you might feel upon jumping off a cliff and discovering that you're buoyant and gliding. That you've given in to the *suchness* of things, the frailty of rock, the solitude of the cypress tree, the fullness of the moon. These are the sorts of things that put a faint smile on the Madonna's face. Only from certain angles can it be discerned, through the milky mist of her porcelain face, behind her inward gaze.

Shlomzion Kenan

NOTES

1
Giorgio Agamben, "On Potentiality," in Giorgio Agamben, *Potentialities: Selected Essays in Philosophy,* trans. Daniel Heller-Roazen (Stanford: Stanford Univ. Press, 1999), 177.

2
Ibid., 178.

3
From Anna Akhmatova, "Where is your gypsy boy, tall one," trans. Ilya Shambat, "Anna Andreevna Akhmatova," accessed April 19, 2012, http://ahmatova.niv.ru/ahmatova/text/stihi/english/english-54.htm.

4
Marie-José Mondzain, *Image, Icon, Economy: The Byzantine Origins of the Contemporary Imaginary,* trans. Rico Franses (Stanford: Stanford Univ. Press, 2005), 13.

5
"What links the economy of the natural and consubstantial image to the artificial icon and prevents them from being confused with each other is the question of *absence* or *emptiness,* which is also the mark of the historical economy" (ibid., 81). Ibid., 90–91.

6
All quotes from *Salome* are taken from Oscar Wilde, *Salome,* in "The Literature Network," accessed April 17, 2012, http://www.online-literature.com/wilde/salome/1/.

7
Maurice Blanchot, *The Space of Literature,* trans. Ann Smock (Lincoln: Univ. of Nebraska Press, 1989), 203.

8
Avital Ronell, *Crack Wars: Literature, Addiction, Mania* (Urbana and Chicago: University of Illinois Press, 1992), 57.

9
Mondzain, 92.

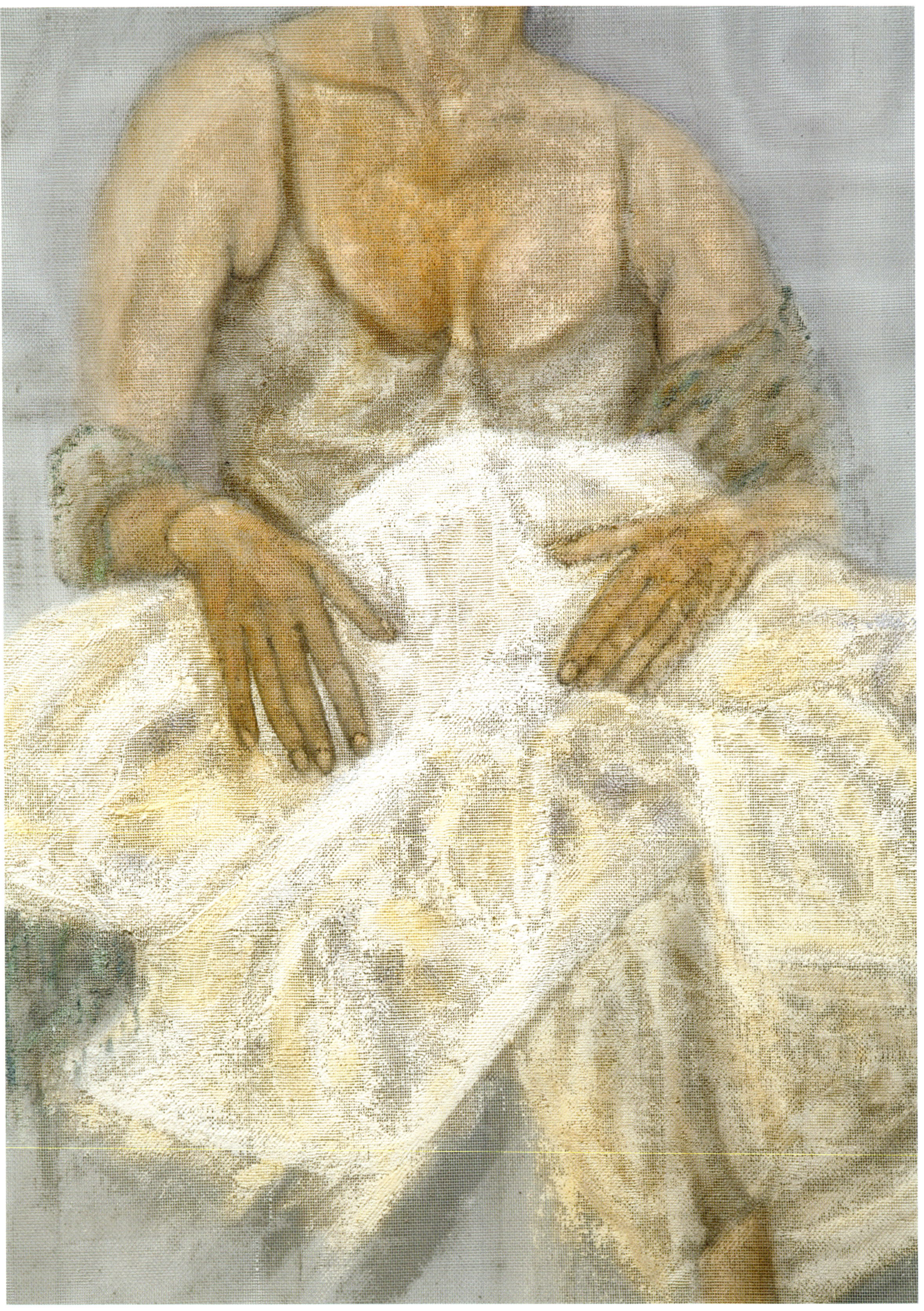

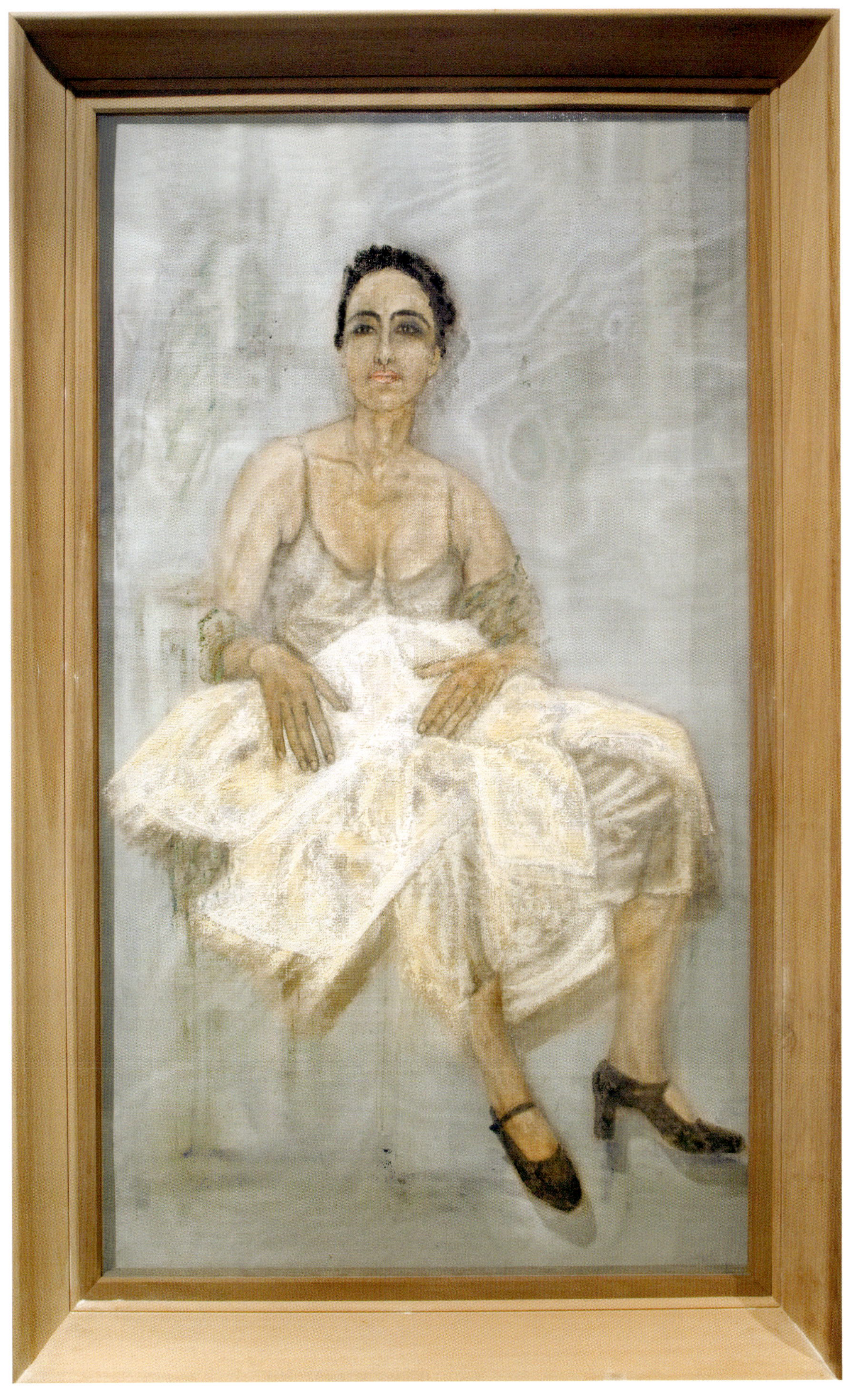

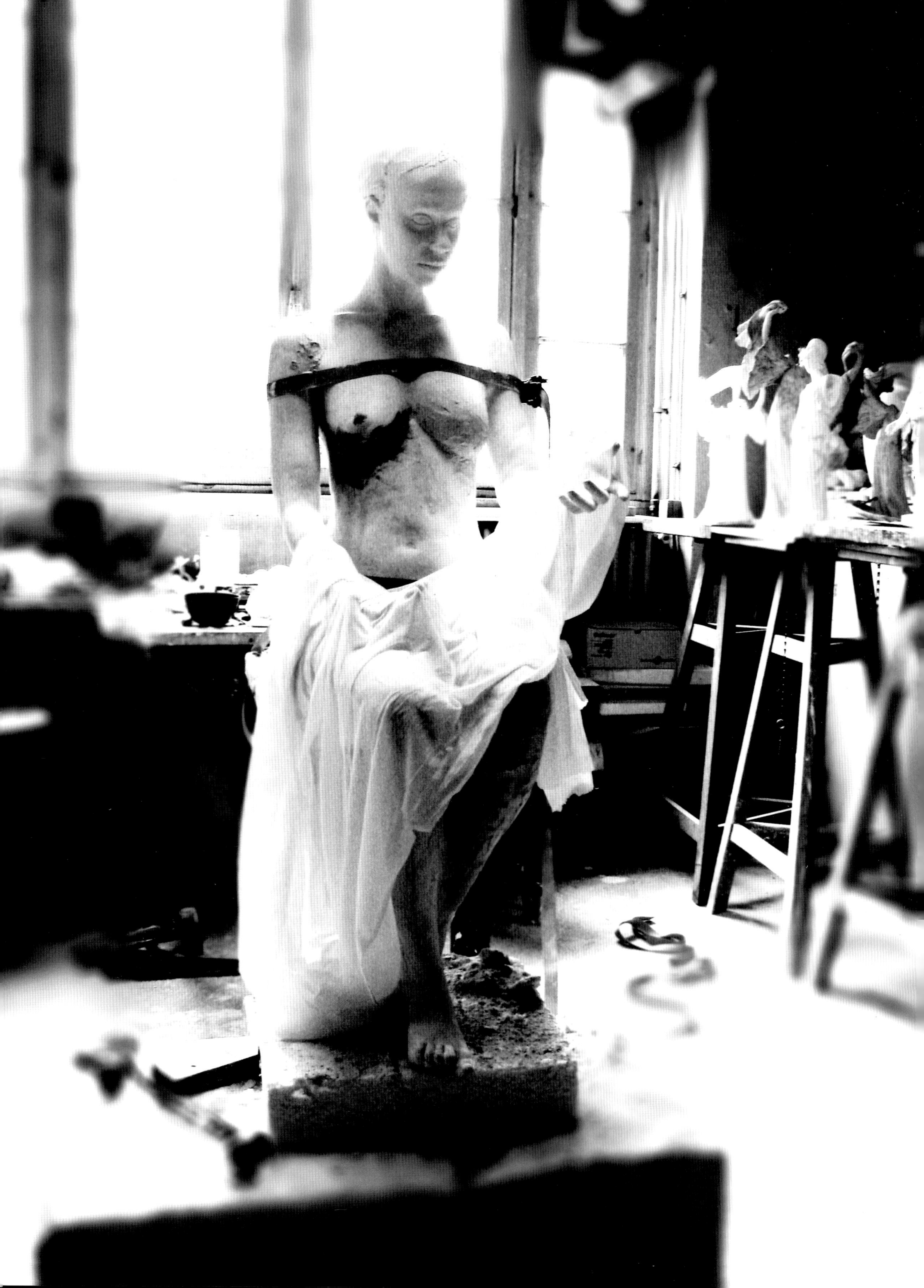

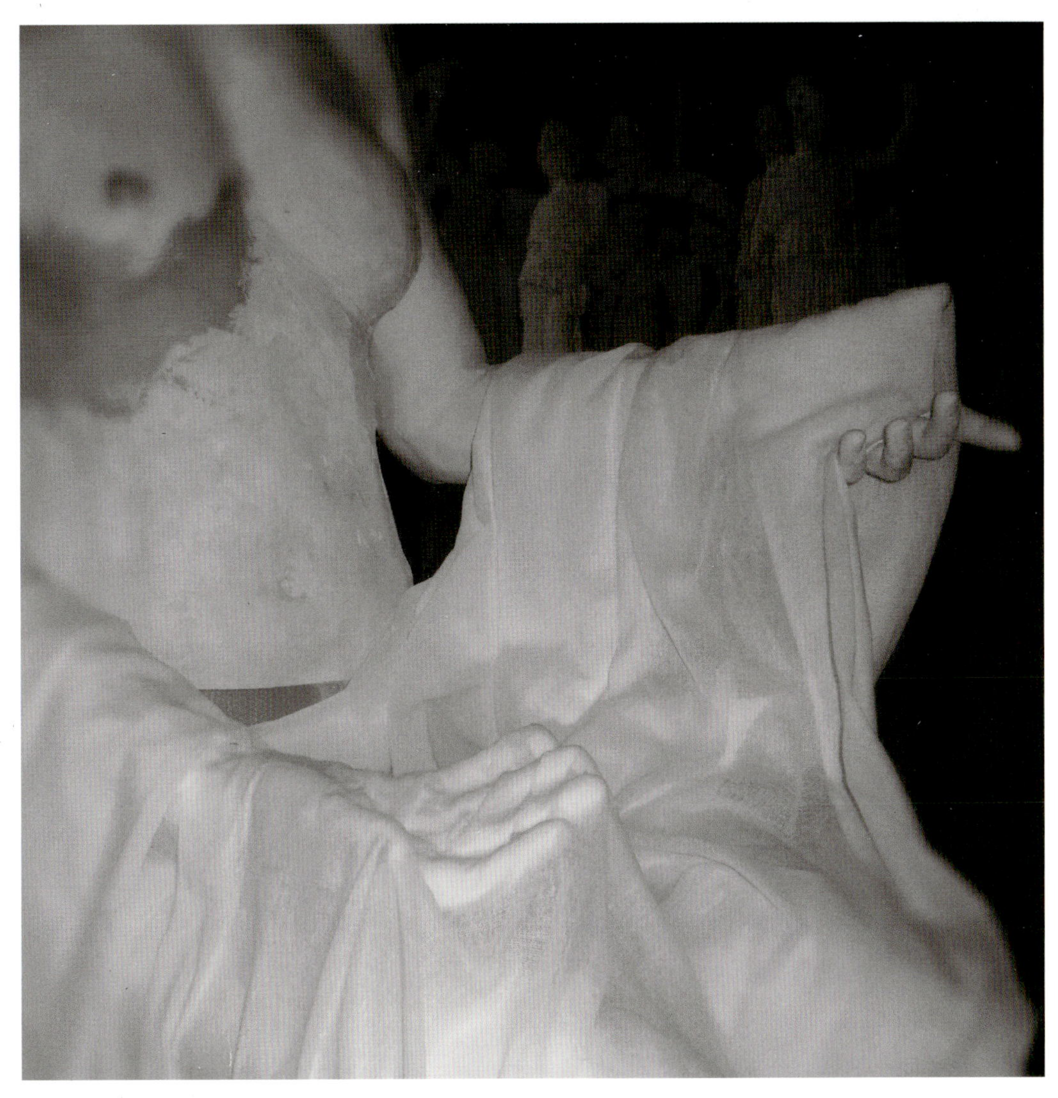

To me, intimacy is freedom. It's important for me to emphasize the intimacy of the human touch and evidence of the creative process, which bring an emotional intelligence.

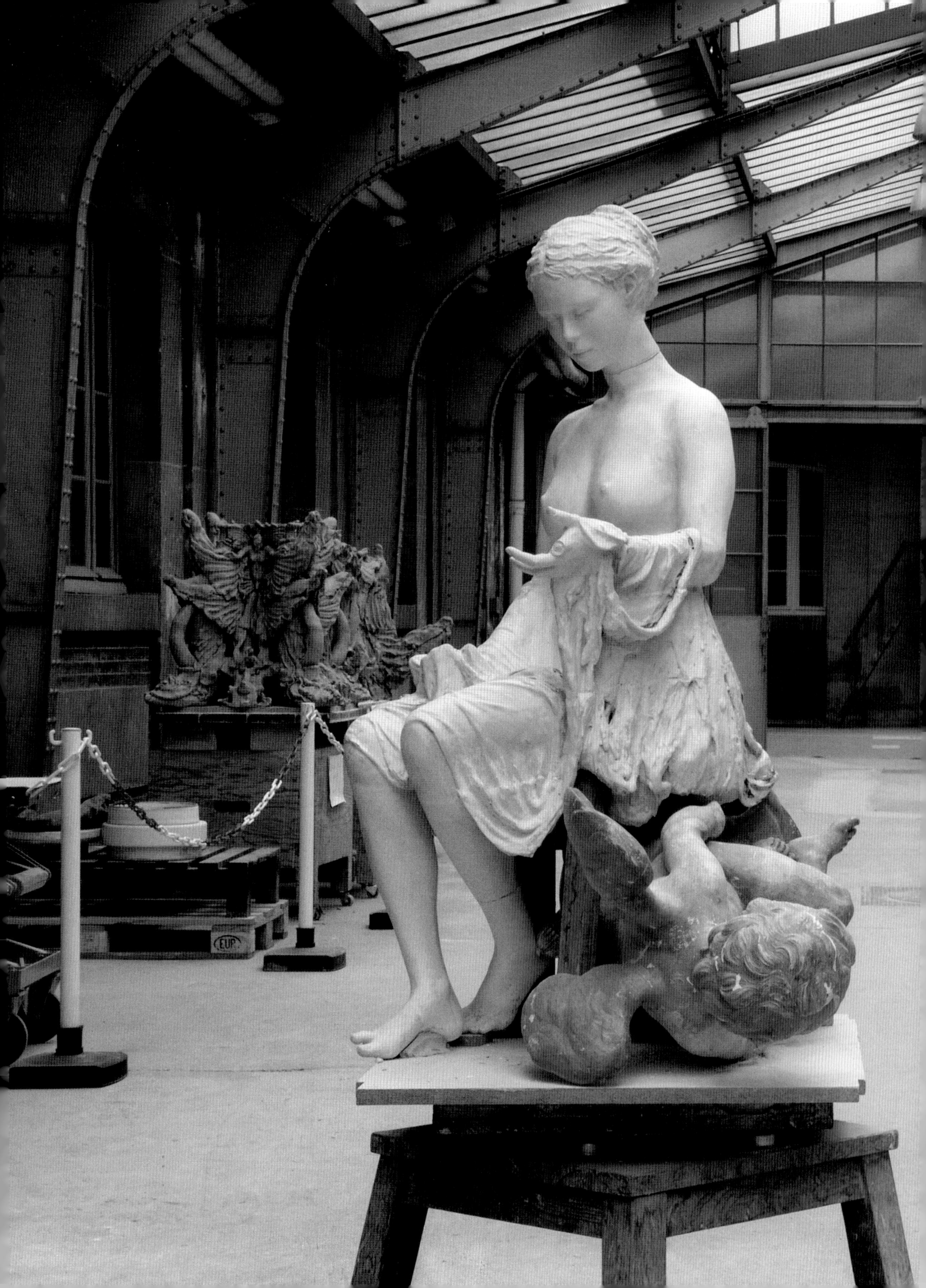

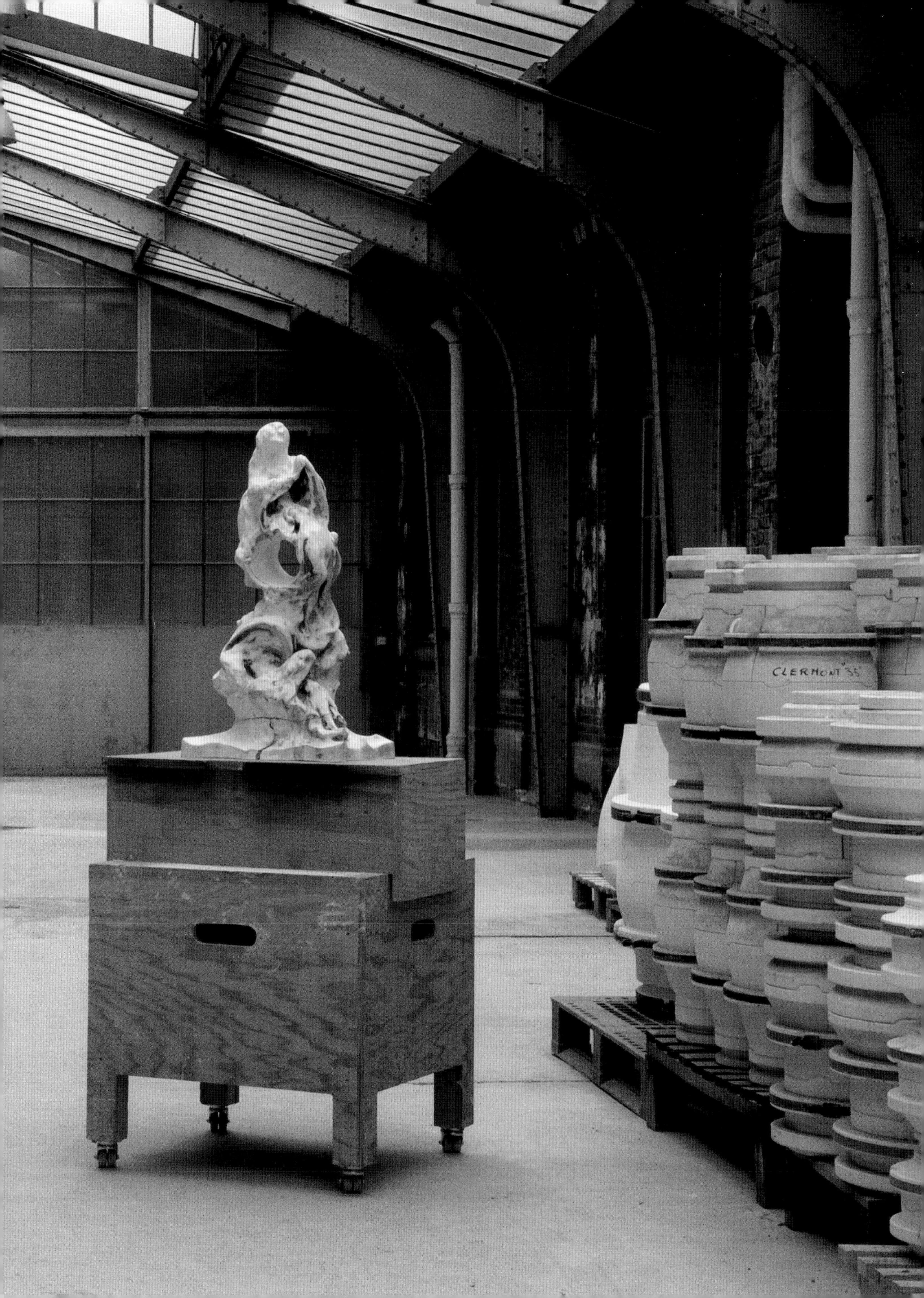
CLERMONT 35

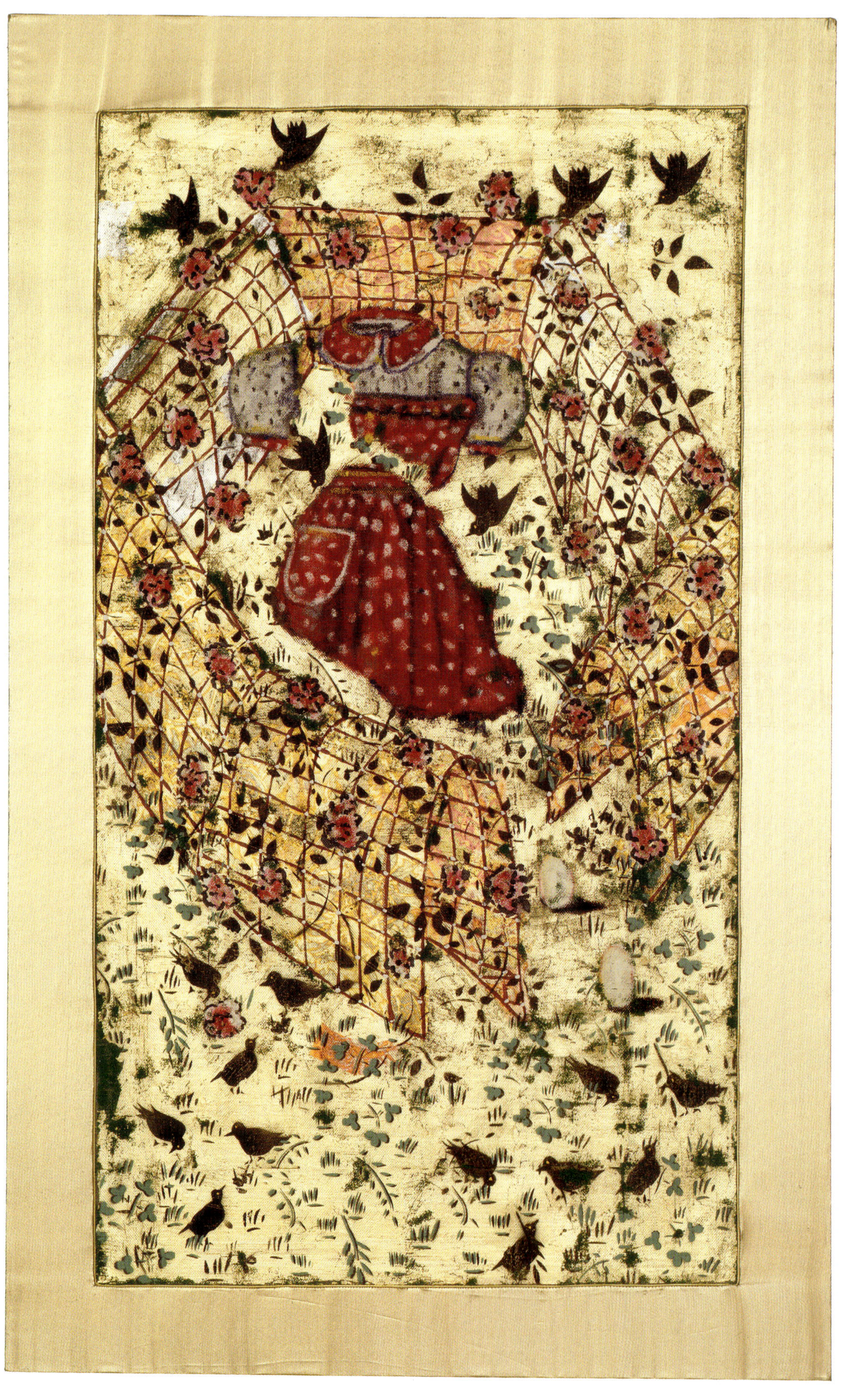

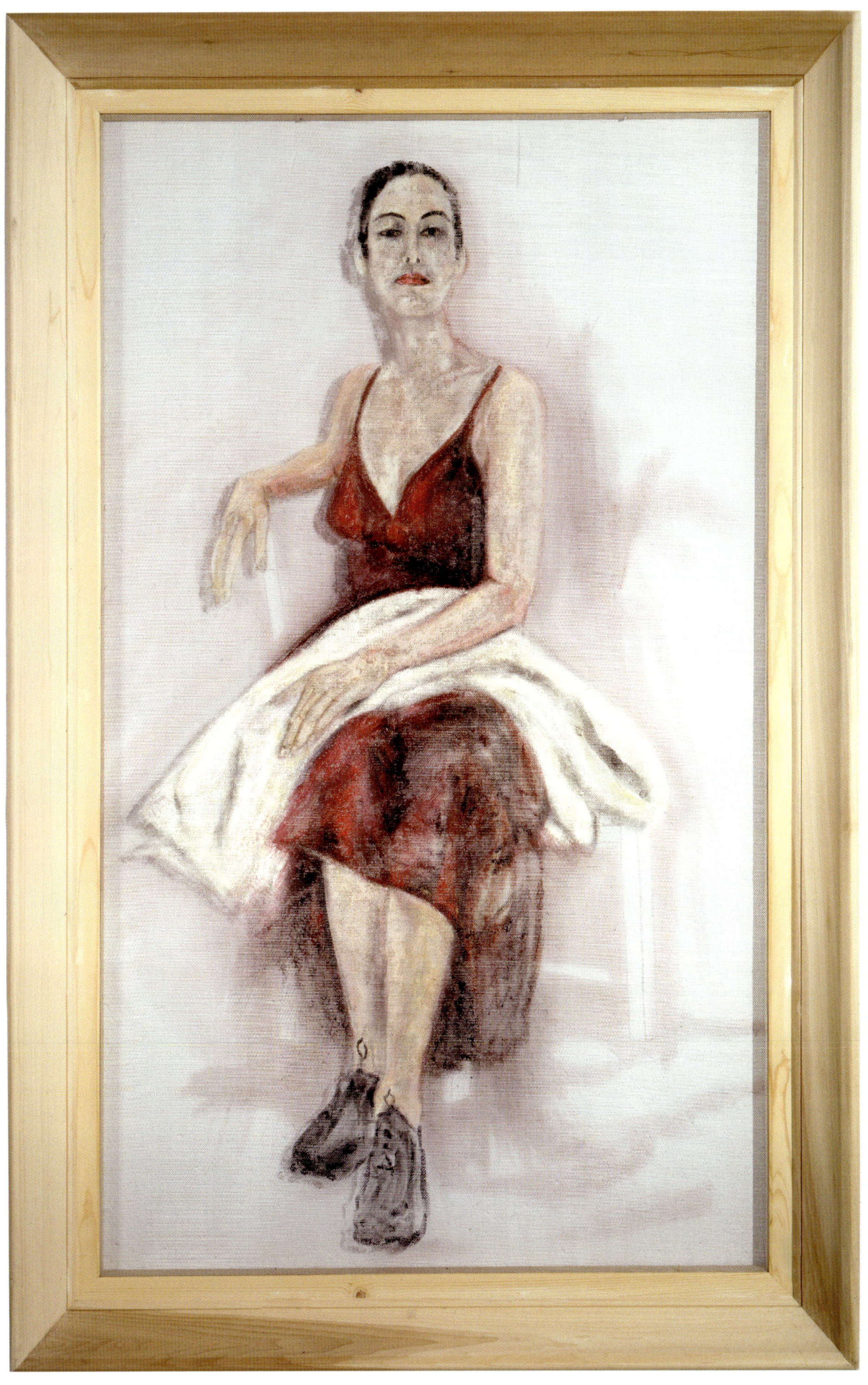

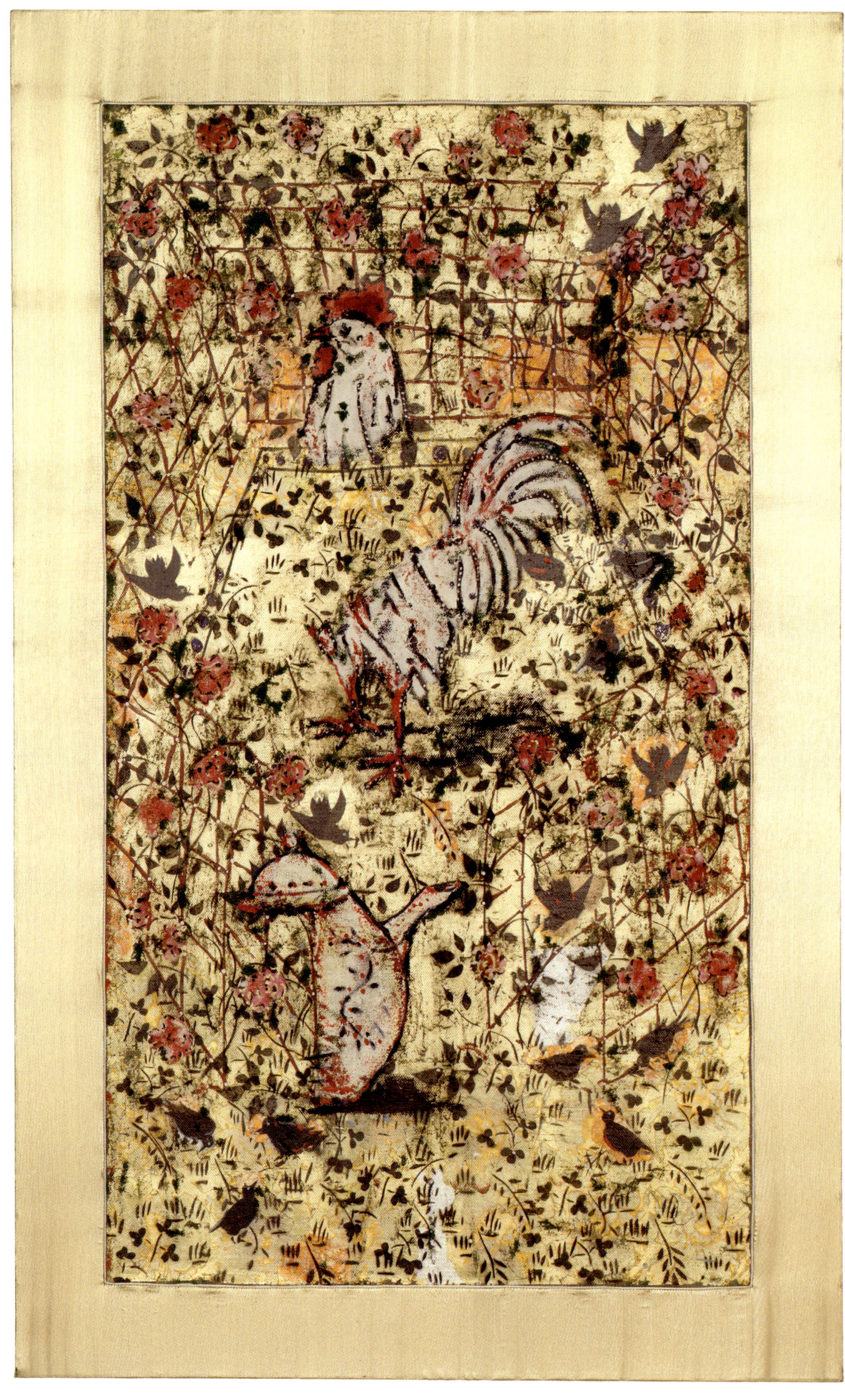

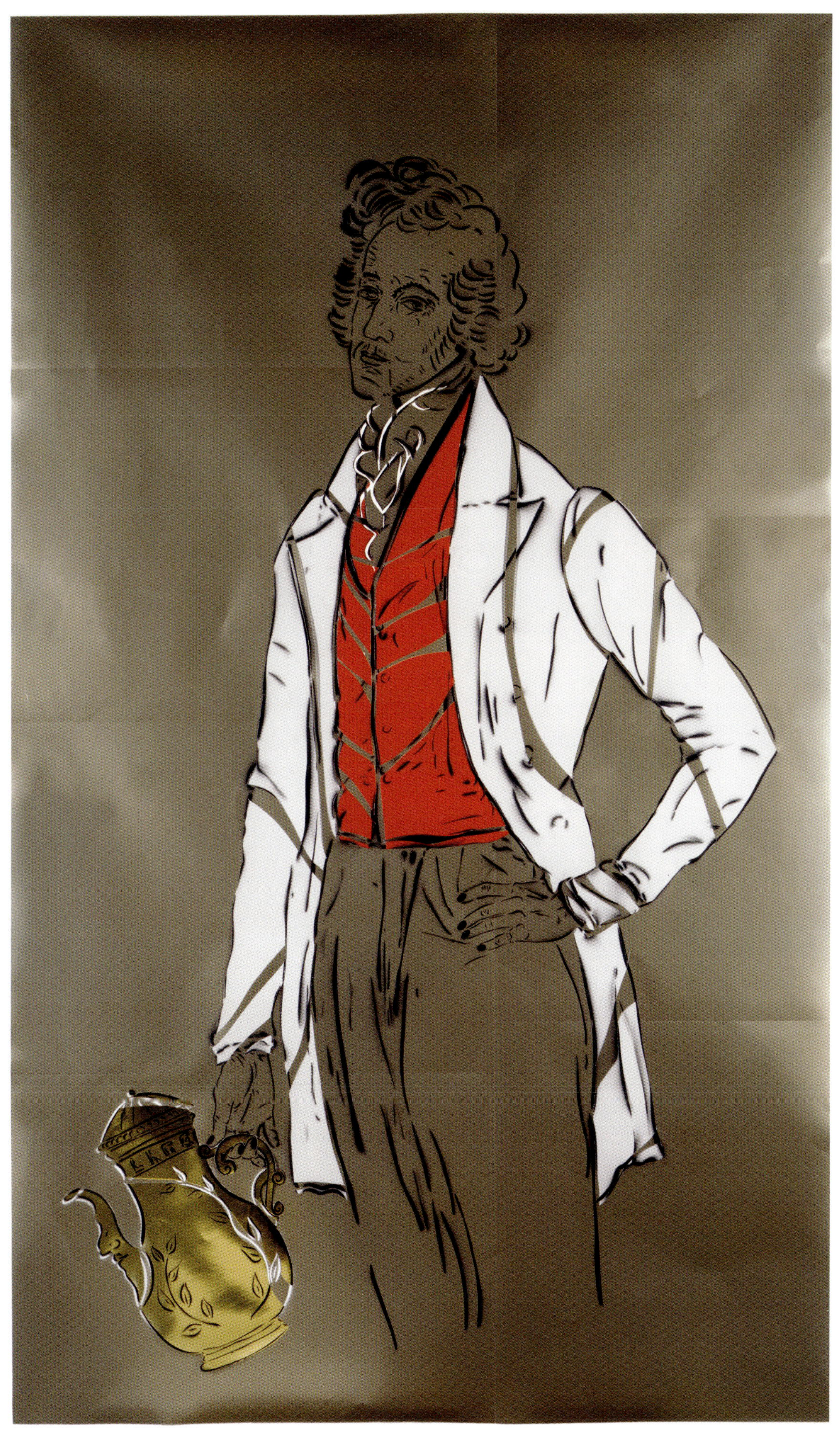

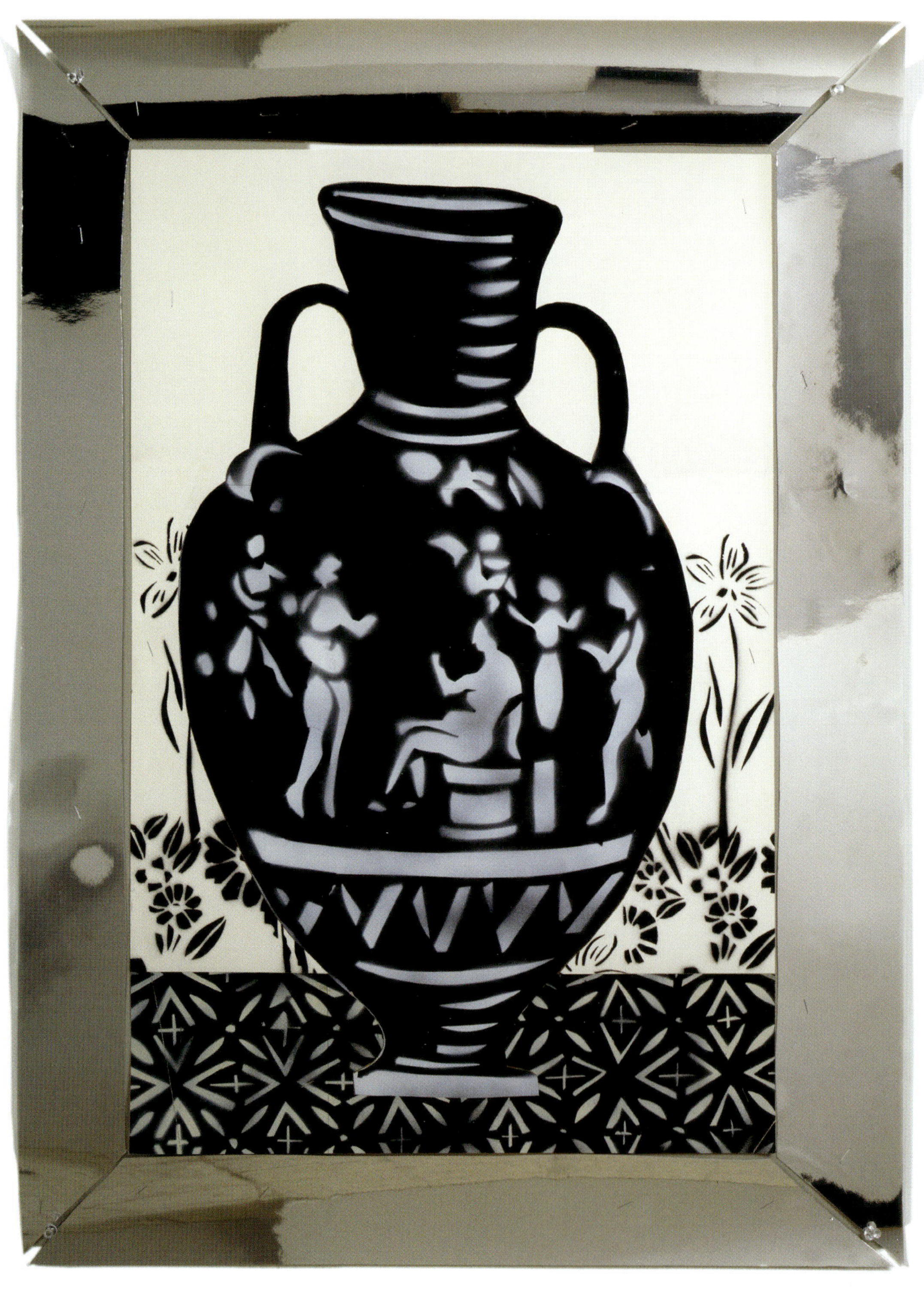

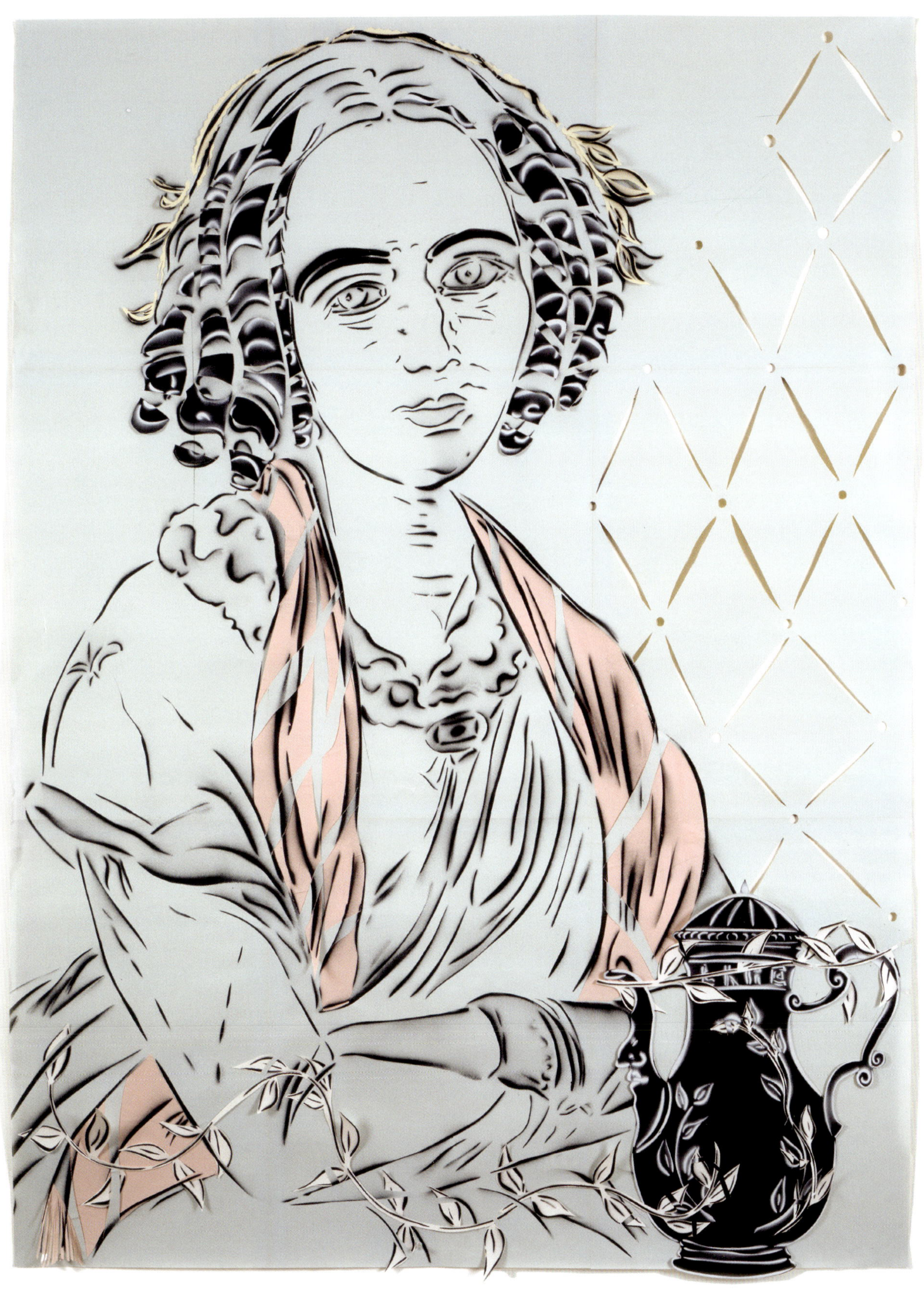

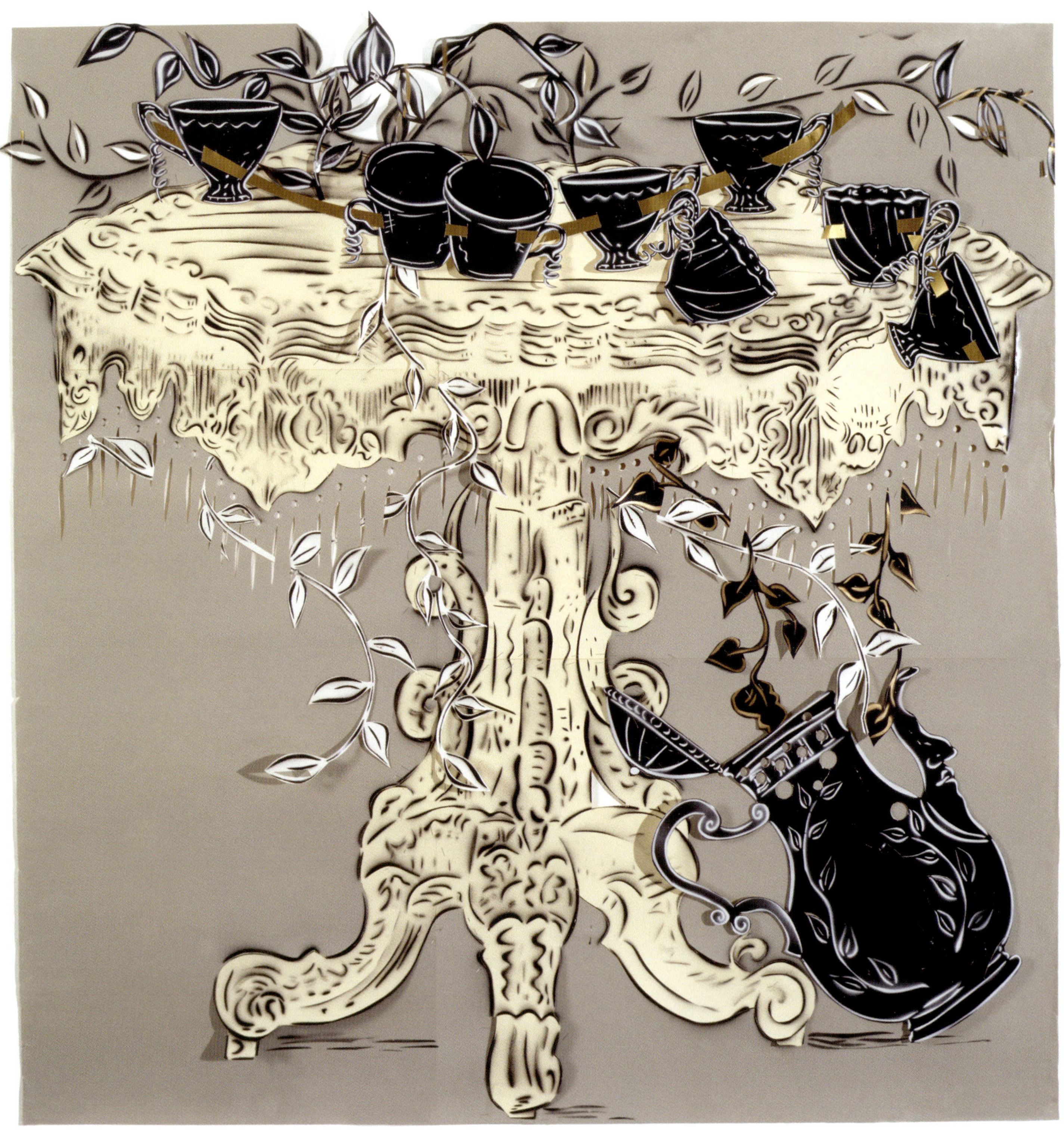

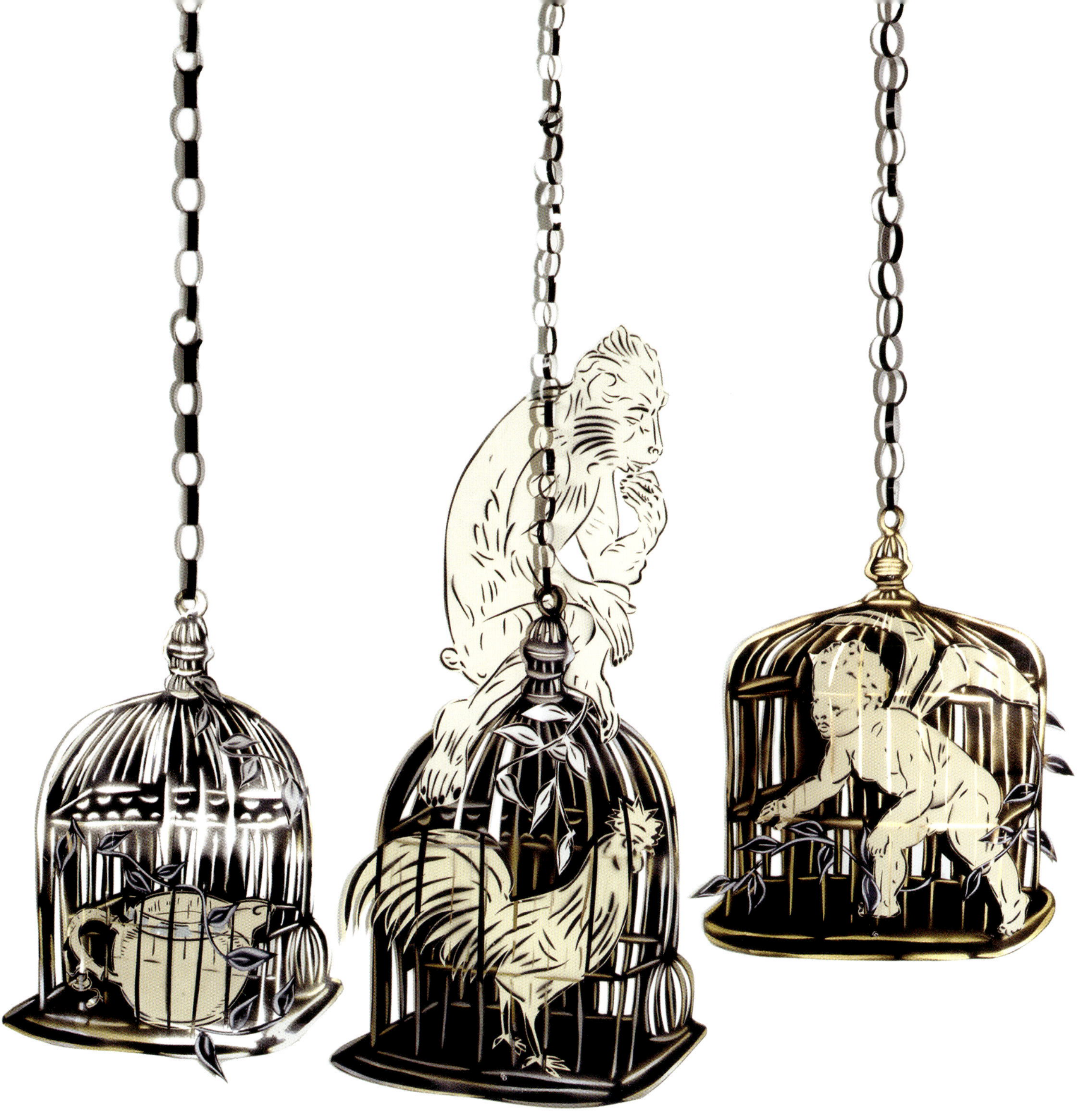

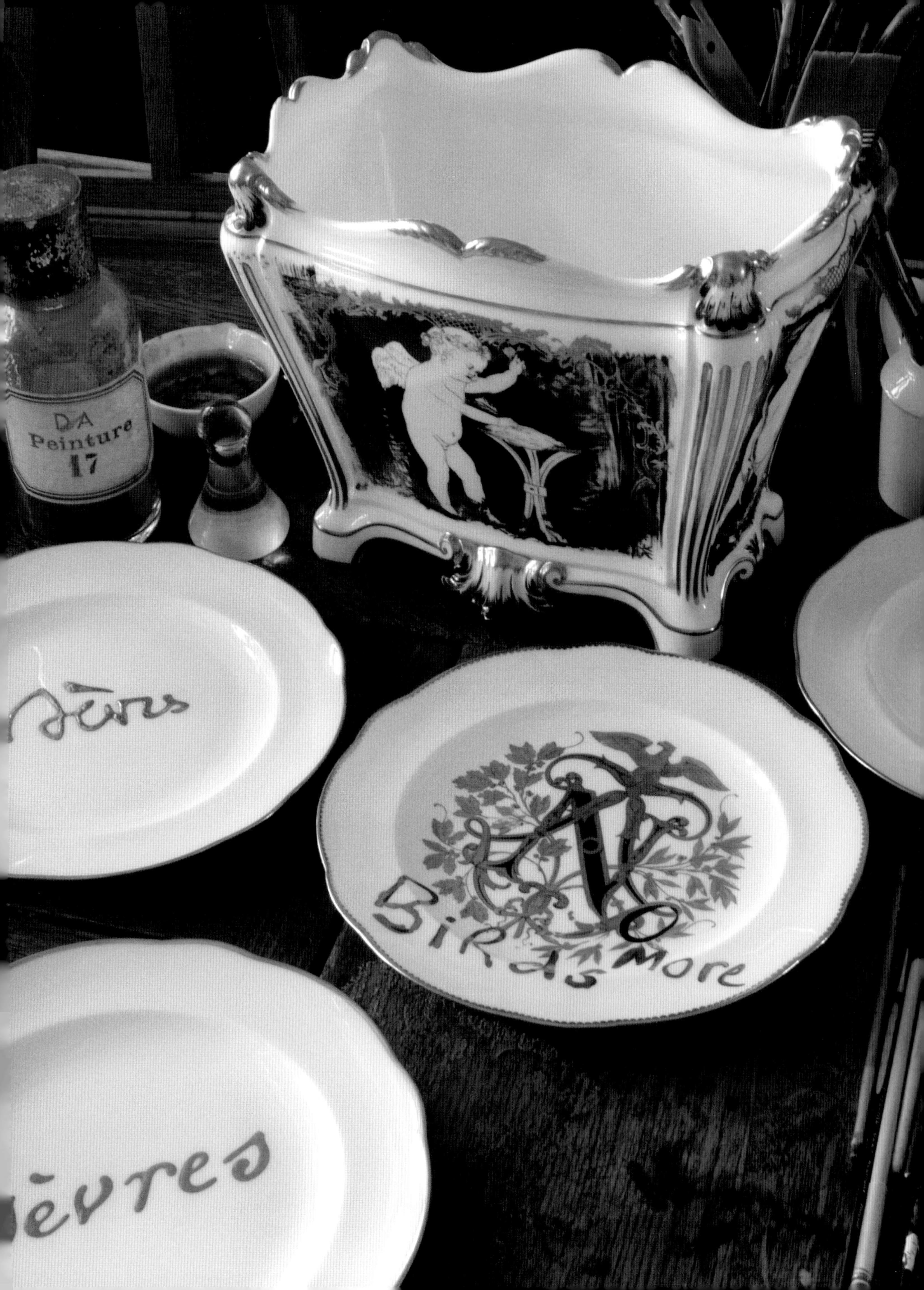

DA
Peinture
17
BiRds more
èvres

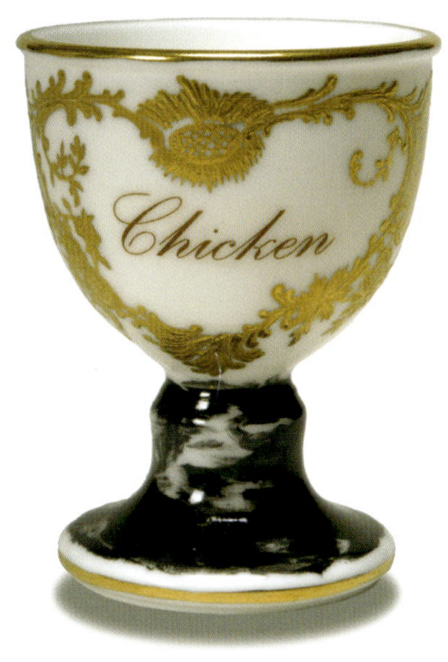

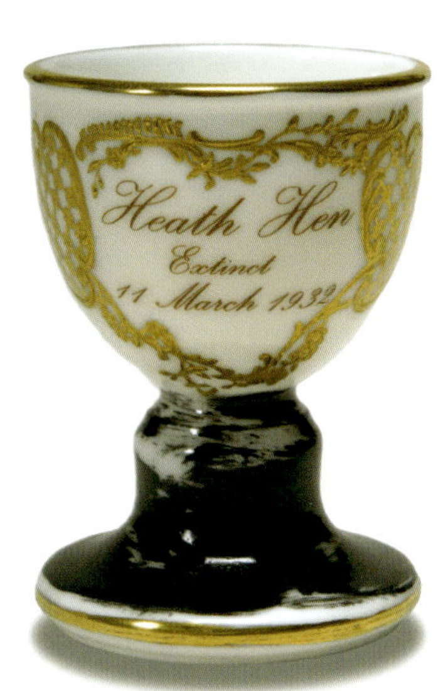

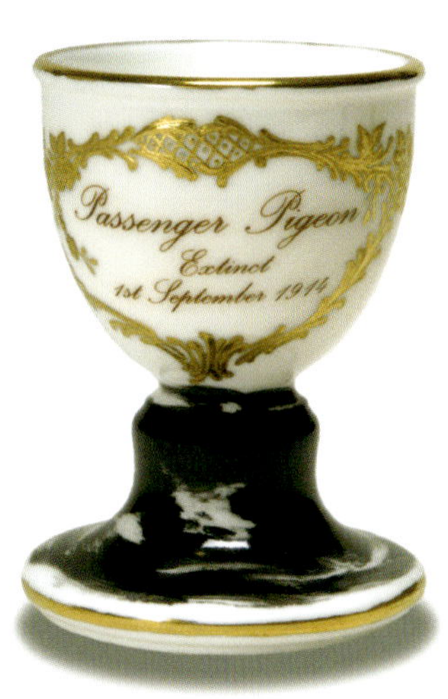

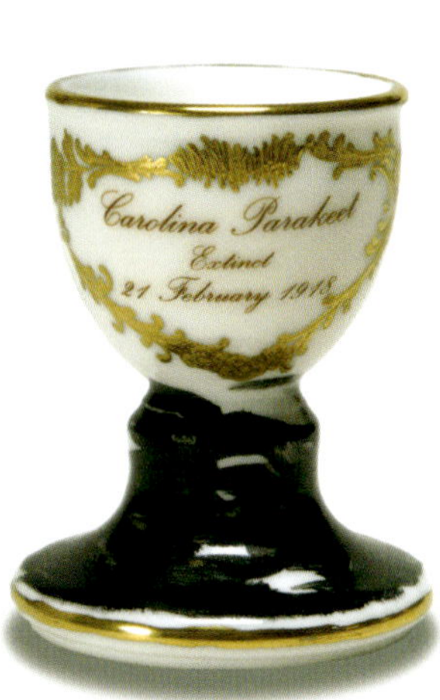

I have always believed that even the most abstract thought needs an object to exist. One of the things I always ask myself is how much body does a work of art really need to exist and to convey its plot. An extinct bird as an empty eggcup.

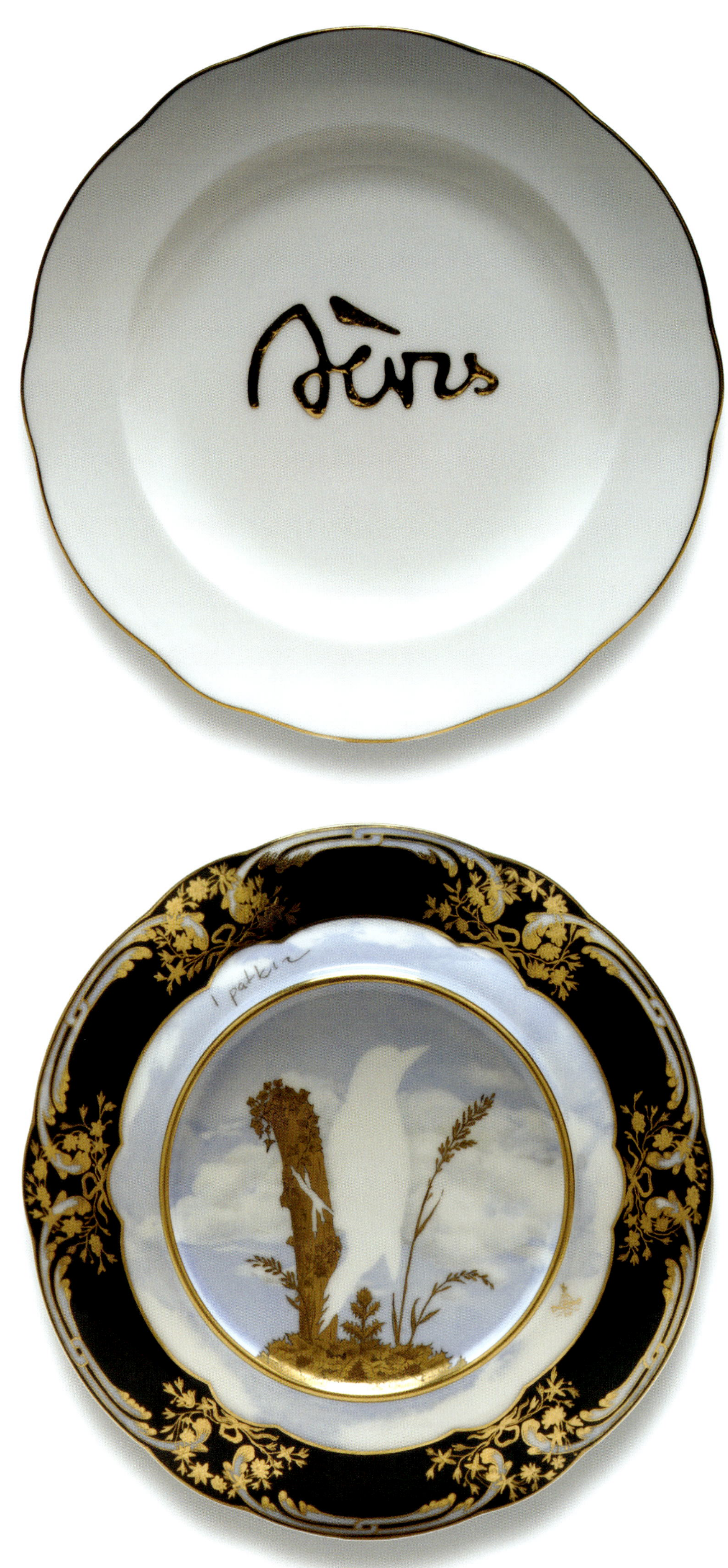

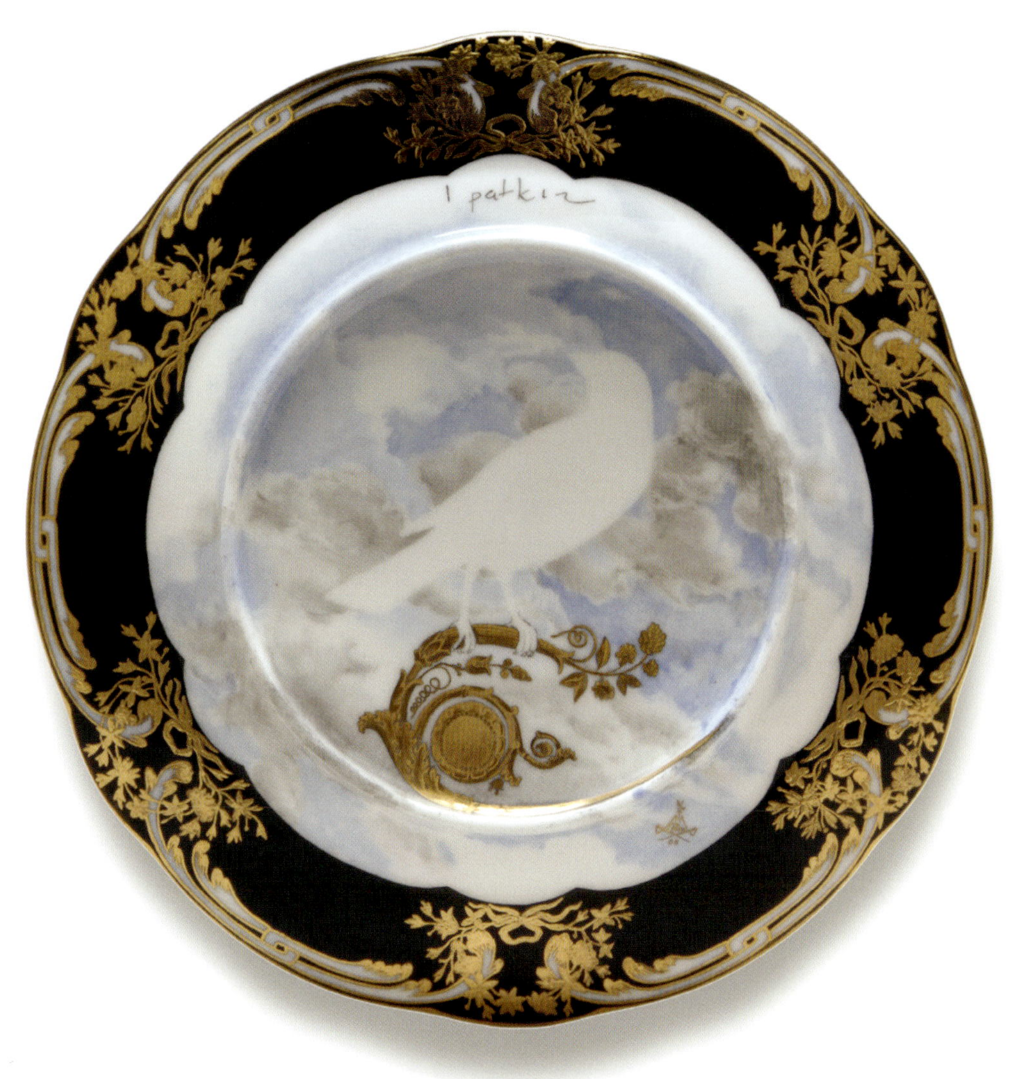

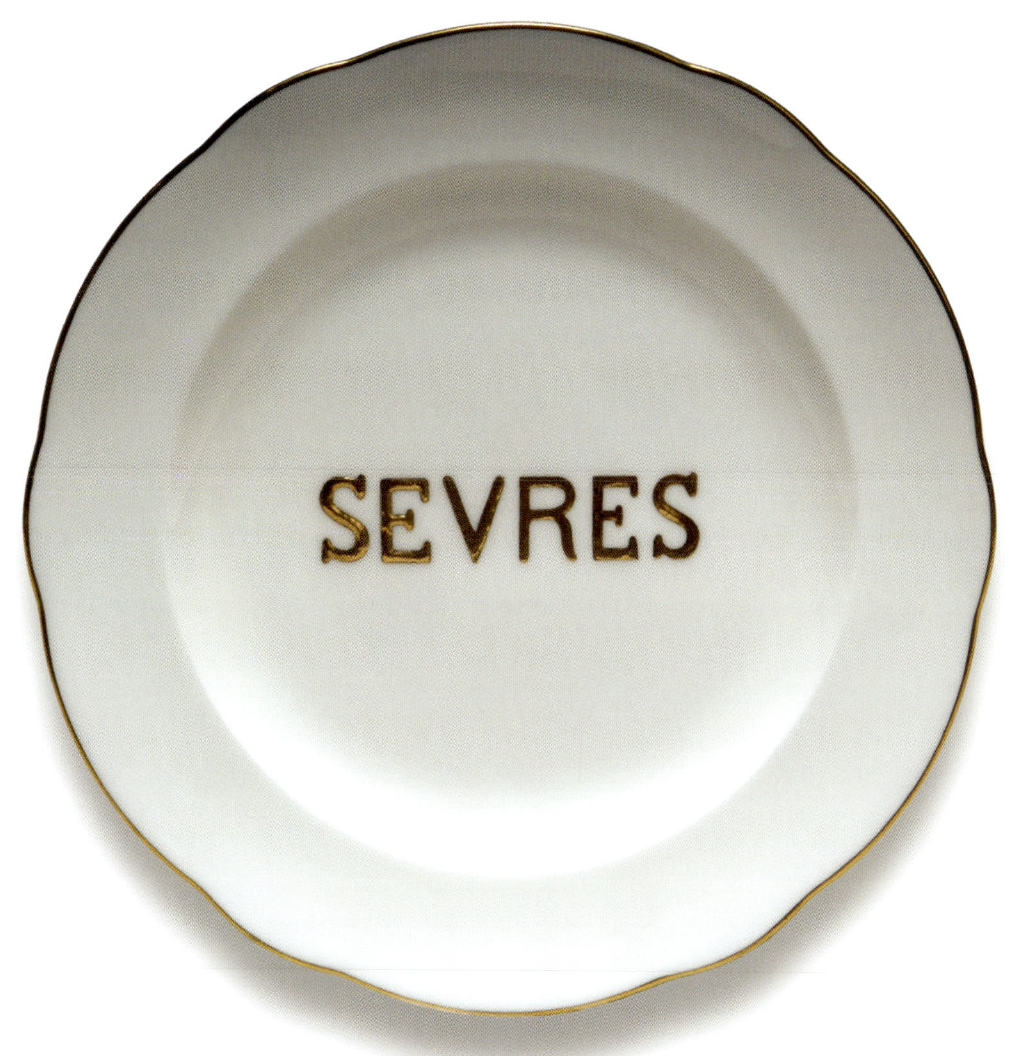
SEVRES

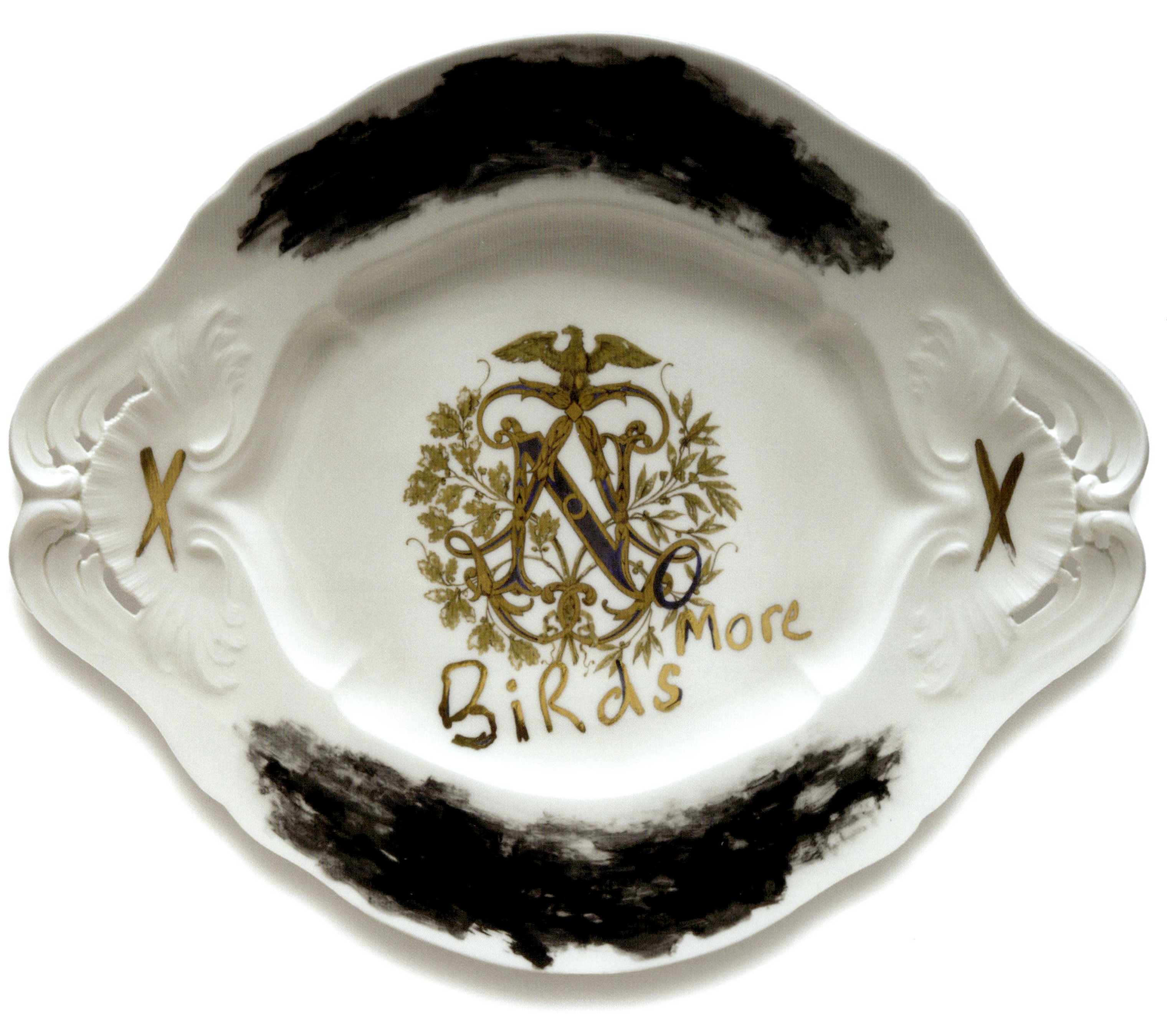
X
X
No
More
BiRds

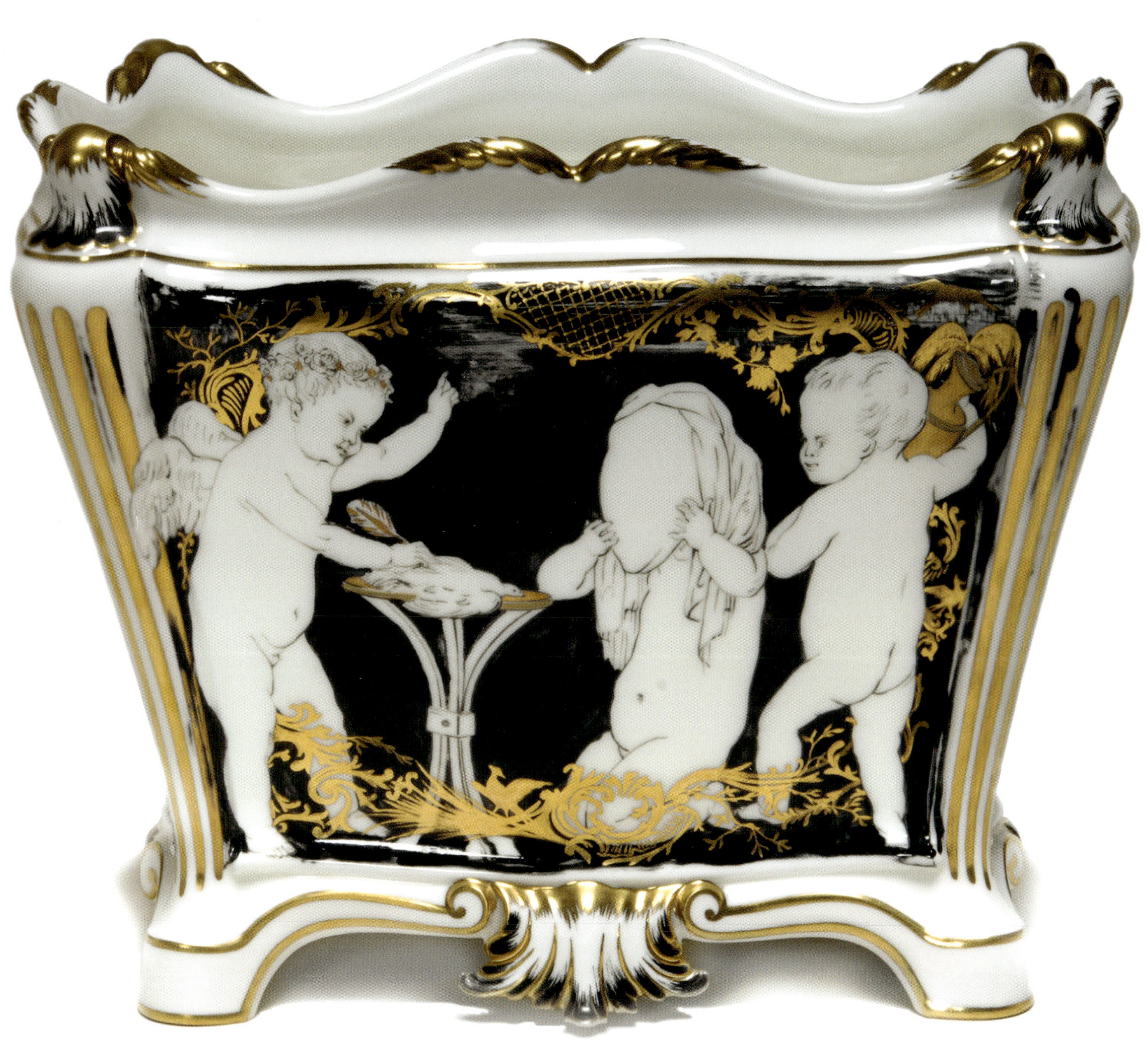

A Complicated Landscape

YOU TELL US WHAT TO DO

When we launched life
on the river of grief,
how vital were our arms, how ruby our blood.
With a few strokes, it seemed,
we would cross all pain,
we would soon disembark.
That didn't happen.
In the stillness of each wave we found invisible currents.
The boatmen, too, were unskilled,
their oars untested.
Investigate the matter as you will,
blame whomever, as much as you want,
but the river hasn't changed,
the raft is still the same.
Now *you* suggest what's to be done,
you tell us how to come ashore.

When we saw the wounds of our country
appear on our skins,
we believed each word of the healers.
Besides, we remembered so many cures,
it seemed at any moment
all troubles would end, each wound heal completely.
That didn't happen: our ailments
were so many, so deep within us
that all diagnoses proved false, each remedy useless.
Now do whatever, follow each clue,
accuse whomever, as much as you will,
our bodies are still the same,
our wounds still open.
Now tell us what we should do,
you tell us how to heal these wounds.

Poem by Faiz Ahmed Faiz
Version by Agha Shahid Ali

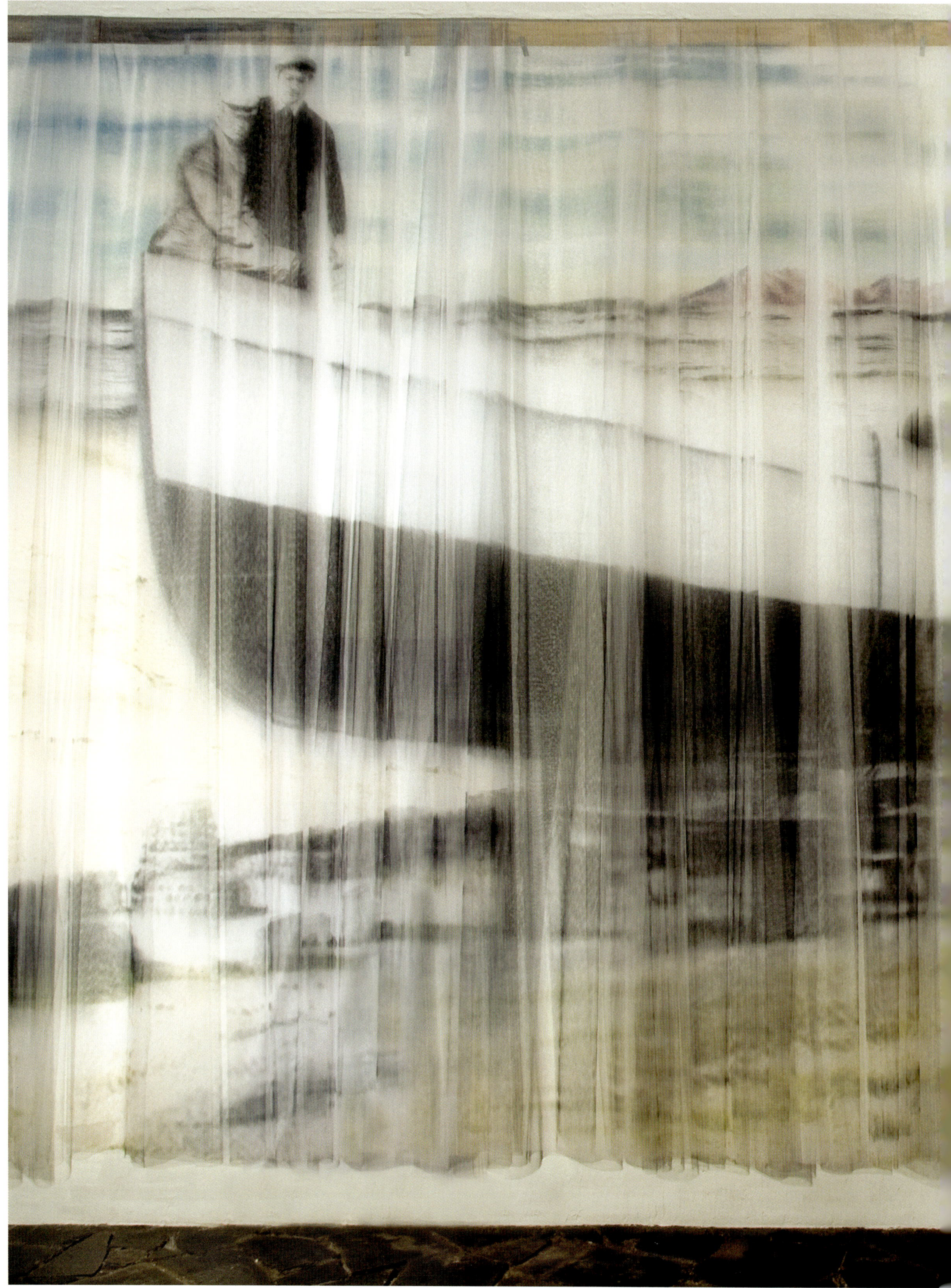

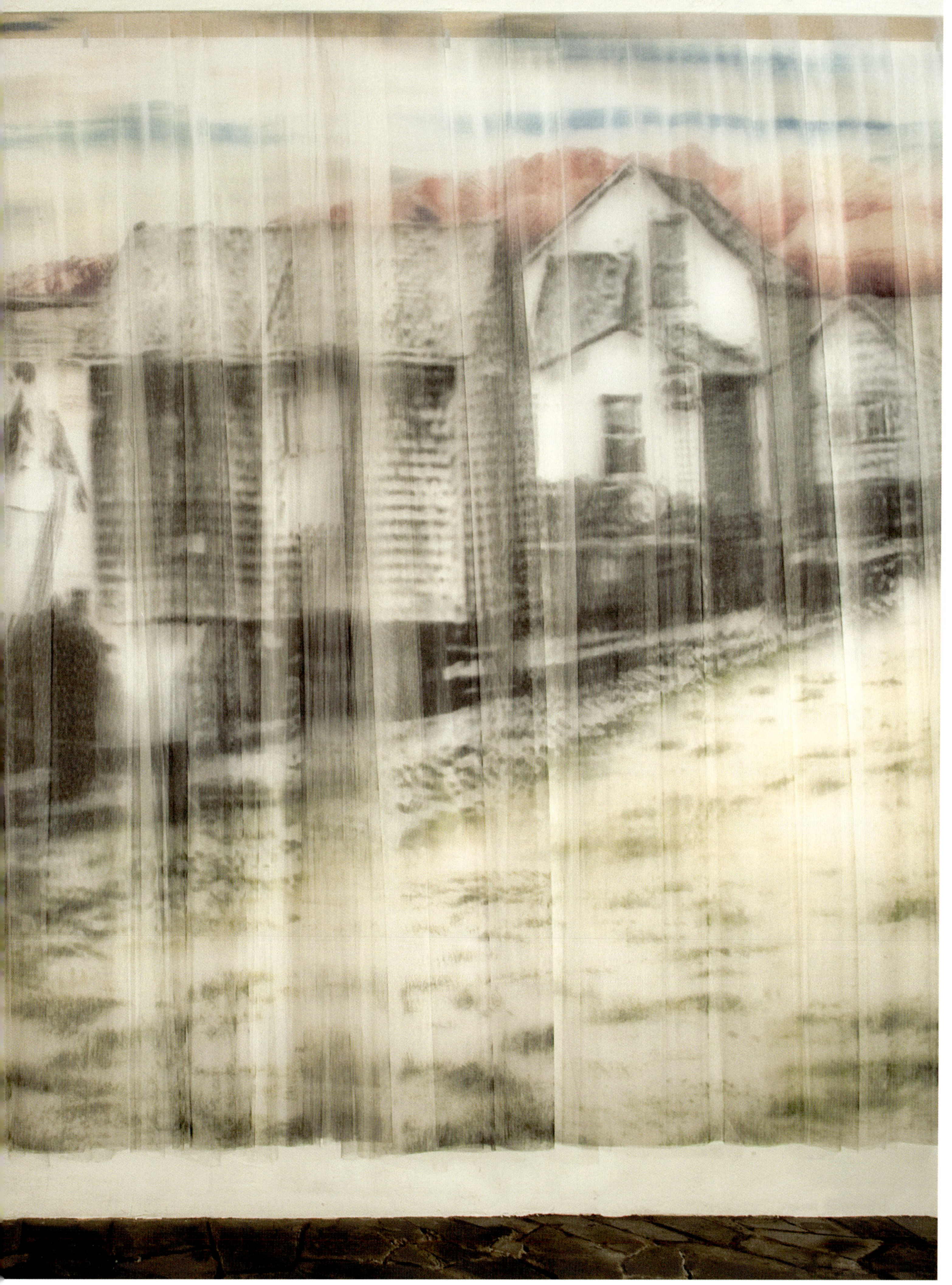

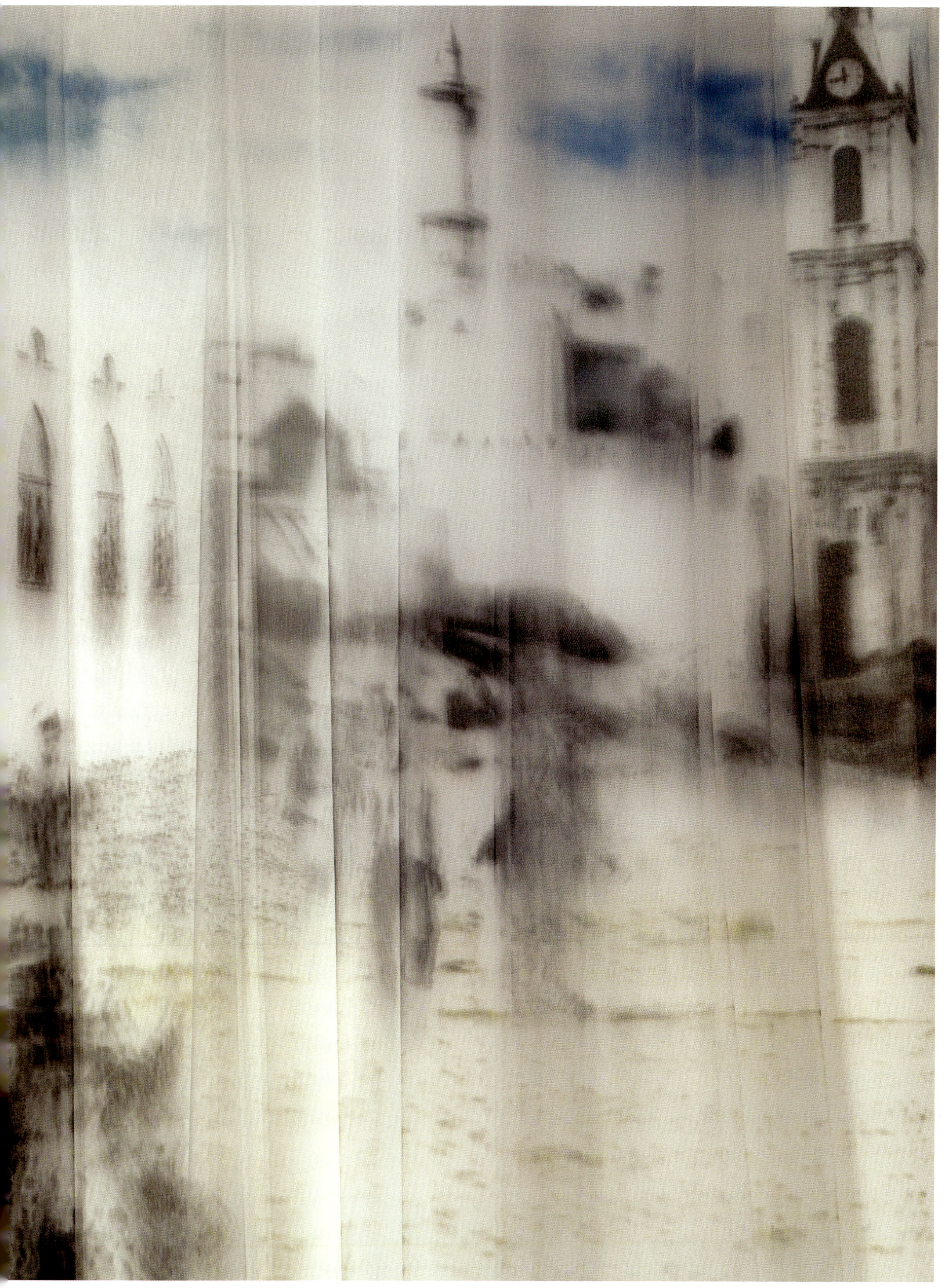

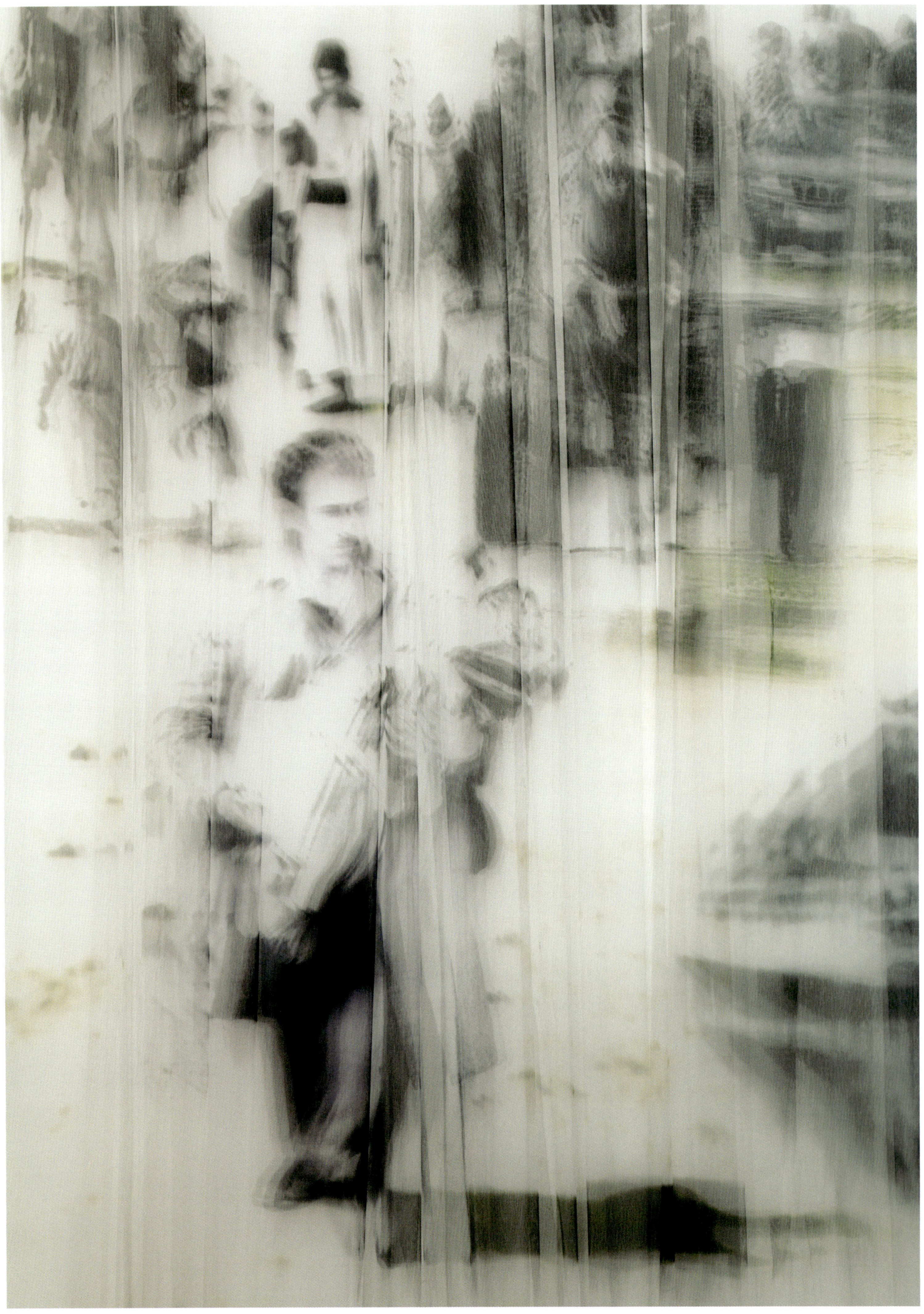

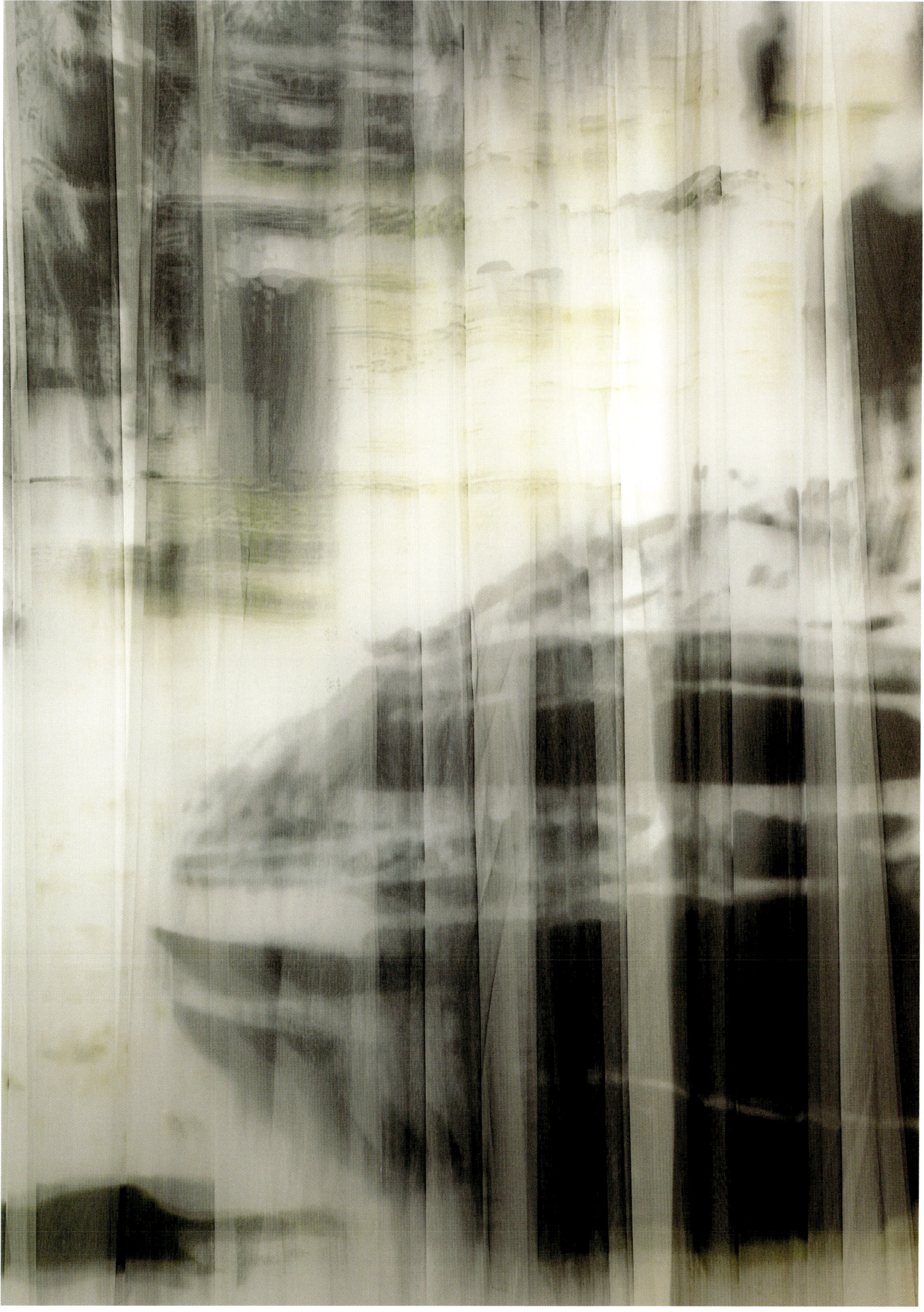

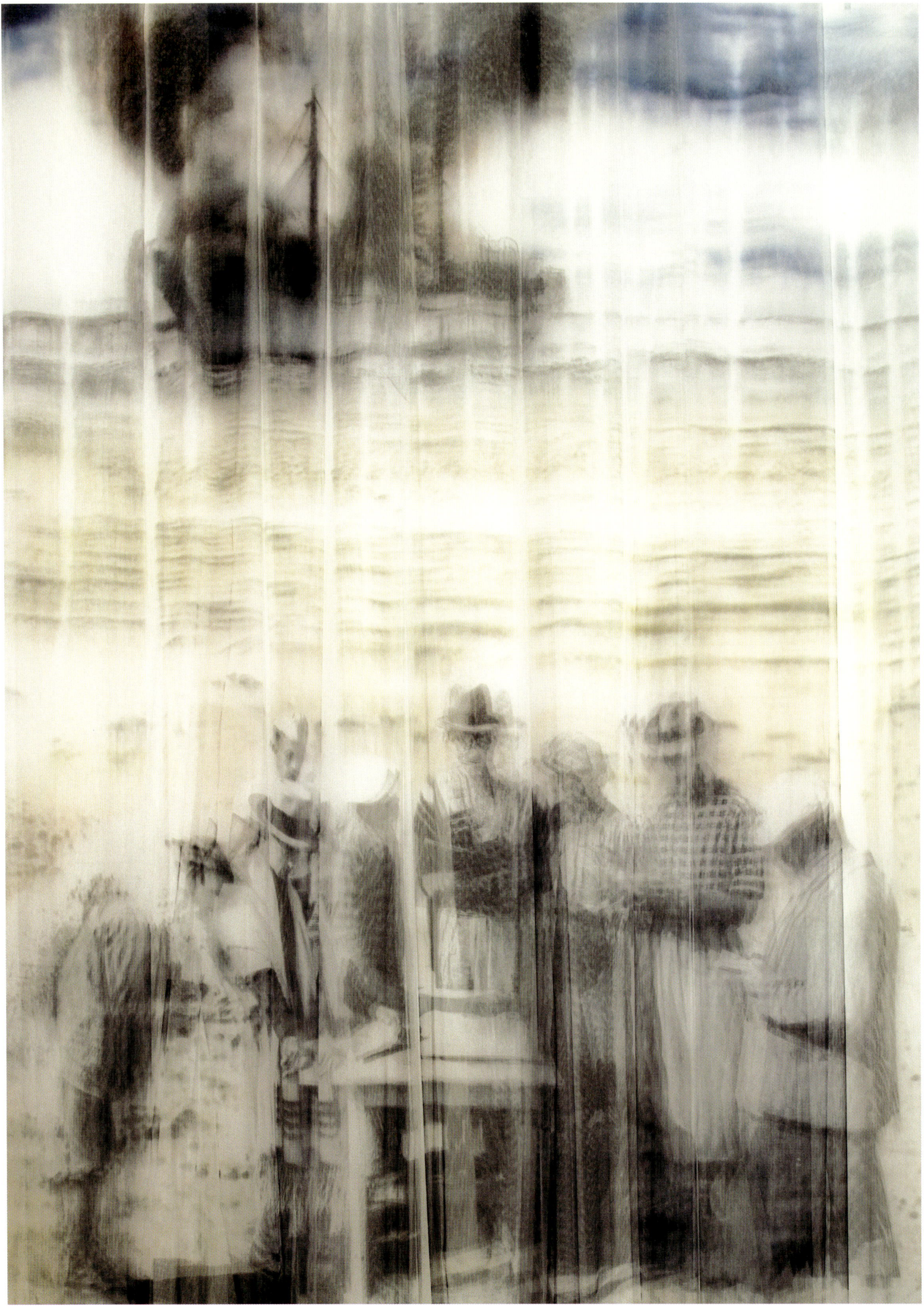

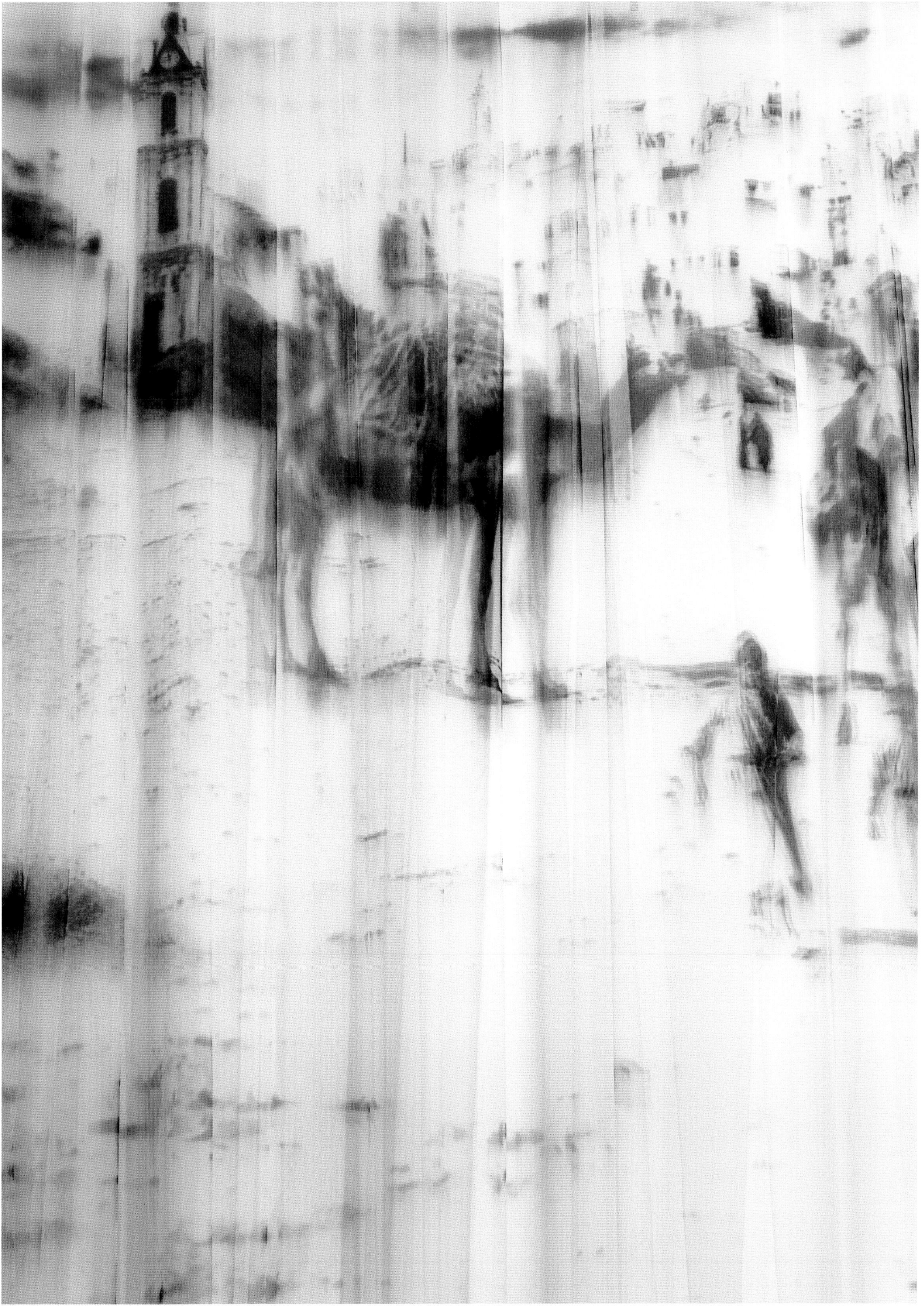

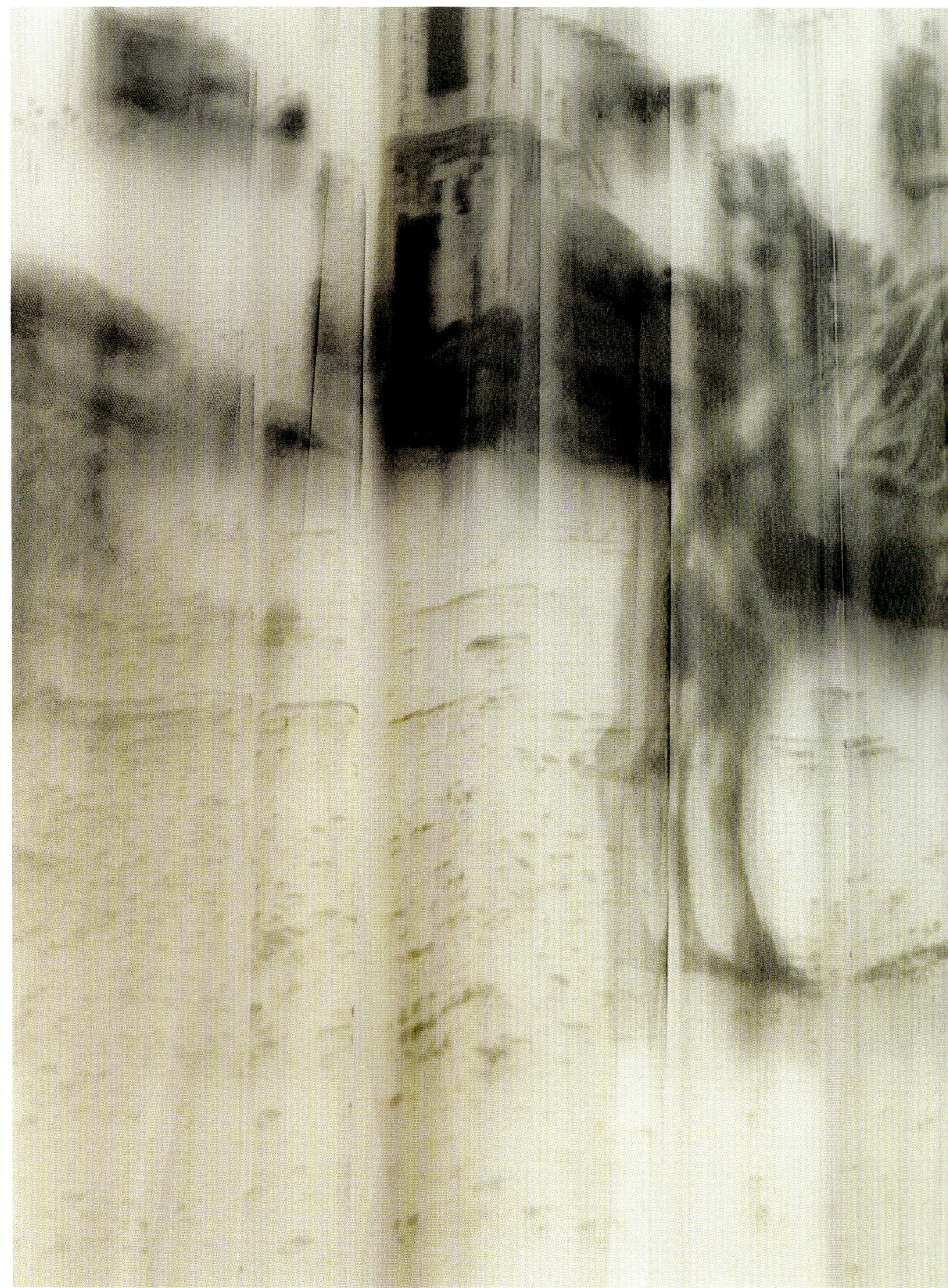

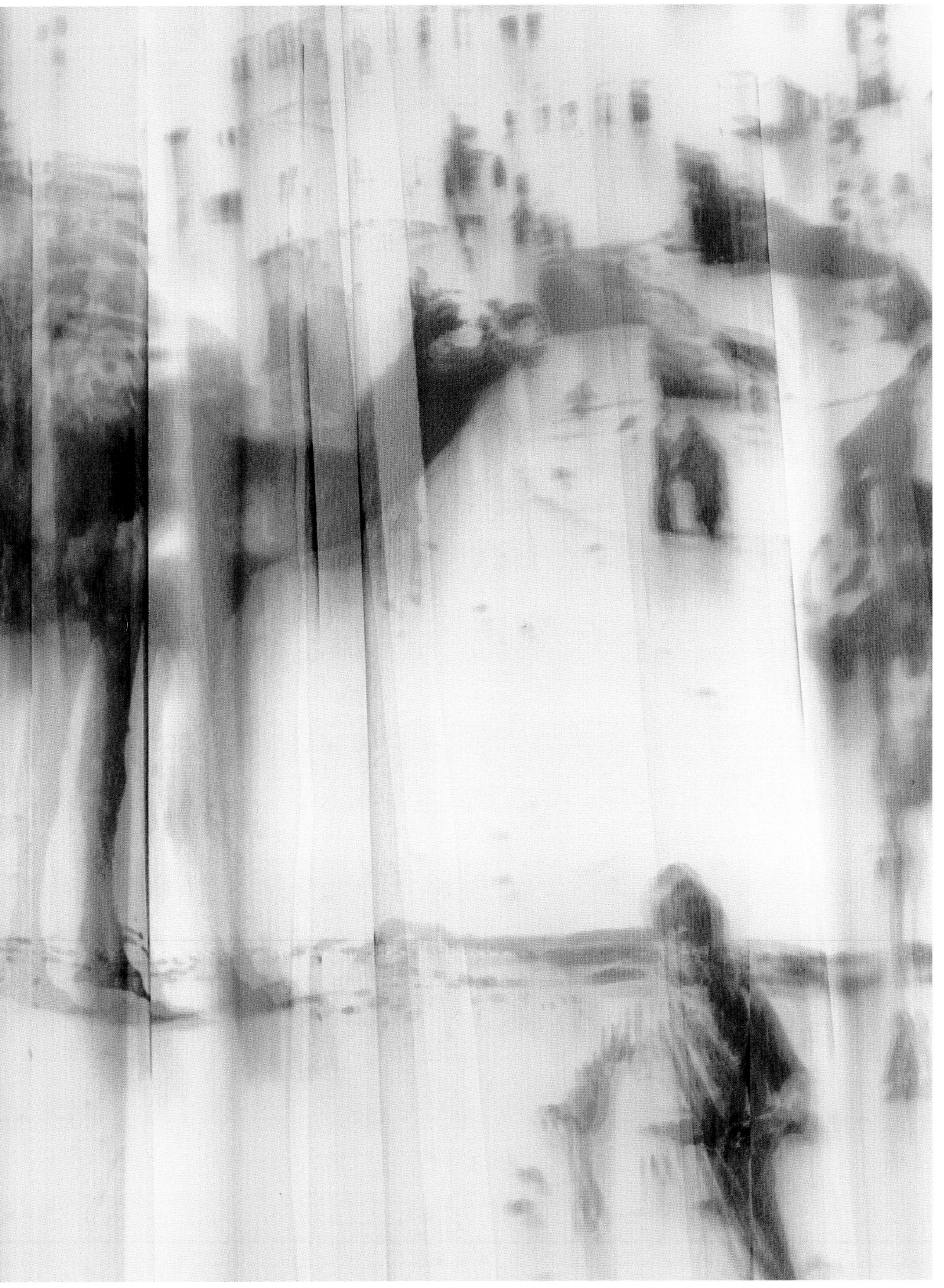

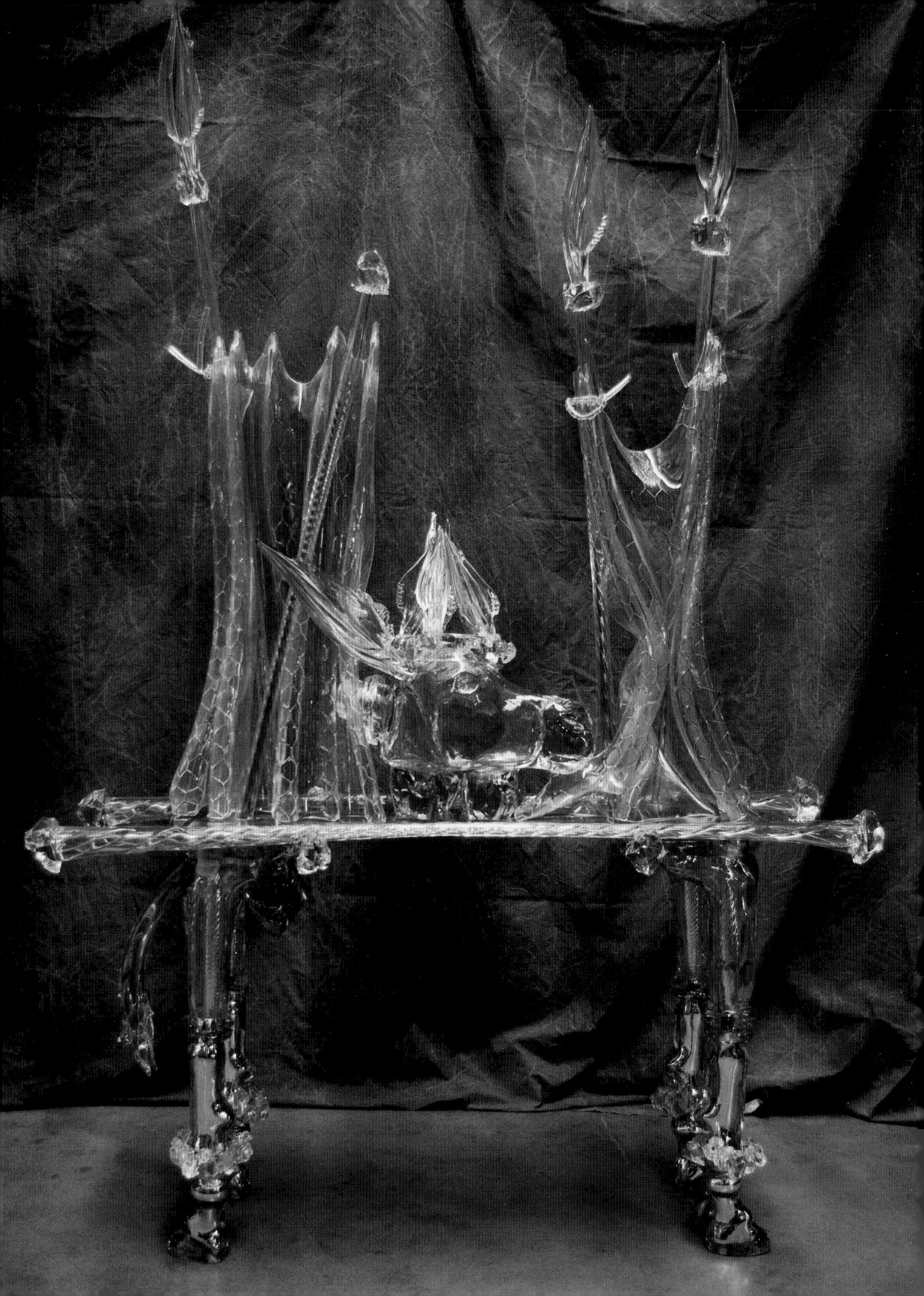

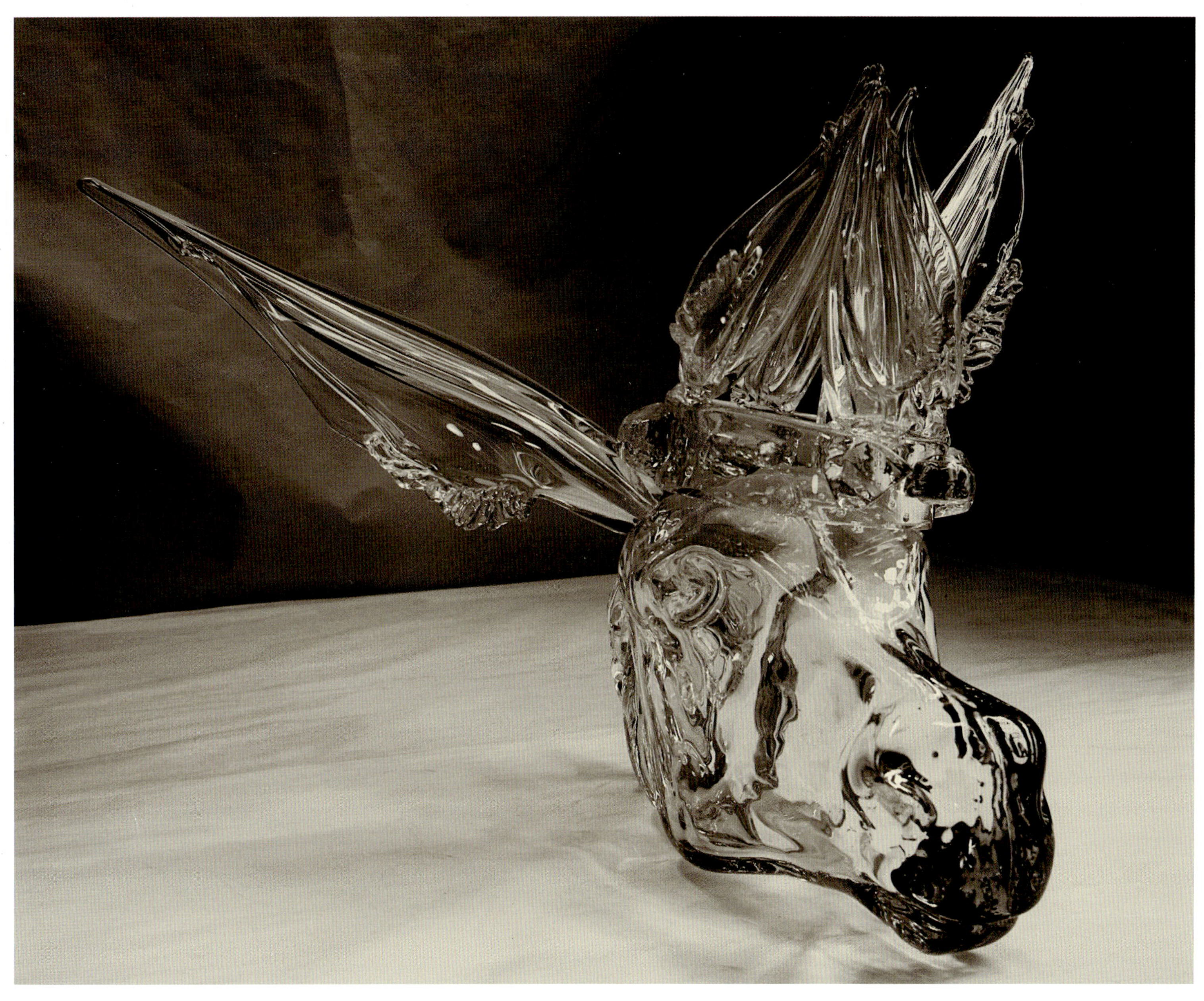

A metaphor gives an idea a body—an objectification. Emotions and words are objects—they have volume and weight. No matter how fleeting they are, they have matter. Translucent matter is bliss.

The Messiah's Ass

Of all the idioms and images whose meaning has changed over the years, none holds as multifaceted a mirror to the turmoil in Jewish history and culture as the iconic Messiah's ass. Its multitude of historical facets—from down-to-earth Old Testament theology to the apocalyptic, manipulative messianic outlooks that have swallowed up most of Jewish orthodoxy in Israel—reverberate in Izhar Patkin's work *The Messiah's glAss* (2003–07; pages 120–21). Familiarity with these diverse facets may help to shed light on the contemporary Israeli and Jewish existential crisis, which extends far beyond the present-day secular liberal "bubble" [1] of Tel Aviv.

The image and notion of the Messiah's donkey originates in the Book of Zechariah, in a story about a savior king who is "humble, and mounted on a donkey." The theological idea is simple and clear: God will anoint as king of Israel not a rich prince in a horse-drawn carriage, but a modest man whose power originates in God alone. A whole world, both Jewish and non-Jewish, was influenced by the original icon of the Messiah's donkey—from Hasidic notions of *Tzadik Nistar* [2] ("hidden righteous one") to socialist and revolutionary outlooks: it is the simple, poor, and unassuming youth that God chooses to rule the world. That is exactly how David, the seventh and youngest son, and Saul, who looked for his lost mules,[3] were chosen.

The donkey was cast in its messianic role because of its humble characteristics and because it is found among the poorest of the poor. The notion of a gentle man mounted on a donkey is set in contrast to the prophet Samuel's admonition to the Israelites foretelling that they will bring upon themselves a tyrannical king who has many horses and will strip them of their possessions. The arrogant horse is contrasted with the donkey, which is perceived as patient, meek, dedicated, and stubborn, just as the simple wooden sheds in which Itzhak Ben-Zvi and David Ben-Gurion, Israel's early heads of state, lived contrast with the glitzy mansions of today's leaders. The attributes of Jesus riding the donkey into the gates of Jerusalem reflect his entire outlook as a prophet and Messiah candidate: "Blessed are the meek for they shall inherit the earth" (Matthew 5:5) and "It is easier for a camel to go through the eye of a needle, than for a rich man to enter into the kingdom of God" (Matthew 19:24).

Since then, the metaphor of the donkey has undergone a sharp transformation. After the destruction of the Temple, Judaism—in exile, tormented, and cut off from its aspirations—became permeated by apocalyptic views in which the cosmic drama between God, man, and Satan played a central role. In this drama, satanic forces constantly threaten man. The dubious honor of serving as Satan's symbols on earth was given to the serpent and the donkey.

The snake has threatened mankind from the dawn of history, and in Jewish mythology—both in the Book of Zohar [4] and before—it is described as having intercourse with Eve. From this union all Gentiles were said to be born, and were therefore considered to be contaminated and not quite human. According to this view, only Jews may be called human, for they are not the snake's progeny but descended from God and Adam.

That the frightening snake was cast in this role is quite understandable, but why the donkey? Why has this handsome beast, with its lovely eyes and funny ears, become a symbol of Samael,[5] Lucifer, and Satan? The donkey's downfall had to do with a single anatomical fact: it is blessed with a large penis. Erect, it reaches the ground. And it is very thick. It is ten times bigger than the bull's, a much larger domesticated beast. The humble nature of the donkey and the fact that it could be found in practically every home were turned against it. It became a symbol of the sexual dangers that lurk everywhere.

Thus a reversal in perceptions occurred. In the Bible sex was perceived as natural, from the admiring views of male dominance to the acknowledgment and encouragement of female pleasure portrayed in the Song of Songs. However, in changing Jewish theology and from the beginning of Christianity, sex became obscene, threatening, and even diabolical.

This reversal became the fate of Balaam and his ass according to canonical exegesis. In Jewish theology, Balaam is considered to be an immensely wise man. "From Moses [the prophet] to Moses [Moses ben Maimon, Maimonides[6]] there was none like Moses"; well, perhaps there was none among the Israelites, but there was one among the other nations. Balaam's[7] wisdom and power was on a par with that of Moses, but on the side of evil. Wise as he was, Balaam only became powerful (according to the Book of Zohar) by having intercourse with his female donkey, thus gaining evil powers. And the donkey became a symbol and servant of Lucifer not only in Judaism, but also in Christianity, its younger sibling. On April Fools' Day, which is also a day of reversals, many villages and monasteries would make the donkey a priest for a day and donkey-masses would be held.

In all this turmoil, Jewish theologians found remedy, as usual, in their friends, the letters. Heinrich Heine regarded Jews as leading their lives in a book, with mountains and rivers constructed of words and letters. Unlike the material world around them, symbolic words were one thing the Diaspora Jews had control over. And so, by a simple transposition of two letters, the ass (in Hebrew, *chamor*) became symbolic of inferior material (in Hebrew, *chomar*), even diabolical.

Thus, instead of symbolizing humility and camaraderie, the Messiah mounted on a donkey came to symbolize a cosmic war in which the spiritual Messiah overcomes the material donkey. The donkey stands for all that is ignoble in the world. The Messiah's masterful donkey ride is akin to the beginning of the Bible, where "on the face of the deep" stands for the cosmic victory of God over the Babylonian Goddess Tiamat,[8] the chaos monster. It is also an extension of the exegesis that sets Jews apart. The Gentile is mounted on a donkey ruled by the beast's materiality, while the Jew has the spiritual fortitude to control lowly matter and redeem it.

The expression "The Messiah's Ass" became a canonical notion in Jewish theology through the Book of Zohar. It was an essential, vital notion, and the longer and more difficult exile became, the more elaborate and profound the image of the struggle against a multitude of diabolical forces. Religious thought embraced the notion of a multifaceted, apocalyptic timetable with the necessary phases that precede redemption. For redemption to take place, a licentious, materialistic generation that revolts against God must first exist and then be destroyed. This generation is called the Messiah's Ass Generation.

This is where Abraham Isaac Kook,[9] the most important Jewish theologian of recent generations, enters the picture—and most crucially so. Kook constructed a myth that was first accepted by a small group of followers. It gradually turned into the foundational myth shaping the worldview of a great majority of Orthodox Jews in Israel, thus affecting all of Israeli society.

Like many other rabbis of his generation, Rabbi Kook, who wrote before the Holocaust, had to tackle the vital question of how to explain three problematic issues. First, there was the persecution of Jews in his time, coupled with the calamity of the First World War and the rise of racism and Nazism. Second, there was the secularization of Jews, which orthodox regard as a catastrophe. And finally, there was the actual redemption of the Land of Israel. Although this resembled the redemption promised by Rabbi Maimonides, the most important religious authority on this issue, it was being implemented by secular Jews who are adulterers and desecrators of the Sabbath.

Rabbi Kook created a myth centered on the symbolic notion of the Messiah's ass. According to him, being secular is neither a sin nor a punishment; it is part of an overall necessary divine plan. Armed with notions of *Tzimtzum*[10] (Contraction of the Divine) derived from Lurianic[11] thought, Rabbi Kook maintained that the material power of Jews, particularly males, weakened in the Diaspora. According to the Kabbalist Rabbi HaAri, it was necessary to use lowly, base matter for the creation of the world onto which God's divine light emanated, followed by the Breaking of the Vessels,[12] whose base matter could not withstand the glory of that light. Similarly, it was necessary to create an inferior materialistic Jewish base in order to bring about the Jews' historical redemption. That necessary matter is the secular Israeli Jew—that is, the ass. According to Kook's myth, this secular ass is an expression of God's will and is meant to use its material power and energy to build kibbutzim, fight, establish the State of Israel, and re-inherit the Promised Land.

That is when, according to Kook's myth, the religious rider, for whose benefit all of this took place, is to assume his entitled seat. Just as God shone his light on the base matter, so will the religious Jew take over, ride, and direct the material State of Israel in accordance with his divine light. Kook's Messiah's ass myth foretold it all. The secular ass was supposed to rebel against the religious hands guiding it toward conquest, occupation, and redemption of the land, a rebellion that would be equivalent to the Kabbalistic Breaking of the Vessels. But this would only strengthen the religious Jews, who would forcefully crush the mutiny and take over the country. In the minds of these followers, this happened with the assassination of Prime Minister Yitzhak Rabin,[13] the secular hero who was about to forego parts of the Promised Land.

Kook's viewpoint became, in fact, the principal guideline for Orthodox Jewry in Israel. It progressed from exerting pressure over the government to having major influence over the entire Israeli society and over Orthodox Jews around the world. This is not limited to the many thousands of people populating the messianic universe of settlements in the Occupied Territories. Nor does it stop with the majority of religious and ultra-religious Jews, who, in fact, lead their lives in accordance with this worldview. The government of Israel is also being induced to take this route.

Izhar Patkin's work may be seen as both contrasting with and complementing Itzhak Danziger's *Nimrod* (1938–39). An attempt at creating indigenous art carved of an ancient rock,[14] Danziger's sculpture is presently on view at the center of the newly refurbished Israel Museum in Jerusalem, the city that stands for categorical theological and mythological doctrines.

In contrast, Patkin's *The Messiah's glAss* seems to have been made to suit the newly expanded Tel Aviv Museum of Art building. It is a sculpture recalling the Holy Ark, the one that was accompanied by cherubs and was emblematic of God's incarnation. This time, it is an ass with huge testicles, evoking the said member that led to the beast's own crucifixion. The secular splendor of the donkey surpasses the veil covering the Ark of the Covenant. It is made of a mythical, fragile material—glass blown in the Diaspora, in southern France, in the land of Rashi[15] (Rabbi Shlomoh Yitzhaki) situated between Ashkenazi[16] and Sephardic[17] Jewry. And it is on view in a venue neighboring the secular square where last summer's social-protest demonstrations started in Israel, in one of several exhibitions celebrating the renewed power of Israel's central secular museum. Thus Patkin's *glAss* stands for the richness of secular Judaism: Israeli, Hebraic, Tel Avivian, sexual, innocent, sparkling, virile, intriguing, gratifying, and reflective in all meanings of the word.

But Patkin's ass is beheaded. There is no substitute lamb in this tale of sacrifice; it is the ass itself that is beheaded here, by political messianic hands. Is it strong enough to reinstate its glorious head? That is for viewers to say, should they survive the foretold apocalyptic war against the Messiah's Ass Generation.

Sefi Rachlevsky

NOTES

1
In the Israeli vernacular, Tel Aviv is often referred to as "The Bubble" in the middle of Israel.

2
A *Tzadik Nistar* is a hidden *Tzadik*, whose righteousness remains unknown to his community. In every generation there are thirty-six *Tzadikim Nistarim* in addition to thirty-six revealed *Tzadikim*. Together they combine to form the seventy-two "bridges" (corresponding to the seventy-two Names of God) described in the Zohar as linking together the concealed and revealed worlds. It requires tremendous self-sacrifice for a *Tzadik Nistar* to reveal himself to the world. This was first accomplished in full by the *Ba'al Shem Tov*.

3
When Saul was looking for his father's lost donkeys, the prophet Samuel found him and anointed him king of Israel: "And as for your donkeys that were lost three days ago, set not your mind on them; for they are found. And on whom is all the desire of Israel? Is it not on you, and on all your father's house?" (1 Samuel 9:21).

4
The Book of Zohar (Hebrew for "splendor, radiance") is widely considered to be the most important work of Kabbalah.

5
Samael is an archangel in Talmudic and post-Talmudic lore. He is seducer and destroyer, and he has been regarded as both good and evil. It is said that he was the guardian angel of Esau and tempted Eve in the guise of the serpent.

6
Maimonides (1138–1204), also known as Rambam, is considered to be the greatest Jewish philosopher of the medieval period. He was a leading rabbinic authority of his time and quite possibly of all time. His works influenced thinkers as diverse as Aquinas, Spinoza, Leibniz, and Newton.

7
Balaam attempted to curse God's people. He failed all three tries, each time producing blessings, not curses (Numbers 22–24) as the Angel of the Lord (Numbers 22:22) was sent to prevent him. At first the angel was seen only by the donkey Balaam was riding, which tried to avoid the otherwise invisible angel. After Balaam started punishing the donkey for refusing to move, it was miraculously given the power to speak to Balaam (Numbers 22:28), and it complained about Balaam's treatment. Balaam was then allowed to see the angel, who informed him that the donkey was the only reason the angel did not kill Balaam. Balaam immediately repented, but was told to go on.

8
In Babylonian mythology, Tiamat is a chaos monster, a primordial goddess of the ocean, mating with Abzû (the god of fresh water) to produce younger gods.

9
Abraham Isaac Kook (1865–1935) was the first Ashkenazi chief rabbi of the British Mandate for Palestine, the founder of the Religious Zionist Yeshiva Merkaz HaRav, a Jewish thinker, a Halachist, a Kabbalist, and a renowned Torah scholar. He is known by the acronym HaRaAYaH (HaRav Avraham Yitzchak HaCohen), which in English means "the evidence," or simply as HaRav (*the* Rabbi). He was one of the most celebrated and influential rabbis of the 20th century. While Rabbi Kook is exalted as one of the most important thinkers in mainstream Religious Zionism, he was quite critical of the more modern-orthodox Religious Zionists, whom he saw as naive and perhaps hypocritical in attempting to synthesize traditional Judaism with a modern and largely secular ideology.

10
Tzimtzum ("contraction" or "constriction") is a term used in the Kabbalistic teaching of Isaac Luria, explaining his concept that God began the process of creation by "contracting" his infinite light in order to allow for a "conceptual space" in which a finite and seemingly independent world could exist. This contraction, forming an "empty space" in which creation could begin, is known as the *Tzimtzum*. The ability of God to become hidden from perception is what makes creation possible, because God can become "revealed" in a diversity of limited options.

11
Isaac (ben Solomon) Luria Ashkenazi (1534–1572), commonly known as "the ARI" (meaning "the Lion"), was a foremost rabbi and Jewish mystic in the community of Safed in the Galilee region of Ottoman Palestine. He is considered to be the father of contemporary Kabbalah. Before his writings, all Kabbalists asserted that the *Ein-Sof* (the "Infinite") was made manifest through the processes of emanation and creation. Isaac Luria suggested the opposite: an enormous chasm existed between *Ein-Sof* and the world of emanation. Luria explained this "new" Kabbalah on the basis of three characteristics: contraction, the Breaking of the Vessels, and reintegration.

12
According to Luria, the vessels that were meant to contain the origins of God's light were unable to, and were either displaced or shattered. As a result of this cosmic catastrophe, the *Sefirot*, the archetypal values through which the cosmos was created, are shattered and out of place, and the world within which we reside is composed of the shards of the these

broken values. The Breaking of the Vessels is, according to the Lurianic Kabbalah, a clearing of the decks, a fresh start that we equate with our own civilized life. It is an eruption of chaos into the heart of our spiritual, conceptual, moral, and psychological structures.

13
The assassination of Yitzhak Rabin took place on November 4, 1995, at the end of a rally in support of the Oslo Peace Accords at the Kings of Israel Square in Tel Aviv.

14
Made of red Nubian sandstone, *Nimrod* depicts a naked, uncircumcised hunter, carrying a bow and with a hawk on his shoulder, in a style showing the influence of ancient Egyptian statues.—Trans.

15
Shlomo Yitzhaki, or, in Latin, Salomon Isaacides (1040–1105), generally known by the acronym Rashi, was a medieval French rabbi famed as the author of a comprehensive commentary on the Talmud.

16
Ashkenazi Jews are the Jews of France, Germany, and Eastern Europe and their descendants. *Ashkenaz* is Germany.

17
Sephardic Jews are the Jews of Spain, Portugal, North Africa, and the Middle East and their descendants. The adjective *Sephardic* is derived from the Hebrew word *Sepharad*, which refers to Spain.

Et in Arcadia Ego: A Tale of History and

ON TWO NARRATIVES IN IZHAR PATKIN'S WORK

> *All works of art are nothing but visible imprints of the artist's faculties, presenting and exposing to us, as it were, his entire soul.*
>
> Moses Mendelssohn [1]

Izhar Patkin's decision to engage in this exhibition with issues related to Jewish and Israeli history and culture underscores the nature of his entire artistic oeuvre, which is usually based on narratives—whether historical, personal, or artistic. I would like to address the two key themes at the heart of the works on view at the Open Museum in Tefen: the centuries-old German porcelain called *Judenporzellan* and the twentieth-century Israeli painter Reuven Rubin's pastoral landscapes.

JUDENPORZELLAN: A STORY WITHIN A STORY WITHIN A STORY

Patkin's series *Judenporzellan* (1998–2002; pages 95–99) is based on the accounts of the despicable and petty degradation of Jewish families in Berlin in the late eighteenth century. The story of the *Judenporzellan* (Jewish porcelain) begins in the days of King Frederick of

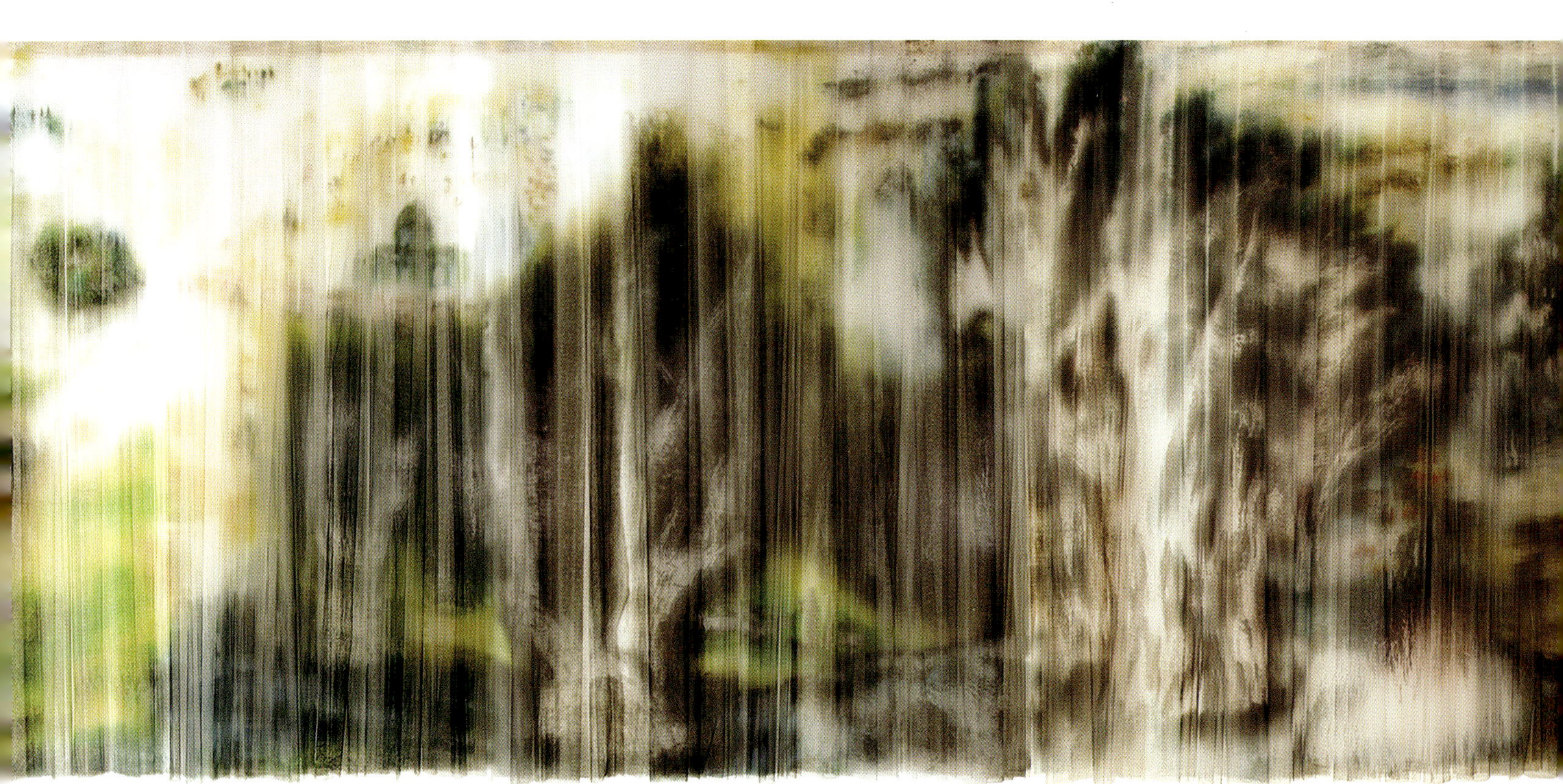

Prussia, who forced Moses Mendelssohn to purchase porcelain monkeys, and ends with the paper collages Patkin created about this historical tale, which he discovered while researching his own family's history.

The idea for the series was born when Patkin visited the German-Speaking Jewry Heritage Museum in Tefen.[2] It was there that he first saw the porcelain ware called *Judenporzellan*. The museum's archive holds letters written by Ben Zion Patkin, Patkin's grandfather's brother, a Zionist Jew who had lived in Sydney, Australia. He wrote the letters to the museum's founder, Israel Shiloni, a German Jew who was exiled to Australia and then detained by the British authorities in the Tantura encampment, approximately 180 kilometers north of Sydney. As he was examining these old letters, the artist noticed the *Judenporzellan* among the museum exhibits: a teapot, a cup, and a saucer from the eighteenth century. Later he said that his first thought was to ask why such ugly ceramic ware would be displayed in a museum. He inquired about it, and heard for the first time the story of how King Frederick of Prussia decreed that all his Jewish subjects had to purchase inferior porcelain from his struggling King's Porcelain Manufacturer (KPM—Königliche Porzellan-Manufaktur) whenever they needed to obtain any kind of official document from the authorities—anything from a home-building permit to a marriage license, or even a birth certificate.

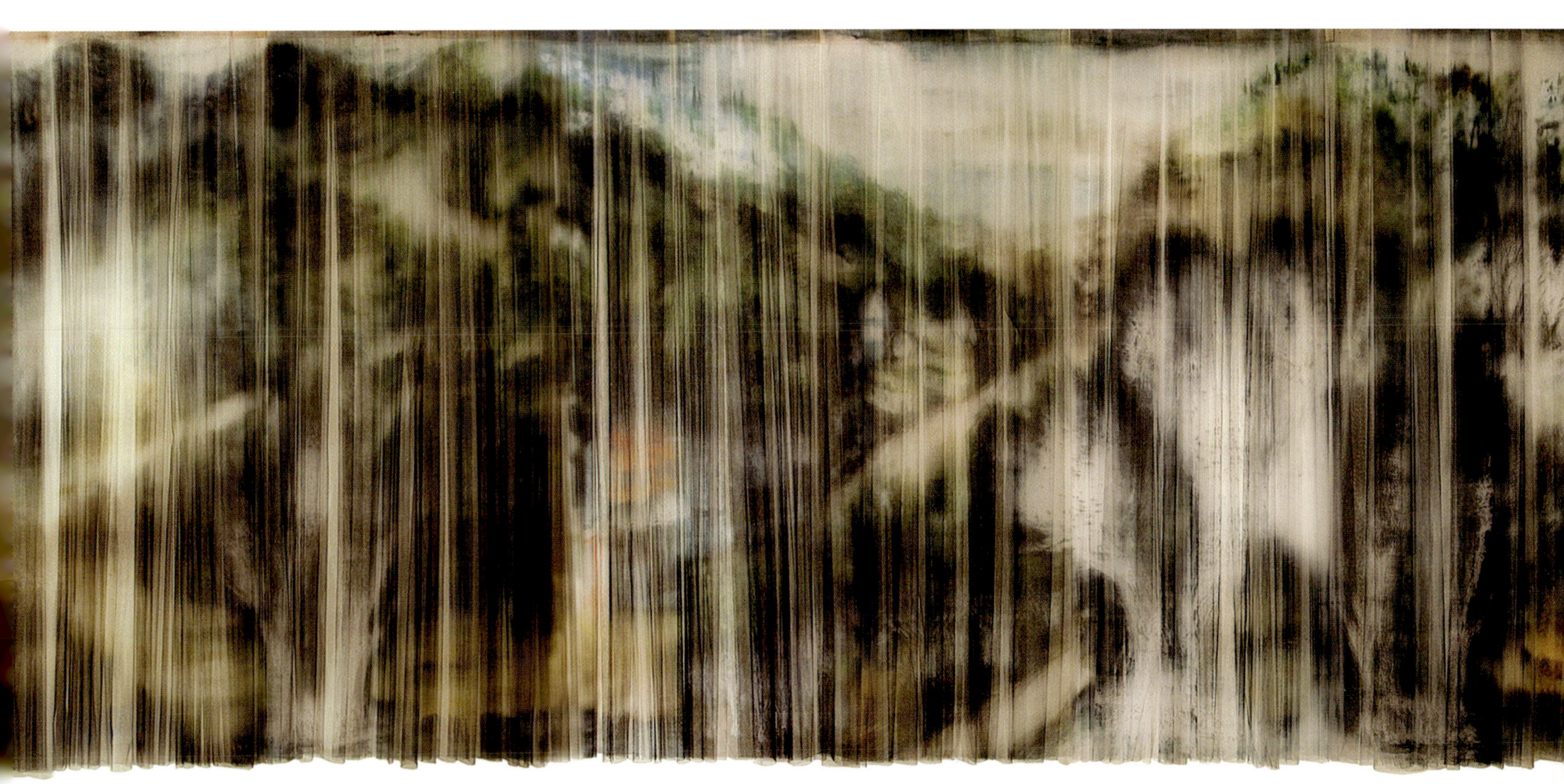

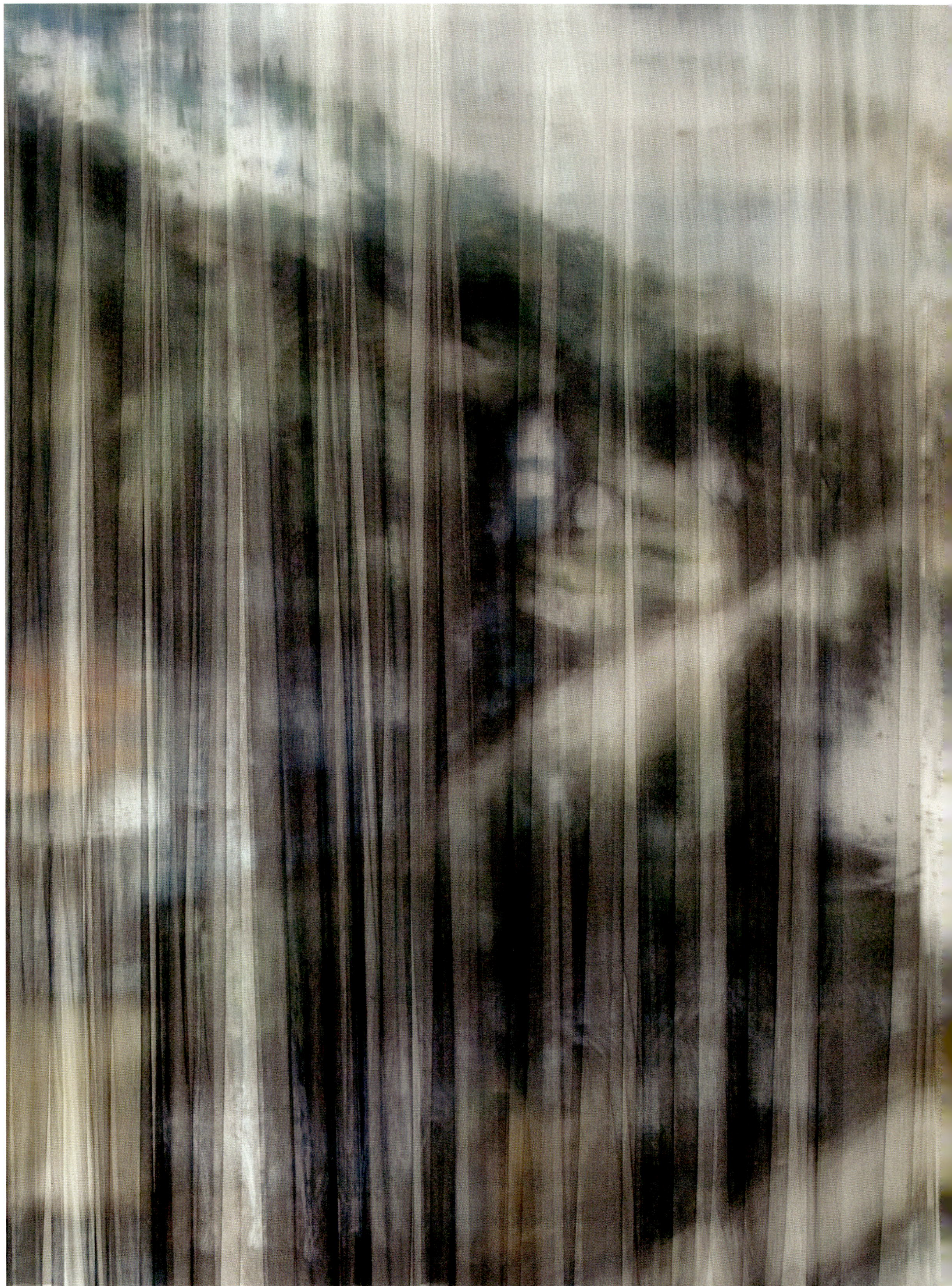

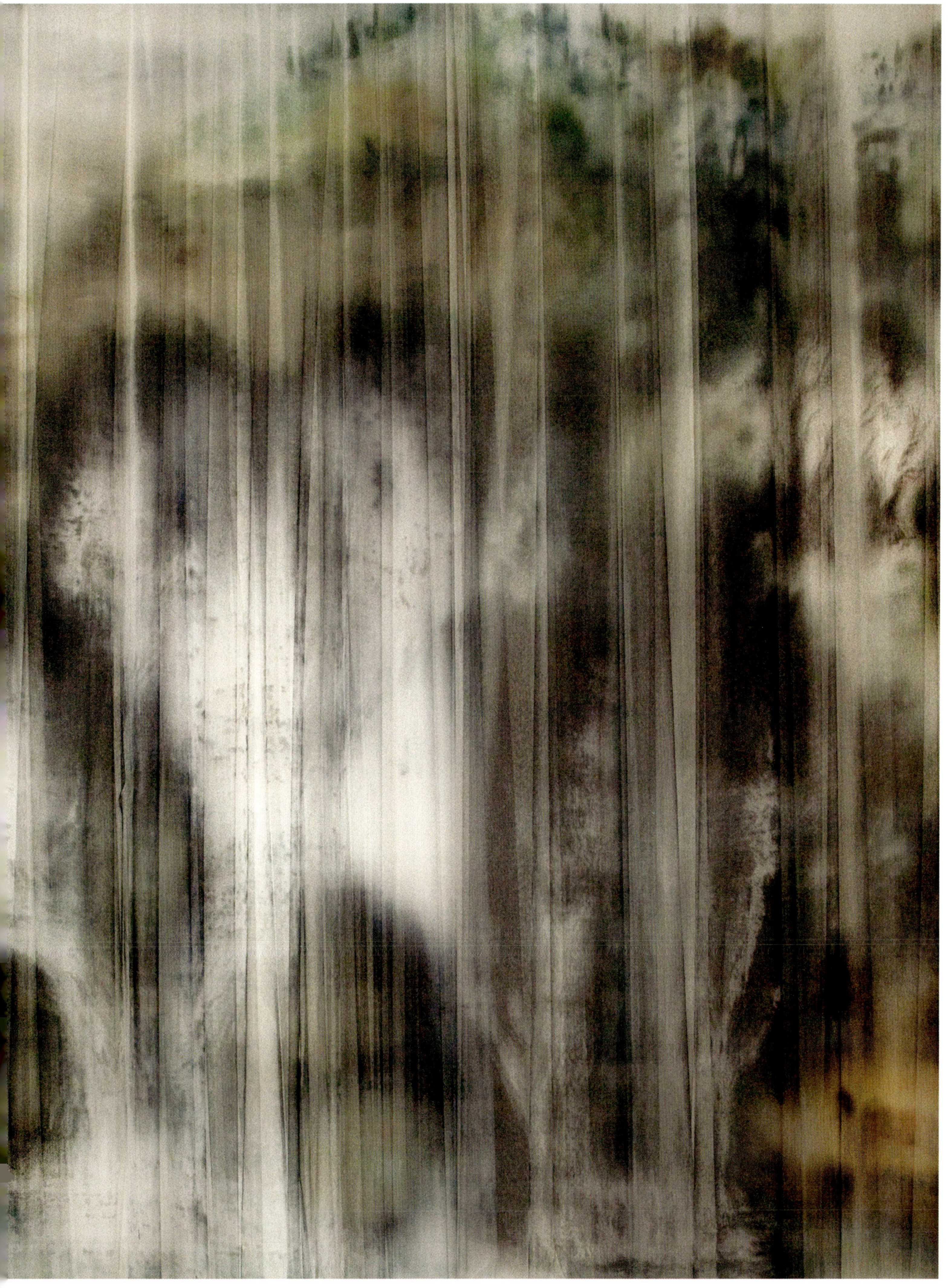

Patkin interwove the story of *Judenporzellan* with that of three generations of a great German Jewish family: the philosopher Moses Mendelssohn (1729–1786); his daughter, the feminist writer and literary salonnière Dorothea von Schlegel (1764–1839); and his grandchildren, the composers Fanny Mendelssohn (1805–1847) and Felix Mendelssohn (1809–1847).

"The use of a traditional folk art for the *Judenporzellan* [series] contributes the touch of sincerity and intimacy to the works and deeply intimates that they tell a story bound to the past not just of Mendelssohn, but of an entire people," as Mark Daniel Cohen has written.[3] Indeed, Patkin made all the works in the series using the folkloristic paper-cut technique that was and still is traditionally used for decorating the sukkah, a task customarily delegated to the children. It was one of the only arts that conformed to the commandment to refrain from making "any graven image, or any likeness *of* anything."

Patkin's works show the figures of Moses Mendelssohn and his family members alongside symbols such as branches of the Wandering Jew plant and objects he invents, like teakettles with lids shaped as skullcaps, side-locks, and kettle spouts shaped like an anti-Semitic depiction of a Jewish hooked nose. The porcelain monkey that Mendelssohn was compelled to buy is also part of this imagery. All the works are pinned on sheets of canvas and displayed in a temporary, sukkahlike construction, built in accordance with Jewish tradition. The magic in Patkin's paper-cut images stems not only from their fine execution, but also from his ability to narrate a complex story through visual means.

For Patkin, these paper collages are not just a journey into childhood memories, but also a challenge to the boundaries of art history. He enters the traditional practice of the children's sukkah decorations into a dialogue with Henri Matisse's paper cutouts, which were initially perceived as childlike. And he positions the sukkah in the gallery context as the mother of all temporary installations.

DISMANTLING ERETZ-ISRAEL'S MYTHICAL LANDSCAPE

In Israeli art, Reuven Rubin's work is emblematic of the Zionist notion of regeneration and of the Orient as naive and unspoiled. Pastoral scenes with divinely lit olive trees and native shepherds became synonymous with Rubin, and he painted them often. His mythical compositions are the key motif in Izhar Patkin's *Et in Arcadia Ego* (2012; pages 128–31, 134–35), whose title is Latin for "Even in Arcadia I am," with "I" referring to death. Patkin has taken several of Rubin's easel landscapes, including *Glory of Galilee* (1966), which hangs in the Knesset government meeting room, and combined them into a single seamless panorama, printing them onto a large, translucent pleated tulle curtain, 62 feet long by 13 feet high, as if they were photographic negatives of the Rubin paintings. He turns the silvery glow of the olive trees in *Glory of Galilee* into bright, blurry whites, enhancing the original's illusory sense of viewing the landscape, as Alfred Werner wrote in 1958, "through misty veils of light."[4] The optical reversal from a positive to a filmlike negative dismantles the fantasy suggested by the virginal scenery. In Patkin's work, the hills and olive trees are at once vaporized and re-created, at the point where an idyllic landscape turns into a menacing and perplexing one.

Through this deconstruction and reconstruction, Patkin portrays the rupture of the Zionist dream. He finds a surprising resemblance in Rubin's landscapes to those of Nicolas Poussin, a seventeenth-century French-Italian painter whose landscapes are heroic and idealized. Like Poussin, Rubin fosters a sense of drama by incorporating into the landscape minuscule figures, thus exaggerating the scale of the hills and trees around them. The association with Poussin's painting *Et in Arcadia ego* (1627–28) intensifies the paradox of horror and death in the myth of pastoral renewal in Eretz-Israel.

In painting the incandescent Rubin pastorals on the tulle[5] veils, Patkin increases their illusory exuberance. At the same time, their Zionist myth of innocence becomes a chimera, exploding like shrapnel. The mythical landscape is ruined, and the utopian Arcadia is revealed as an out-of-focus illusion, slipping away from the viewer's gaze. In his *Et in Arcadia Ego*, as in his *Judenporzellan*, Patkin tackles issues related to Jewish and Israeli identity, regarding his personal narrative and the historical one in a critical, sober manner, as if they were one horizon.

Ruthi Ofek

NOTES

1
Moses Mendelssohn, *Gesammelte Schriften Jubiläumsausgabe* (Leipzig: F. A. Brockhaus Verlag, 1843), 310.

2
The German-Speaking Jewry Heritage Museum is in Stef Wertheimer's visionary industrial park located in Israel's Lower Galilee, which holds several museums under the aegis of the Tefen Open Museum.

3
Mark Daniel Cohen, "The Artist and the Philosopher," in Izhar Patkin, *Judenporzellan* (Tefen, Israel: The Open Museum, 2008), 47.

4
Alfred Werner, *Rubin* (Tel Aviv: Massadah Publishing, 1958), n.p.

5
Tulle is the French term for illusion netting, sometimes known as bridal illusion. Patkin's use of tulle is another allusion to Rubin's virginal pastorals.

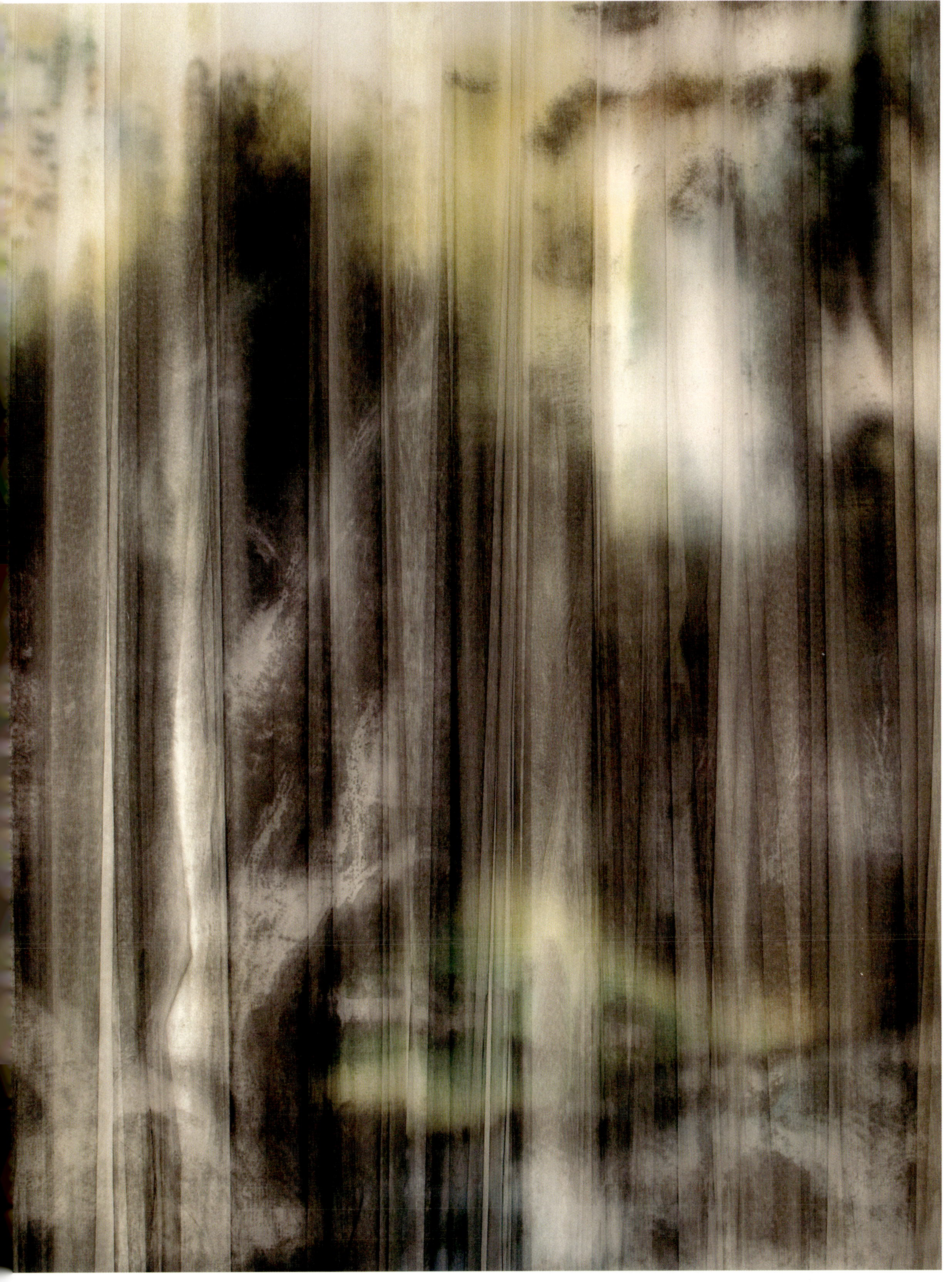

The Dream Corps

The art critic Harold Rosenberg wrote an essay in which he asked: What is Jewish art?[1] Art produced by Jews? Art depicting Jews? Or art charged with Jewish symbolism? Rosenberg analyzed various objects that appear in the Old Testament, ordinary objects that became vessels of miraculous revelation: a shepherd's staff, smooth stones from a brook, a burning bush, a fleece of wool, the jawbone of an ass. In a world of miracles, there was no need to *create* specific ceremonial objects that would be either a representation or a manifestation. Rather, these common objects were tools of an abstraction: a faceless, invisible god. Any place or object could be imbued with mysterious powers. This led Rosenberg to wonder: If in biblical times it had been possible to conceive of a Jewish, or any other, art museum to exhibit these everyday yet magical objects, would representational paintings and sculptures of the Madonna and saints have captured people's imagination?

There is a connection between Rosenberg's imaginary Jewish museum of sacred objects and Izhar Patkin's work. For example, when Patkin employs sukkah ornaments[2] (pages 95–99) or the *Simchat Torah*[3] flag (page 36) in his work, he recalls how, when he was a child, these traditional holiday ornaments were vessels of pure, unmediated magic; it did not matter what religious meaning they were meant to convey. When those mundane paper garlands were pinned to the sukkah fabric walls and pulled open, they revealed their secret cutout patterns and became wondrous.

Magical objects of sacred manifestation are not unique to Judaism. What about venerated Christian objects, such as fragments of the Shroud of Jesus and of the Cross—or the bones of saints? And what about the hair from Muhammad's beard on display at the Topkapi Palace in Istanbul? Aren't these relics, in the same way, magical objects? Are portraits of the Madonna and statues of Christian saints "merely" second-degree mediated *representations*, rather than unmediated magical objects of *manifestation*? Is the distinction between an object that is a *representation* and one that is a *manifestation* indeed so sharp? Or should we regard all these sacred objects as remnants of pagan objects that have made their way into the monotheistic religions?

Just as Rosenberg questioned the status of a biblical stone from a brook, we might also wonder whether to regard any common objects as art at all? Could we have done so prior to their discovery by Dada? When Marcel Duchamp placed a urinal, a bicycle wheel, and a typewriter cover in an art gallery, he elevated his *objet trouvé* into a manifestation of art. This is conceivably how religions managed to venerate their objects for millennia. Perhaps Duchamp's common object gains an aura by being exhibited in the "sanctity" of an artistic venue, but it never loses the Dadaistic outlook of humor and irony, skepticism and criticism. And while it lowers art, it also lifts the profane.

It is in this perspective—which is pan-religious and multicultural, one that involves both representation and manifestation (as much post-Dada as post-Conceptual)—that we may contextualize Patkin's work more coherently. His ambivalent stance toward the relentless religious dimension in all of our vocabularies, both visual and verbal, distances his work from the spirit of Pop, even when he contemplates objects and images that seem to be items culled, ready-made, from our collective archive of populist iconography. His sculpture *The Messiah's glAss* (2003–07; pages 120–21) is a Jewish icon of the Holy Ark. It is also a magnificent glasswork produced by some of the best glassblowers in the world. For an earlier sculpture, Patkin used glassblowers from Murano, Venice, a magical city that appears in many of his works, both overtly and covertly. *The Messiah's glAss* has Gothic, Baroque, even Rococo overtones. But at the same time there is a grotesque twist in turning the traditional angels' wings of the Holy Ark into donkey's ears and making both the Holy Ark and the donkey that carries it one and the same. And so with the title of *The Messiah's glAss*, we return to the Bible, where the miraculous is manifested through this brute animal: the Messiah's donkey, Balaam's ass, the lost donkeys of Saul, and Samson's jawbone of an ass. It is precisely because it is so gray, so wretched, and so lacking in glorious sacredness that the lowly donkey, the embodiment of the material world, gains a magical status. In Hebrew, donkey is *chamor*, and *chomar* is matter contrary to spirit—the two words are anagrammatic—thus the profane, the quotidian, and the sacred coalesce. As do Israeliness, Judaism, and Christianity. The Holy Ark and the ass merge into a hybrid creature. The sacred object is contrasted with its own carnivalesque version. Similarly, the carnival aspect is also in the play between "ass" and "glass." Patkin's objects contain a measure of Purimic[4] wanton licentiousness, a theater of disguises with a proverbial wink, which crosses the boundary into an "upside-down world" and lays bare the concealed. Even his melancholic works display an impudent joy of life. His elegiac works of mourning are erotic works.

In the 1970s Patkin met the artist Itzhak Danziger, who opened a door for him to radical, post-Conceptual, and yet mythological artistic thought. Danziger regarded an oak grove or a sheikh's tomb as equally sacred places. A Nabatean stone trough, an abandoned Palestinian orchard, and the rocky wall of a quarry were for him ready-made artistic arenas. While Duchamp "found" objects and Joseph Beuys found materials charged with energy, Danziger was finding *places* charged with energy.

Danziger's quarry, grove, and orchard are perhaps distant ancestors of Patkin's sukkah, tent, or veiled rooms: places charged with myth. Every carpet painting is an embodiment of Eden; every room in the exhibition is a magical, ceremonial, festive place—a reincarnation of the Tent of Congregation.

Patkin's ritualistic rooms have the quality of a manifestation: an illusion, an apparition, or a mirage. Just as a recounted dream is never the dream itself, one has to be in the rooms themselves. As with a pilgrimage, one has to experience them in situ, dream them, and be dreamed by them.

In the painting *Arik Patkin WTC* (2006; pages 38–41), the image of Patkin's father appears on a large, gauzy tulle curtain. He is seated on a bench slab that appears to be floating in front of the World Trade Center in New York. The legs of the bench are erased and a large shadow cast by the slab is stretched on the ground beneath him. The father seems to hover in the air, like an angel or Madonna, turning the entire gossamer curtain into a cloud. Patkin created the work after his father's death, which occurred shortly after the World Trade Center disaster.

Patkin creates a hybrid place, a conflation of times and stories between New York and a Jewish-Israeli shtetl.[5] The World Trade Center, now history, stands alongside the weathered houses of Tel Aviv-Jaffa (page 117) and Patkin's great-grandfather's old synagogue in Netanya, Israel (pages 36, 112–13). The early twentieth century merges with the turn of the twenty-first century. Father and grandfather star in his "big screen" veils alongside Yiddish movie actors (pages 215, 221). In his porcelain sculpture *Madonna and Child* (2007–12; pages 88–91), which draws on the same Yiddish movies, Patkin casts the Mother as the Virgin who turns, body and soul, to the savior child. The characters are not just icons; they are profoundly personal.

Anchored in biography, geography, and history, this hybrid place, this locus, belongs to the realm of dreams. Memories fold in, one on top of the other. The vision is grounded in both the artist's private archive of images and the collective one. Geography and history turn into mythology.

The artist, narrator of myth, is also a director in a theater of dreams. The translucent curtains invoke the feeling of a hallucinatory, evanescent space. In *The Veil Suite* (2007; pages 68–75), a requiem work made after the last poem written by late Kashmiri poet Agha Shahid Ali, a vast snowy desert is a field of clouds. *The Meta Bride* (1982; page 225) is both a black bride and Snow White. In *Evening* (2008; pages 176–85), trees turn into shrines, which turn into ruins, while a magician suddenly appears on a gondola against the backdrop of a Venetian sunset, releasing a cloud of shadowy black birds. In Patkin's metaphors, everything keeps metamorphosing as if bewitched. In his dreams, places merge together and are compressed into each other, and every identity is a palimpsest of associations. Objects split up or fuse together. Opposites blend with one another. Nothing is fixed. Everything flows. *Panta rhei.*

In the work *You Tell Us What to Do* (2010; pages 110–19), the viewer is surrounded by a vista of the Tel Aviv-Jaffa seashore: a mosque and a synagogue, Arab and Jewish refugees, smoke billowing from the ship *Altalena*, lying sunk on her side.[6] But the multitude of refugees by the sea also brings to mind the Exodus—the Flight from Egypt. The historical aspect is a stepping-stone to a mythological pageant. *The Messiah's glAss* installed in this room, which is also the Holy Ark palanquin carried by two poles, also alludes to the Exodus, turning the entire room into The Tent of Congregation and Tel Aviv-Jaffa into a transient station.

A tent is a transient home, a place that is no-place, a pause between landscapes. Patkin's world is one of wanderings. Meaning is always on the move, like immigrants and refugees traveling away from home or toward it, in between here and there, both this and that. Transience is a recurring theme. In his Murano glass sculpture *Where Each Is Both* (1994; pages 200–201), even God is depicted as an exile from the Garden of Eden.

R. B. Kitaj writes about diasporist art as inhabiting at least two places and stemming from various cultures.[7] Patkin's collaborator, the poet Agha Shahid Ali, is quoted as saying: "When I say 'exile,' I mean an entirely new kind of geography, an entirely new kind of sensibility became available to my poetry . . . when you write in English, in India, you are in some ways an exile in your own land." Judaism has no monopoly over the diaspora experience. However, the Jewish culture of wandering is a gateway to that experience, which is universal. Who among us does not live in several time zones and several places, straddling different cultures and languages, history and mythology?

In Hebrew, the word *avodah,* "to work," also means "to worship." Patkin grew up in an iconoclastic Jewish-Israeli culture, in the land of "The Want of Matter."[8] He often refers to *his* country, but he is an "exile" from his mother tongue and works in foreign visual languages: the Christian language, the Buddhist language, the pagan language. He speaks about his mother tongue of lack and absence in the language of profusion and abundance. A rich visual language of dreams, pageantry, and theatricality.

Patkin has no desire to speak a "universal language." He is not an artist looking for a reductive common denominator, but, rather, seeks a multitude of denominators. Much like the artist Arie Aroch, who was Russian, Israeli, and European (Patkin refers to Aroch in his 2001 series of paintings *Host Culture: Homage to Arie Aroch*; pages 142–43), Patkin wanders among a multitude of languages—all of which are *him,* yet none quite *his.*

The *exilic* artist lives the crisis of language and cannot fully escape calamity—be it war, permanent leave-taking, disappearance, or muteness.

Patkin works with the anguish of our voices. Our language. His metaphors and images are a painting of a dream threatened with oblivion and evaporation. For a moment, he weaves together love and longing, fear and wonderment, mirth and calamity, the sorrow of loss and the joy of creation.

Itamar Levy

NOTES

1
Harold Rosenberg, "Is There a Jewish Art?" *Commentary,* July 1966.

2
A sukkah is a temporary hut topped with branches, constructed for use during the weeklong Jewish festival of Sukkot. The sukkah is often decorated with handmade paper cutouts, which are pinned onto its cloth walls. The decorations are traditionally of autumnal, harvest, or Judaic themes.—Trans.

3
Simchat Torah (literally, "Rejoicing with/of the Torah") is a celebration marking the conclusion of the annual cycle of public Torah readings and the beginning of a new cycle. During the Simchat Torah festivities, the synagogue's Torah scrolls

are removed from the Ark and carried around the sanctuary, with the congregation dancing and singing. Children are often given paper flags, candies, and treats. The flags often feature 3D pop-open windows, recalling the doors of the ark.—Trans.

4

Purim is a Jewish holiday of public feasting and rejoicing that is characterized by wearing masks and costumes. It commemorates the deliverance of the Jewish people in the ancient Persian Empire from destruction in the wake of a plot by Haman, a story recorded in the biblical Book of Esther.—Trans.

5

Shtetl is the Yiddish word for a small nineteenth-century Eastern European town with a large Jewish population (until the Holocaust).—Trans.

6

In June 1948 the newly formed Israeli Defense Forces shot down the cargo ship *Altalena*, which carried weapons and fighters for the Irgun, a right-wing Jewish paramilitary group, as it approached Tel Aviv.—Trans.

7

R. B. Kitaj, *First Diasporist Manifesto* (London: Thames and Hudson, 1989).

8

One of the most influential art movements in Israel cumulated in a 1986 exhibition: "Dalut Ha'chomar" ("The Want of Matter: A Quality in Israeli Art"). It is characterized by poverty of means and a secular, Israeli outlook (as opposed to Jewish or traditional European art). This Israeli movement is often likened to the Italian Arte Povera.—Trans.

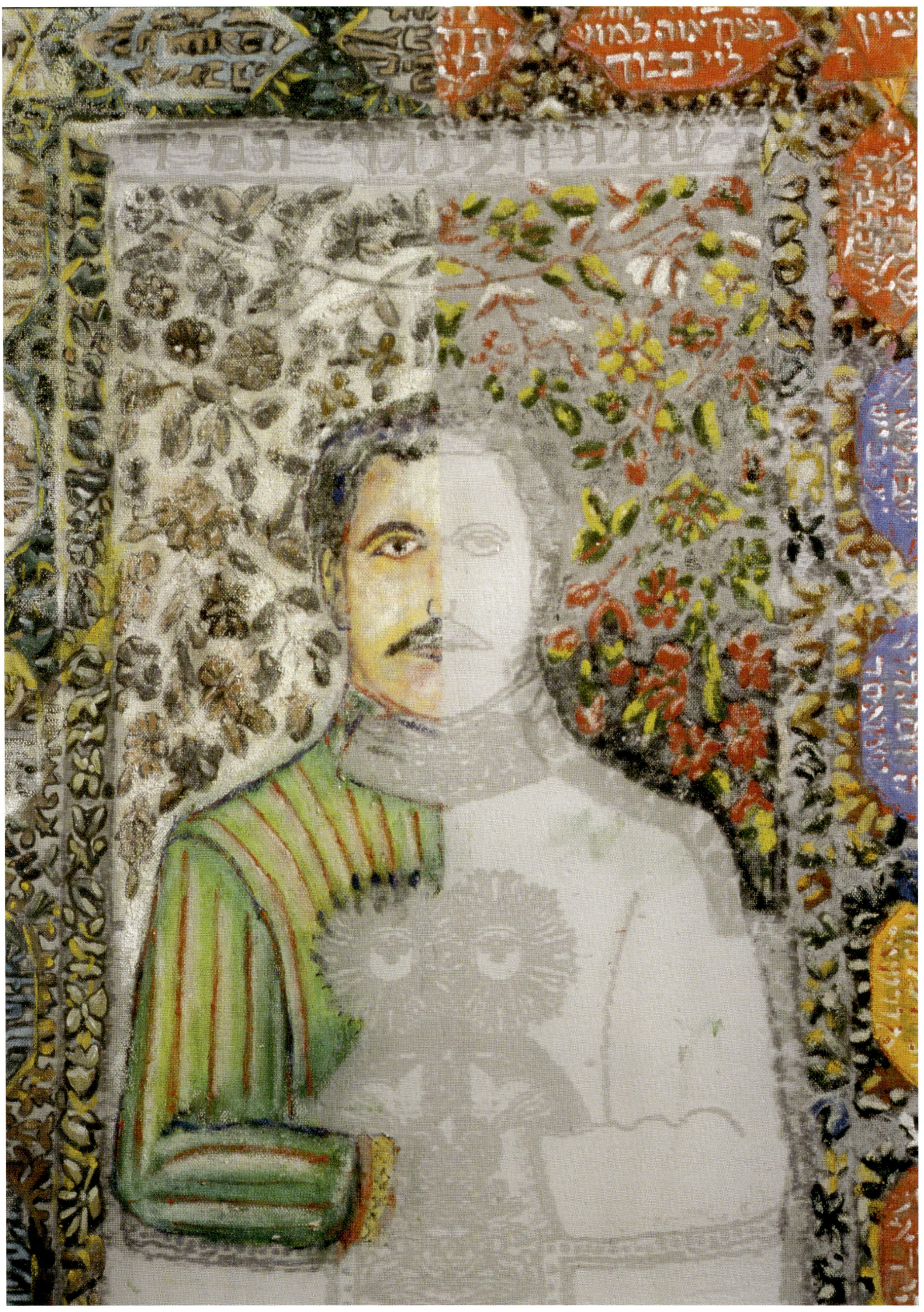

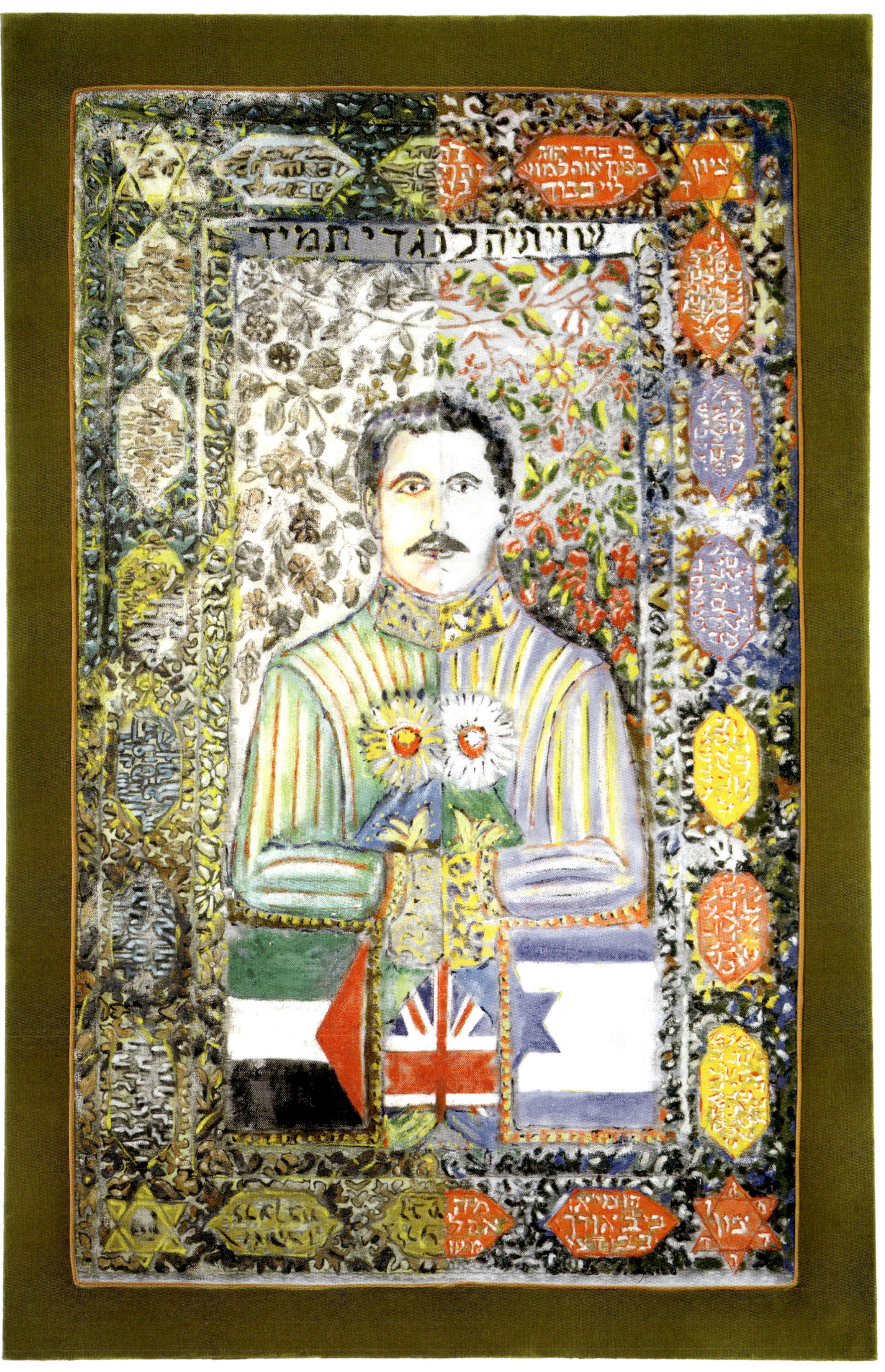
שויתי ה לנגדי תמיד

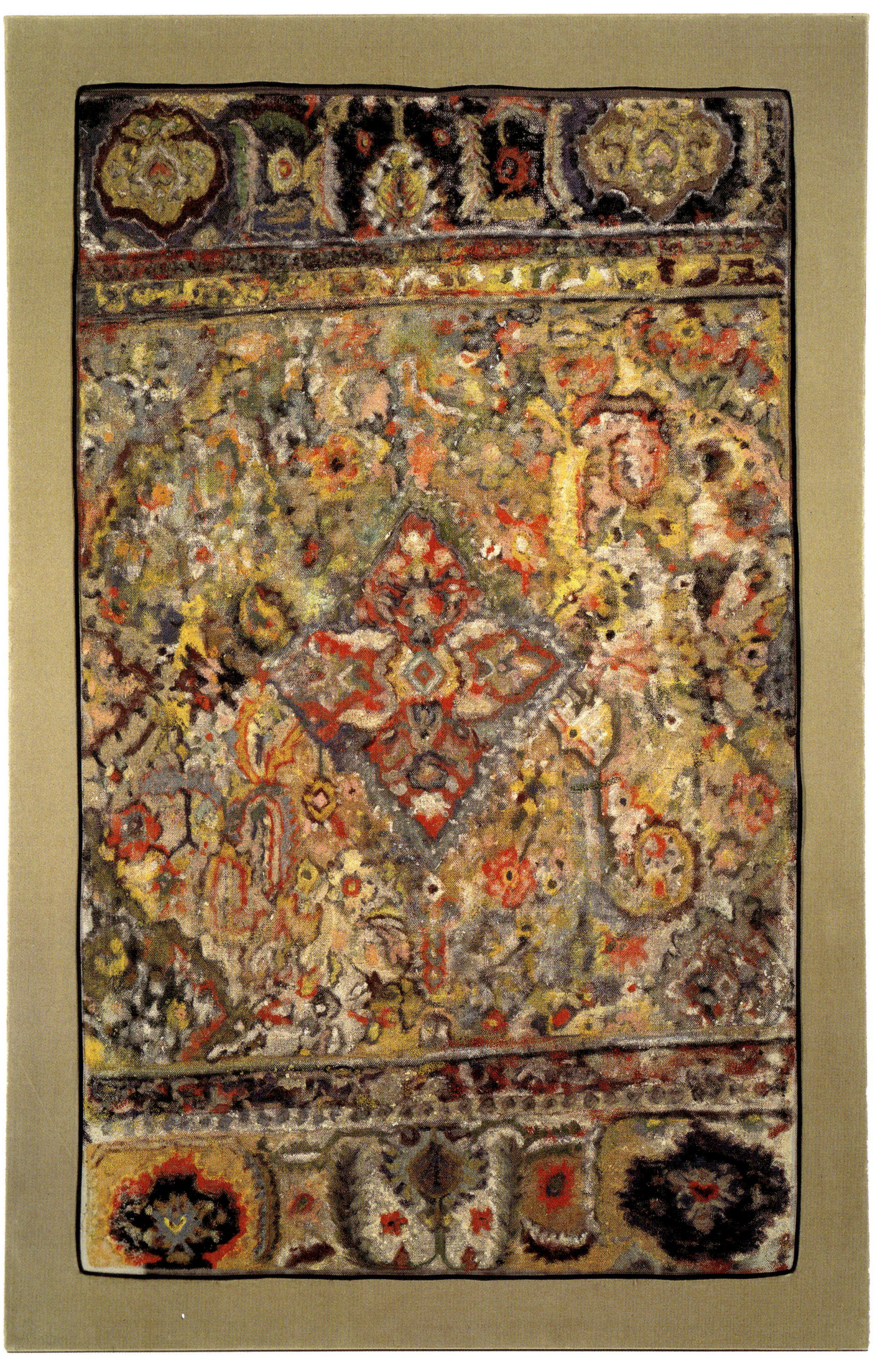

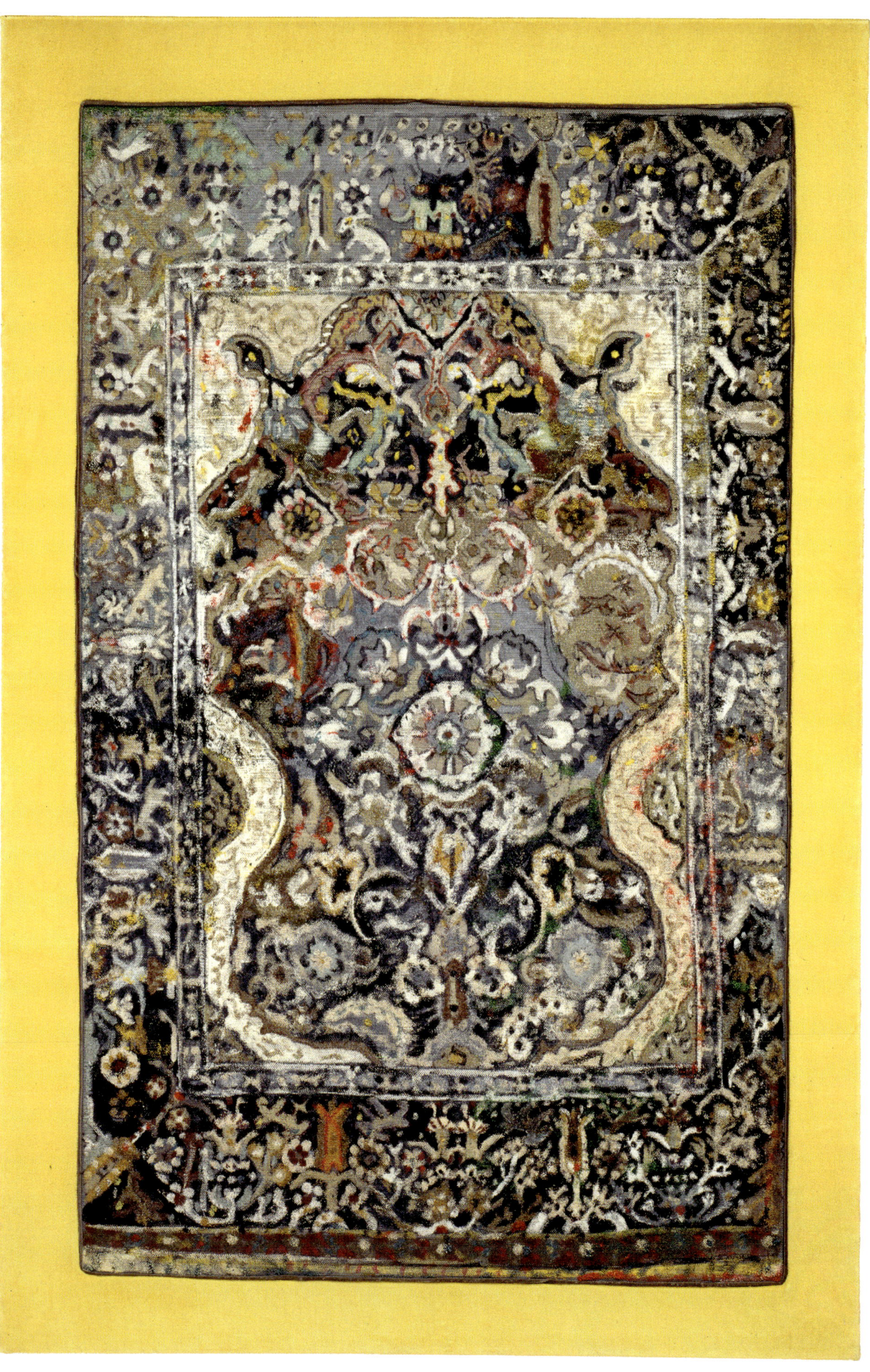

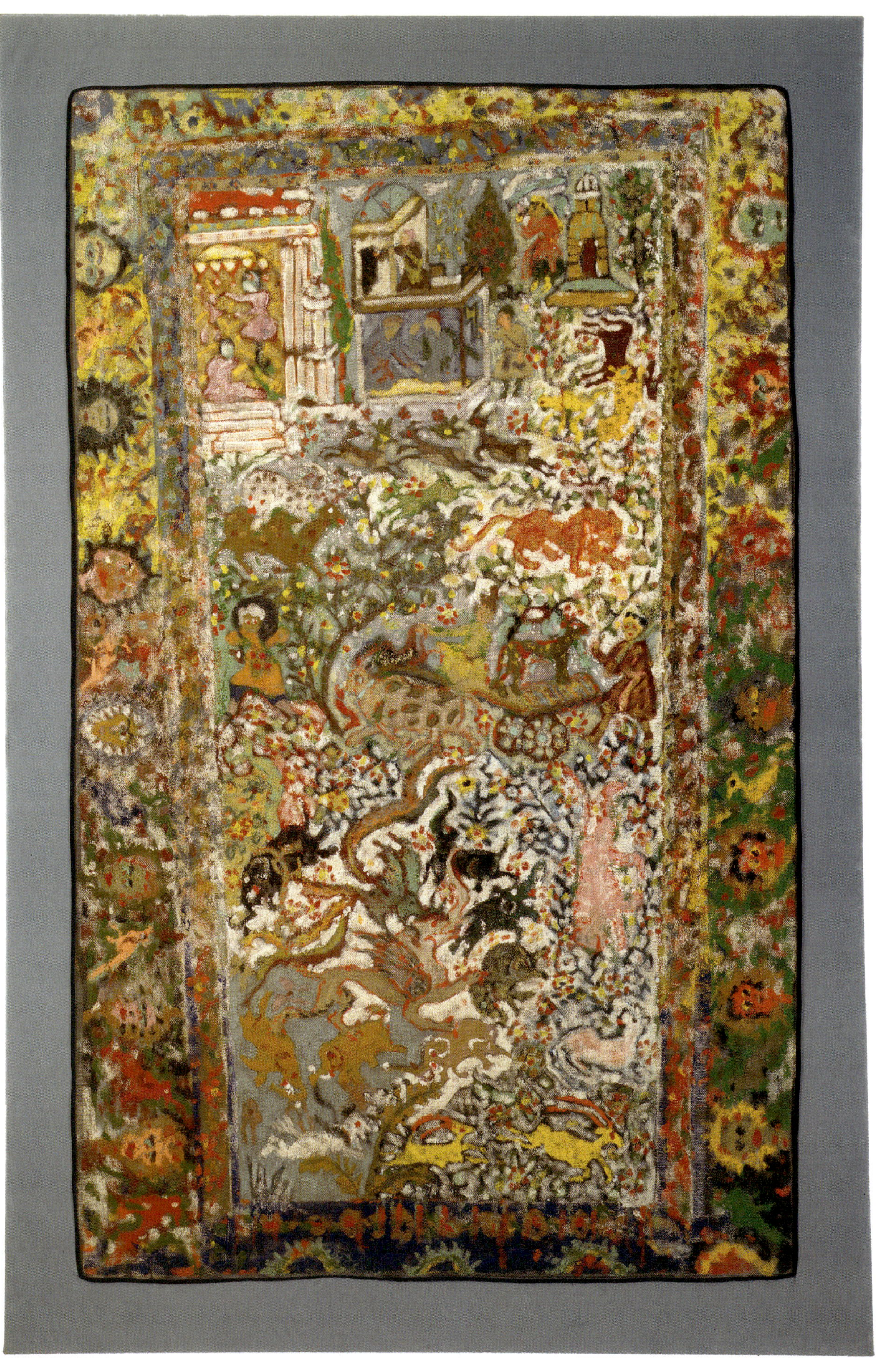

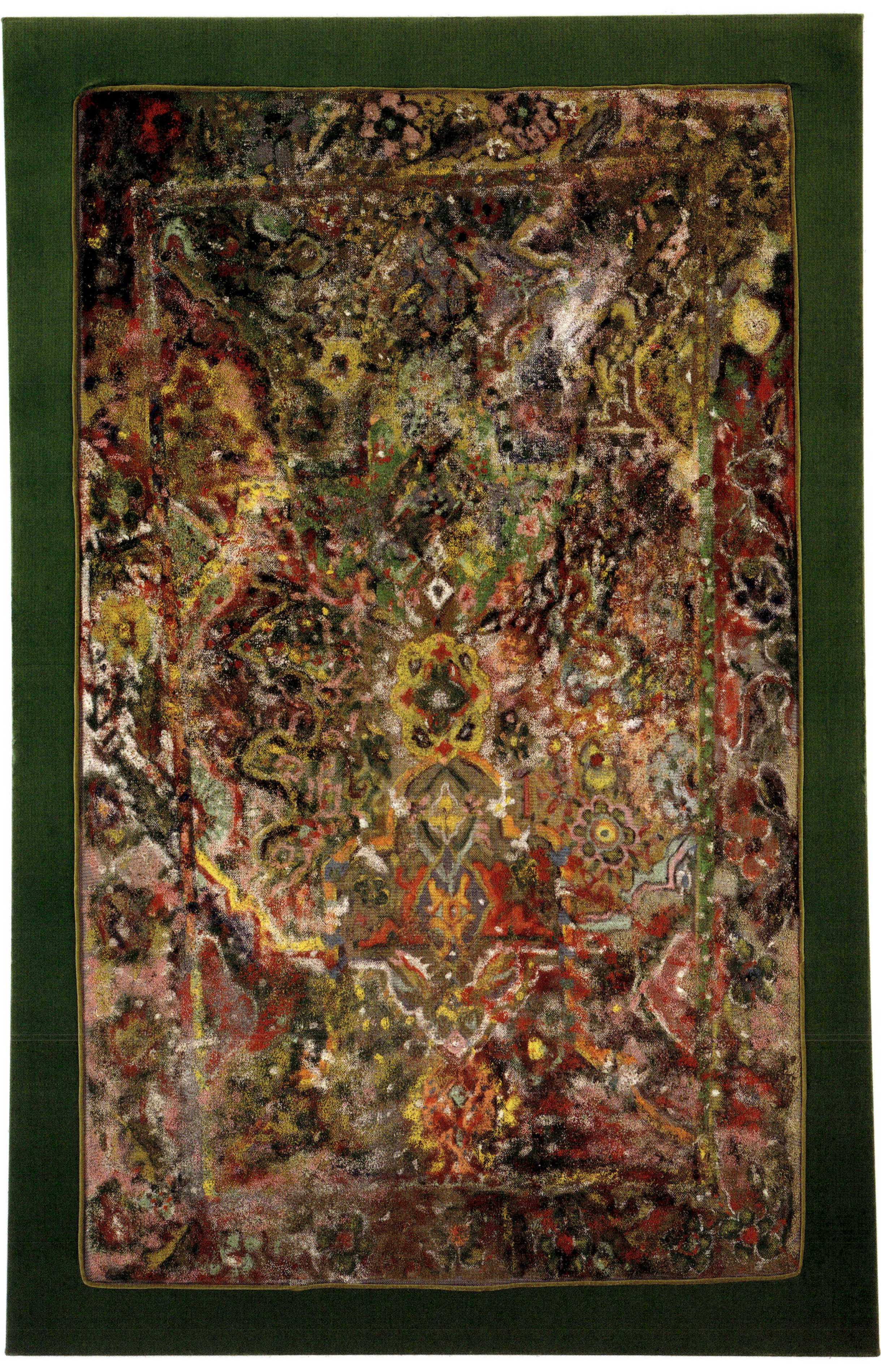

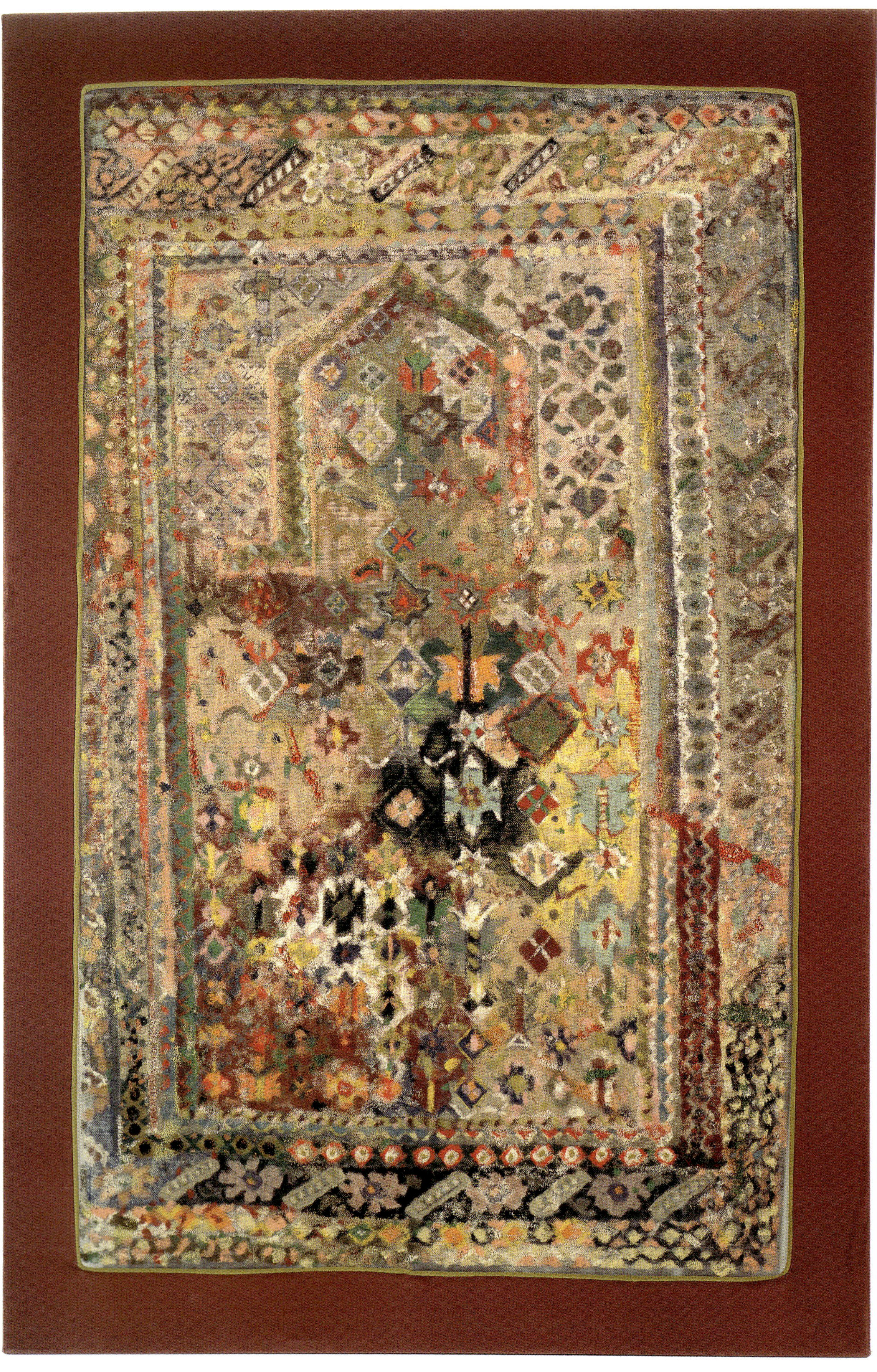

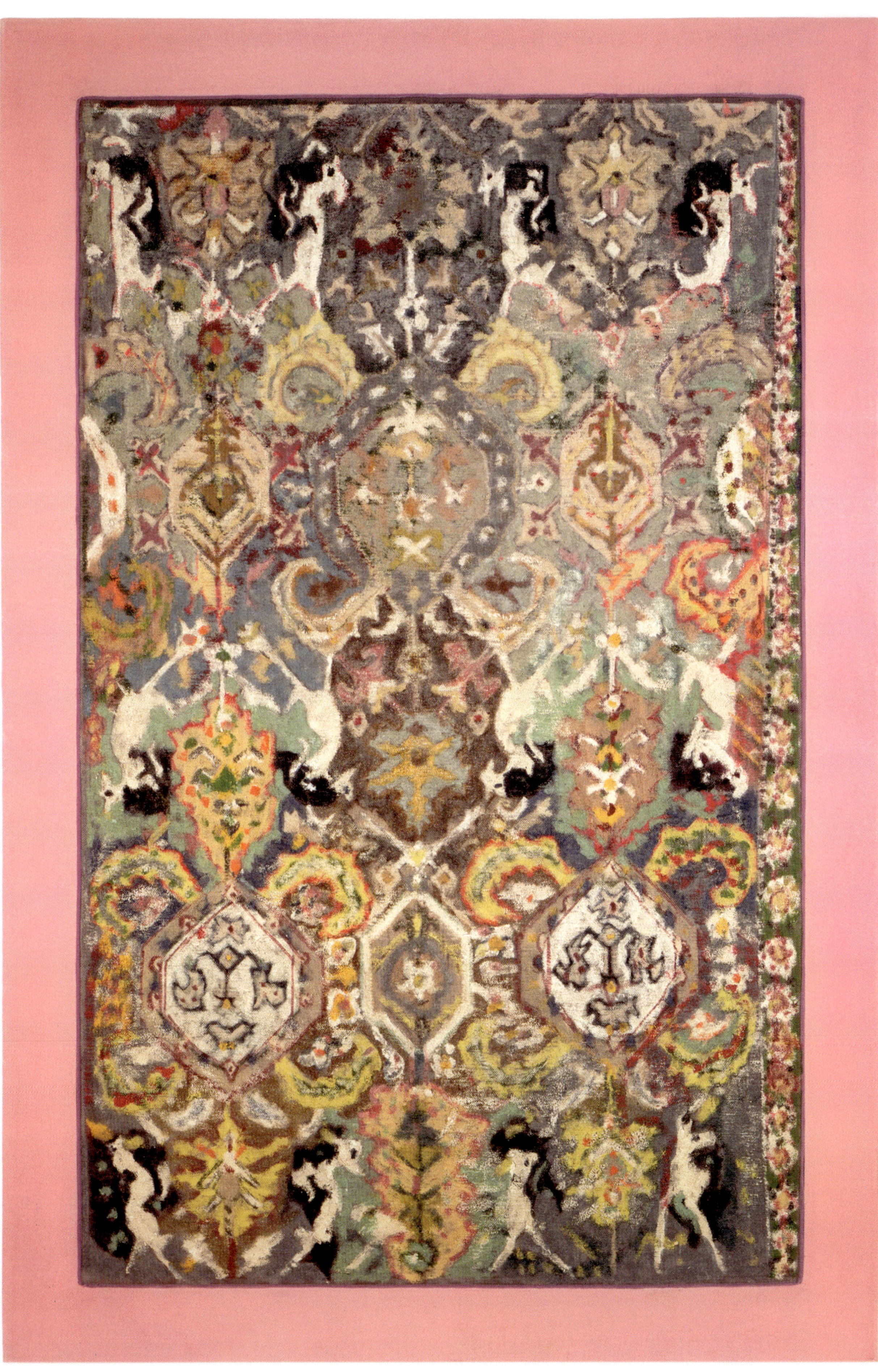

Where Each Is Both

THE DEAD ARE HERE. LISTEN TO THE SURVIVORS

The dead are here. Listen to survivors
search for screams to place on the corpses' mouths.

The self is lost, erased at this moment.
So reveal, quickly, a secret to me:

When, at last, that hour comes, who will lead me
through the catacombs to the swordsman's arms?

Will it be a long-lost friend, speaking of her,
of her hands digging out turquoise perfumes

from the air's mines? Will he bring a message
from her eyes, so far away now, gazing

at a dream in which the ghosts of prisoners
are shaking the bars till iron softens

into a song—everywhere the shadows
of my voice, everywhere a smokeless fire?

Tonight the air is many envelopes
again. Tell her to open them at once

and find hurried notes about my longing
for wings. Tell her to speak, when that hour comes,

simply of the sky. Friend, speak of the sky
when that hour comes. Speak, simply of the air.

Poem by Agha Shahid Ali

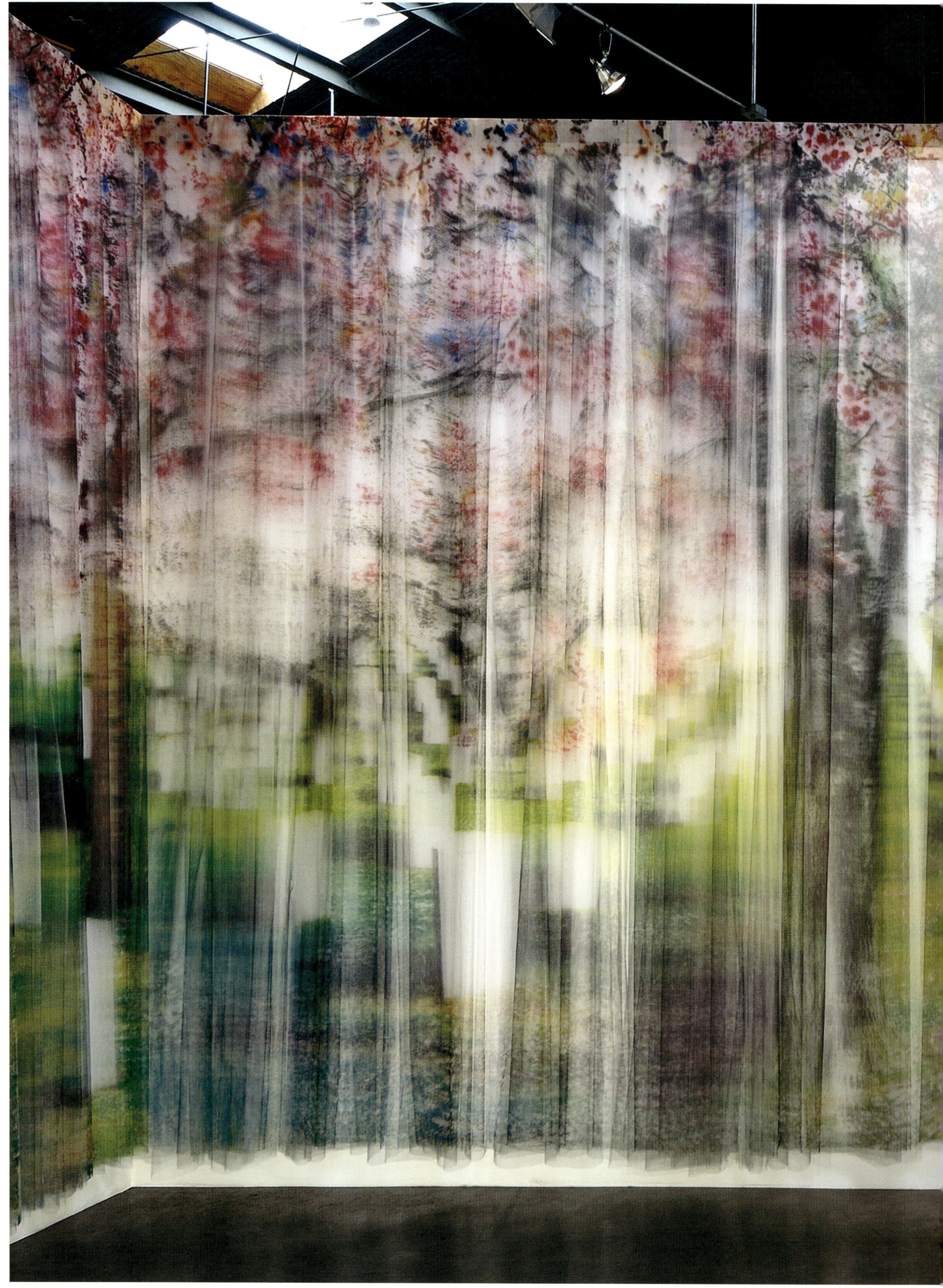

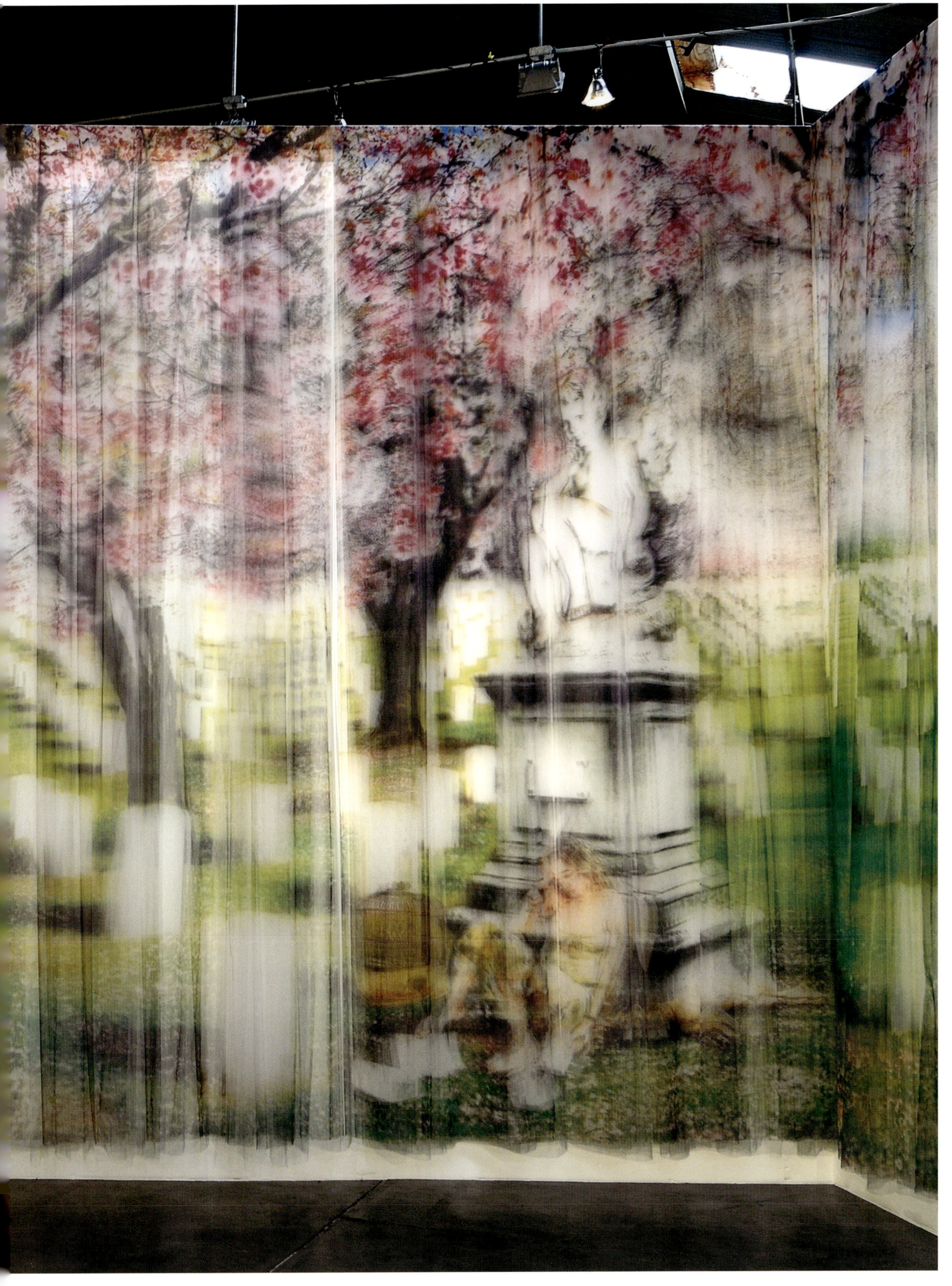

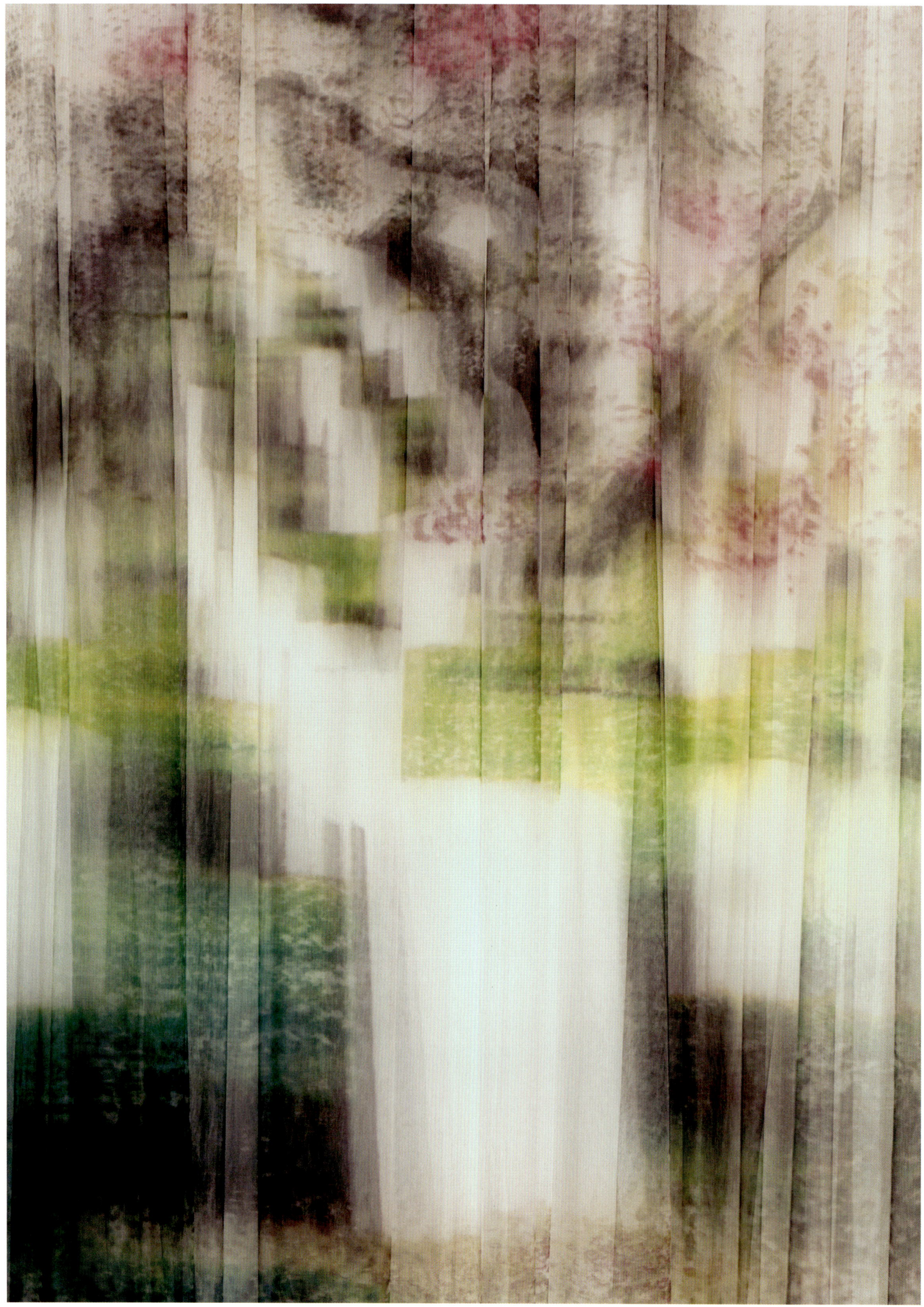

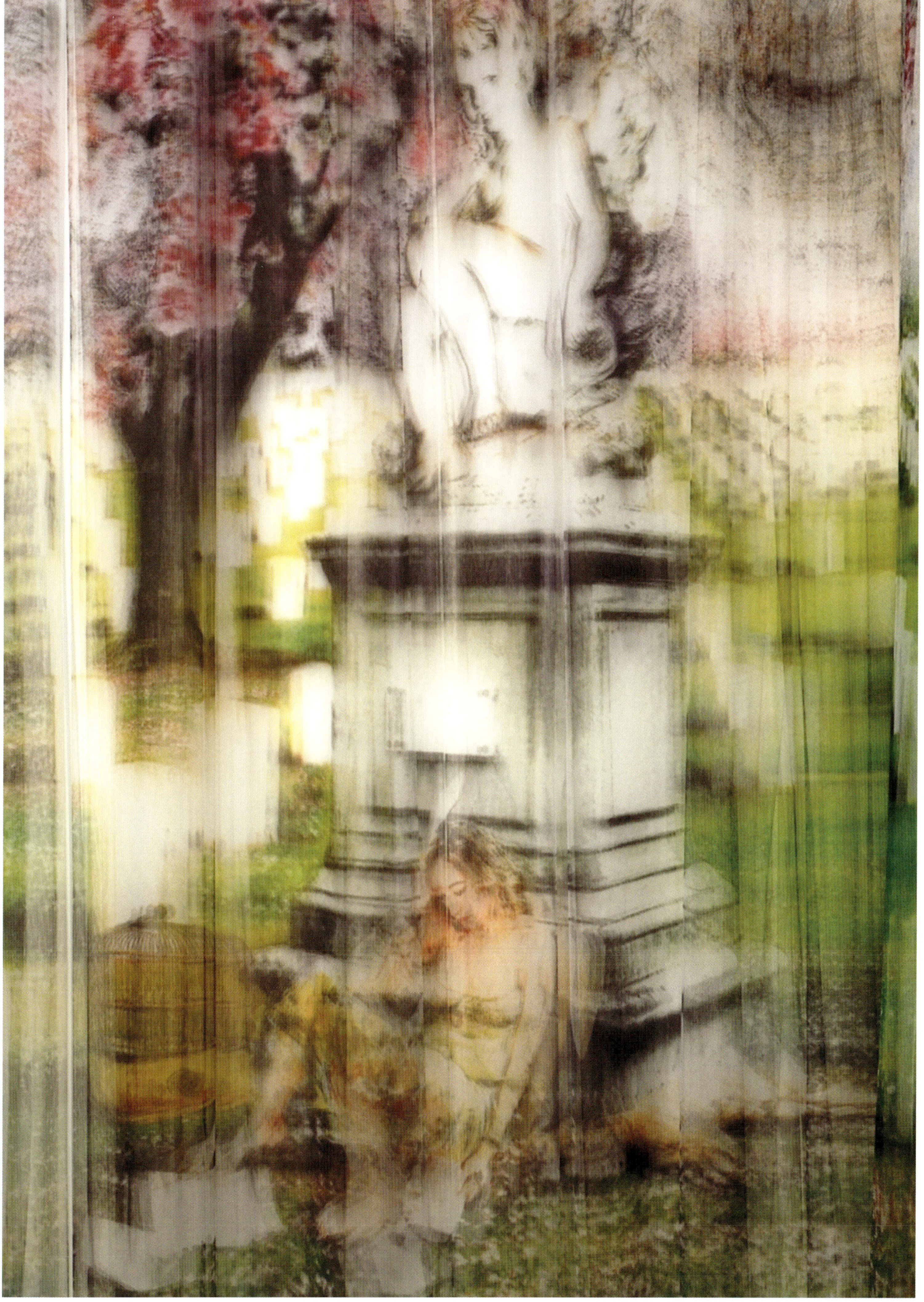

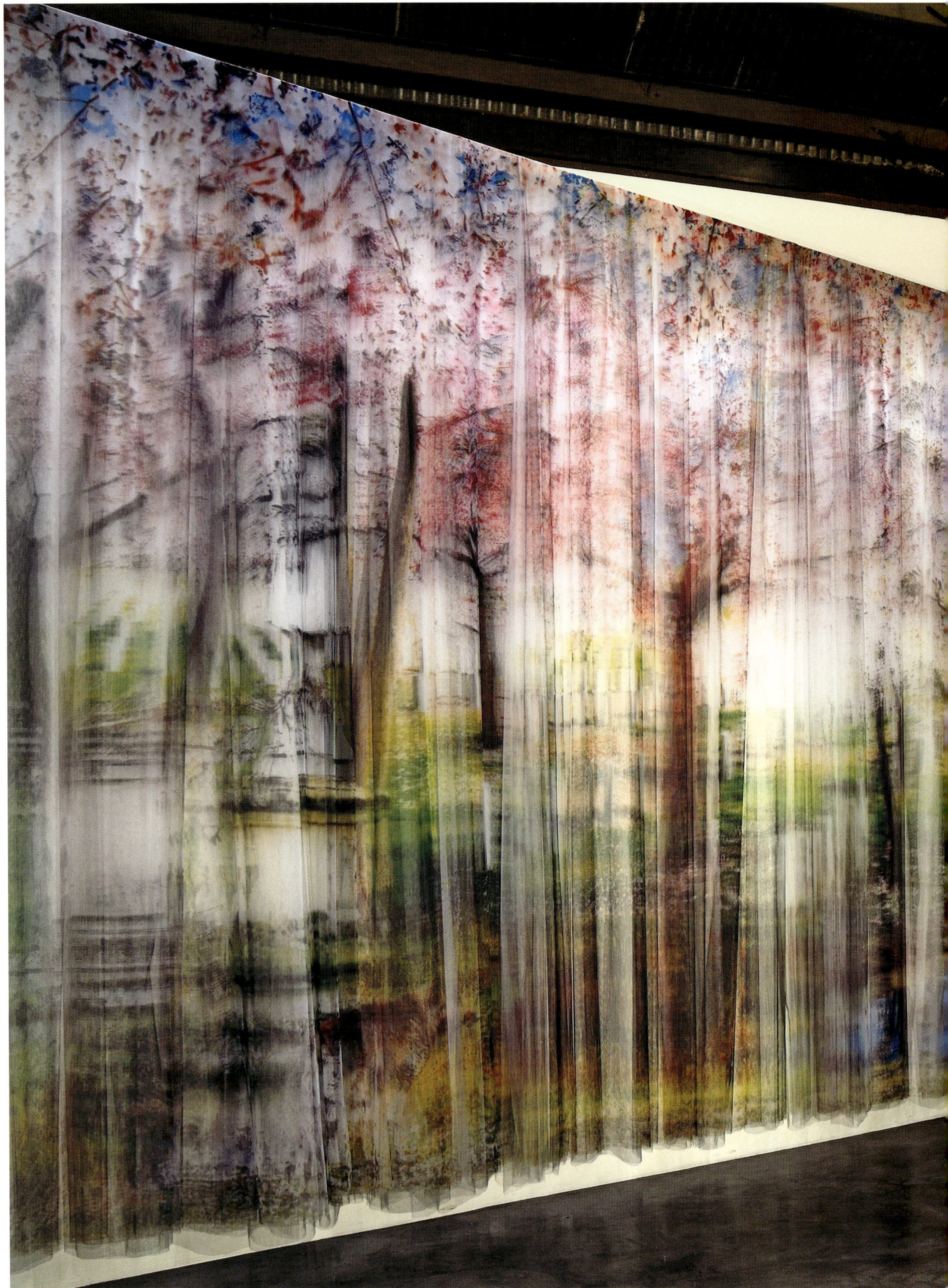

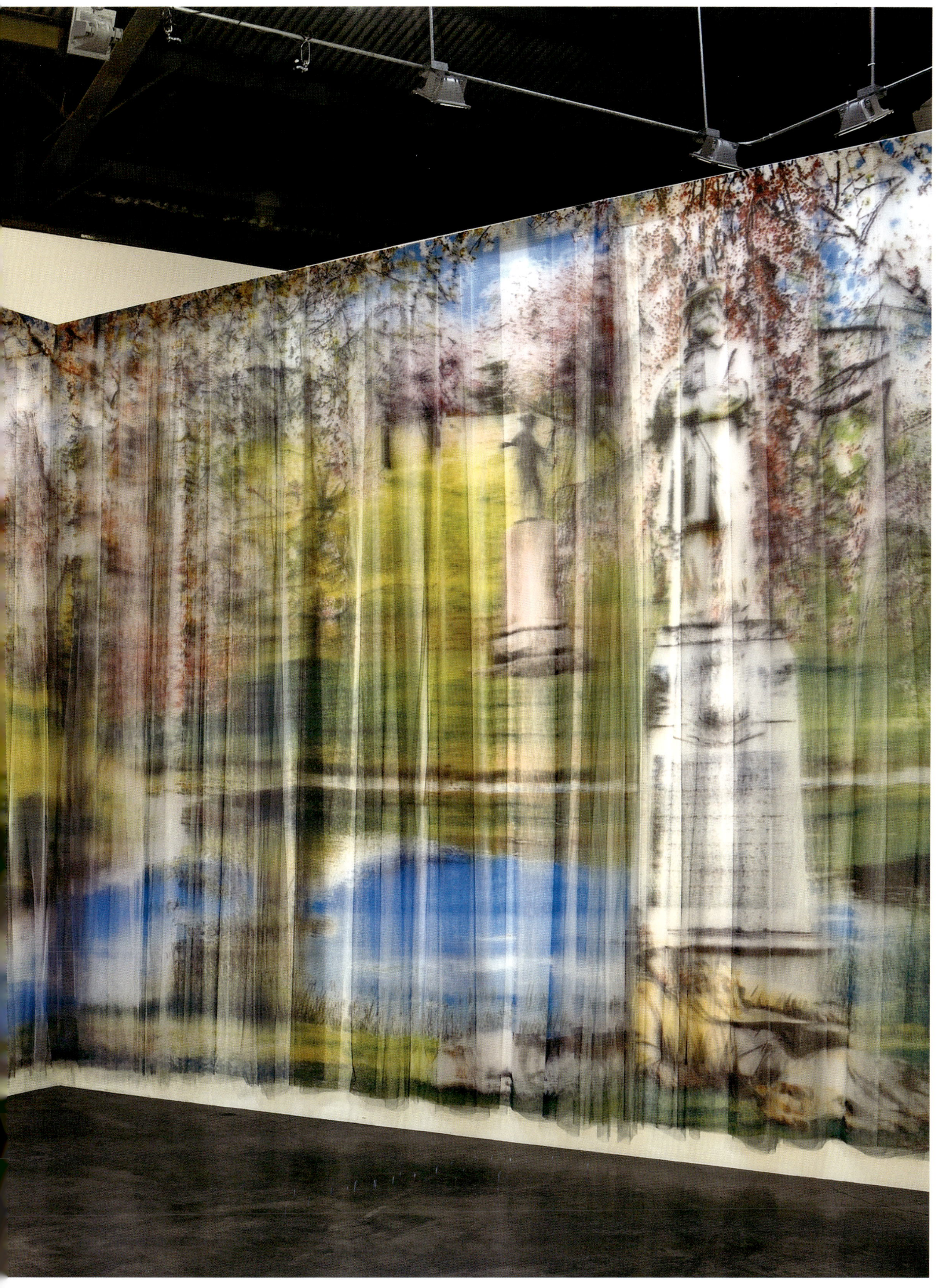

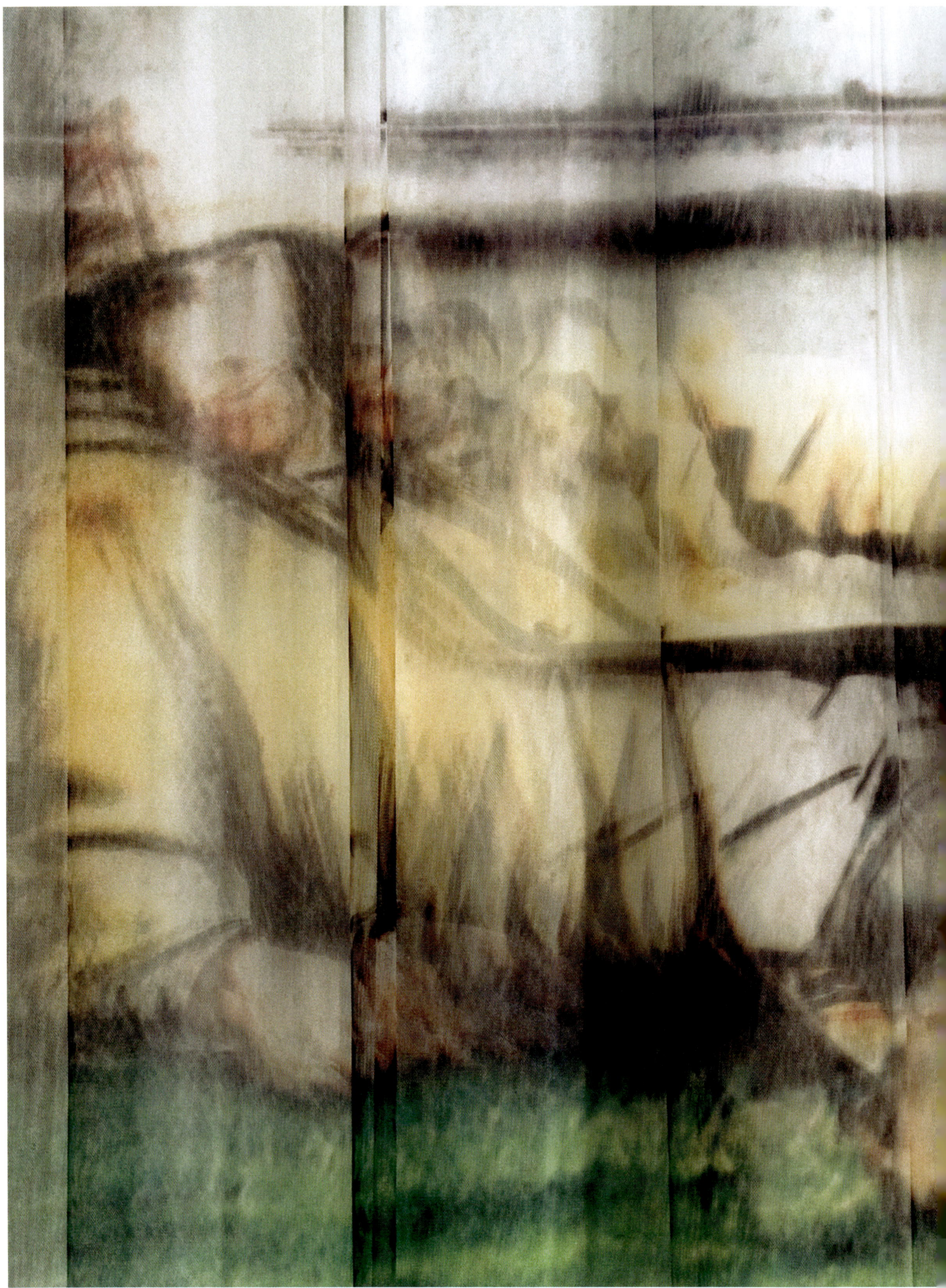

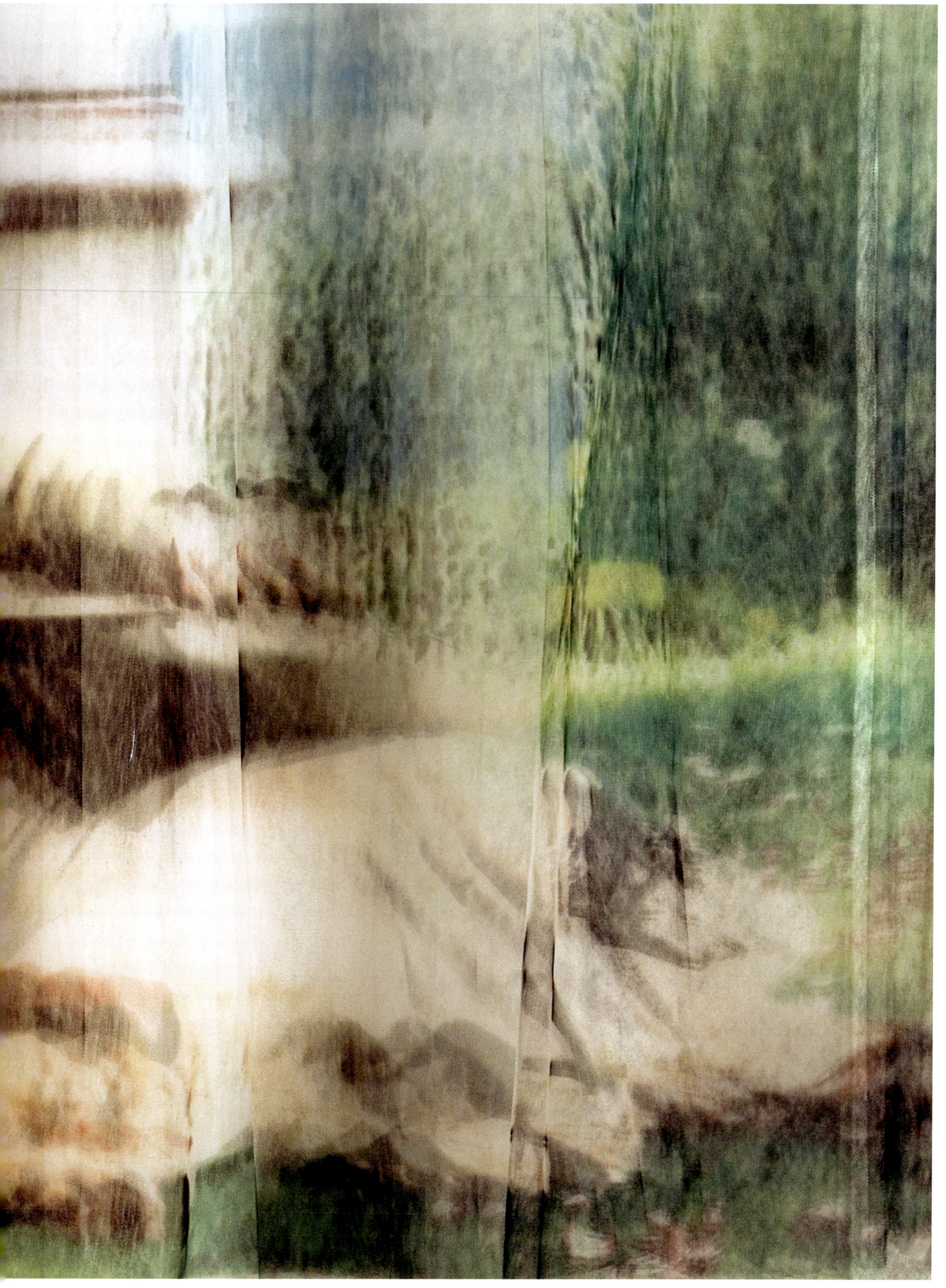

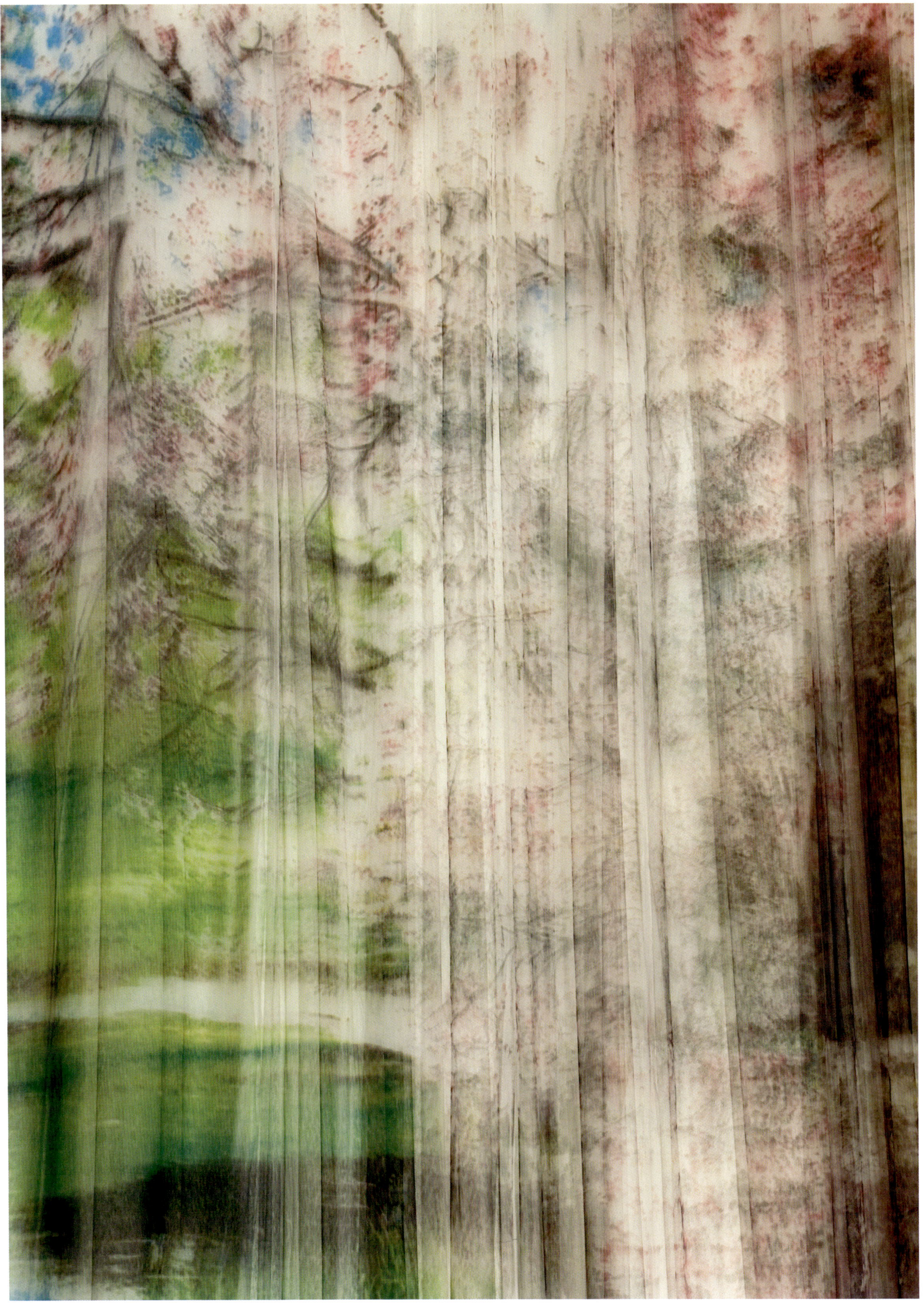

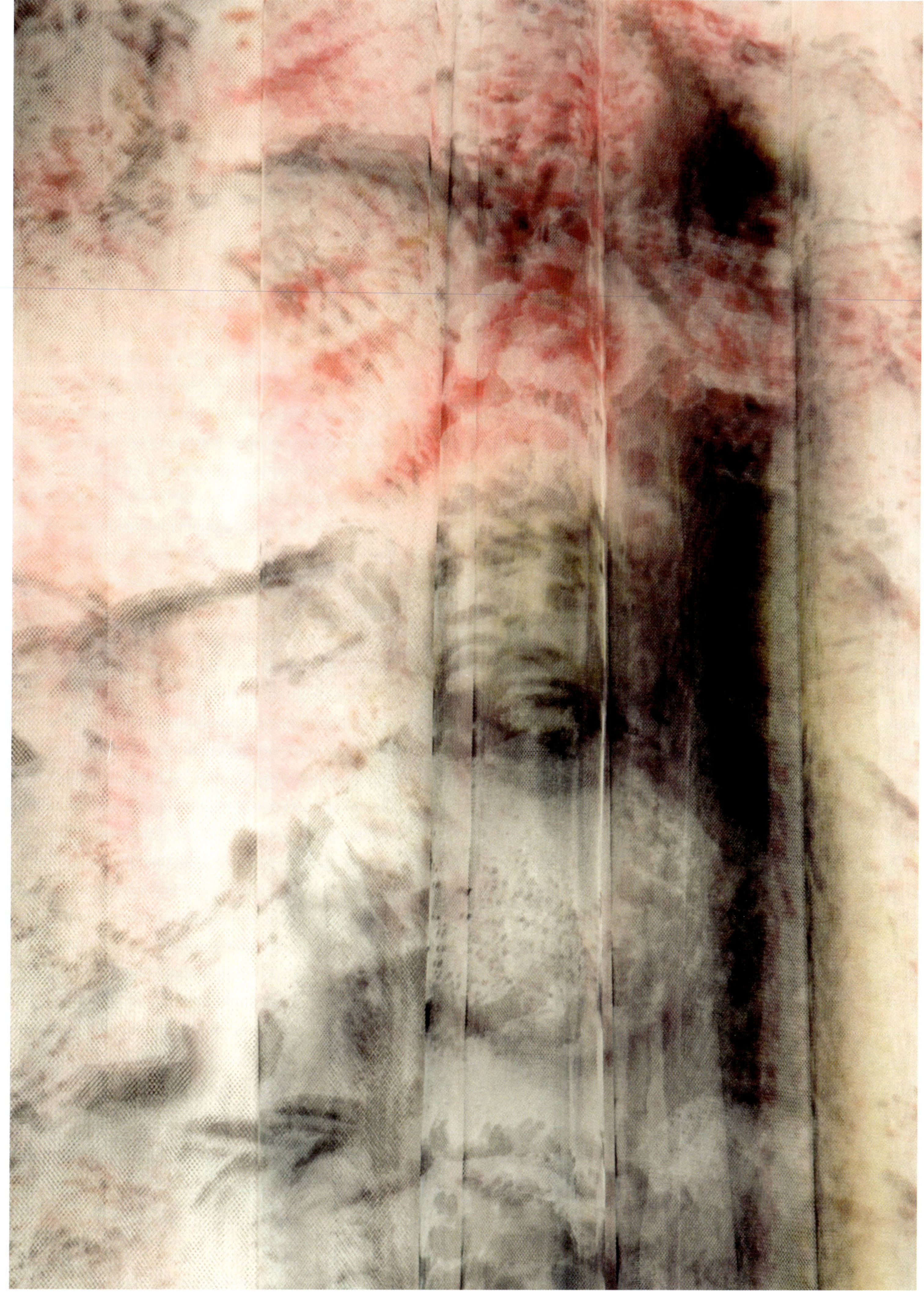

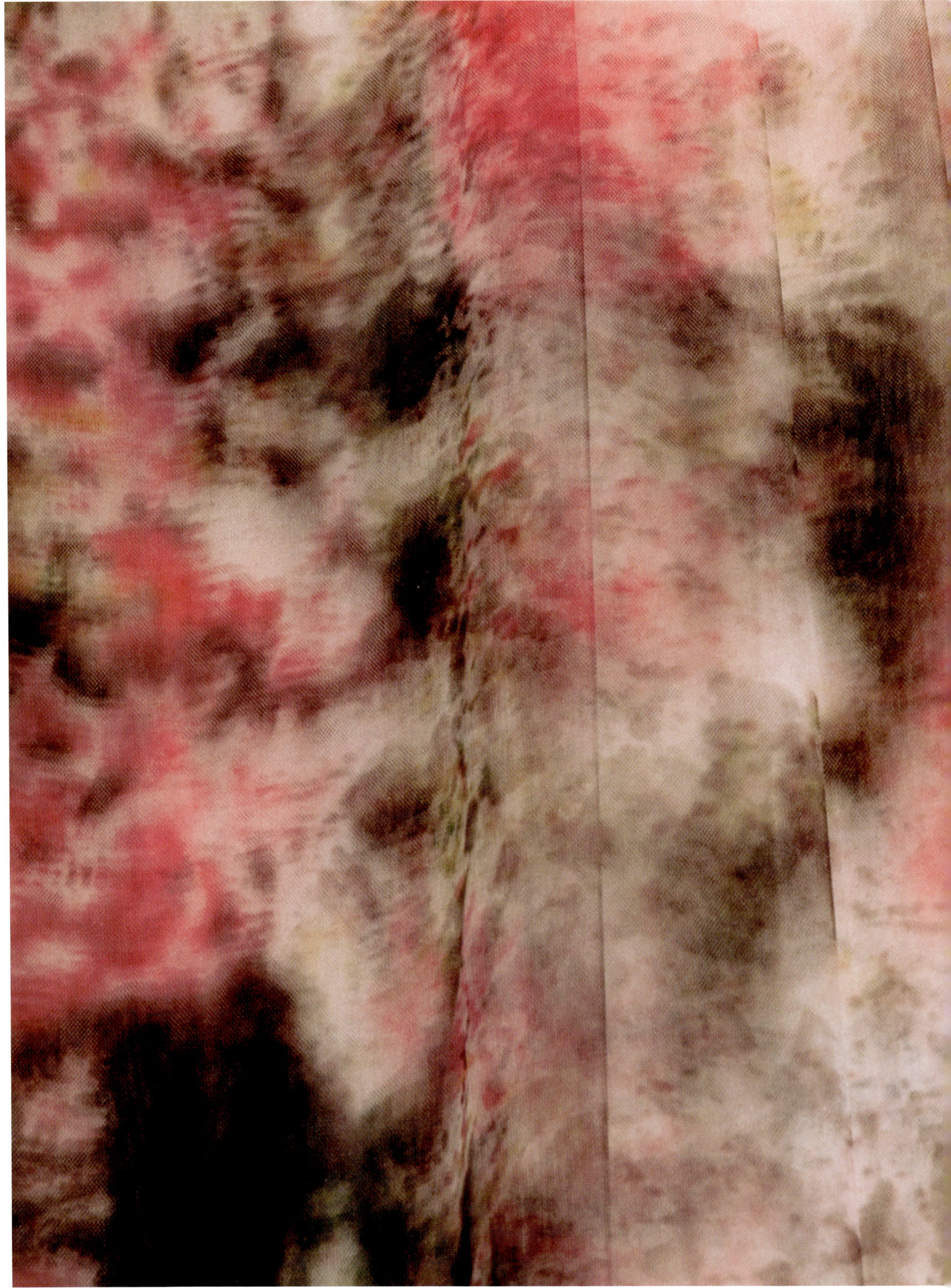

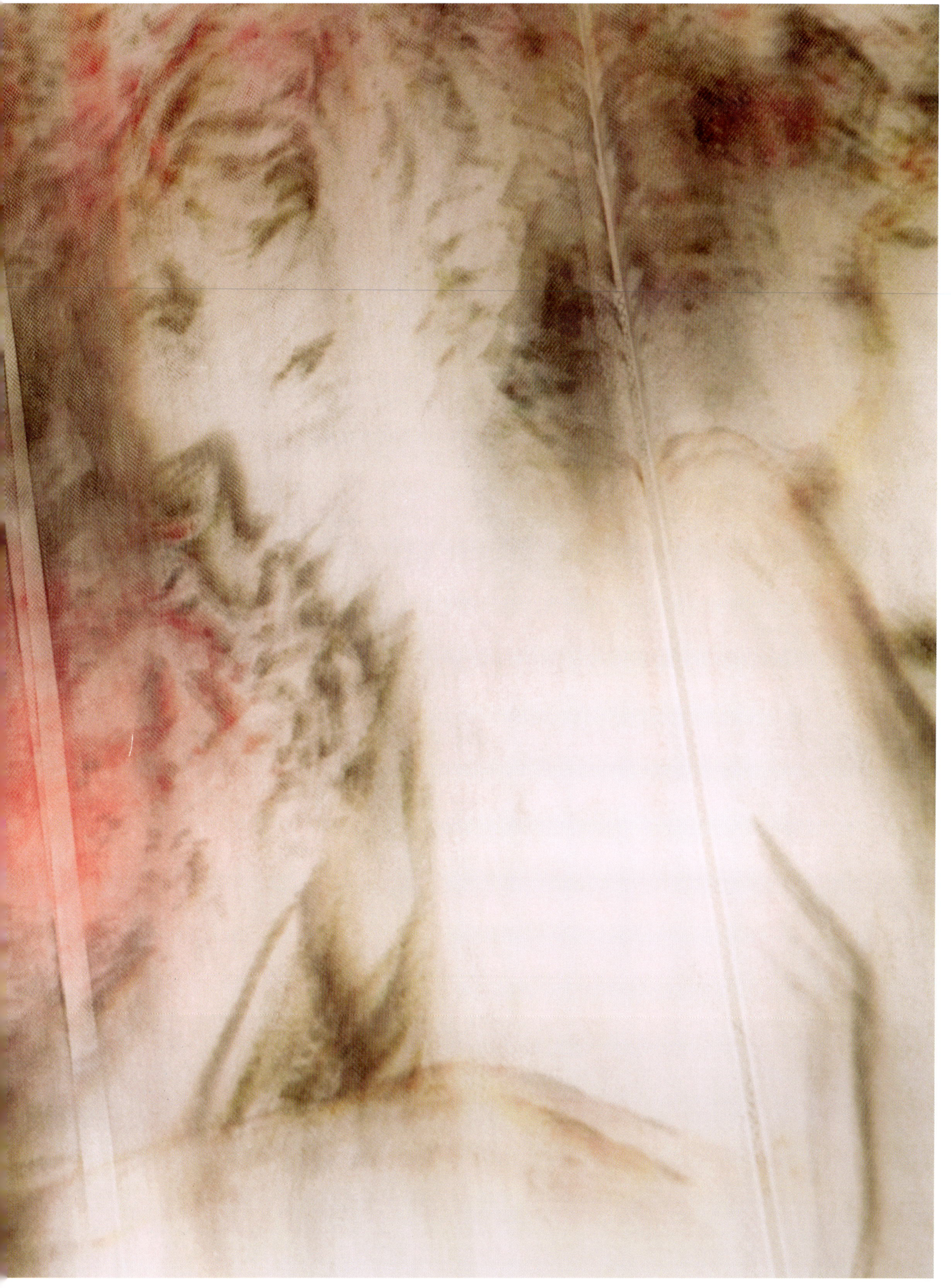

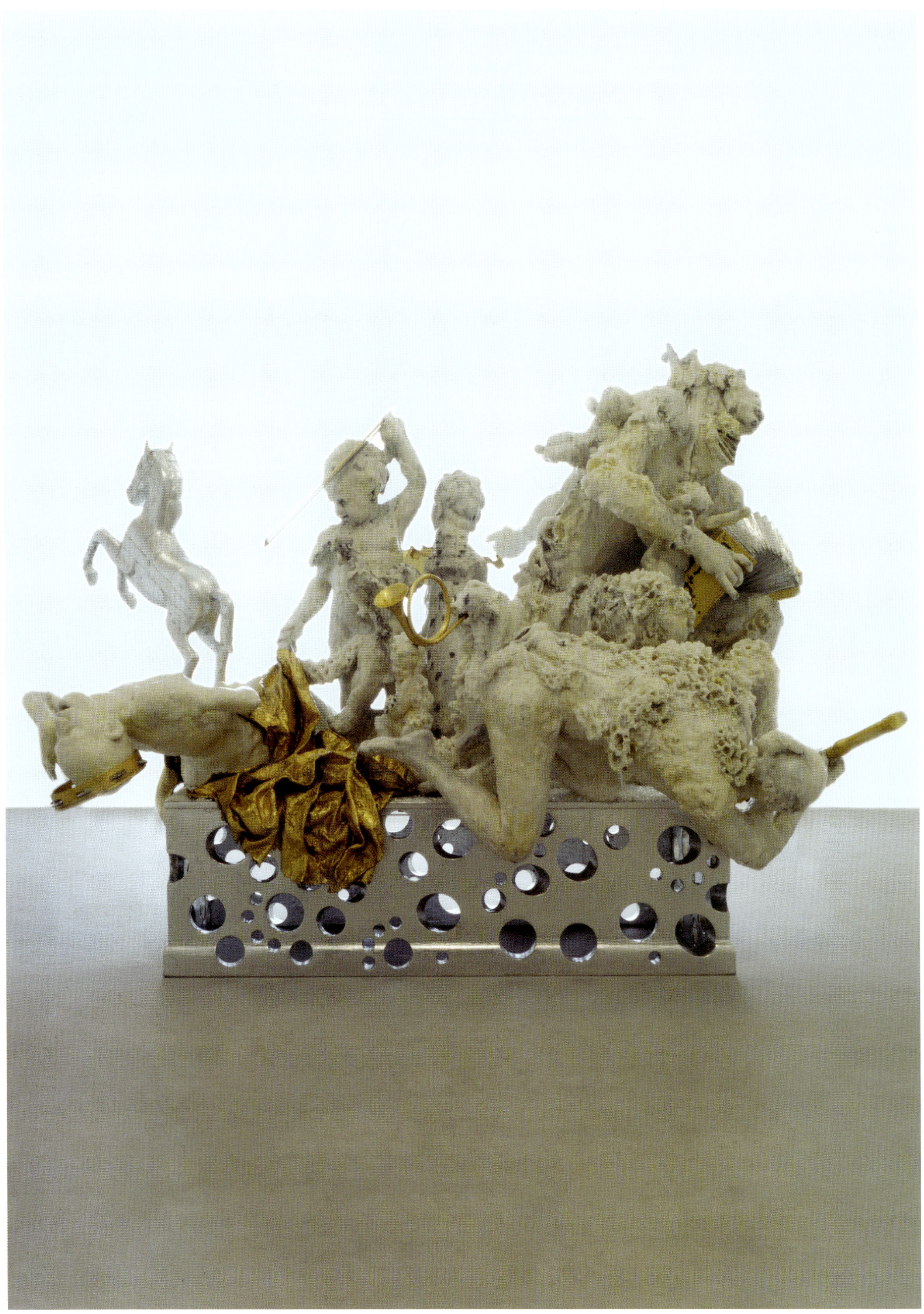

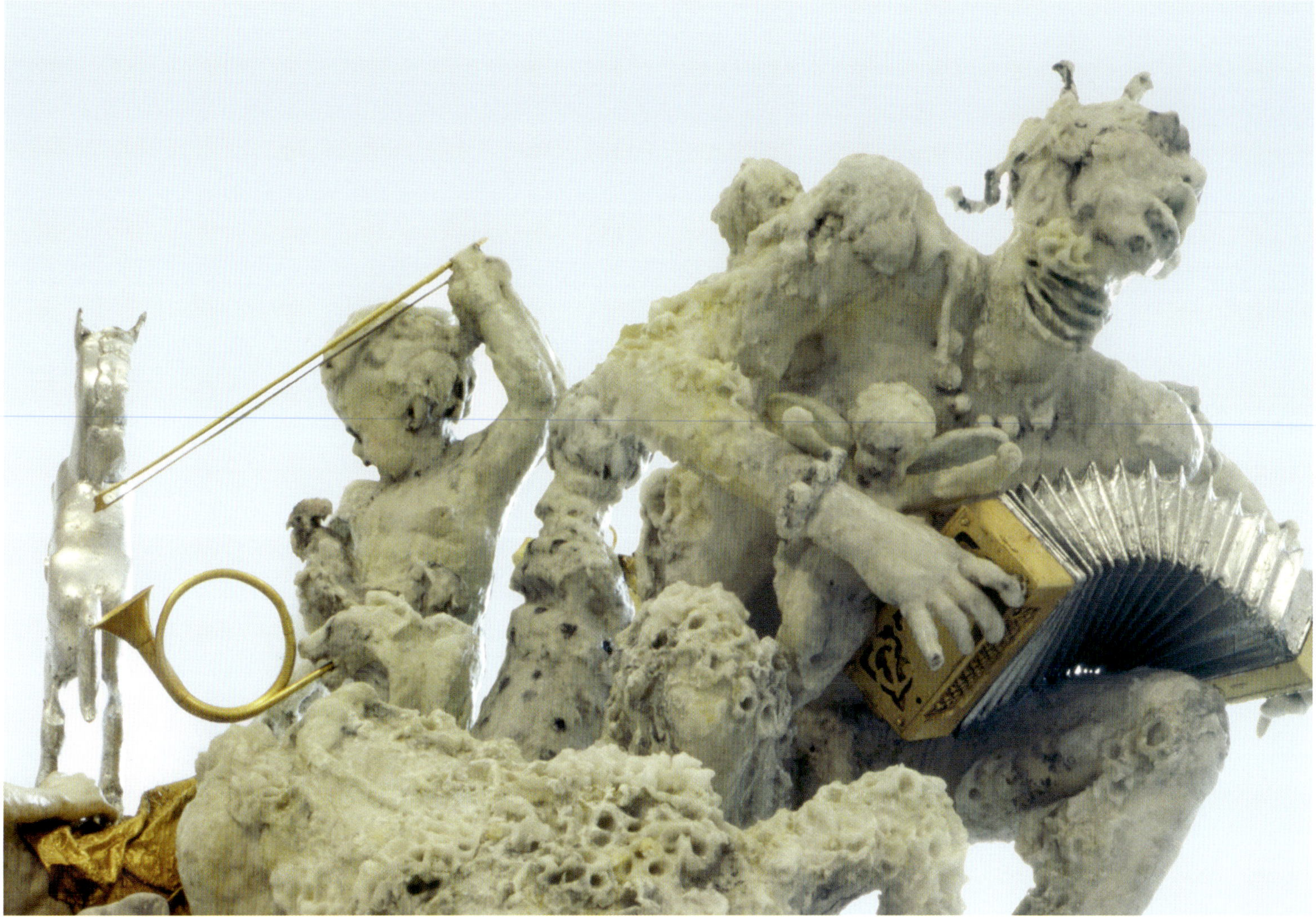

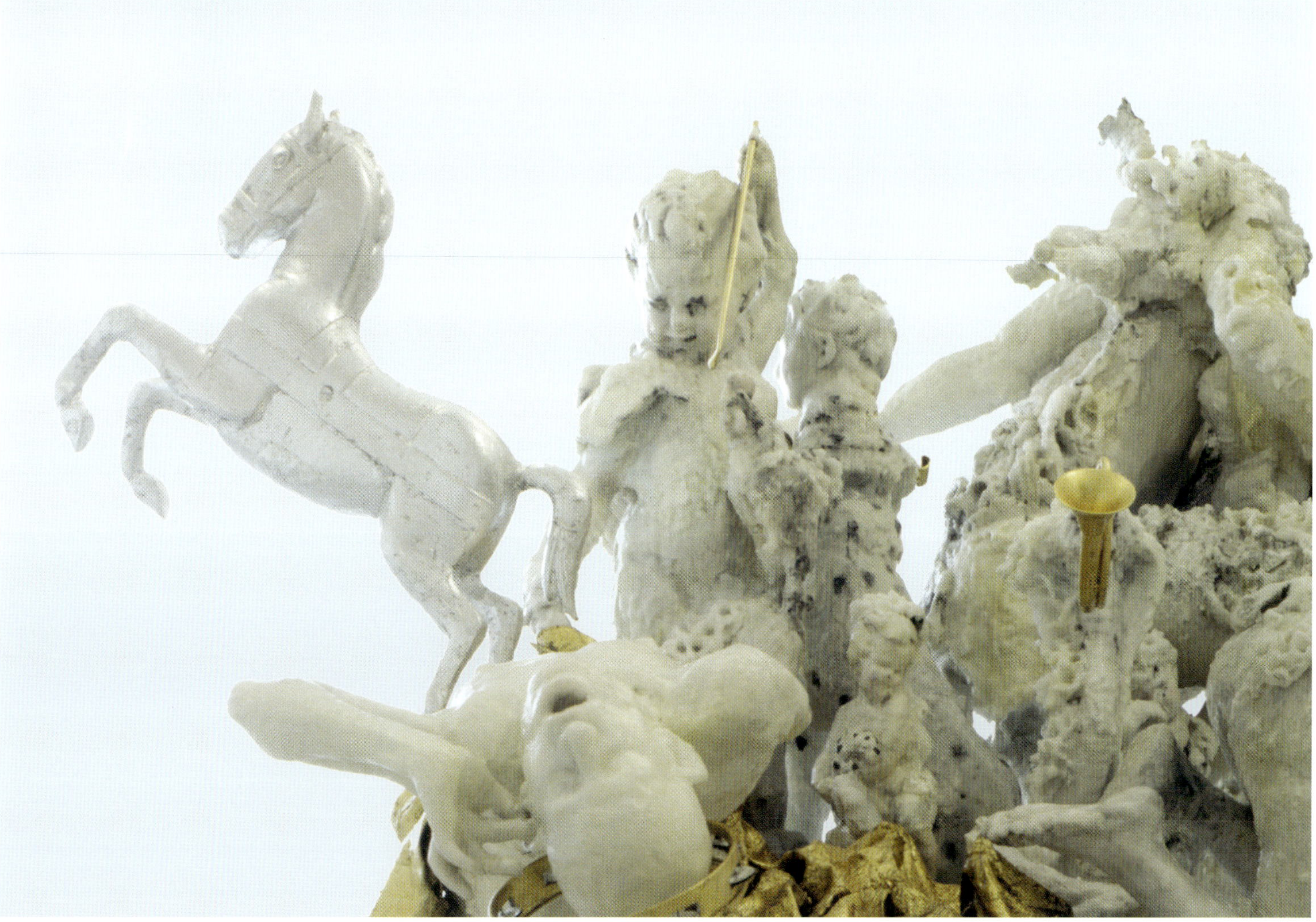

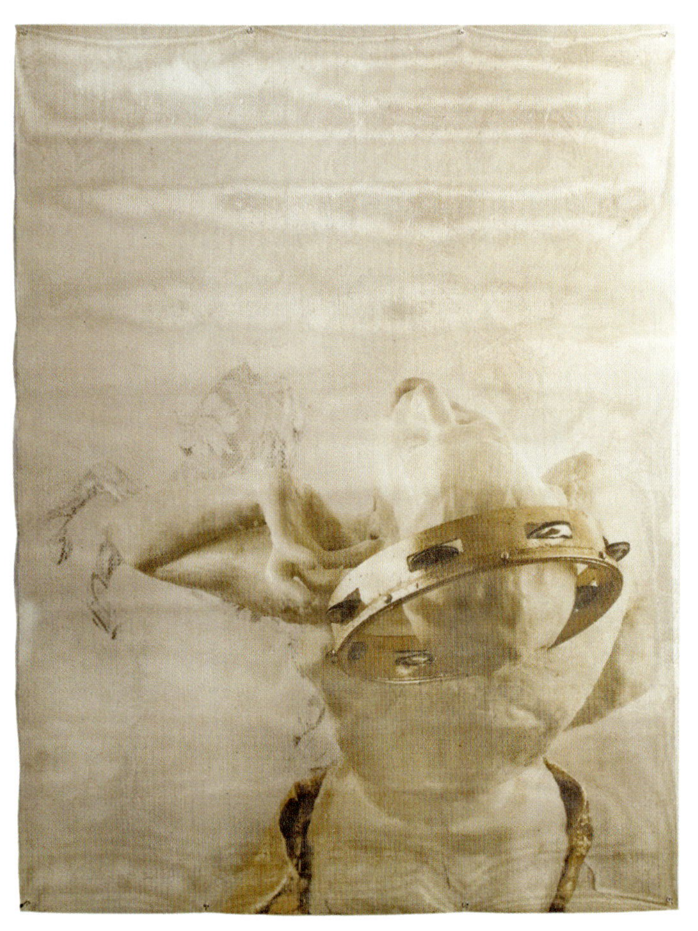

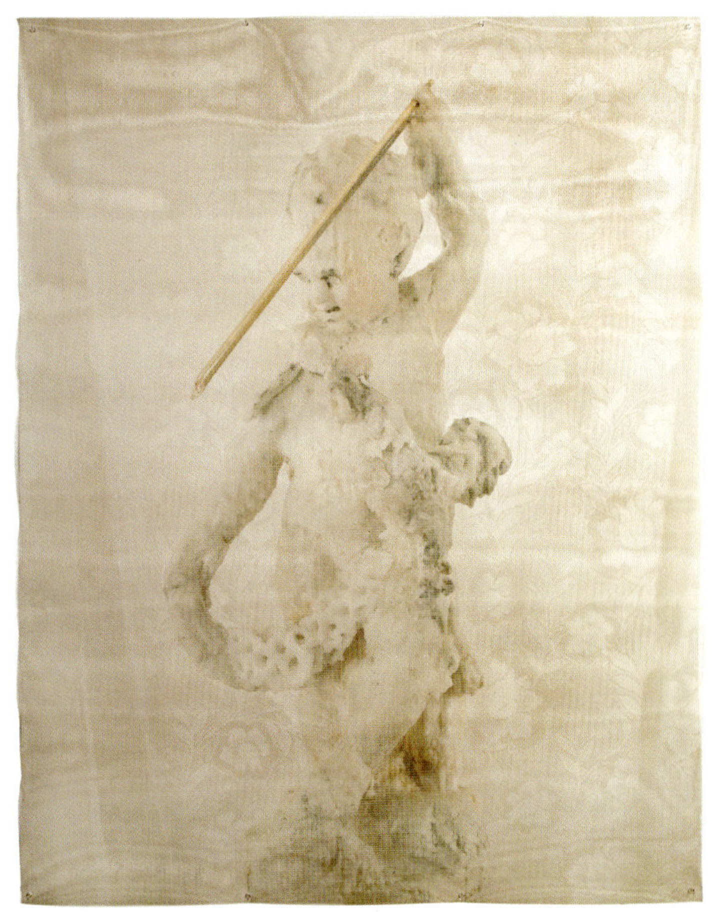

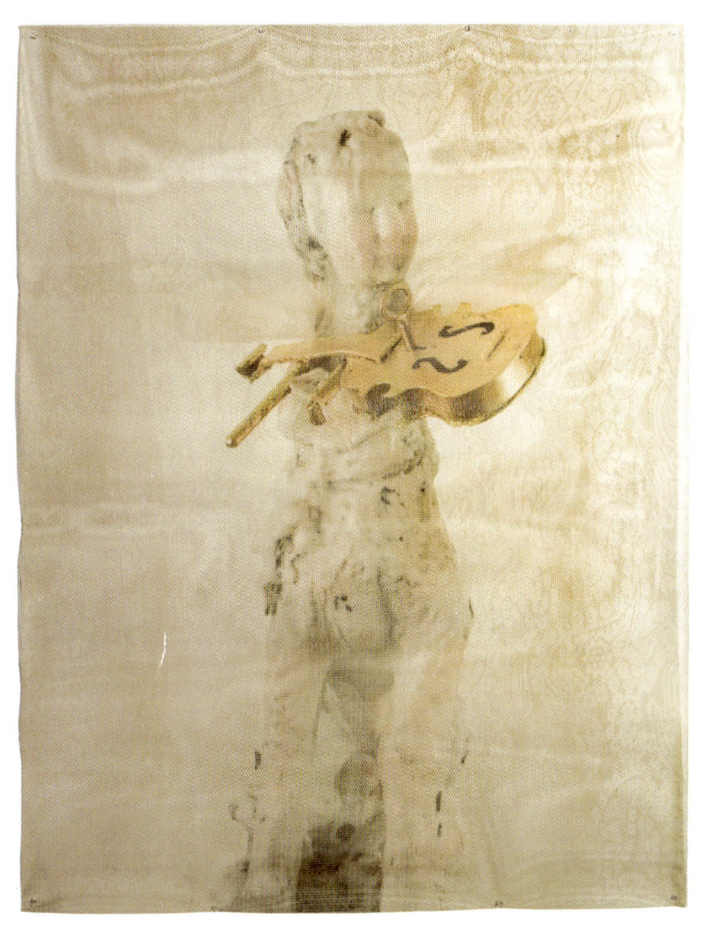

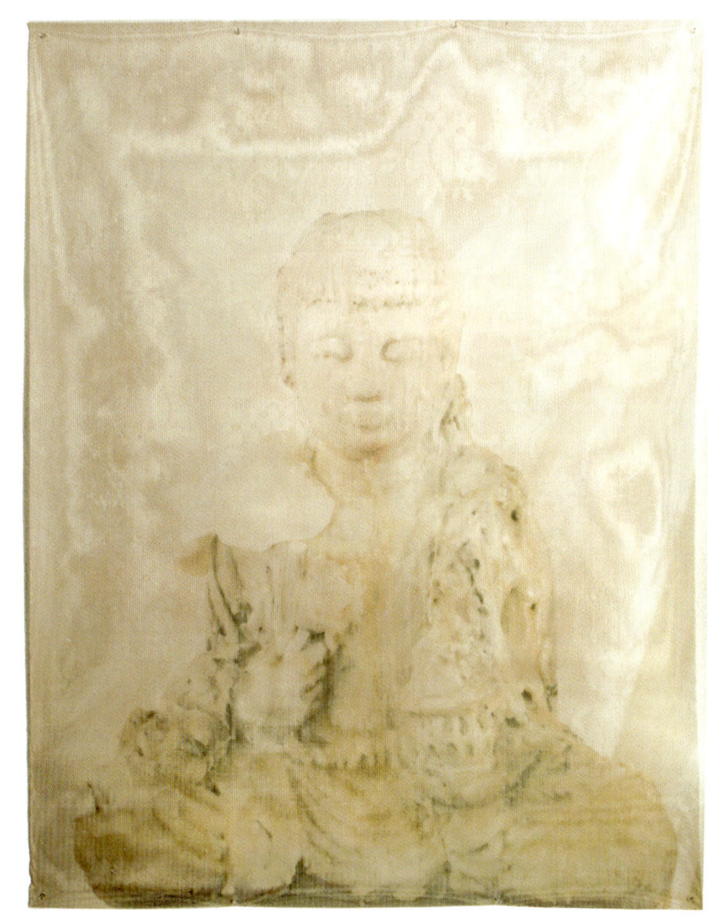

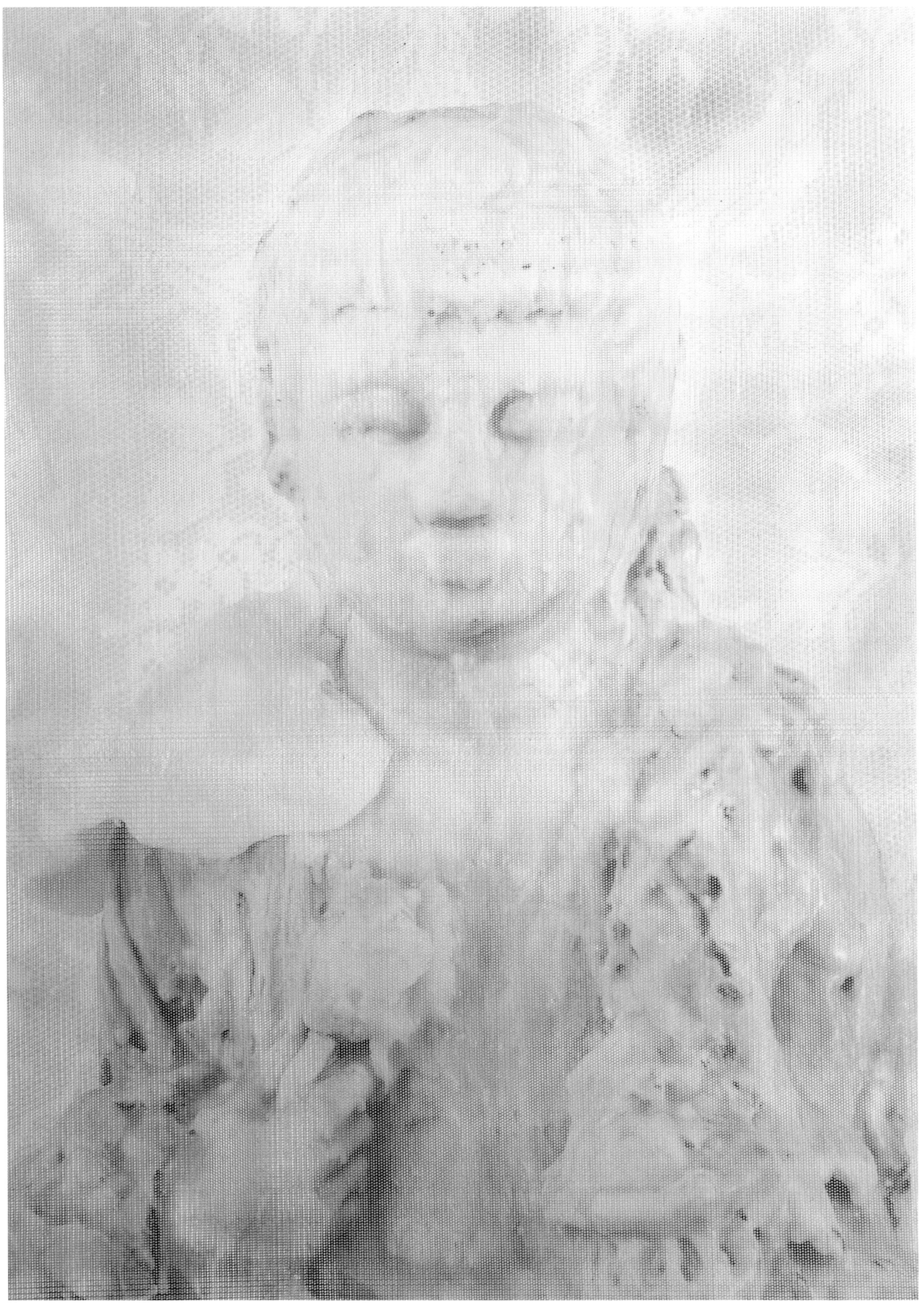

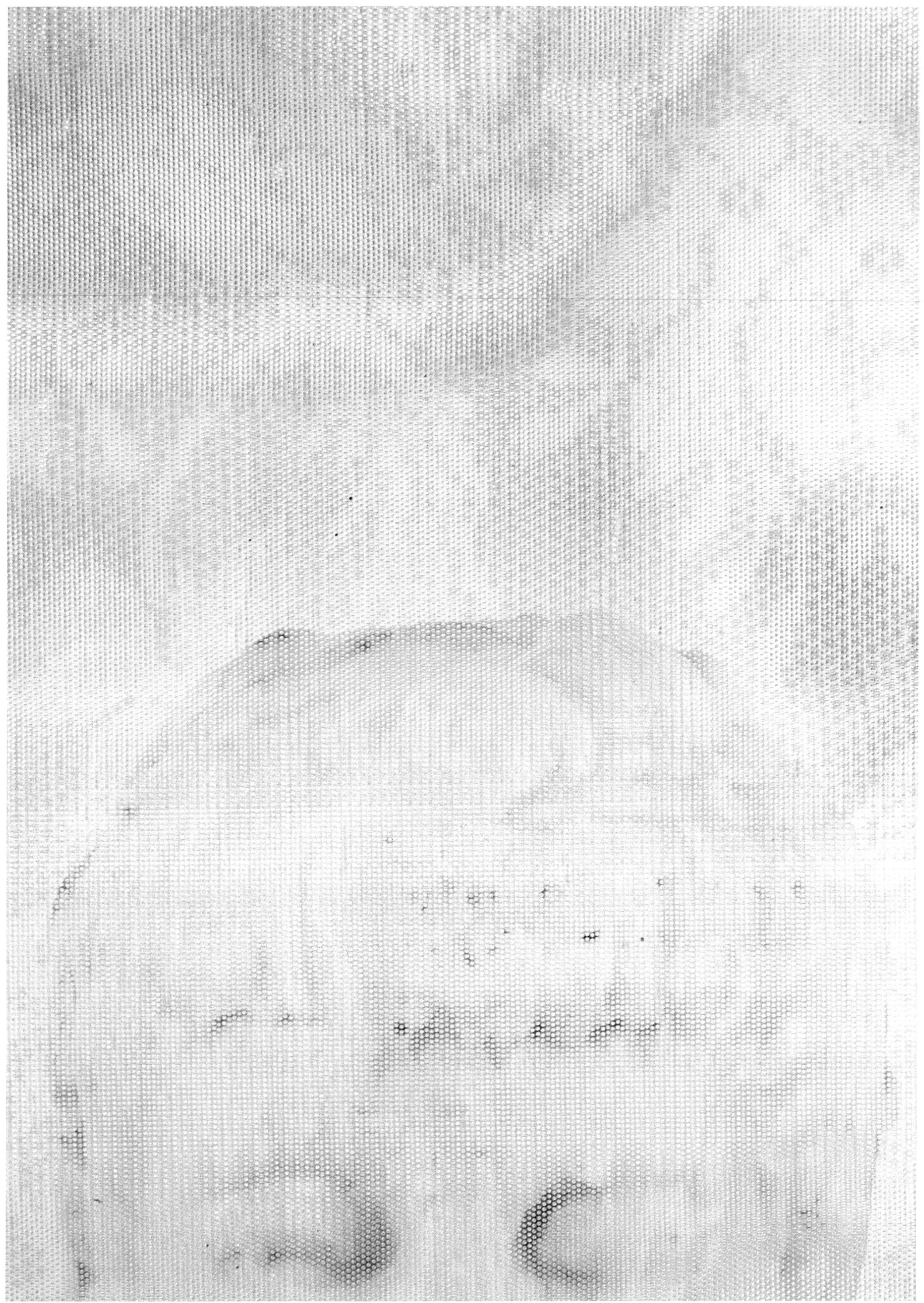

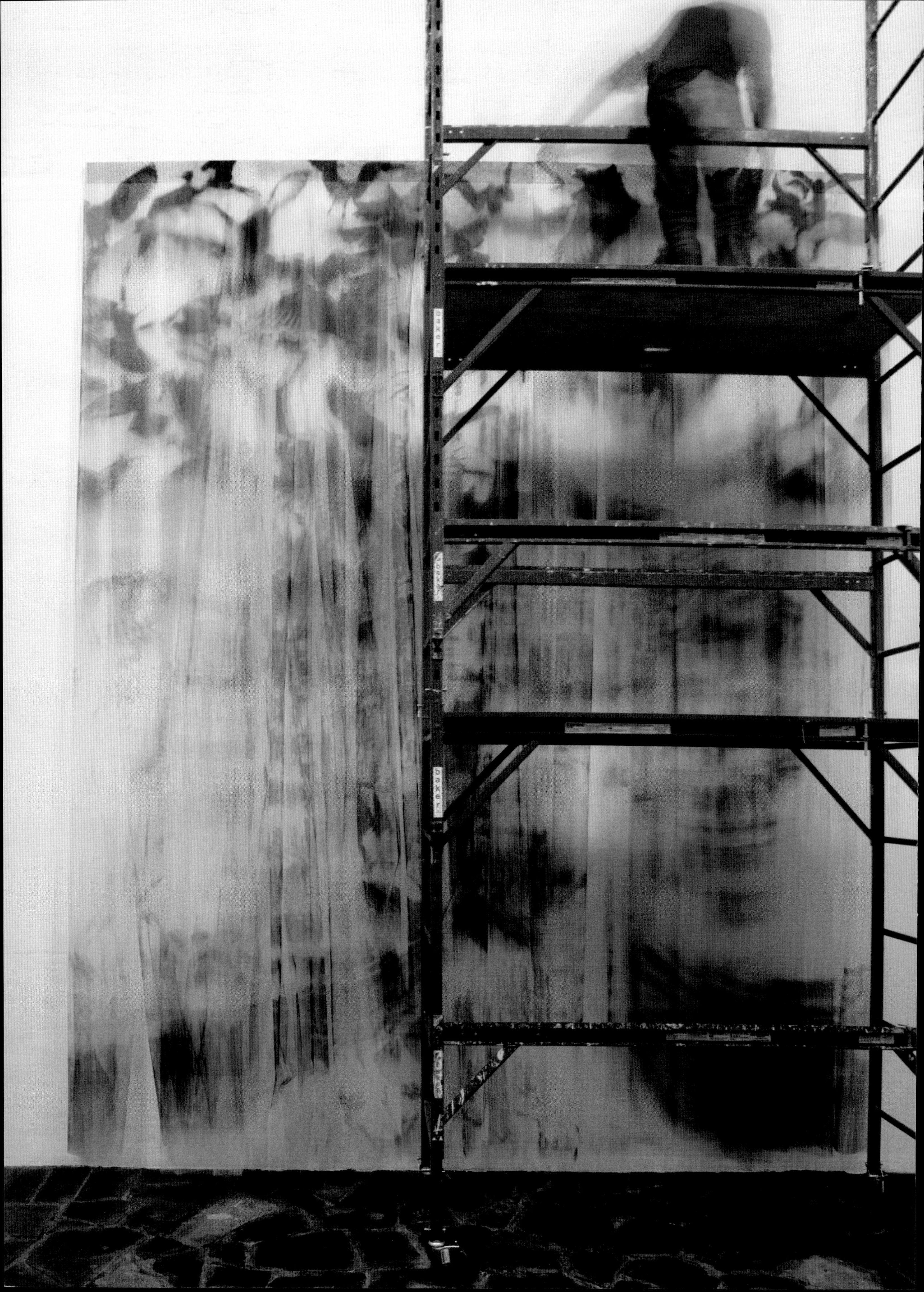
baker
baker

The painted veils may seem unorthodox, but they are unwaveringly paintings because they have the logic, intention, and concerns of a painter. I employ digital printing. In my “reverse” screen paintings, I don’t use a brush either. Yet there is so much hand in those paintings.

EVENING

The trees are dark ruins of temples,
seeking excuses to crumble
since who knows when—
their roofs are cracked,
their doors lost to ancient winds.
And the sky is a priest,
saffron marks on his forehead,
ashes smeared on his body.
He sits by the temples, worn to a shadow, not looking up.

Some terrible magician, hidden behind curtains,
has hypnotized Time
so this evening is a net
in which the twilight is caught.
Now darkness will never come—
and there will never be morning.

The sky waits for this spell to be broken,
for History to tear itself from this net,
for Silence to break its chains
so that a symphony of conch shells
may wake up the statues
and a beautiful, dark goddess,
her anklets echoing, may unveil herself.

Poem by Faiz Ahmed Faiz
Version by Agha Shahid Ali

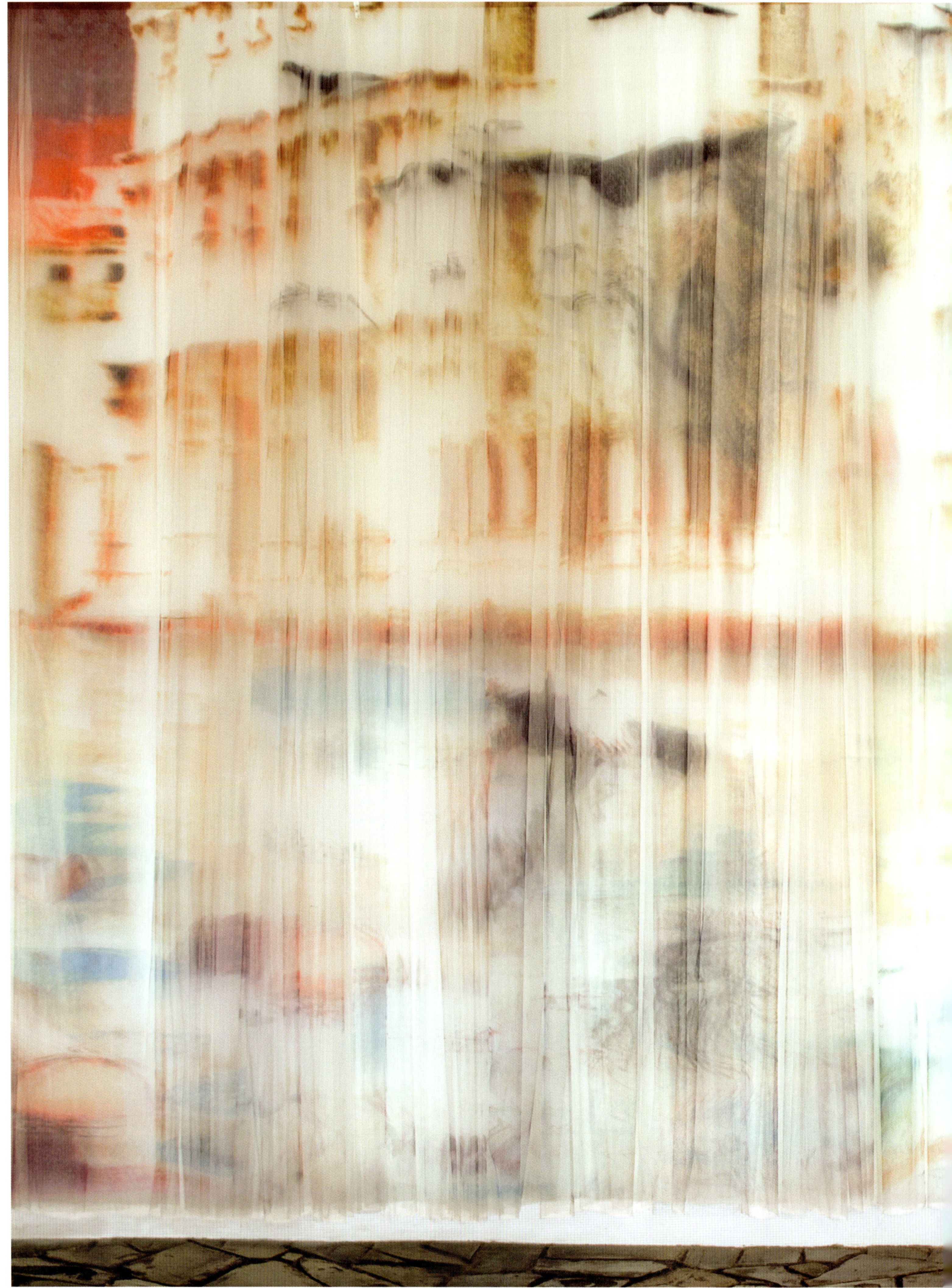

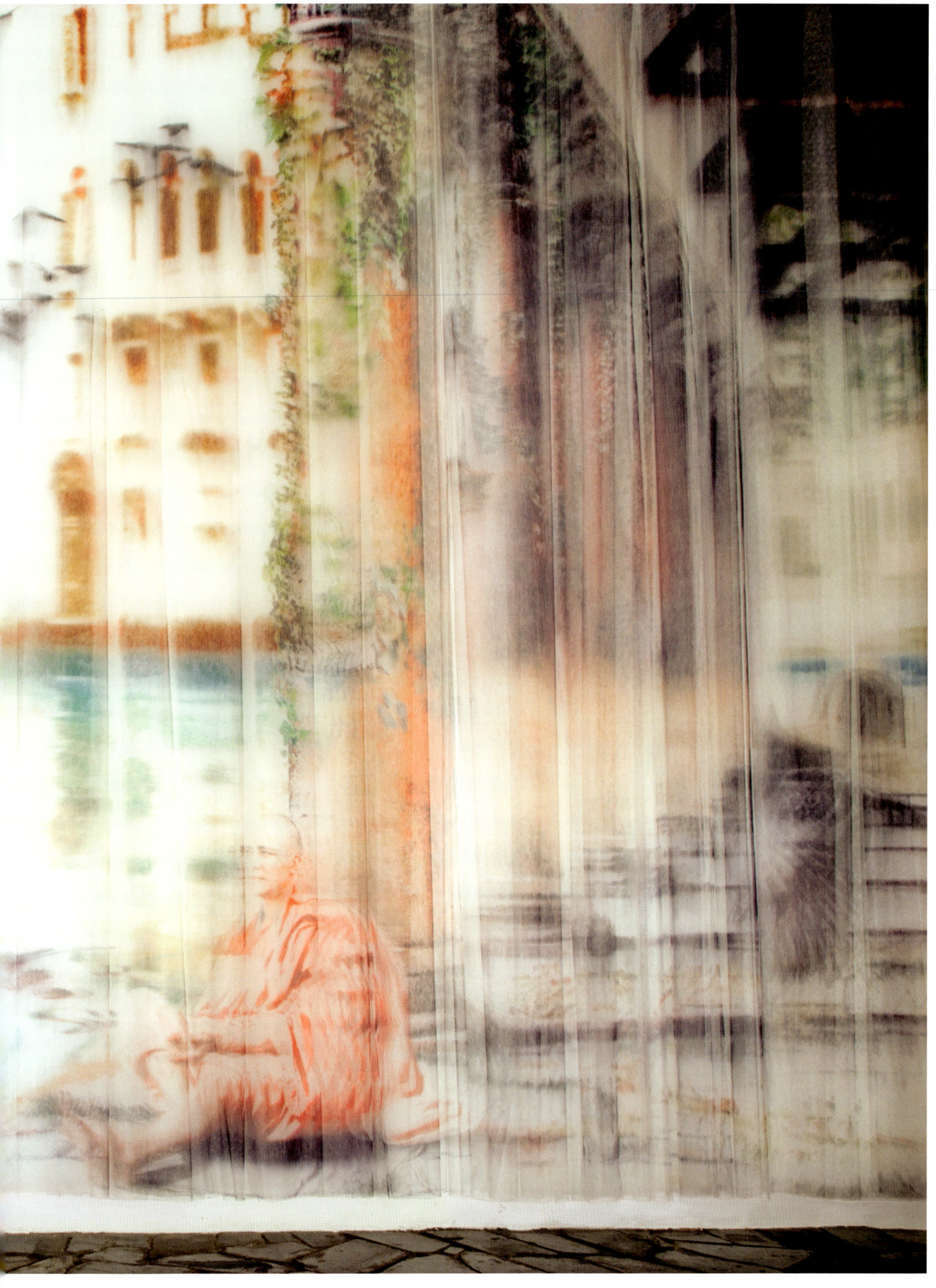

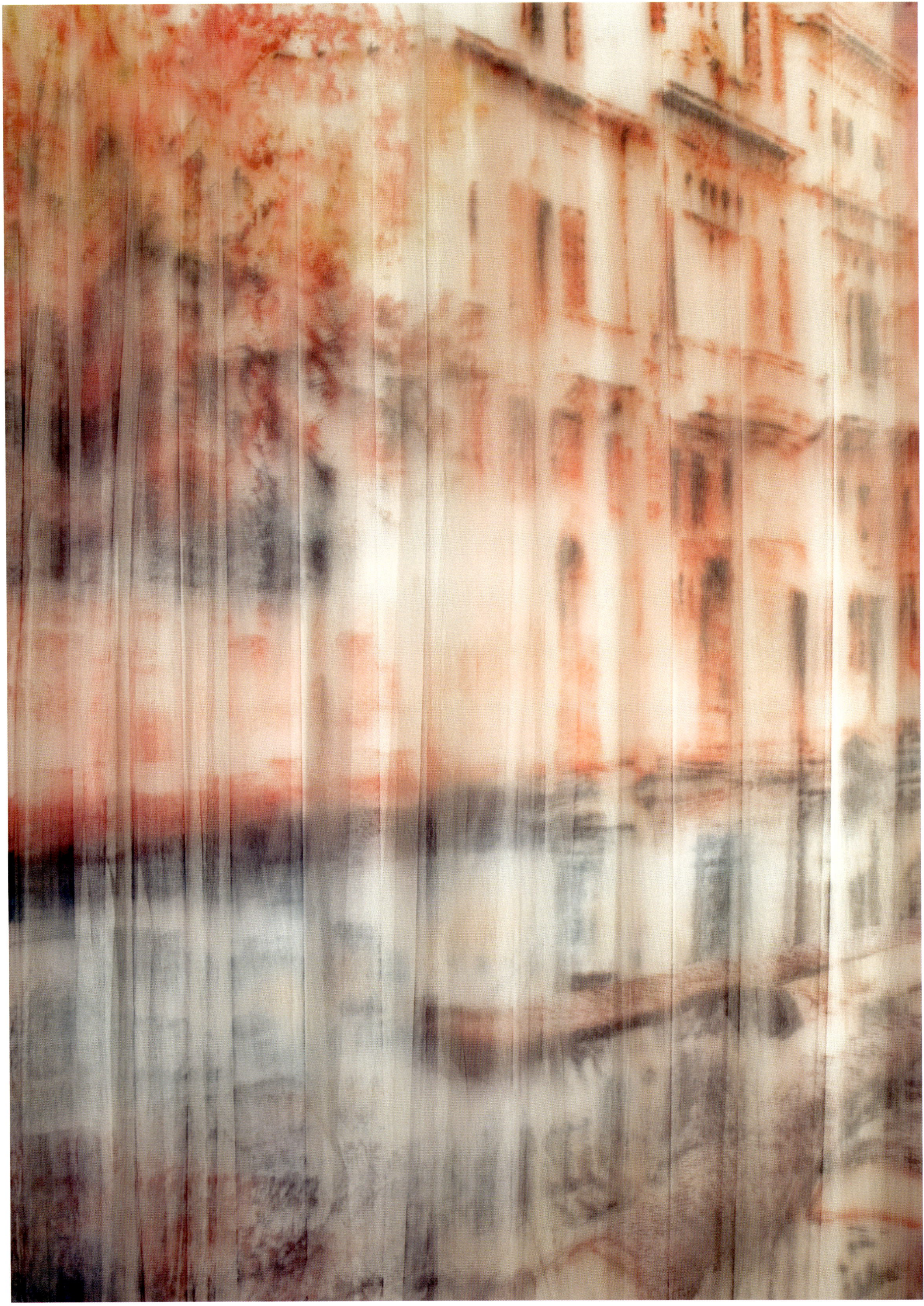

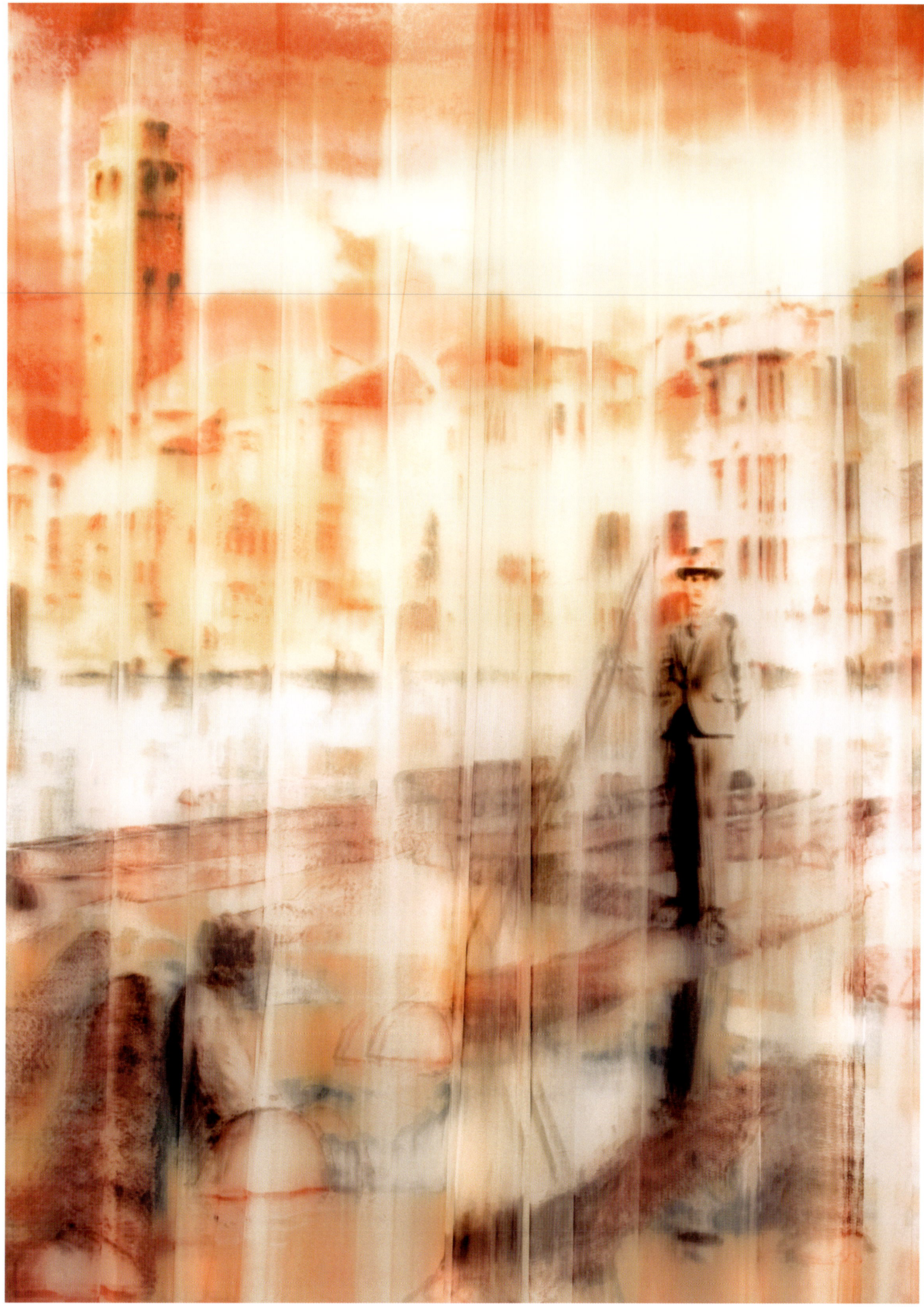

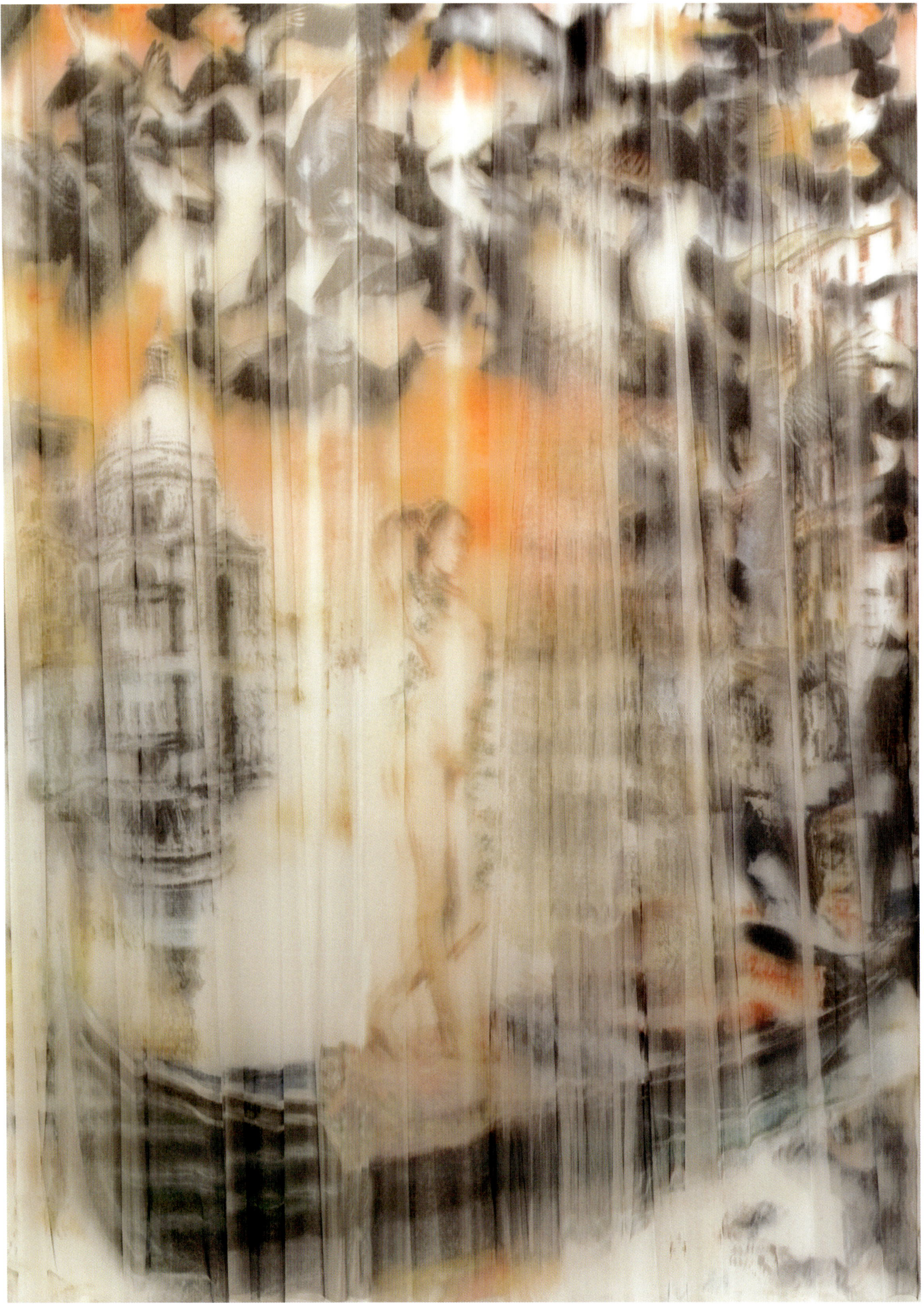

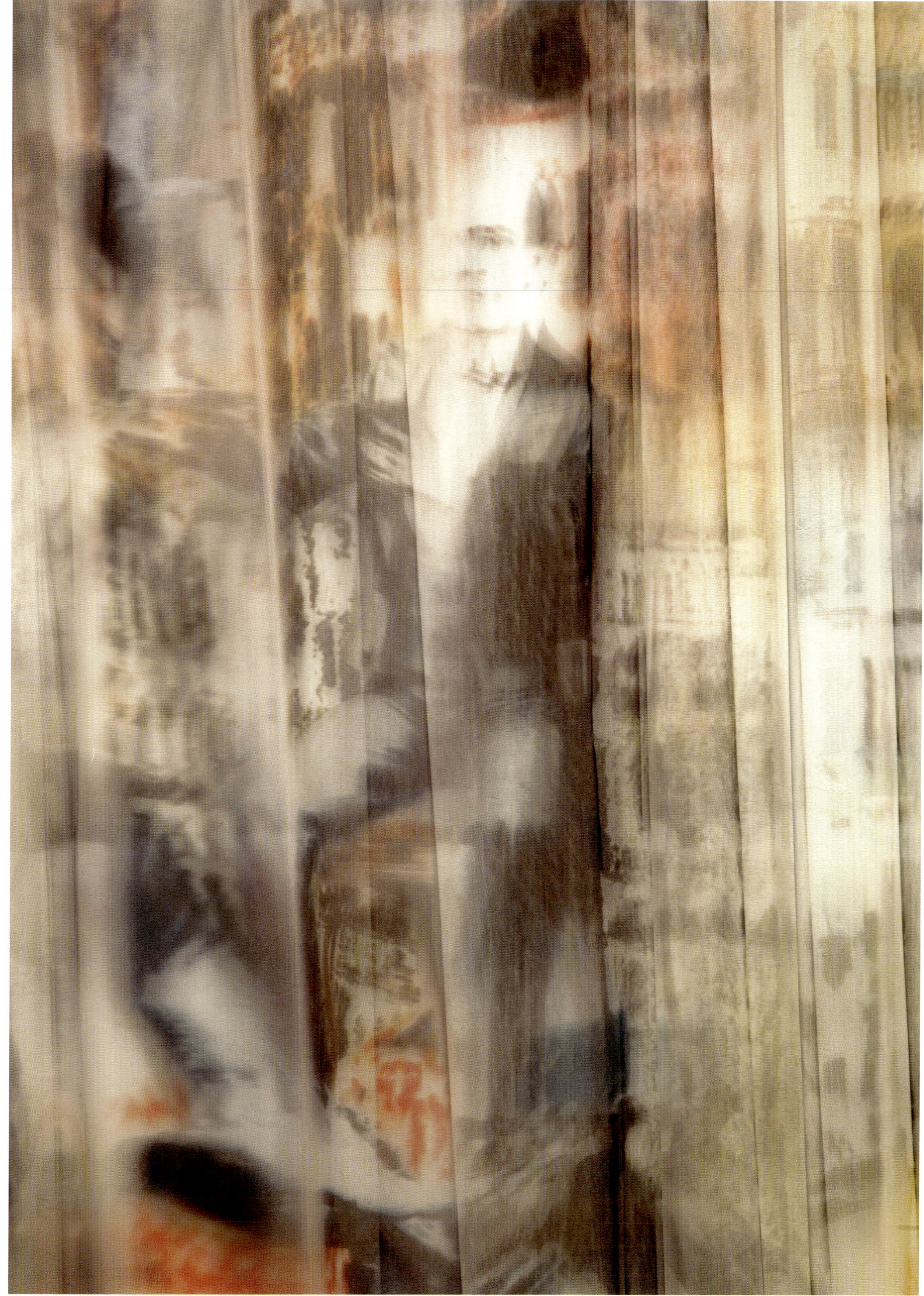

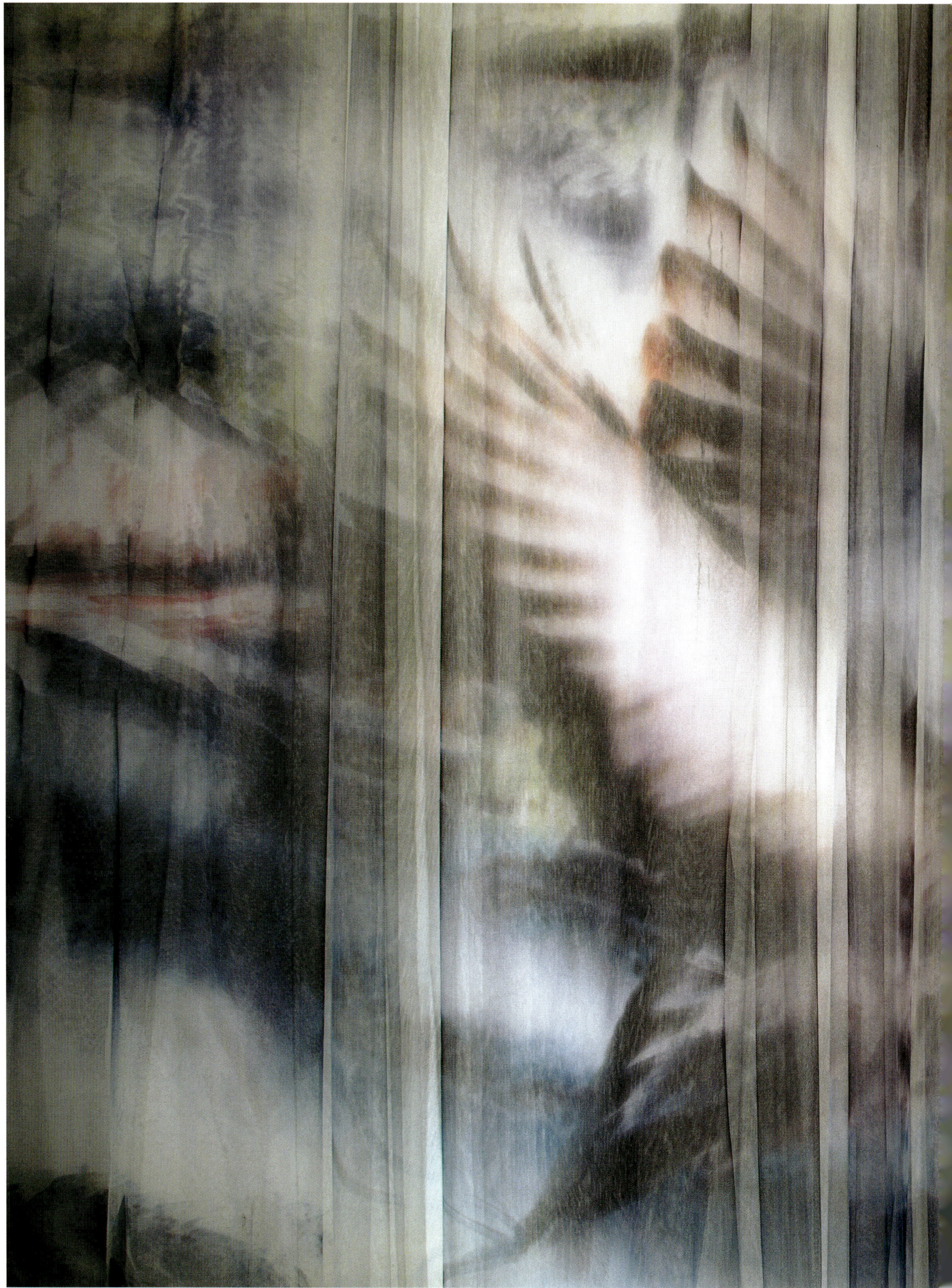

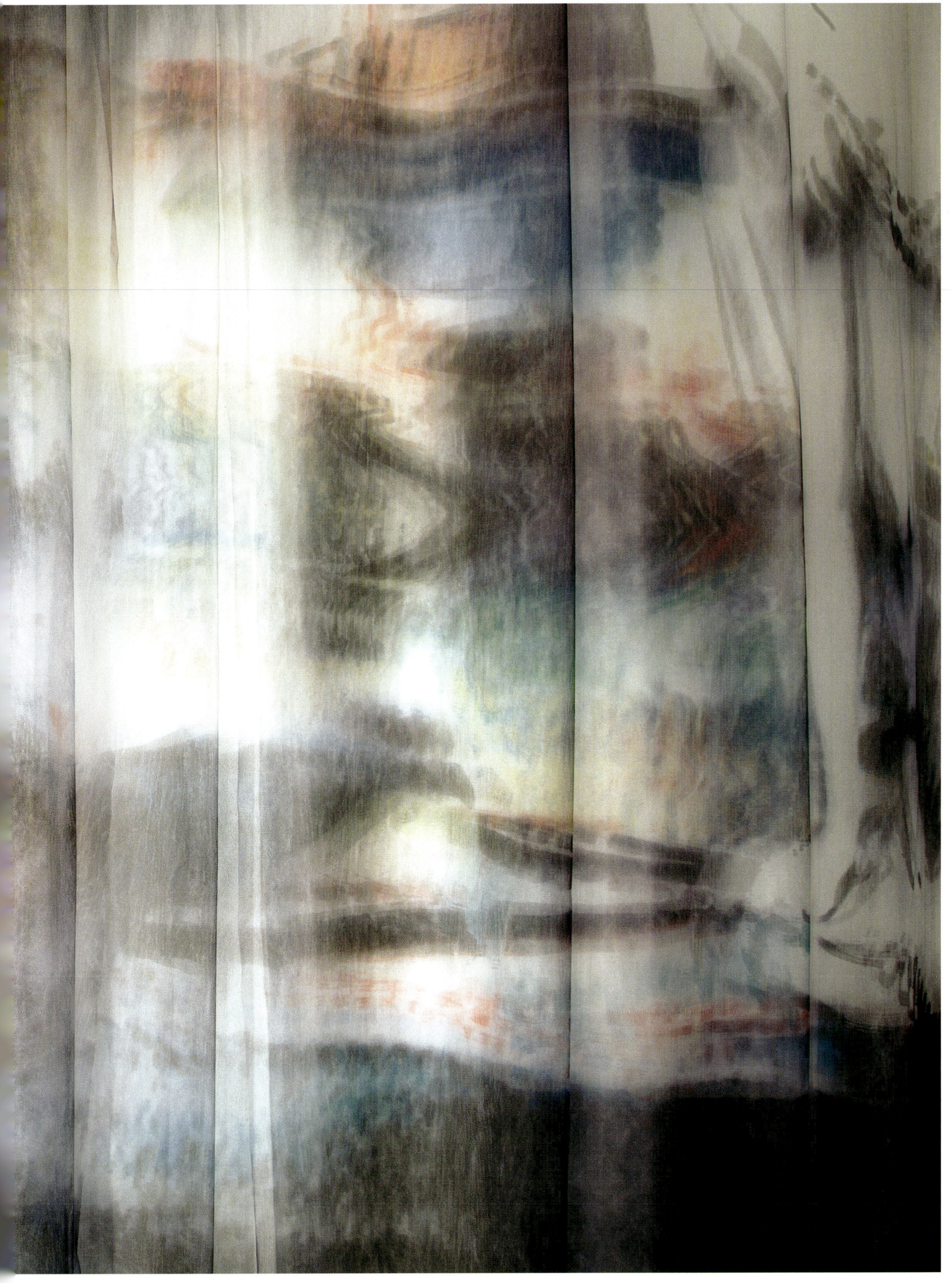

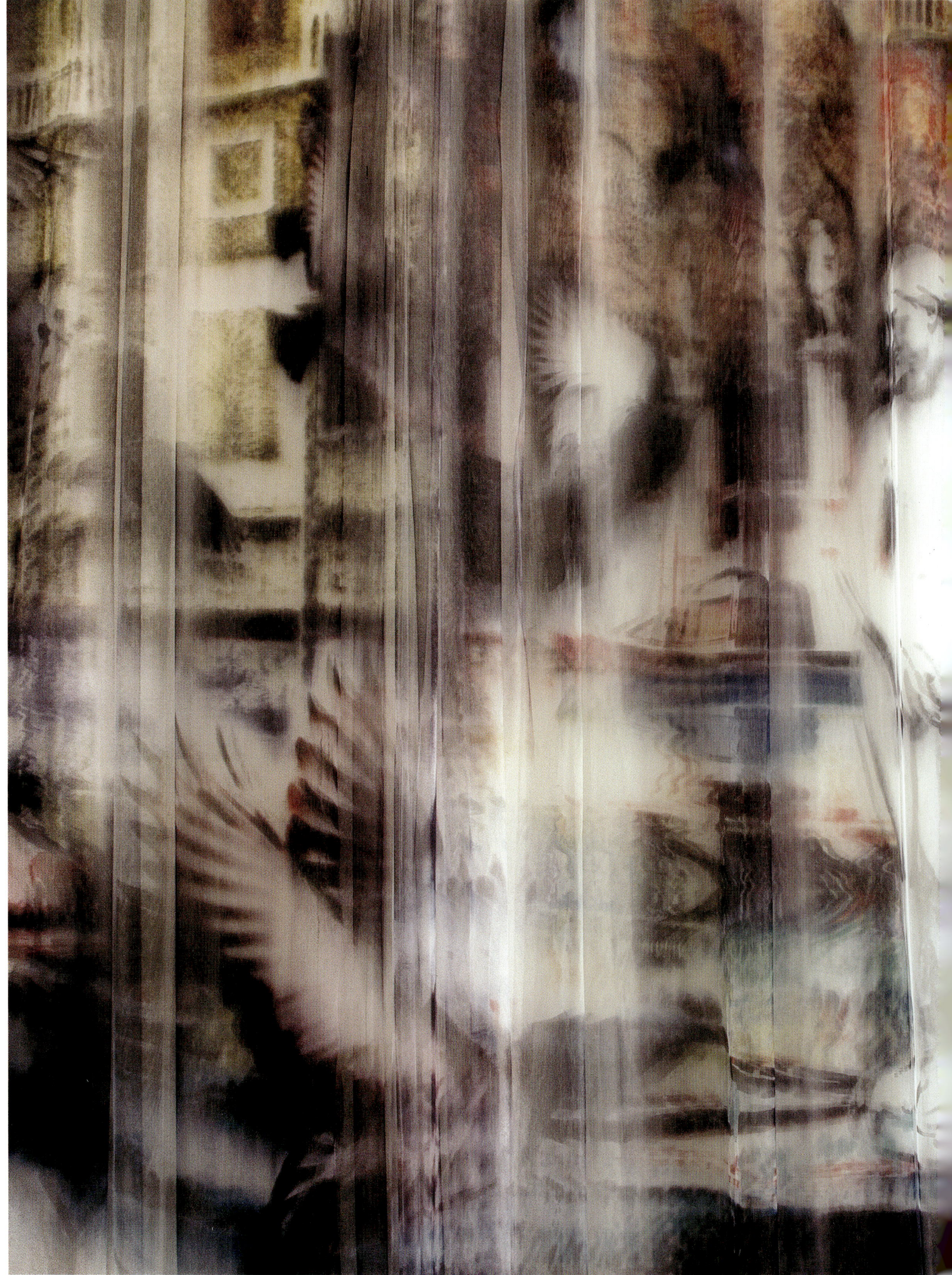

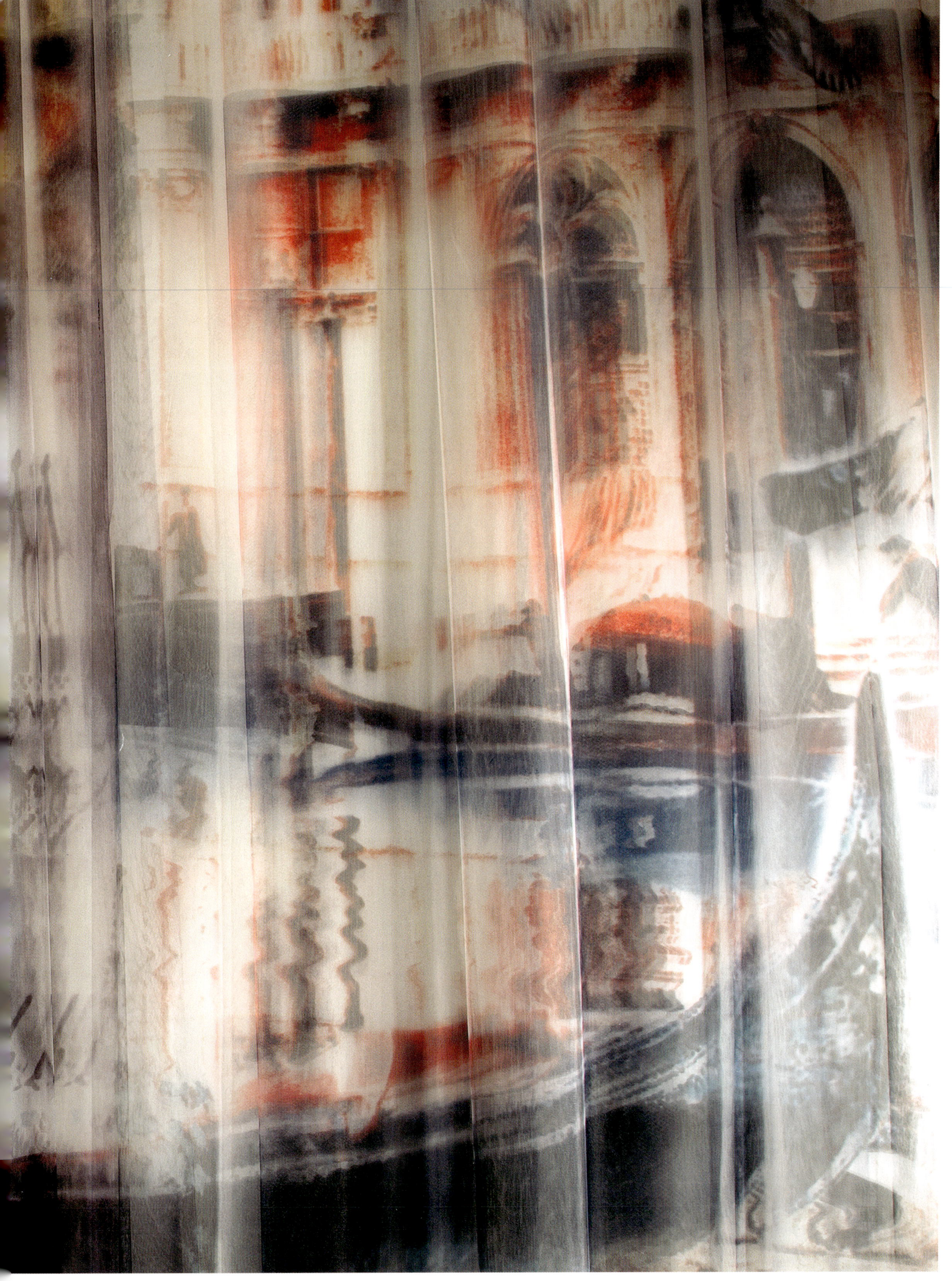

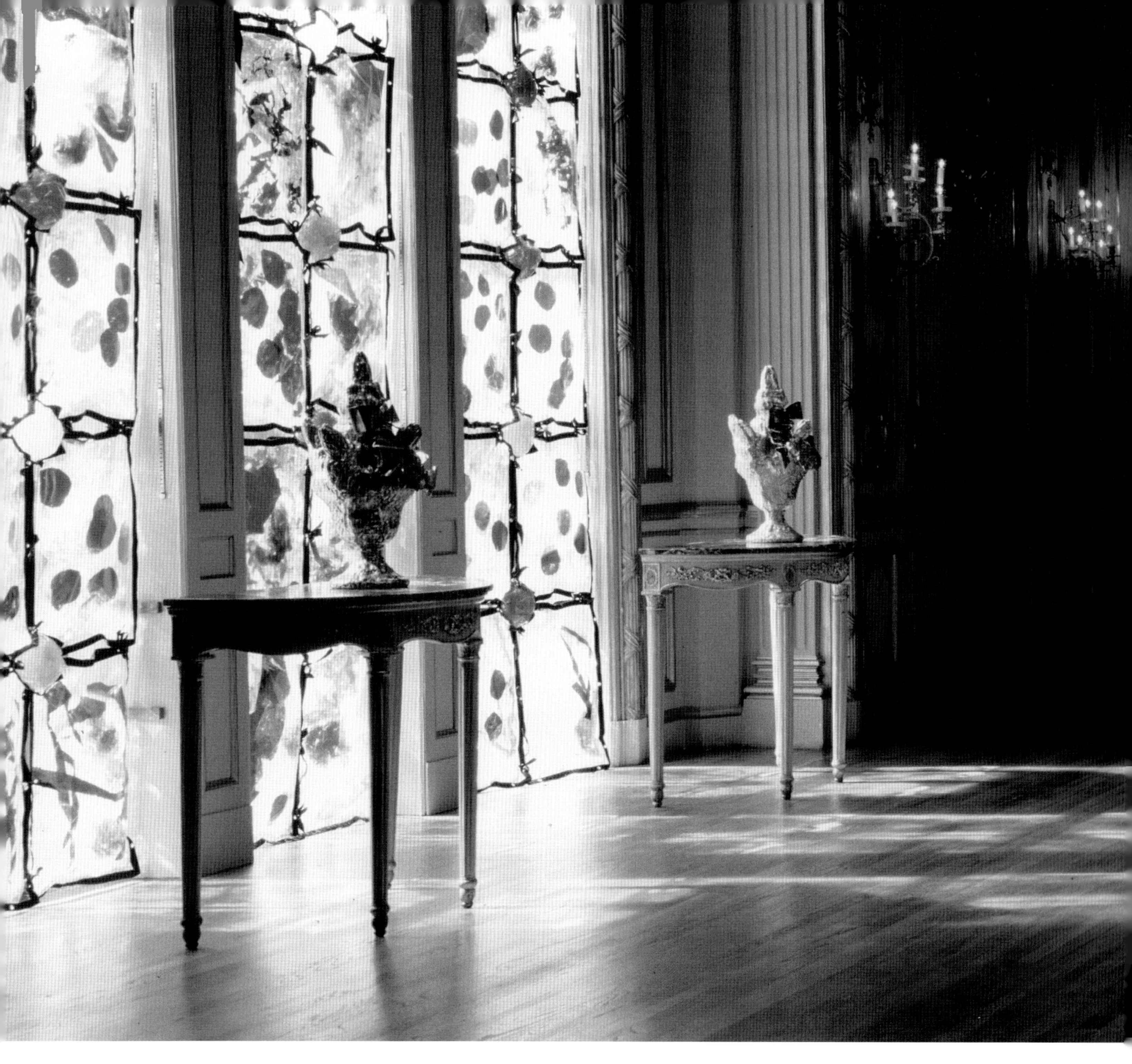

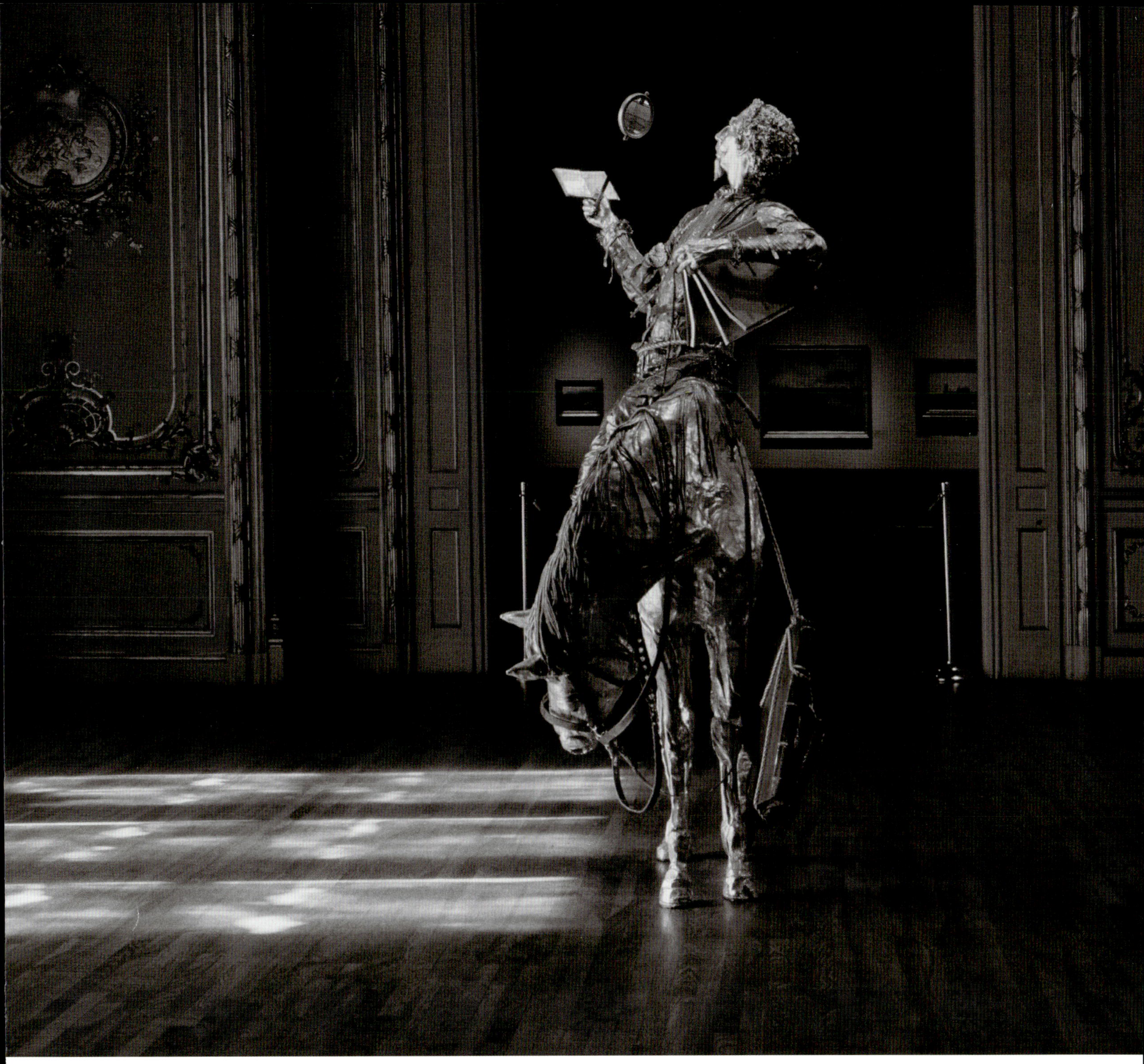

I wander among cultures. The chasm between abstraction, representation and manifestation is embodied in my story. Characters develop in the tension between the material and the image.

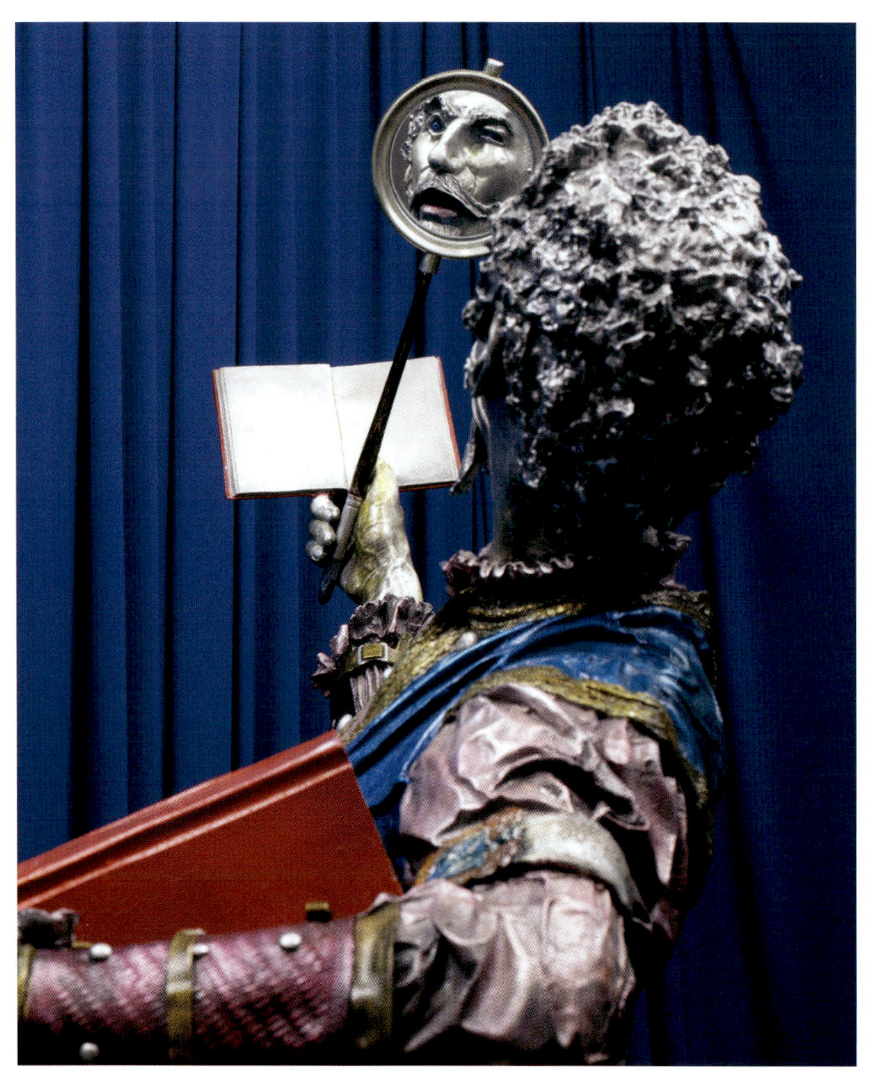

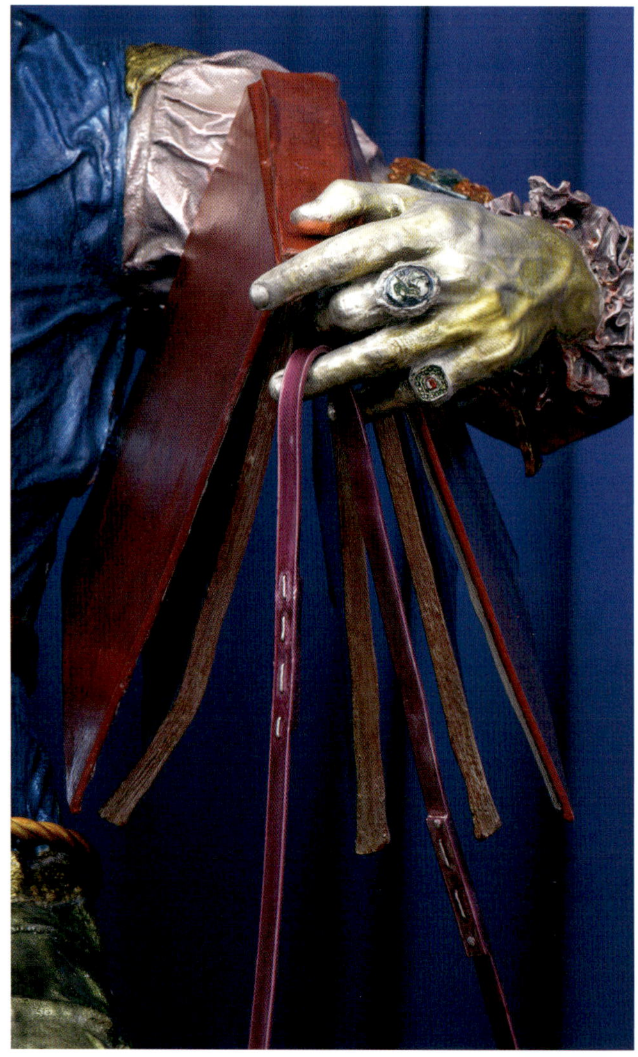

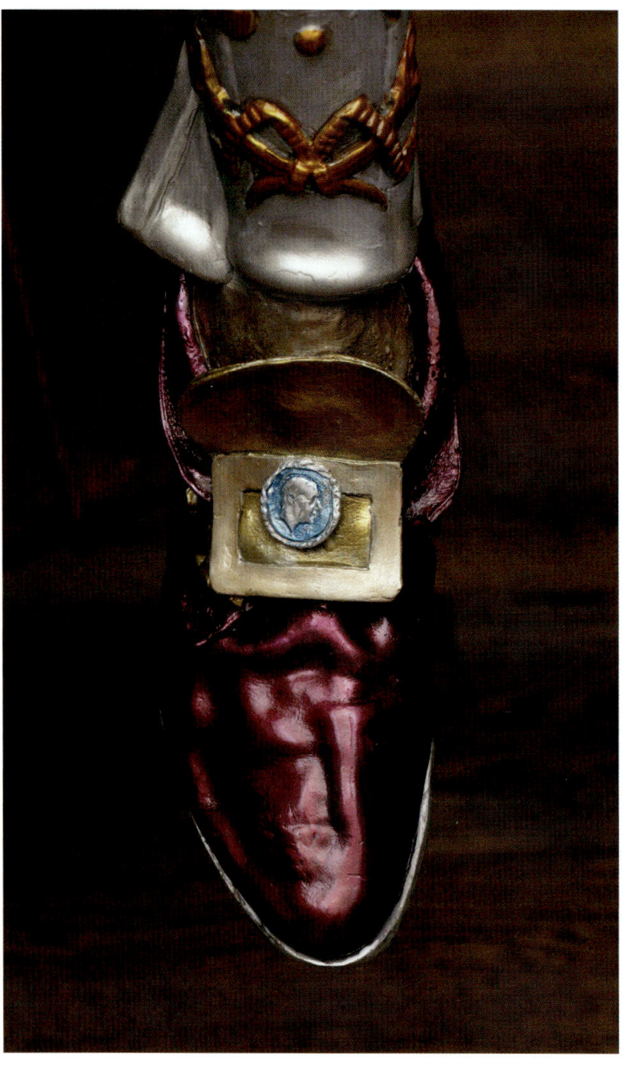

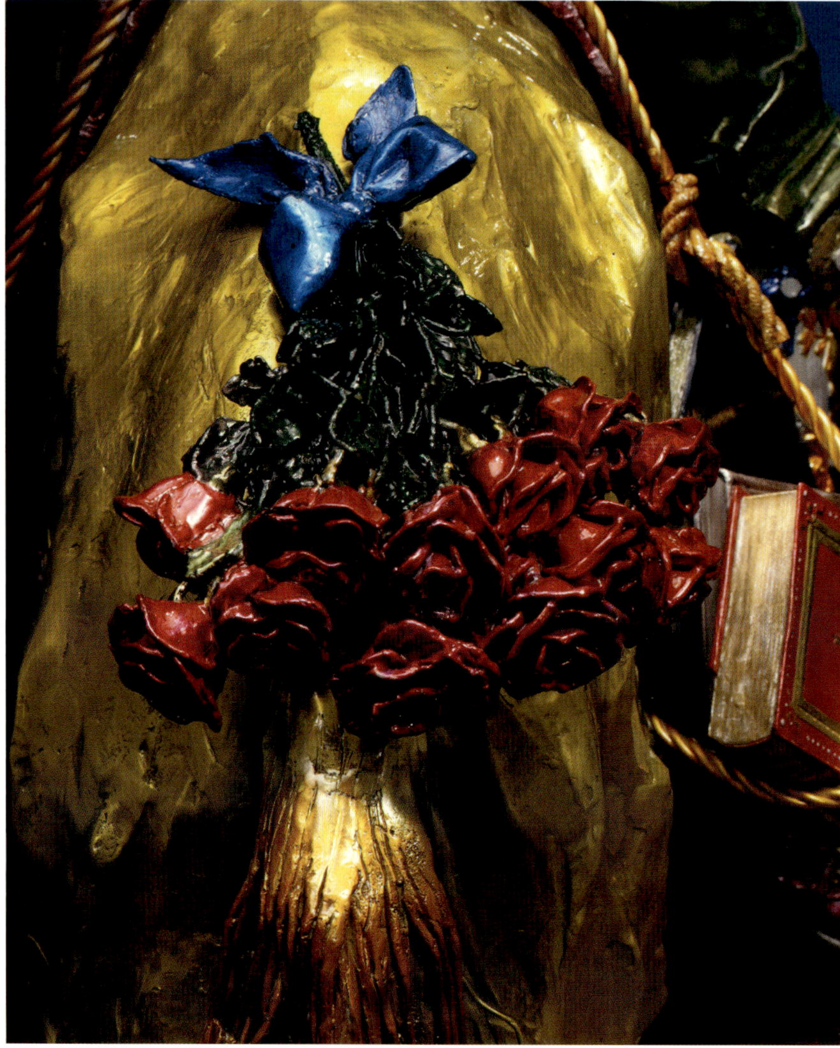

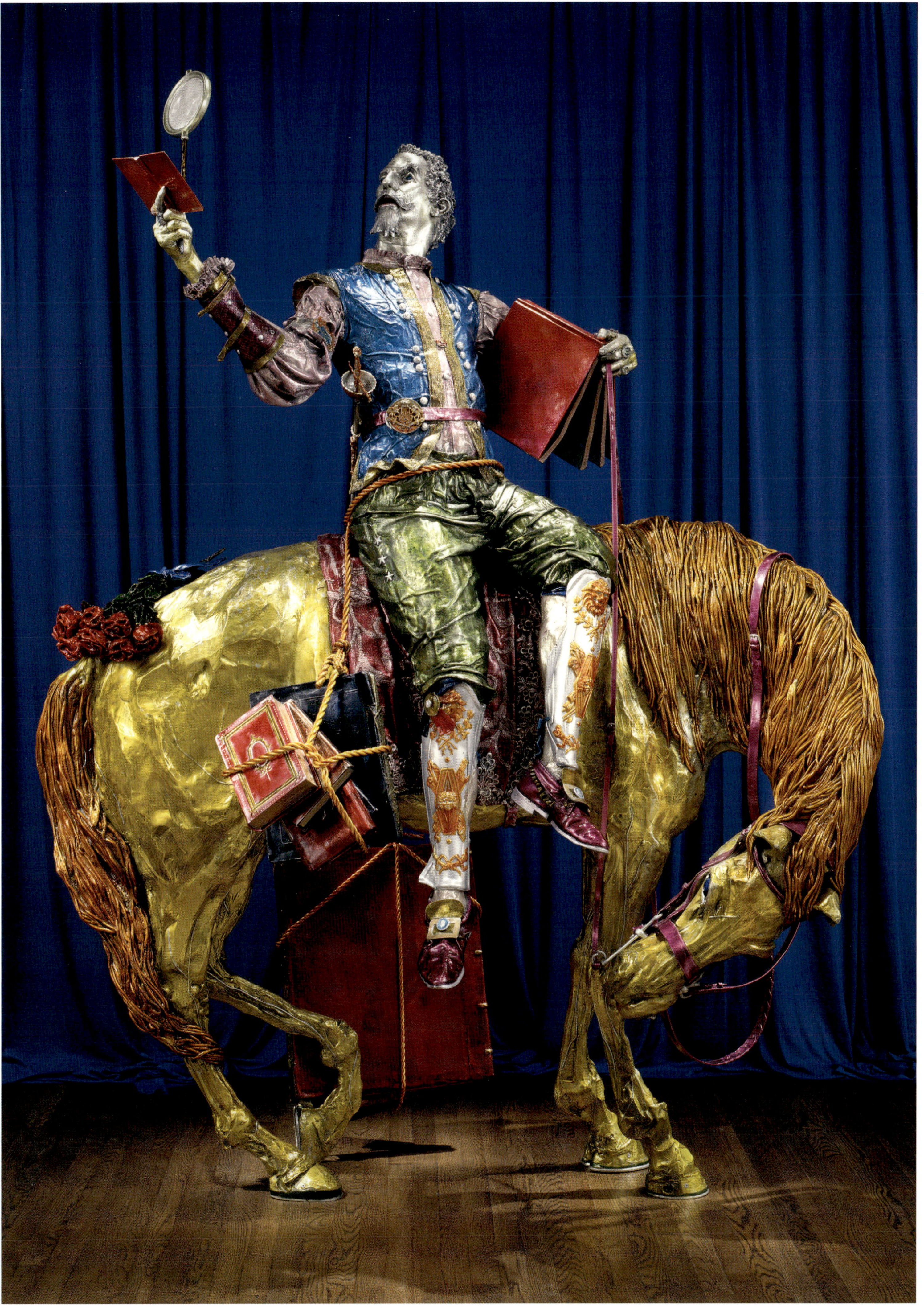

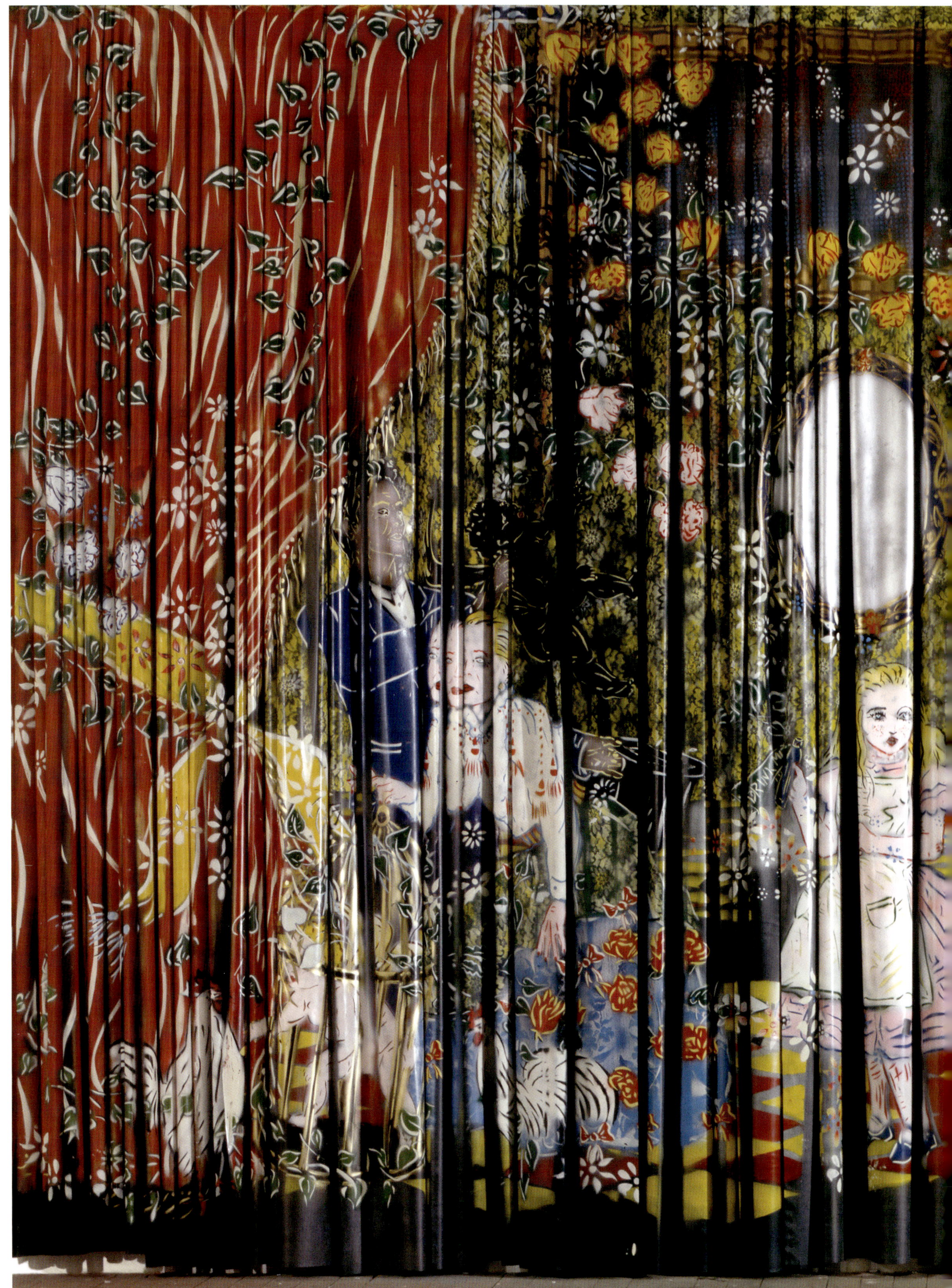

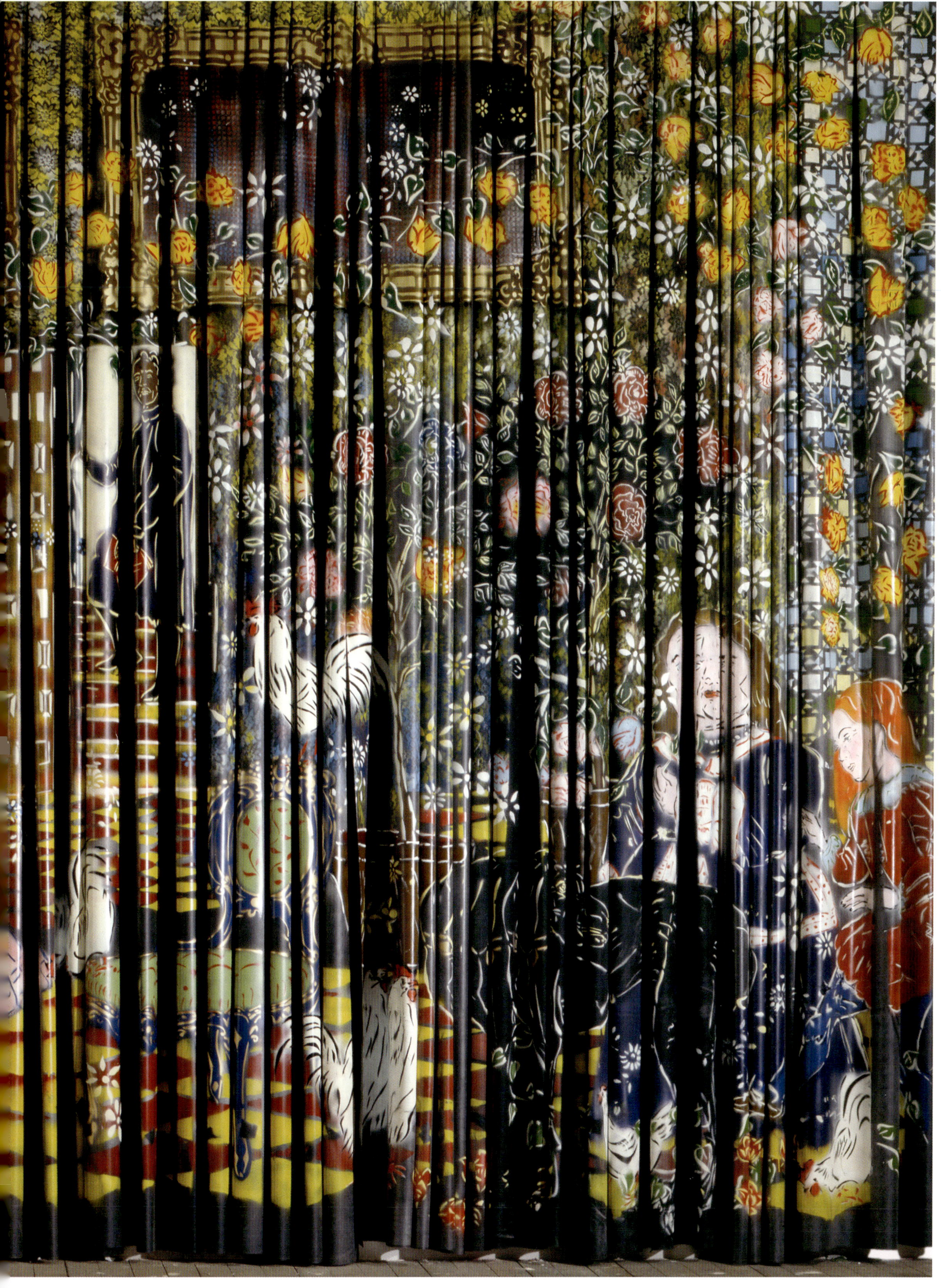

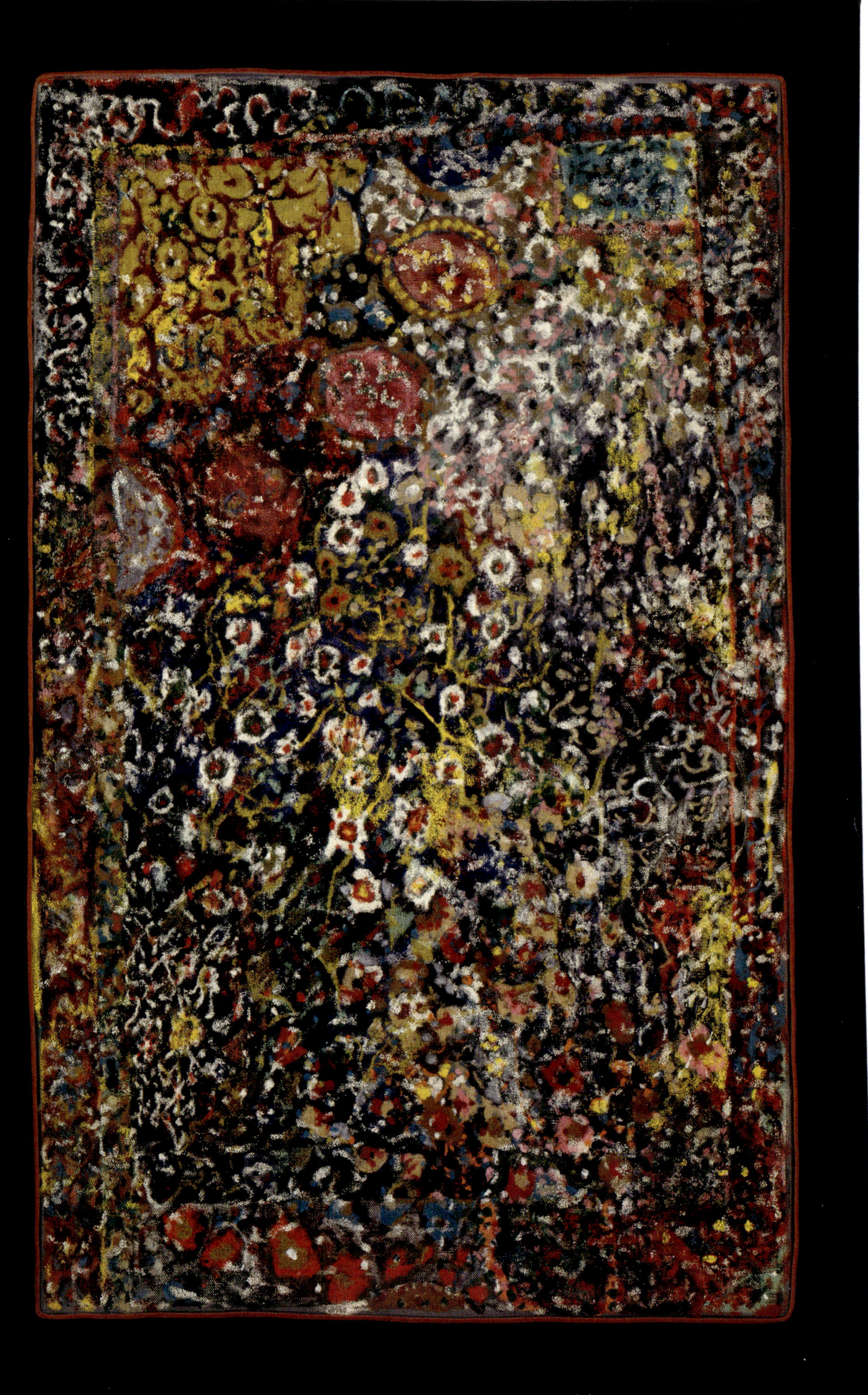

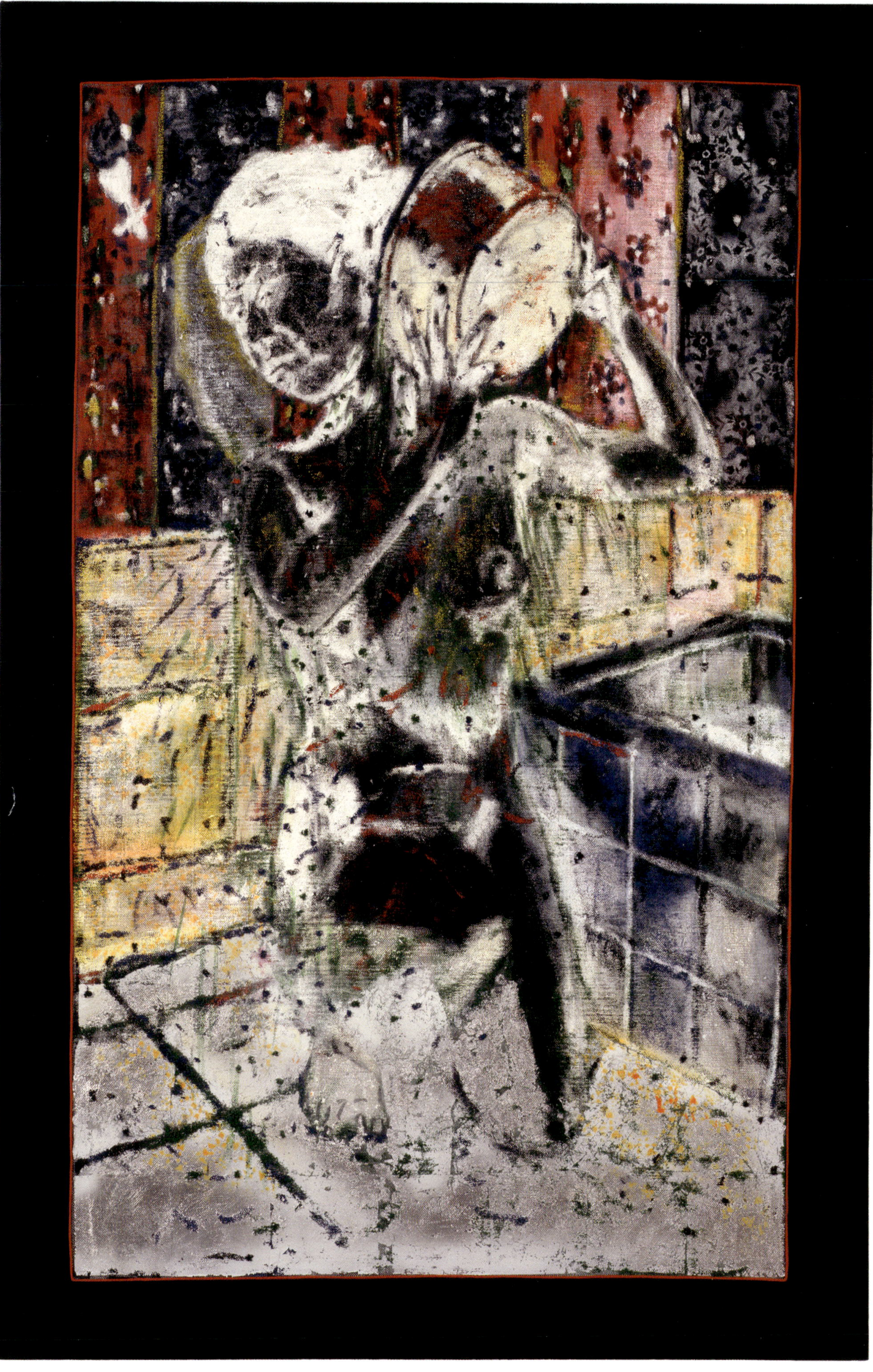

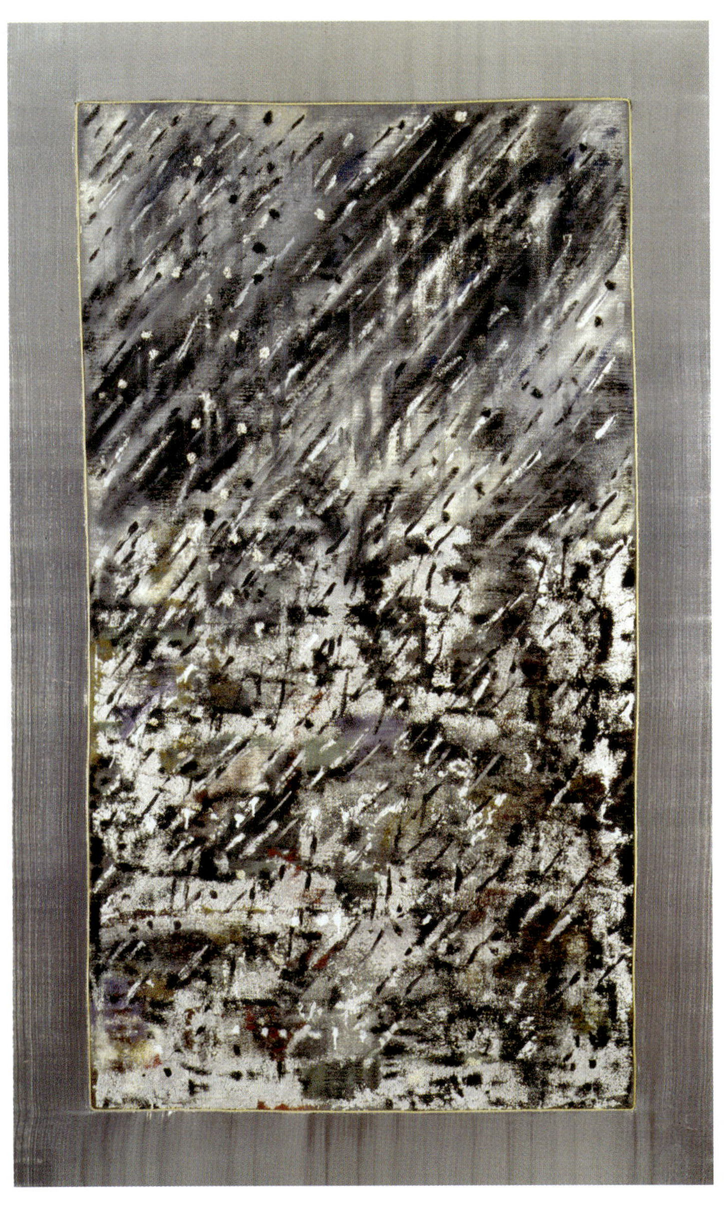

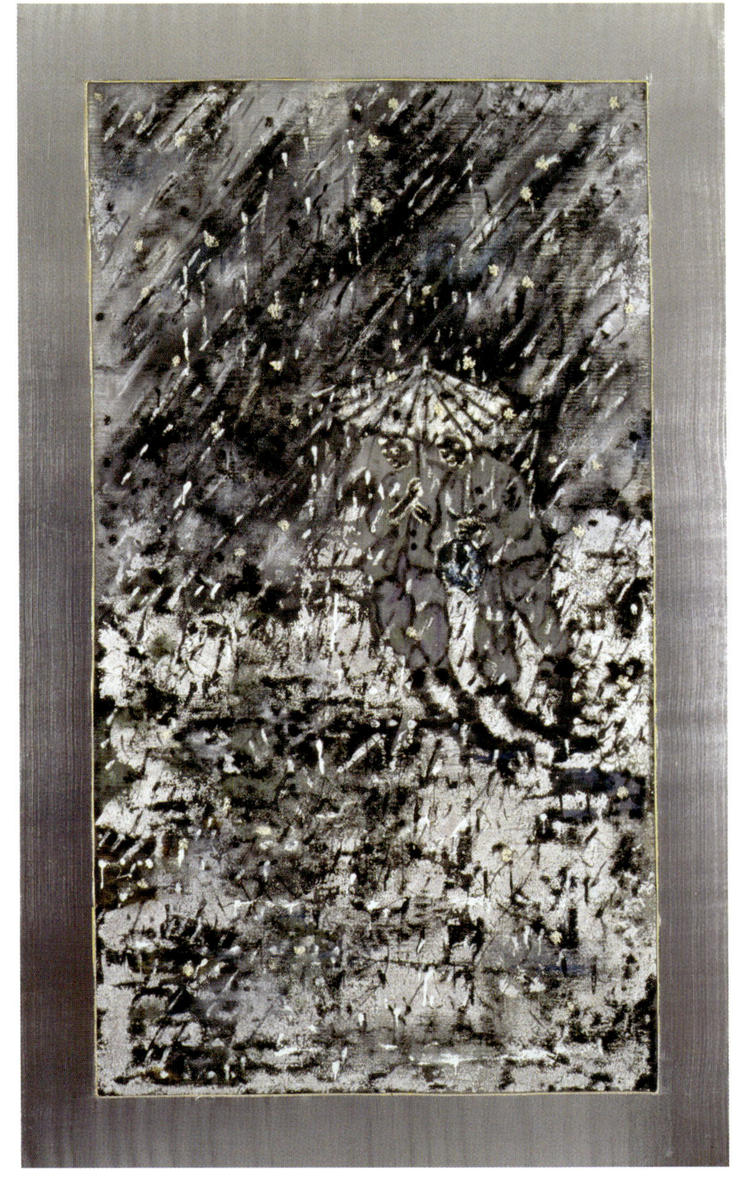

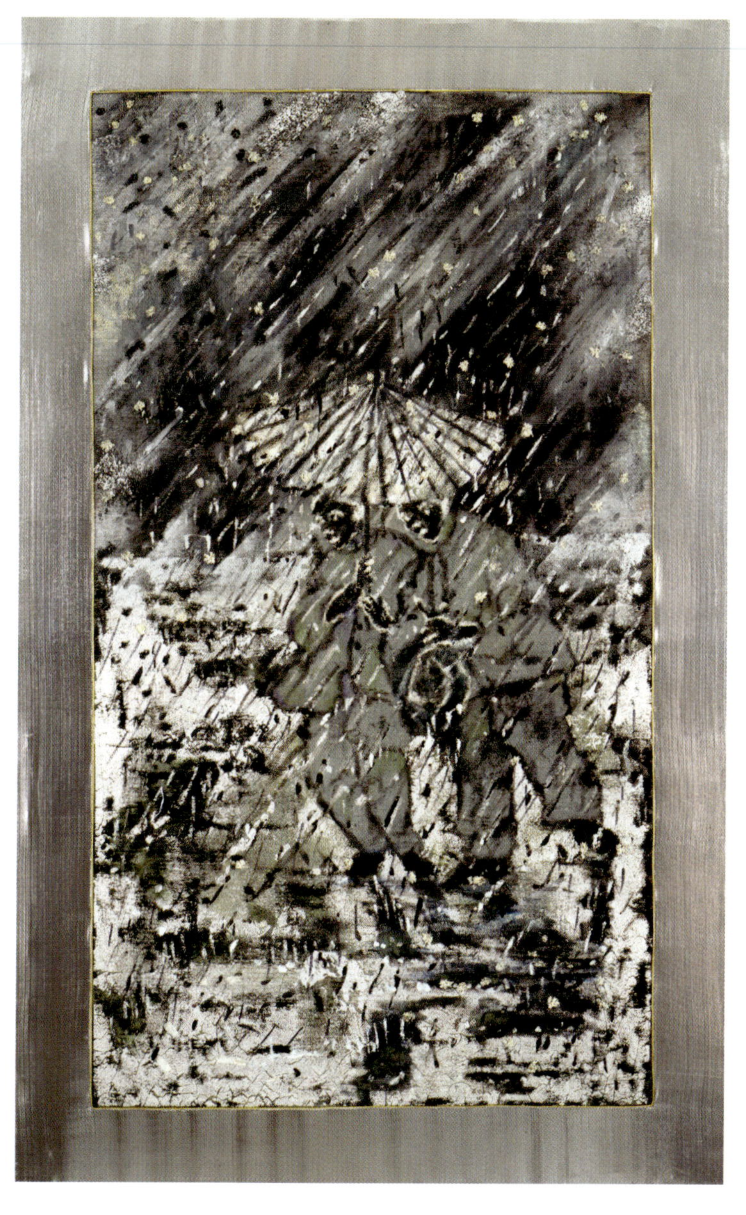

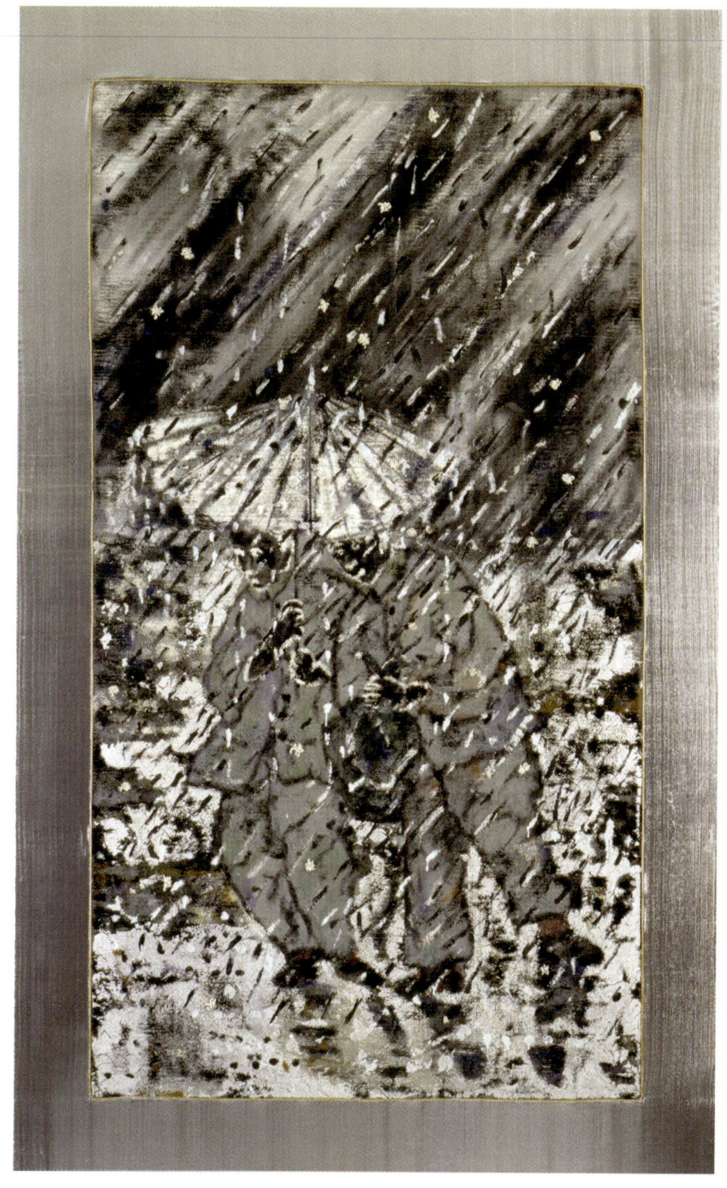

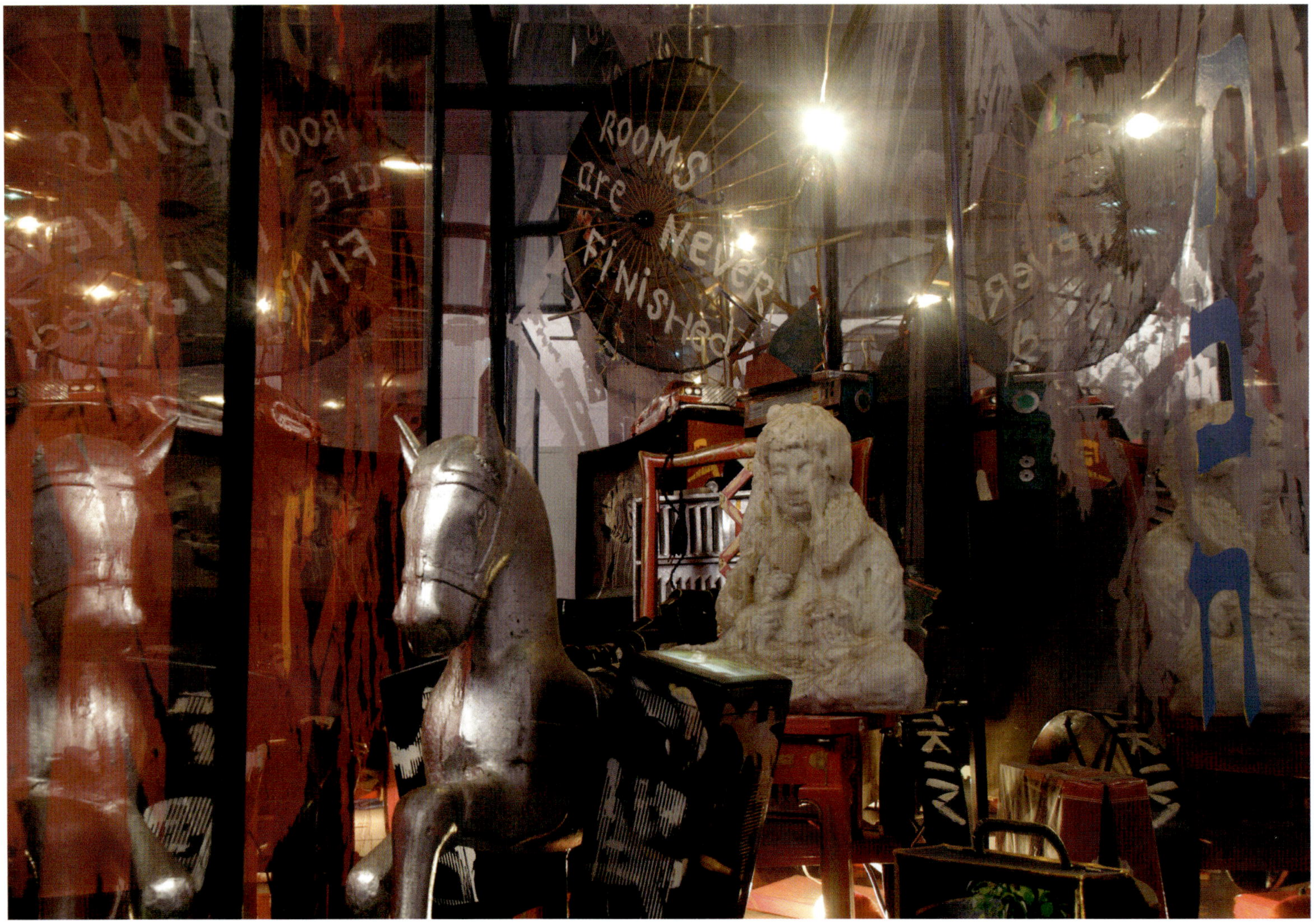

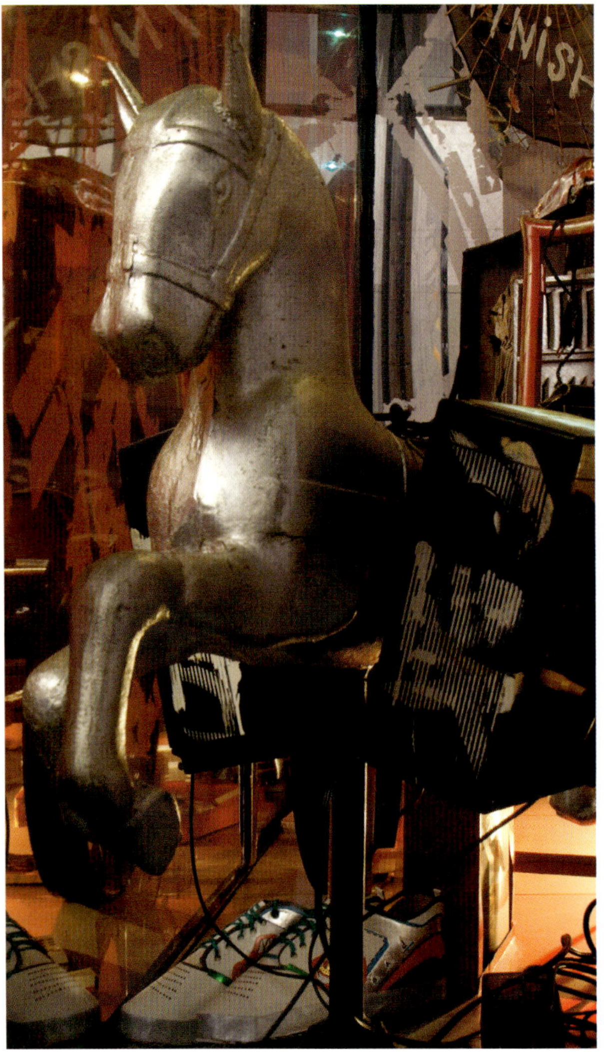

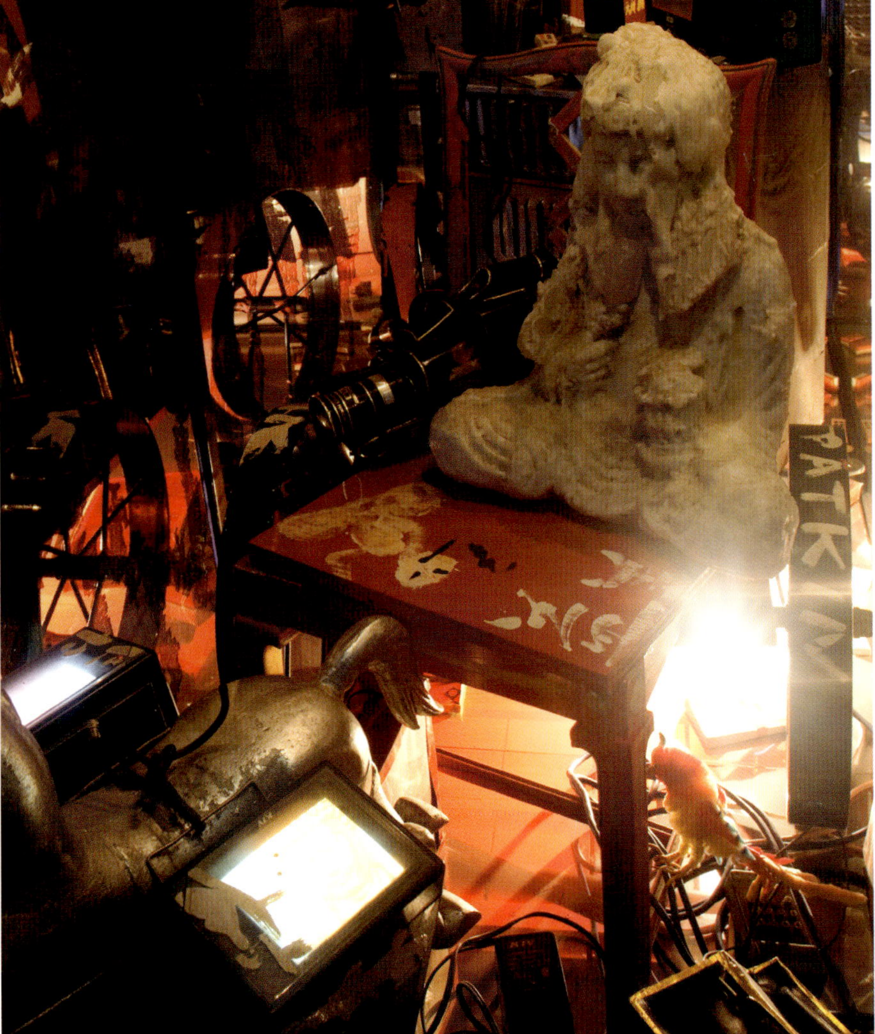

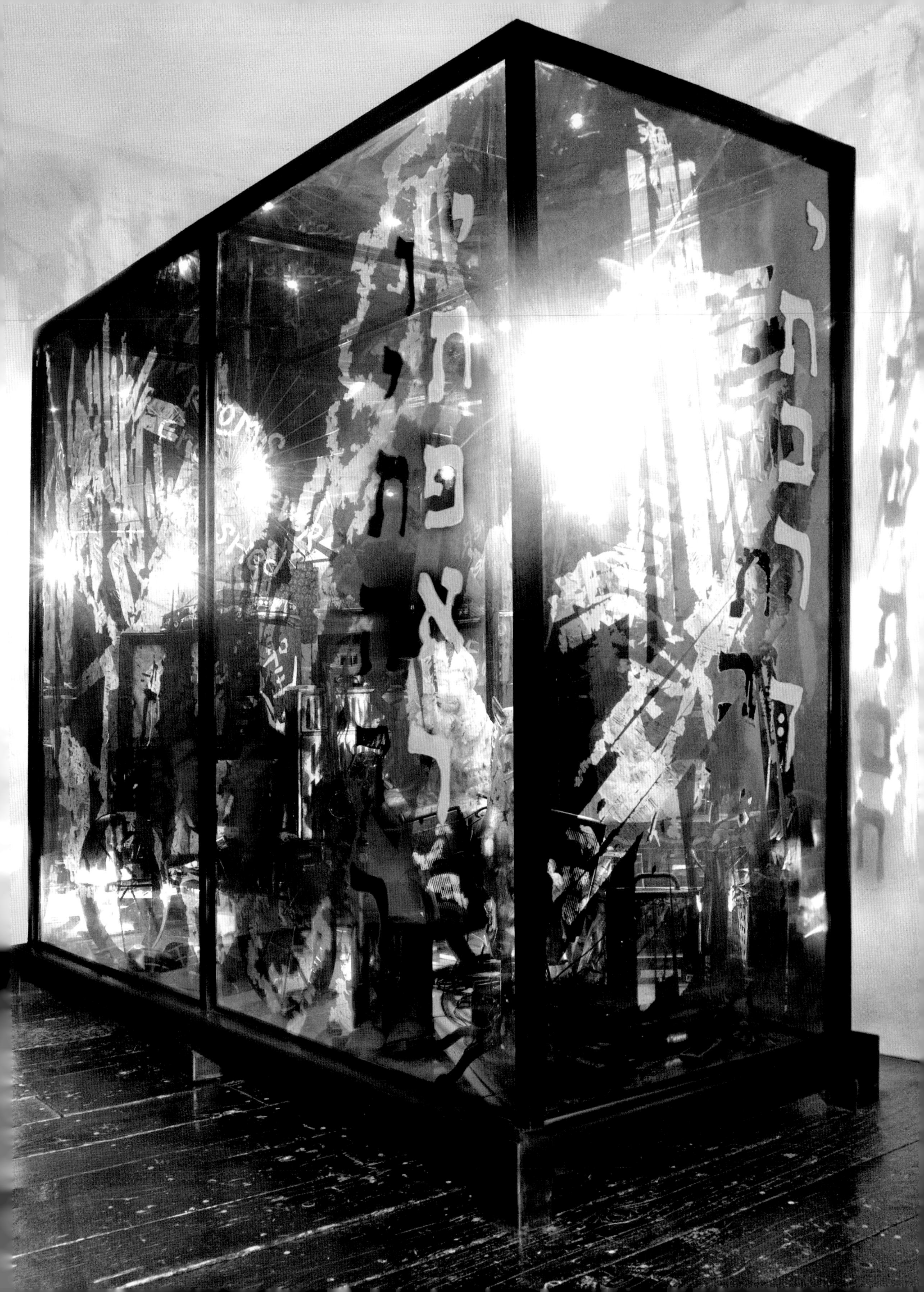

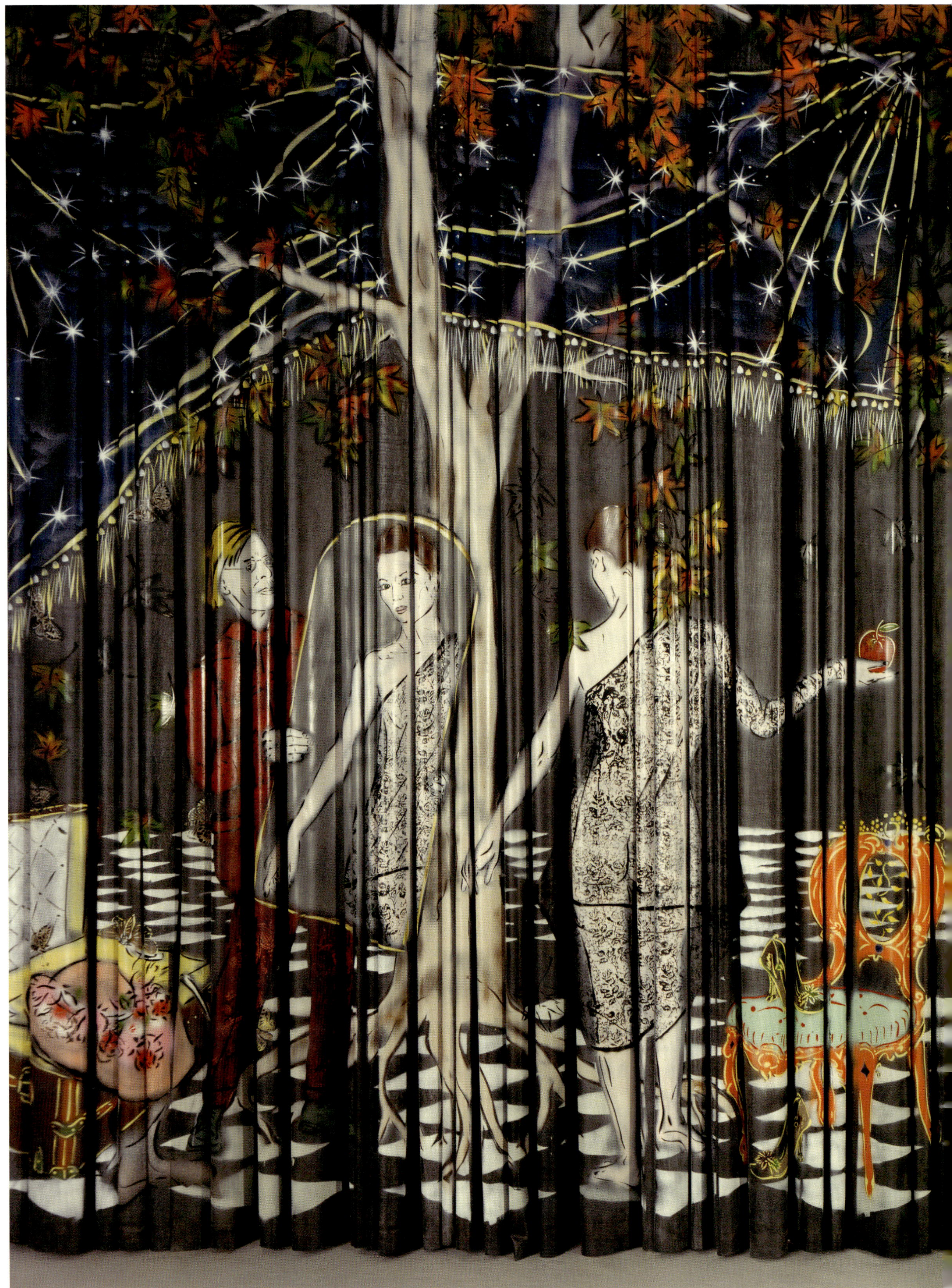

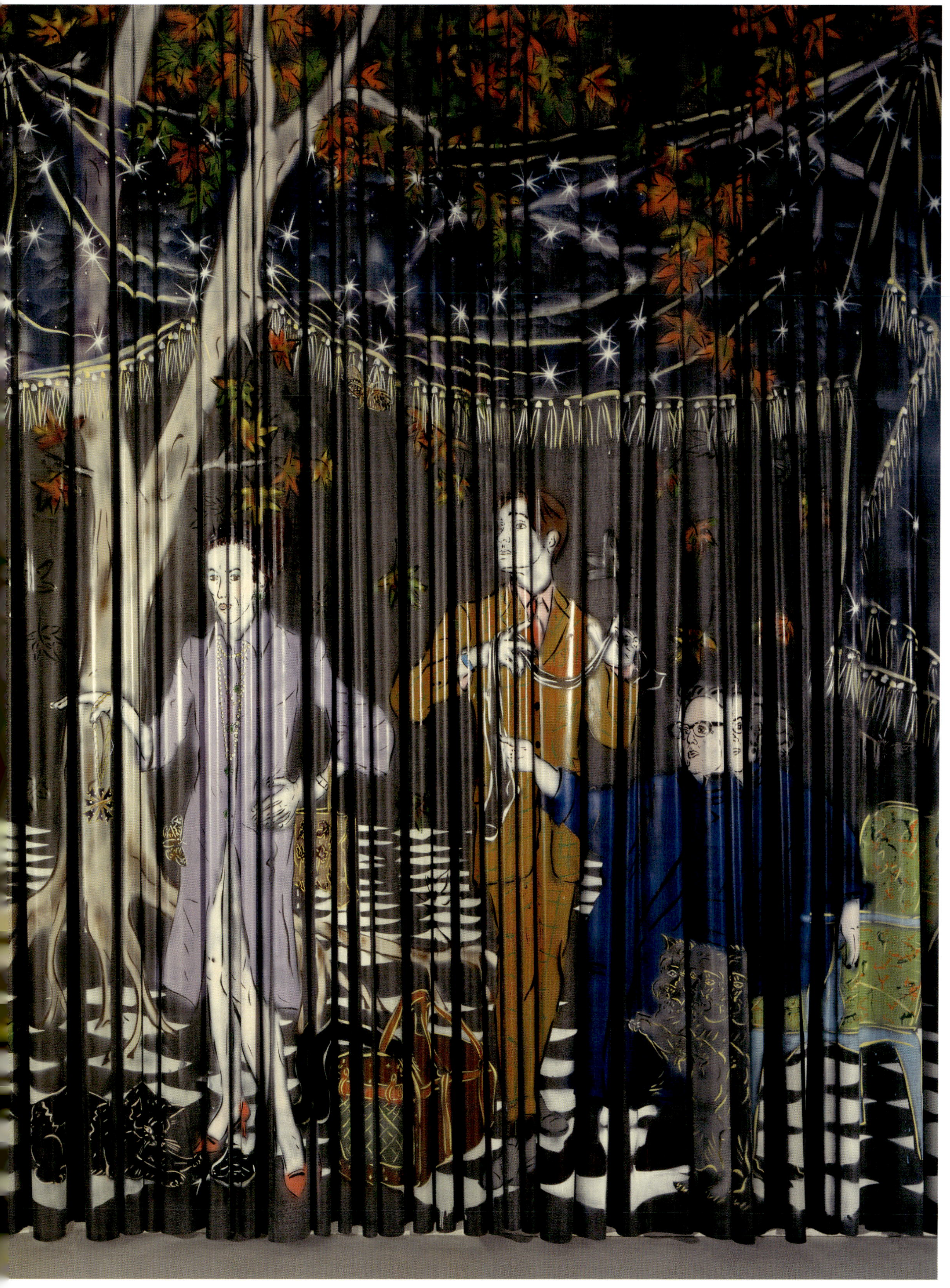

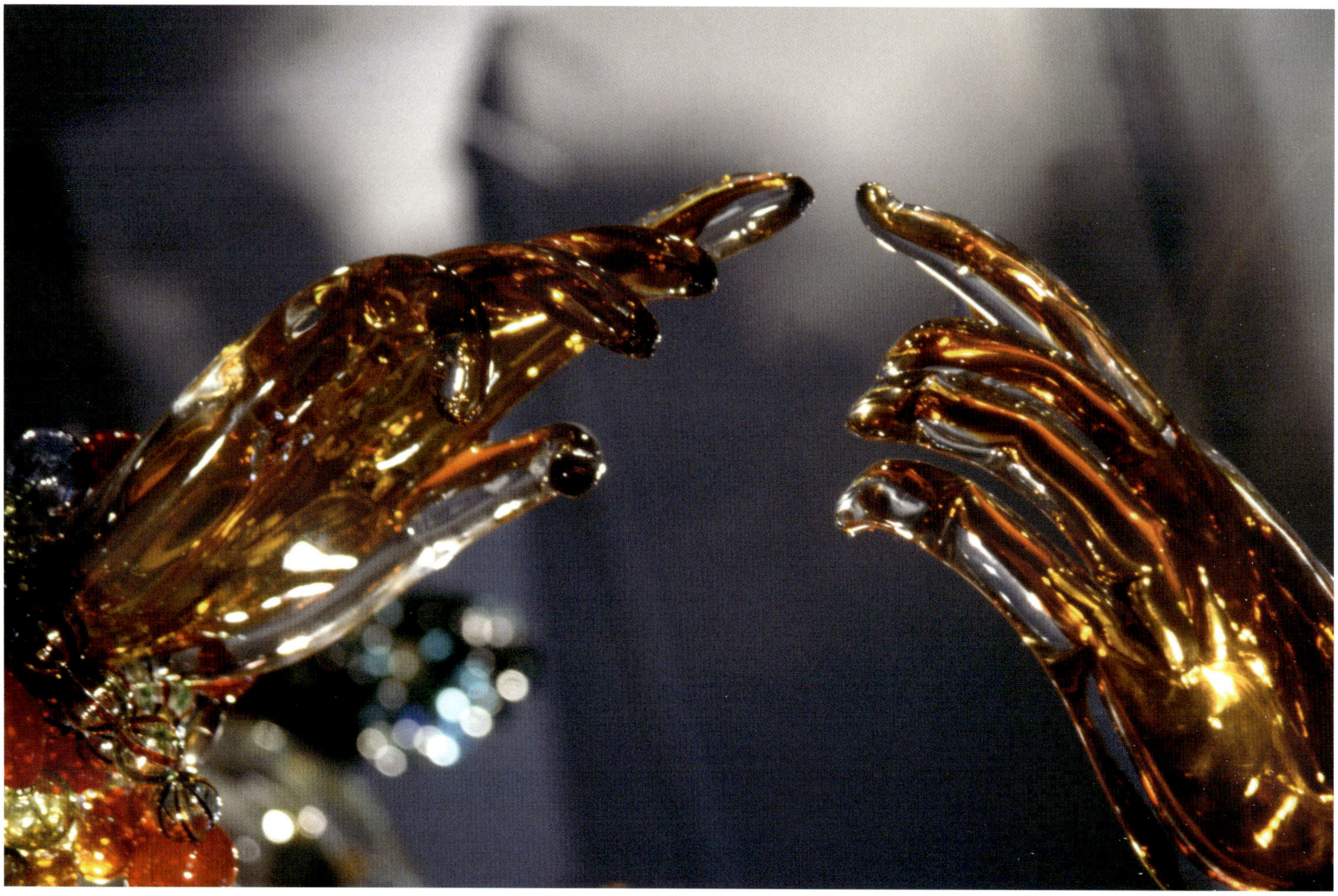

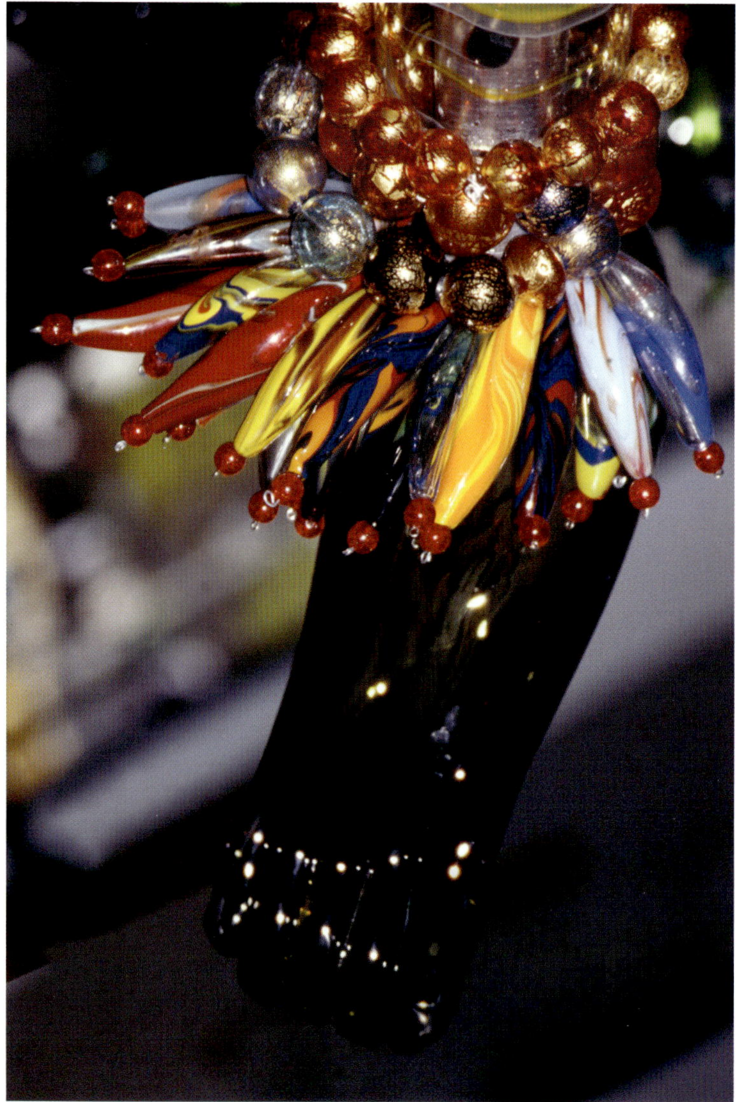

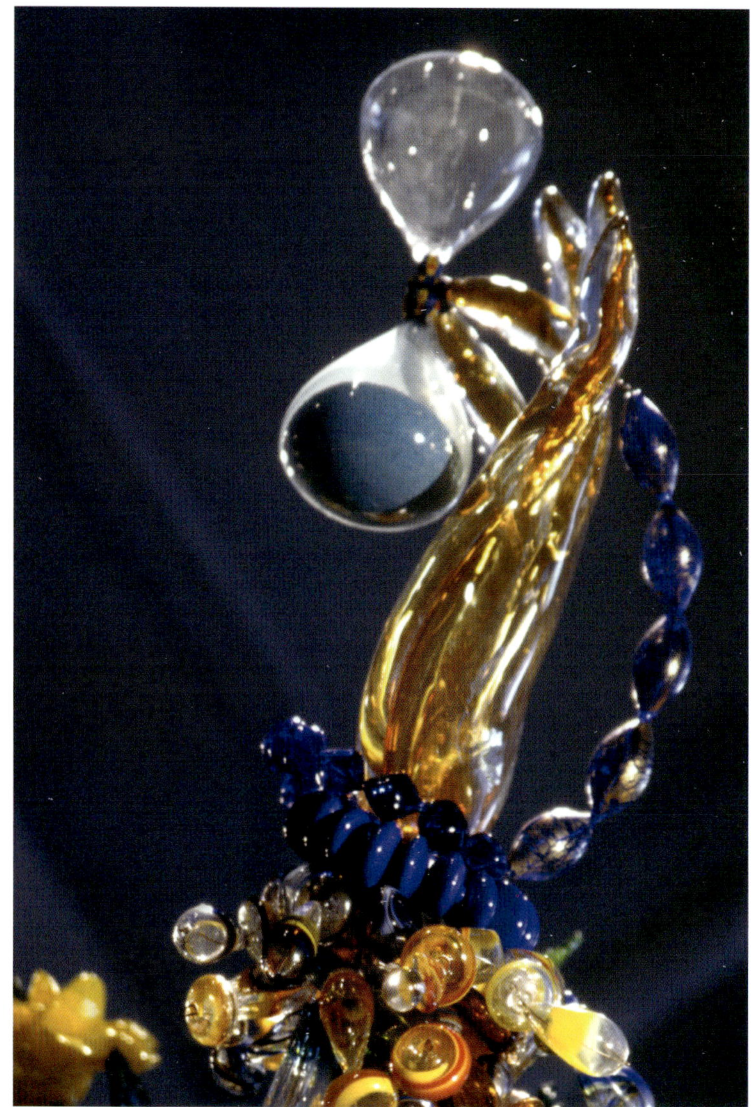

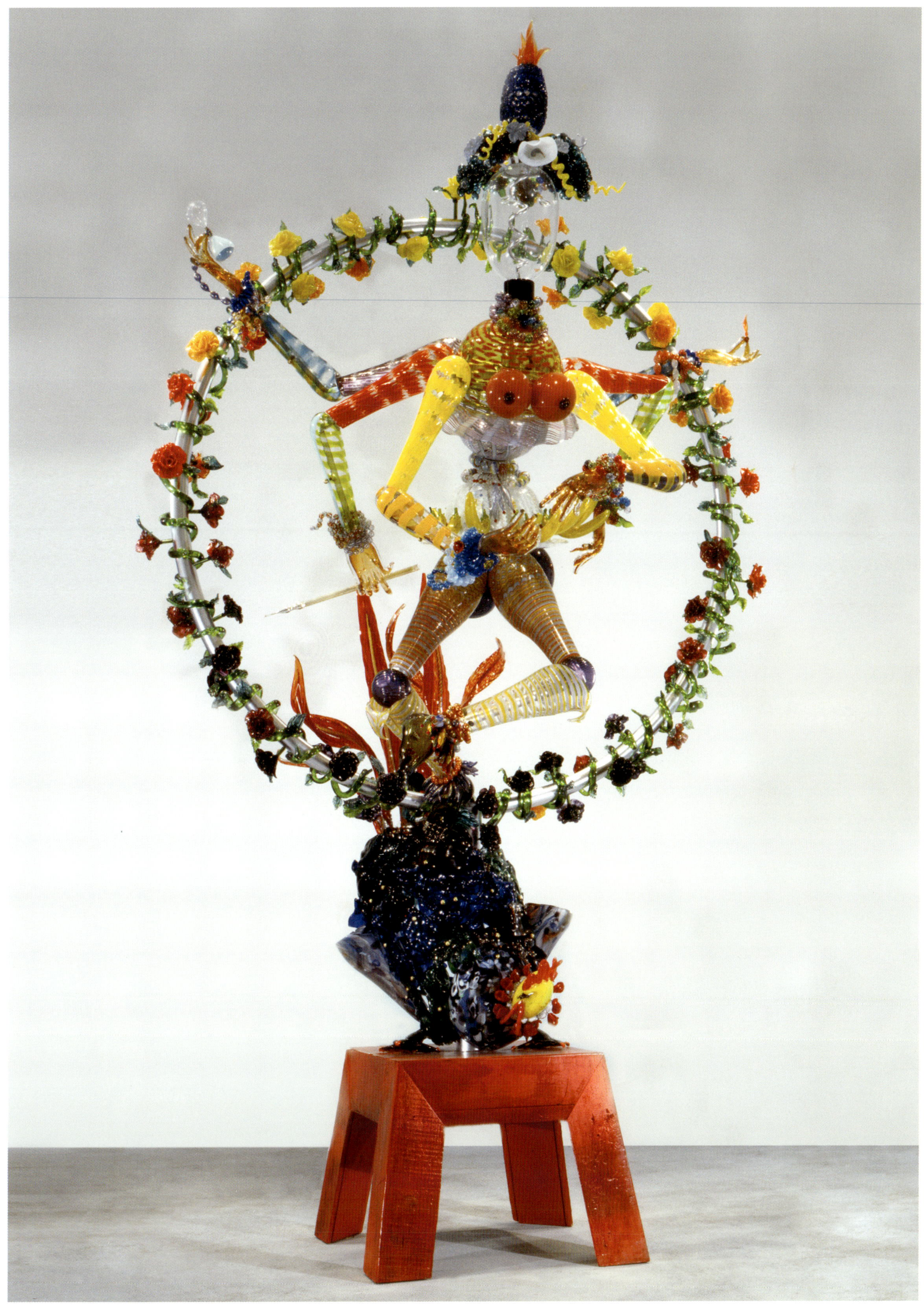

Black Shadows White Ghosts

God at Breakfast, Fallen Angels Over Toast

SPRING 1986, NEW YORK CITY

HERBERT MUSCHAMP: One of the surprise entertainments of *The Black Paintings* (1985–86; pages 212–17) you showed last spring (at the Limbo Gallery, New York City) was to watch the reaction of the viewer. It was as though you took them by the hand over the threshold into the idea of narrative in contemporary art—it was done on such a big scale and with such an explicit literary connection to Genet's play that they couldn't miss it, but once they were inside there seemed to be a language problem. It was like watching a group of travelers entering a foreign country and trying to order a meal. There was food all over the place, but no Berlitz handbook. The waiters didn't understand the useful formalist words and phrases. So I thought we could begin our conversation by describing some of the philosophical features of Narrative Country.

IZHAR PATKIN: Well, the terrain is the voided center left by the Enlightenment's dismissal of God, and the reason for the language problem is that the idea of narrative has been so long suppressed, sacrificed, to the cult of form because of its notorious ties to that exiled central authority. The idea was to establish the autonomy of art by liberating the artist from the job of illustrator to the Master Storyteller. The point of using narrative today, in turn, is to walk off the job of illustrating the Master Story of Modern Art. Or maybe just to look for a better job, something a bit more rewarding than moving the shapes around.

HM: To recognize, in other words, that formalism's pretense of objective truth was itself a romantic narrative, which began as a bill of rights and ended up as a gag order.

IP: Calling my show "The Black Paintings" was polemical in that sense, because even formalists like Reinhardt and Stella used black metaphorically, to tell a story of which they were acutely conscious about Modernism as a tale of our collective progress. My intention in the paintings was to fluff up the narrative structure of the form-making process so that you couldn't miss it.

HM: Some viewers, though, were concerned that they might be missing something in the work because they weren't familiar with Genet's text and couldn't "read" it from your work. But the point you seemed to be making is that with narrative painting you don't have to know "the story," but you might want to know the story.

IP: People are right to be suspicious about narrative, because the old form of narrative said that you have to know a Bible. But formalism became a Bible, too. The new form of narrative is about making room for stories that you do not know. It is not a literary process. The work is not illustrating the narrative; it is generated by it in a visual medium. We had our Modern grid, it was generated by one story, and we made it very well. Now let's look at some others.

HM: We had our church, we had our steeple, now let's open all the doors and see all the people. Narrative is just a tool for ordering experience: I went out, I traveled, I met a man, I heard a story, here it is. Years before "appropriation" became a standard visual tactic, Joanne Kyger wrote something great: "Even if I only repeat what others say, it becomes mine." It may be dumb or smart, true or not, but it's my version.

IP: Narrative is about allowing yourself to be a narrator, about empowering your internal authority to write its own script. You don't have to be God to be a narrator; you're allowed to do it because you woke up that morning, had coffee, made some phone calls, heard some great gossip. You don't have to run a marathon to get to the center of things before you've got your story.

HM: So behind your curtains lurks a different model of self.

IP: It's not the self as a candidate for the vacant center. It's me; it's not, "Please, Lord, let it be me." It's the self as a messy drawer or container. It is enough that the information, the notes, the memories, projects, emotions are all in it. They don't have to be organized in any hierarchy.

HM: Unless you're in a hierarchical mood that morning.

IP: Yes, the center as a mood; god at breakfast, fallen angels over toast at lunch.

HM: What was impressive about *The Black Paintings* was not your use of narrative, but your openness in doing so, your refusal to be enigmatic about it. The story of "the enigma" seems to be the story of being afraid about the professional consequences if you break the gag order.

IP: Even in figurative and abstract painting today, there is a denial of narrative and a celebration of ennui; this is an acceptable form of "passing" as form. Everyone would be scared to death if Napoleon really showed up, but they also get alarmed when someone refuses to put on their Napoleon costume, or puts the hat on backward with the price tag dangling. I'm more interested in breathing than heroics. *Funnels and Trumpets: Portrait of the Self as a Breather* (1986; page 32). Take it in, dump it out. Narrative comes into play when you discover that the air around you doesn't exist in the same way without you, but you don't own it. And it doesn't own you; ripping up the script if the part doesn't suit you is an important function of narrative. I want to shred the script that identified art exclusively with heroic struggle.

HM: That's a traditional function of the comic script. Aristotle's theory was that the origins of tragedy and comedy lay in the two parts of the ritual of succession in the ancient Greek fertility cult. Tragedy arose from the *agon* in which the young pretender challenged the old ruler and fights him to the death. Comedy arose from the *kosmos*, the wedding procession and celebration. In the ritual of Modern Art, young pretenders are called upon to challenge and defeat the rule of stale convention in order to ensure the fertility of the culture. Your work seems to be about inaugurating the second part of the cycle, about the use of comedy as "the ultimate civilizer," as (George) Meredith called it.

IP: For me, this cycle started with the *Meta Bride* work (1982–83; pages 224–25) I showed at Holly Solomon a few years ago. It was about a black bride torn apart by a Snow White complex. The importance of comedy to me is that it allows more stories to enter into our homogeneous experience, and it infuriates a lot of people that it does this. It is not just black and white fighting till the death; the audience has a story to tell, too.

HM: Rather than strive for the idea of essence, your work seems to go for the doorway, the threshold where the dualisms collapse.

IP: One of the points of black paintings is that you cannot separate color from a metaphoric use, but you can transform the metaphor. People aren't black and white; they are brown or pinkish maybe. Every painter knows that there is no pure black or pure white; try to find the polarities with blue-black, green-black, red-black. Dualisms were invented for the upper hand's gain of power. My objective was not a reversal, not to put black where white is usually put, but to liberate the metaphor from the stereotype. Black isn't hell, bad luck, the eclipse, evil, darkness, the abyss. In Genet's play the blacks try to live up or down to these stereotypes, and they fail. But in my work they don't even have to fail, and they don't have to succeed either. They are playing a game that I invented.

HM: I thought the power of the show lay not in the ceasefire of the battle between black and white, but in the collapse of the dualism between self and environment. This is something that probably can't be understood through photographs of the work; it depended on the way the work surrounded the viewer, the way the viewer entered into the room through the work itself, changing it on their entrance; on the scale of the figures, the fact that the figures were at once flattened into the two dimensions of a picture plane and also, because of the curtain folds, protruded into the spectator's space.

IP: The most common interpretation of Genet's play, and of his instruction that the play be performed by black actors before a white audience, concerns the idea of the Other. But I wanted to suggest that the "other" can be experienced on a more fundamental level than alienation or cultural exoticism; that the entire environment we move through, everything from the skin outward, is "the other." The world is "other" even when it's our own world, even when the environment is nothing but a screen for our own projections. You can flatten it, give it more dimension, get scared by it, turn it into wallpaper, flirt with it, feel sorry for it, just as any figure in the environment can do all these things to you.

Herbert Muschamp, 1986

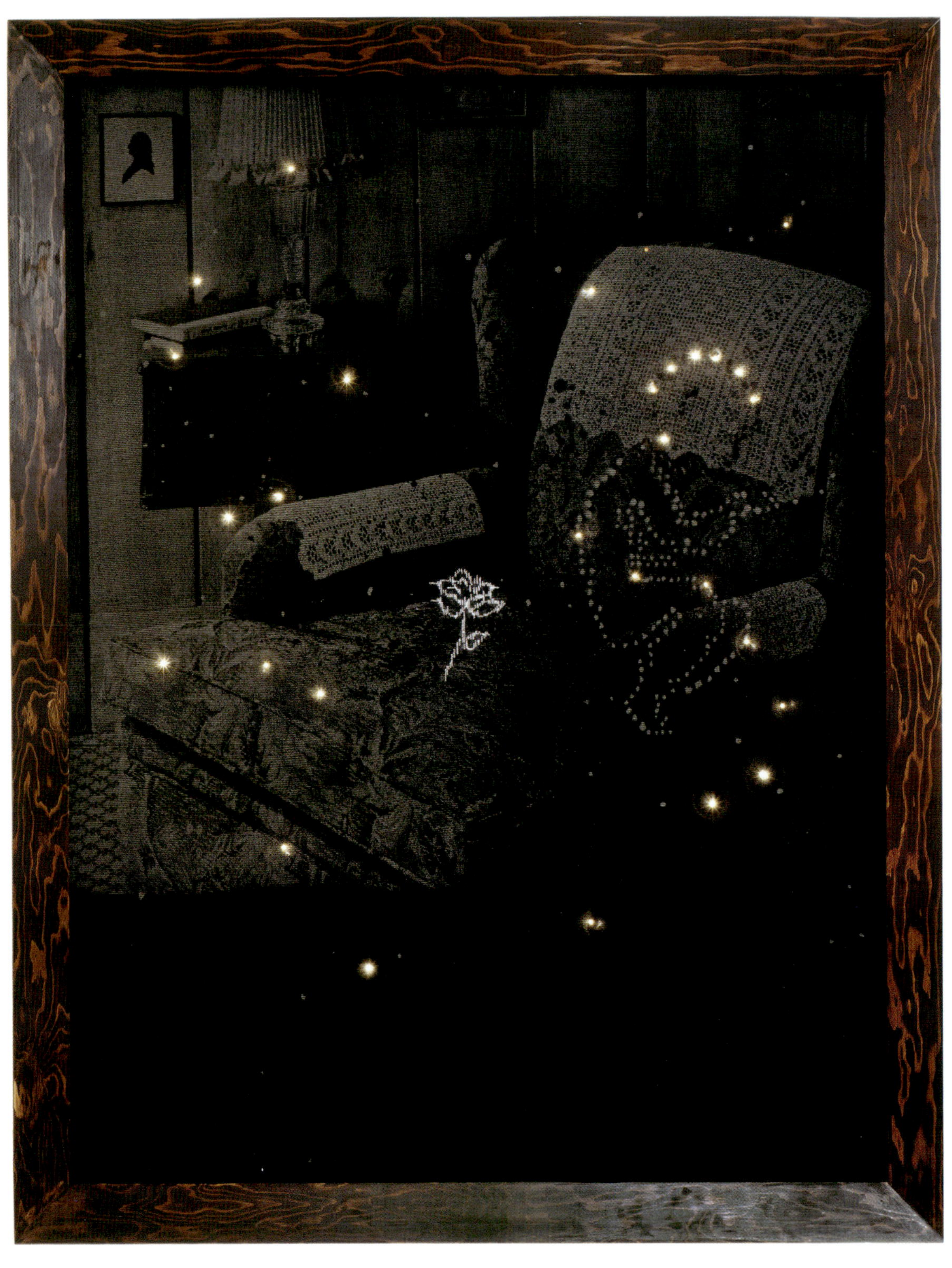

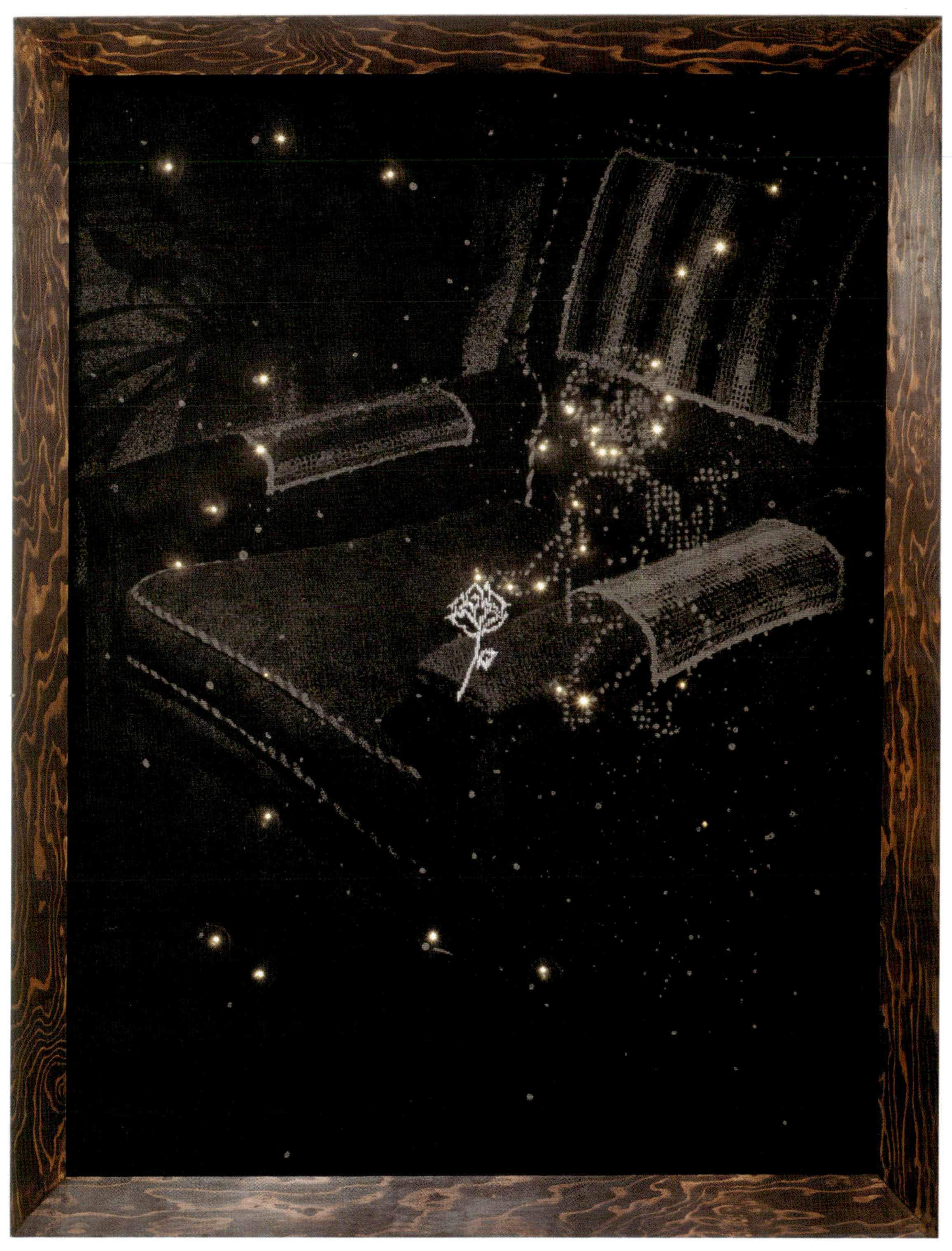

Great Curtains I Have Known

When I was a child, my parents had a summerhouse at the shore with big picture windows and an unobstructed view of the Atlantic, but to me the most luxurious thing about the house were the curtains in my parents' bedroom. They were heavy, lined, and patterned with pictures of seashells against a dark green background. You pulled a cord to open them. The curtains covered a bay window about seven feet wide. There was a ledge about two feet off the ground with enough headroom for a small boy to stand on it, and there, on rainy days, I put on stage shows for an audience that consisted of my older brother and the maid. The performances were mostly variations on me standing there with a grin, though later I added one or two tricks with cards and spoons, but all of this was beside the point. The real trick was pulling the cord. The point was the magic of curtains.

That magic enchanted me for years. I used to go every Wednesday to hear the local orchestra play in a very lovely hall, but one time I went there for an evening performance of the opera and saw, for the first time, the stage hung with a sumptuous gold curtain. It was as though the Cinderella I'd known for ages had suddenly dressed up for the ball. And there was a movie theater I used to frequent just because it had two sets of curtains that closed and opened before each show: one that pulled open horizontally and another that opened vertically in gathered folds.

And then, many years later, I had the opportunity to watch Izhar Patkin paint *The Black Paintings* (1985–86; pages 212–17), in a big, filthy, unheated room on Broome Street. I used to visit this studio almost daily while the work was in process. I rarely stayed very long, but the painting changed each day, and I didn't want to miss a thing. And the painting wasn't the only thing that changed. Graham Greene once said that the difference between writing a short story and writing a novel is that the person who has finished a novel is not the same person who started it. Half the spectacle, which drew me to Broome Street, was watching this change in someone. The extraordinary thing was that you could see this as a physical process, played out in hundreds of ordinary acts: punching a staple gun; climbing a ladder; scrambling over a floor that daily grew thicker with the accumulation of paint droplets, discarded stencils, props, and coffee cups.

Inevitably, the day arrived when the painting departed from the sketches, virtually architectural, that Patkin had unrolled on the floor of my living room months before, and from that point onward it was as though the artist's feet had left the ground and he became a creature of the air, jet-powered by the pressure of spray paint in his travels around a room whose walls had dissolved to reveal cities, highways, night skies, classical ruins, tribal battlefields, dance floors, fashion shows, the Museum of Modern Art. Anyone who hasn't discarded the word "inspiration" from their vocabulary will understand how a witness can feel like a participant under such circumstances.

Pauline Kael once wrote, "There is nothing like that moment when the lights go down and all our hopes are concentrated on the screen." I'd say there's nothing like that moment when the lights go up on a curtain, illuminating an architecture of occasion, the use of a form to create an event. It's the visual equivalent of the drumroll, the heightening of expectation. For the Modernists, as we know, the curtain was anathema. They resisted its connotations of artifice, its division of theater from life. Surely they were right to make the absent curtain a metaphor for releasing art's power into the everyday world. And just as surely, and for much the same reason, we should call the curtain back for a curtain call: not as a wall between a real world and a fake one, but as a portable screen to place anywhere you need to concentrate your hopes, to watch what you thought was ordinary turn into something special. As when a fellow inmate of Genet famously placed a set of dentures atop his head, where it glistened like a queen's tiara; as when Genet's prison jerk-off fantasies became literature, the thief himself Sartre's saint.

Herbert Muschamp, 1990

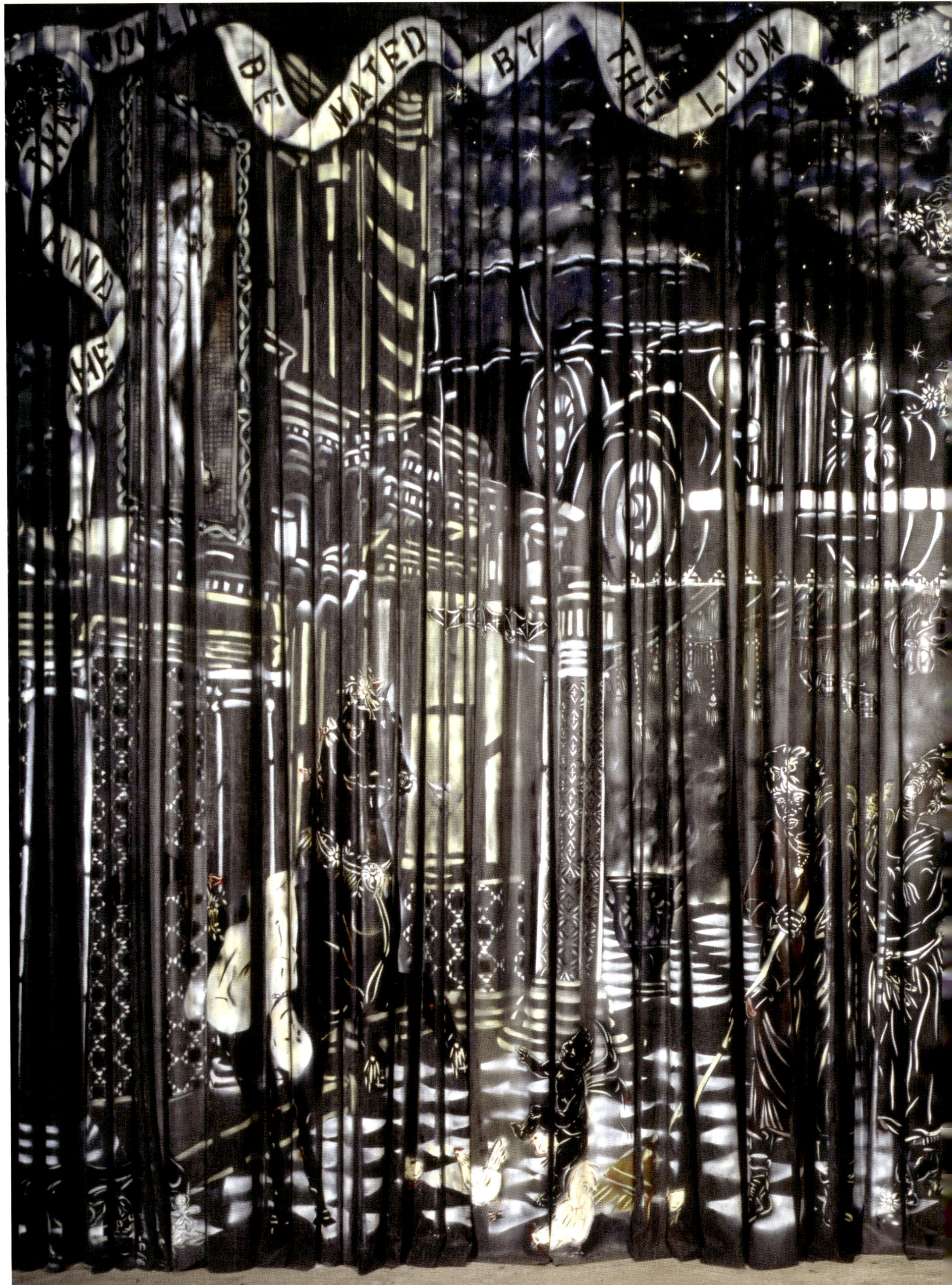
BE MATED BY THE LION

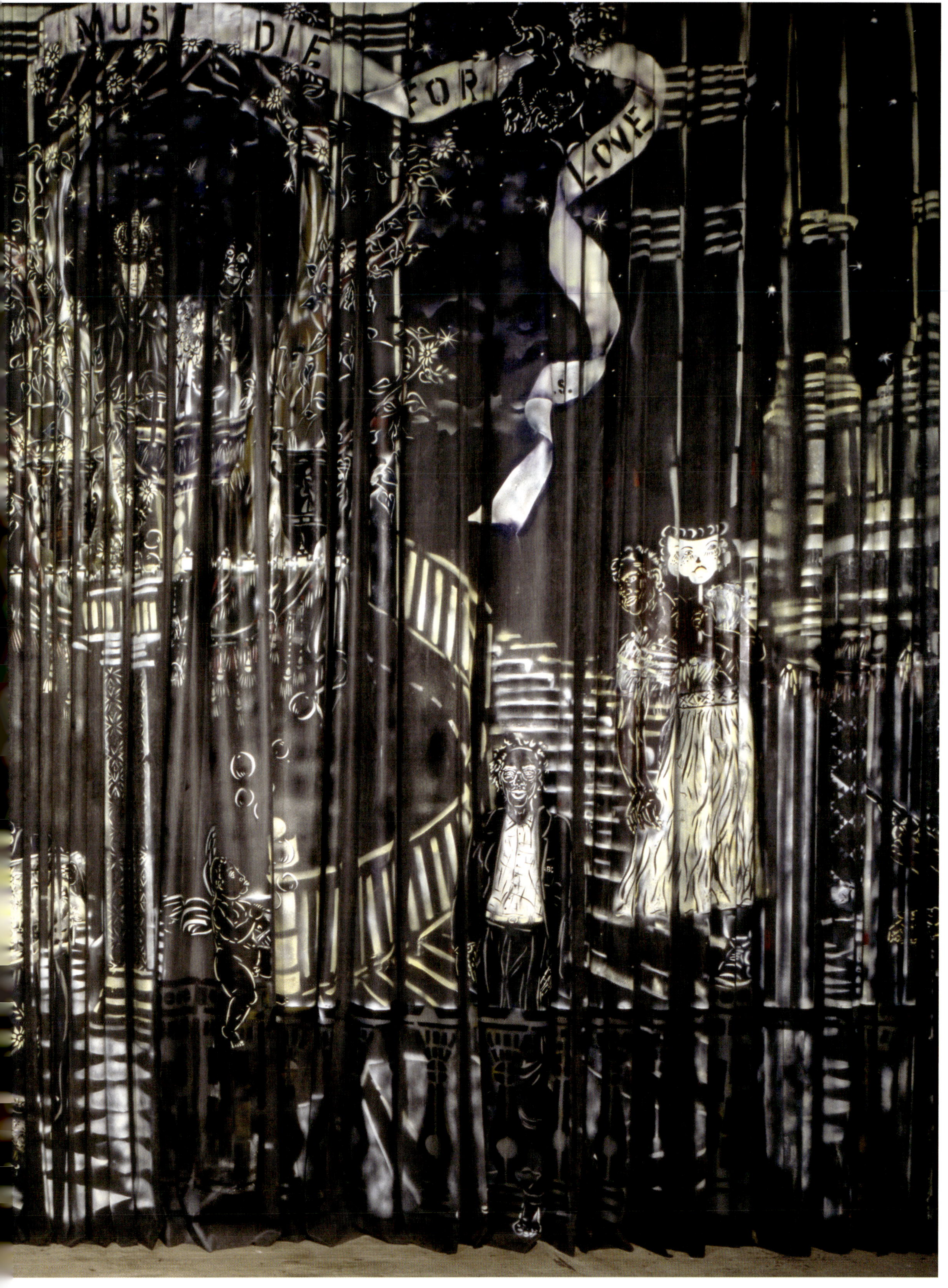
MUST DIE FOR LOVE

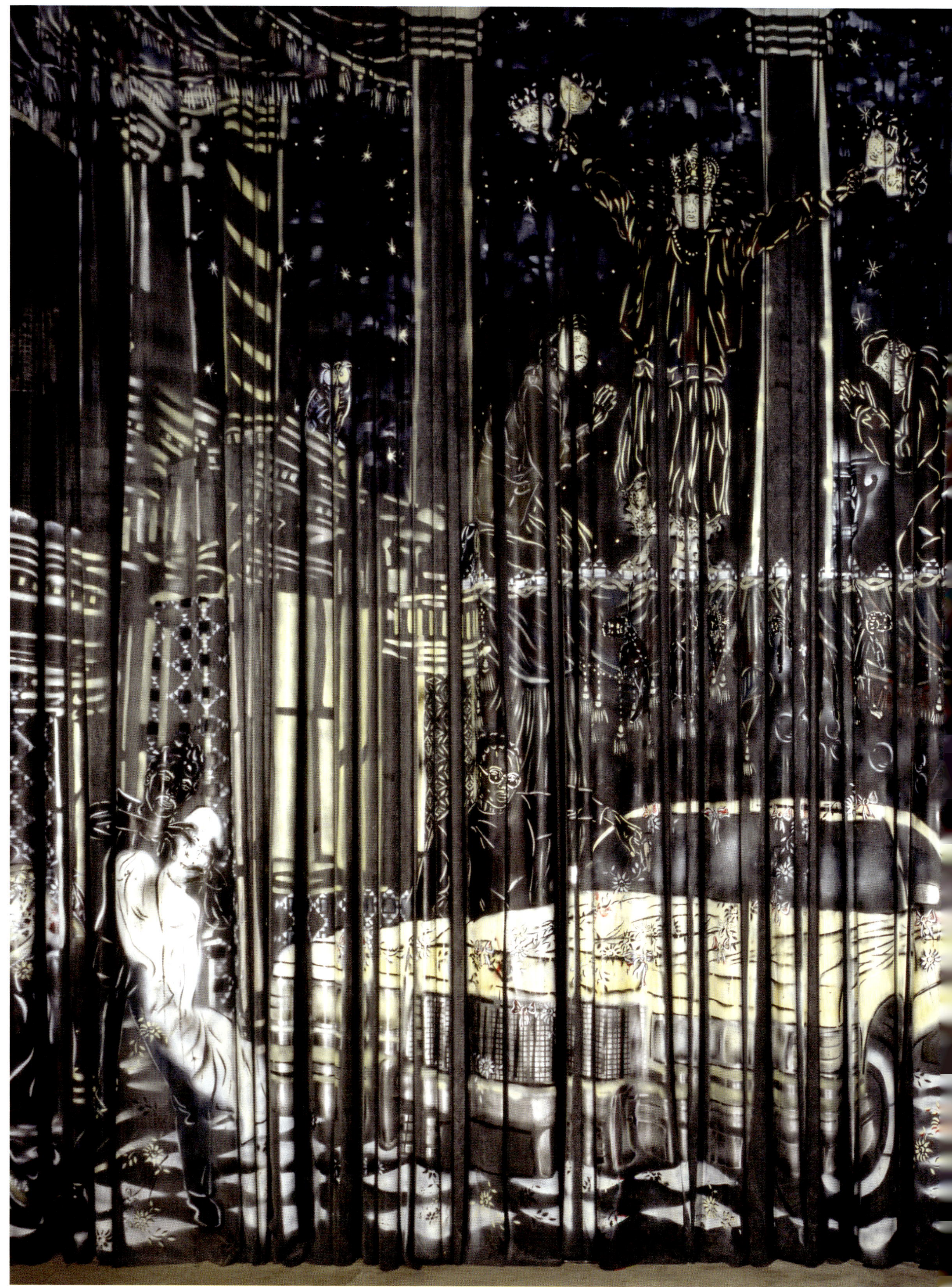

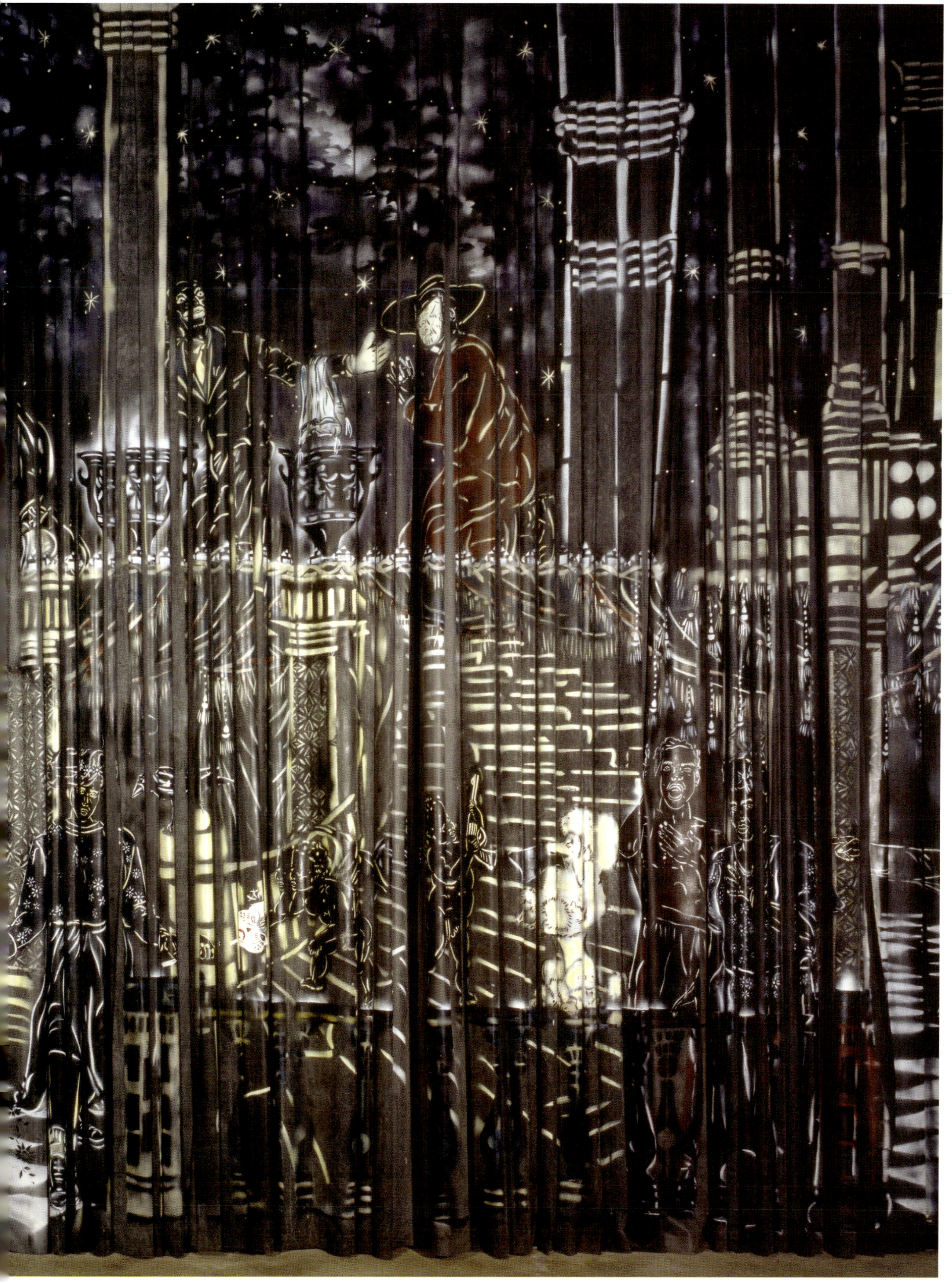

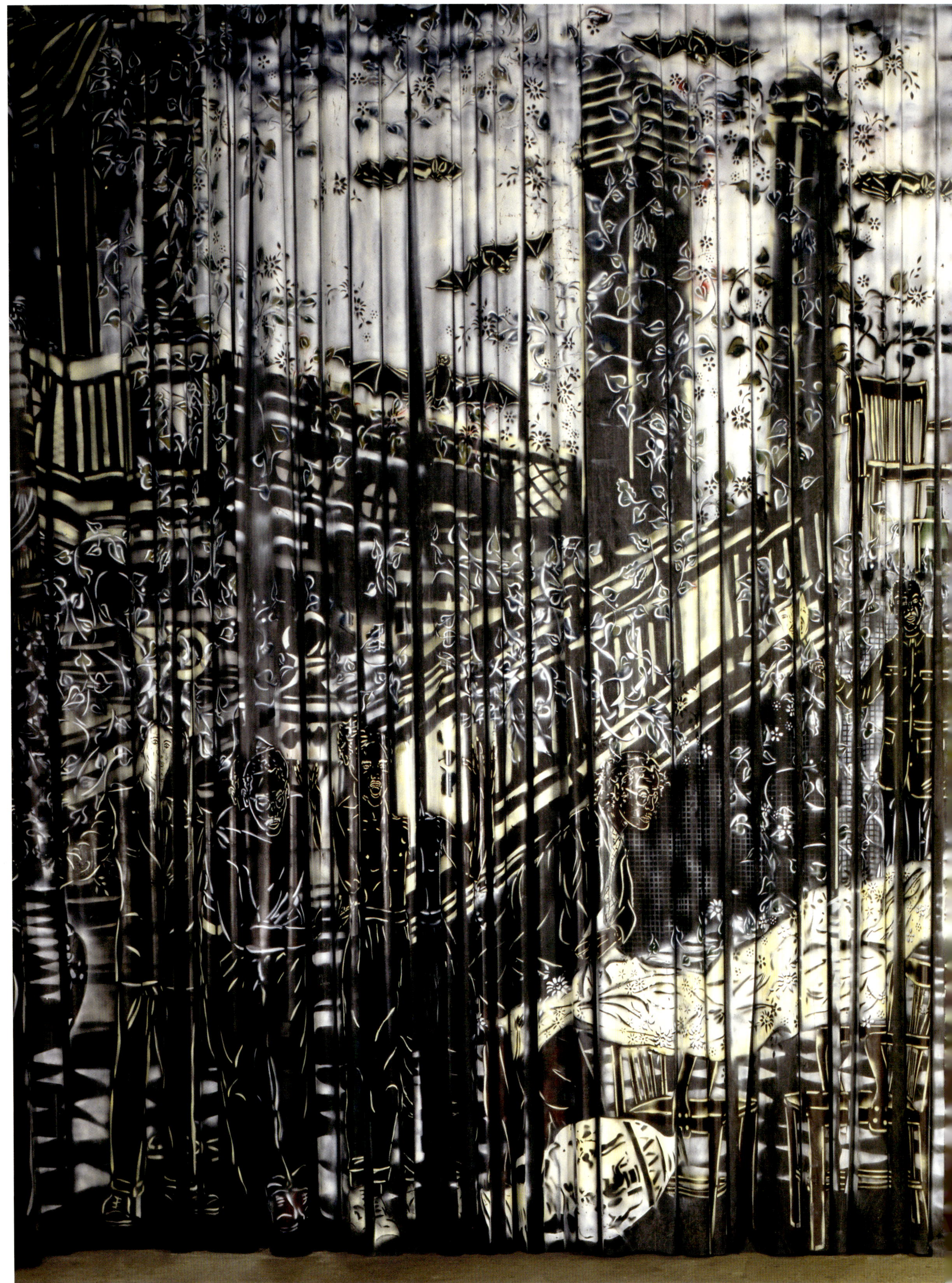

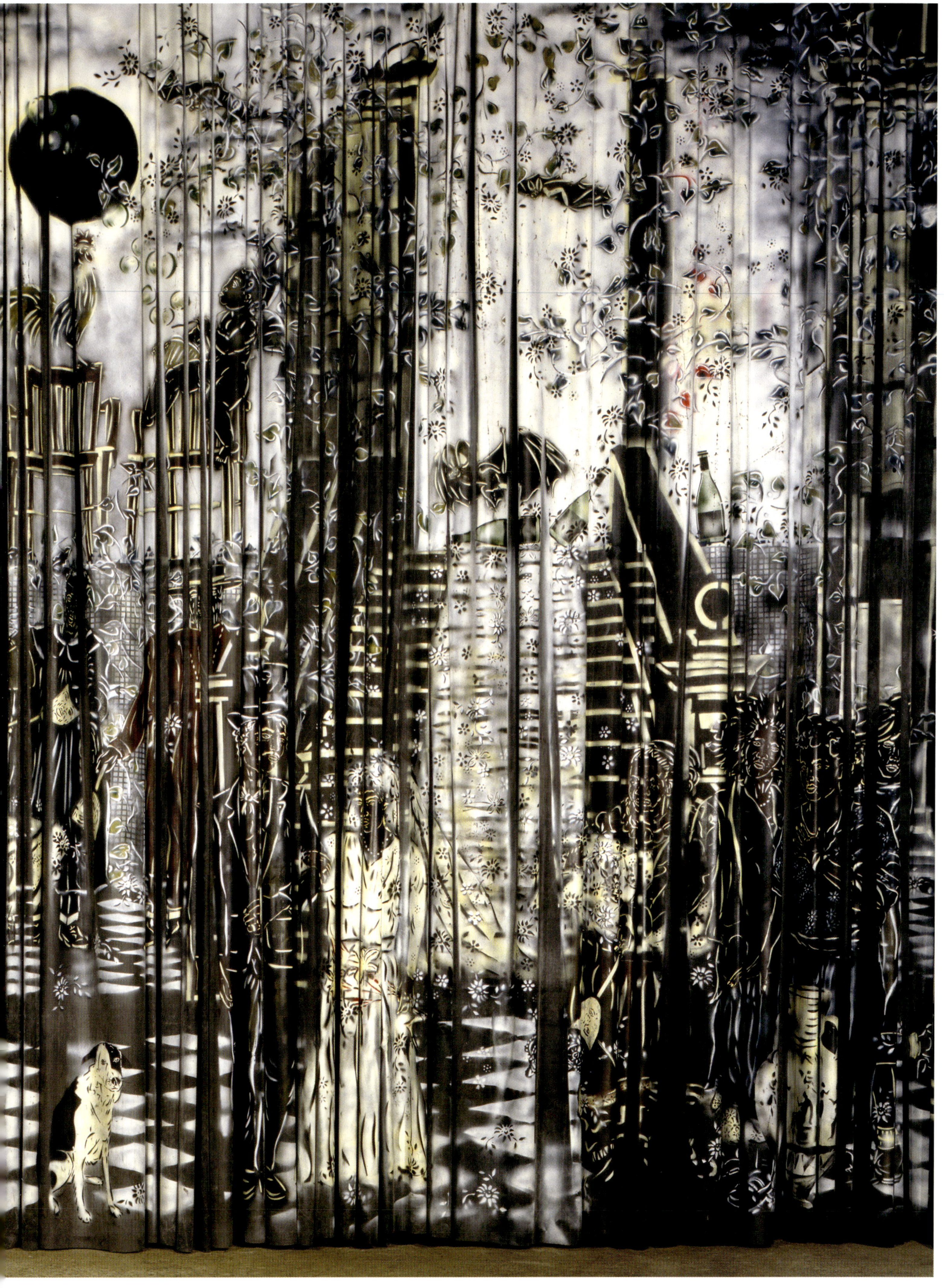

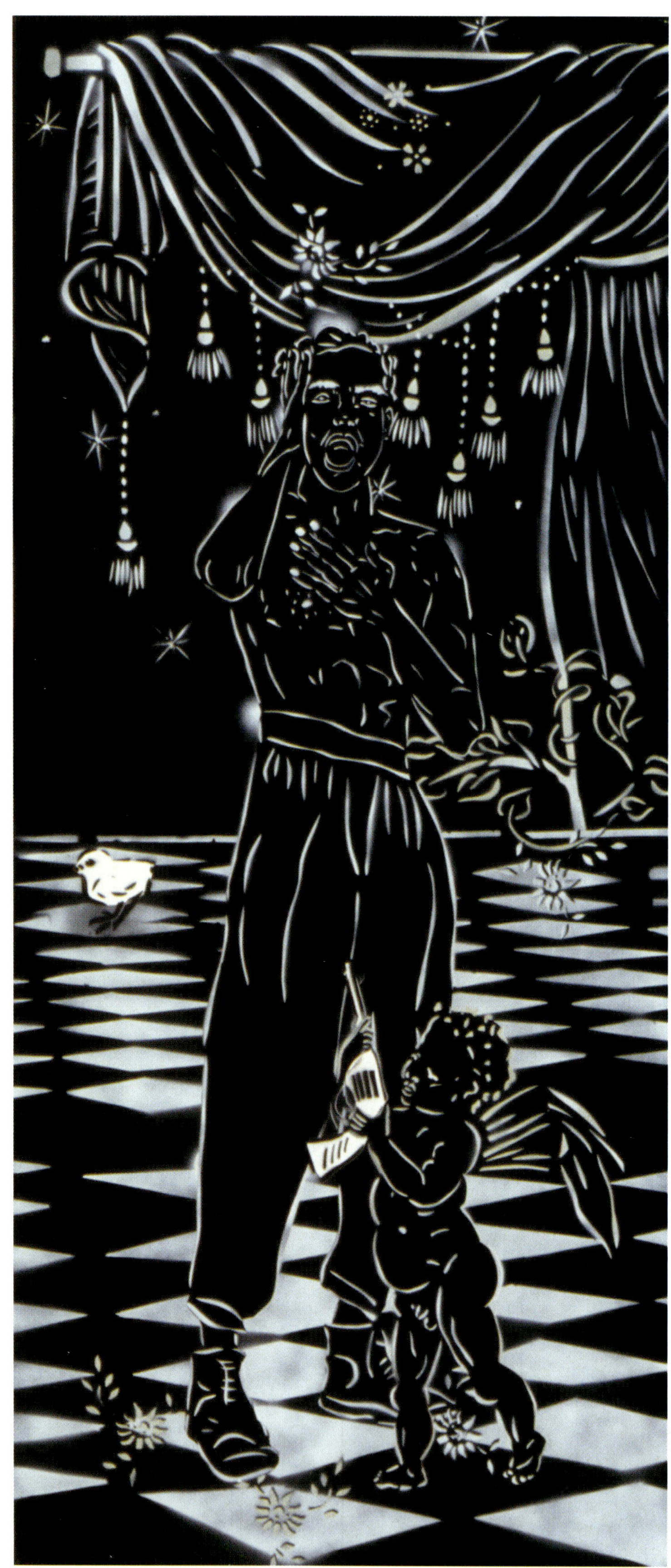

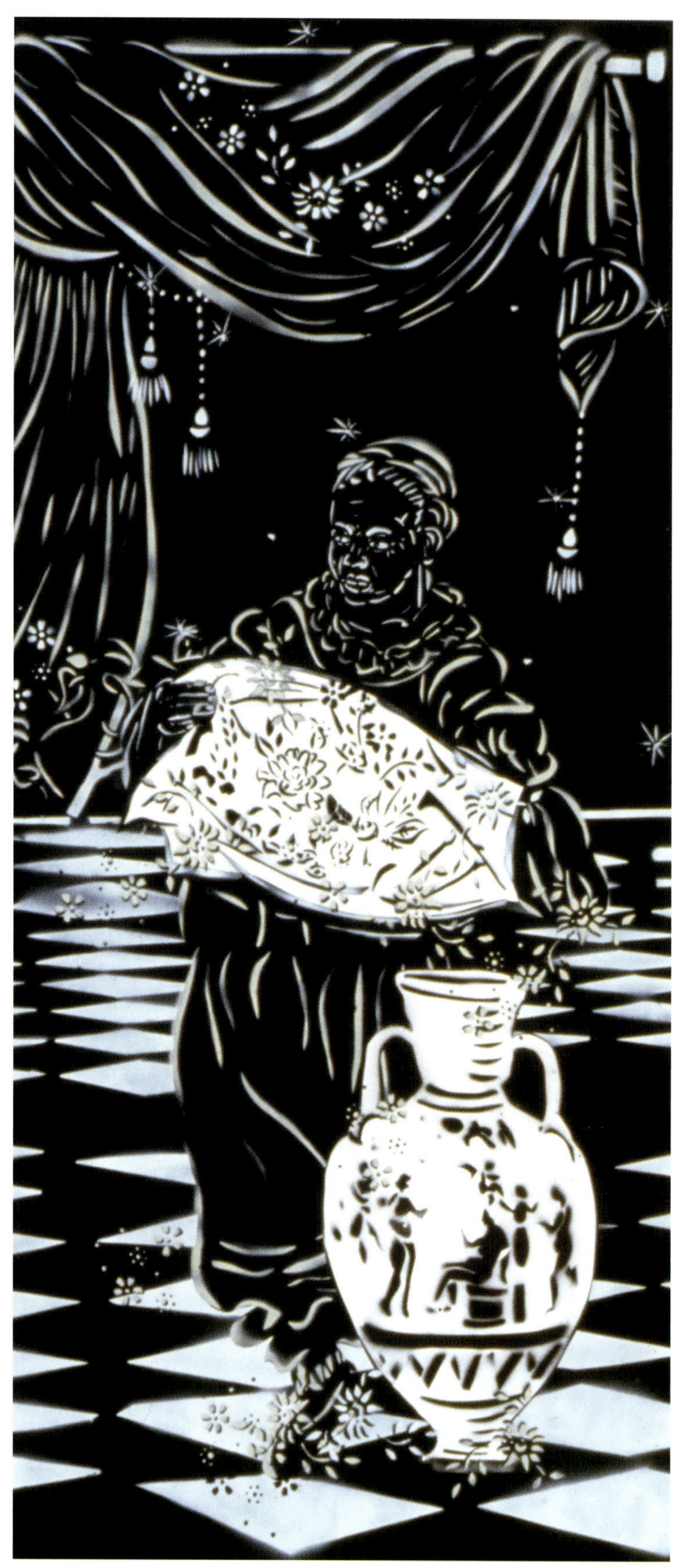

I used the idea that black and white are not in opposition, that they are in play.

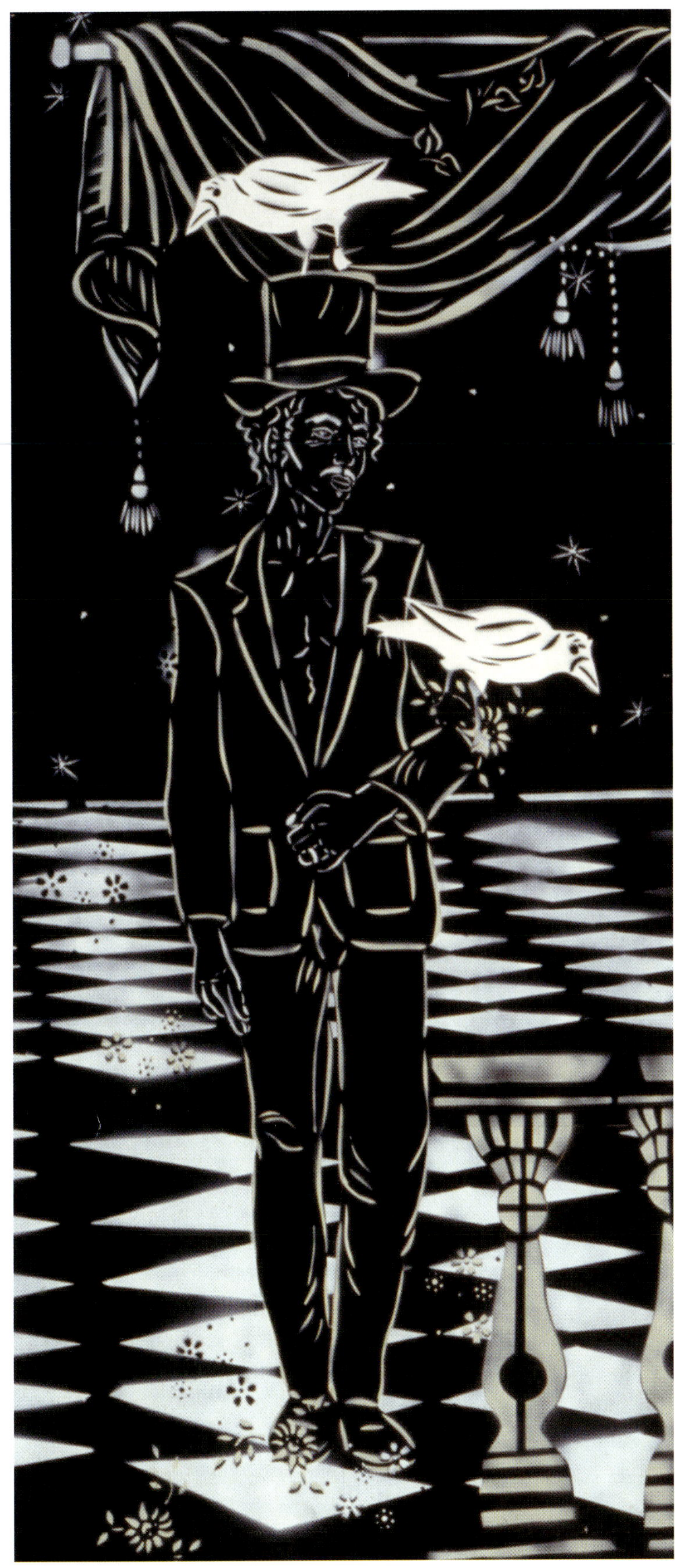

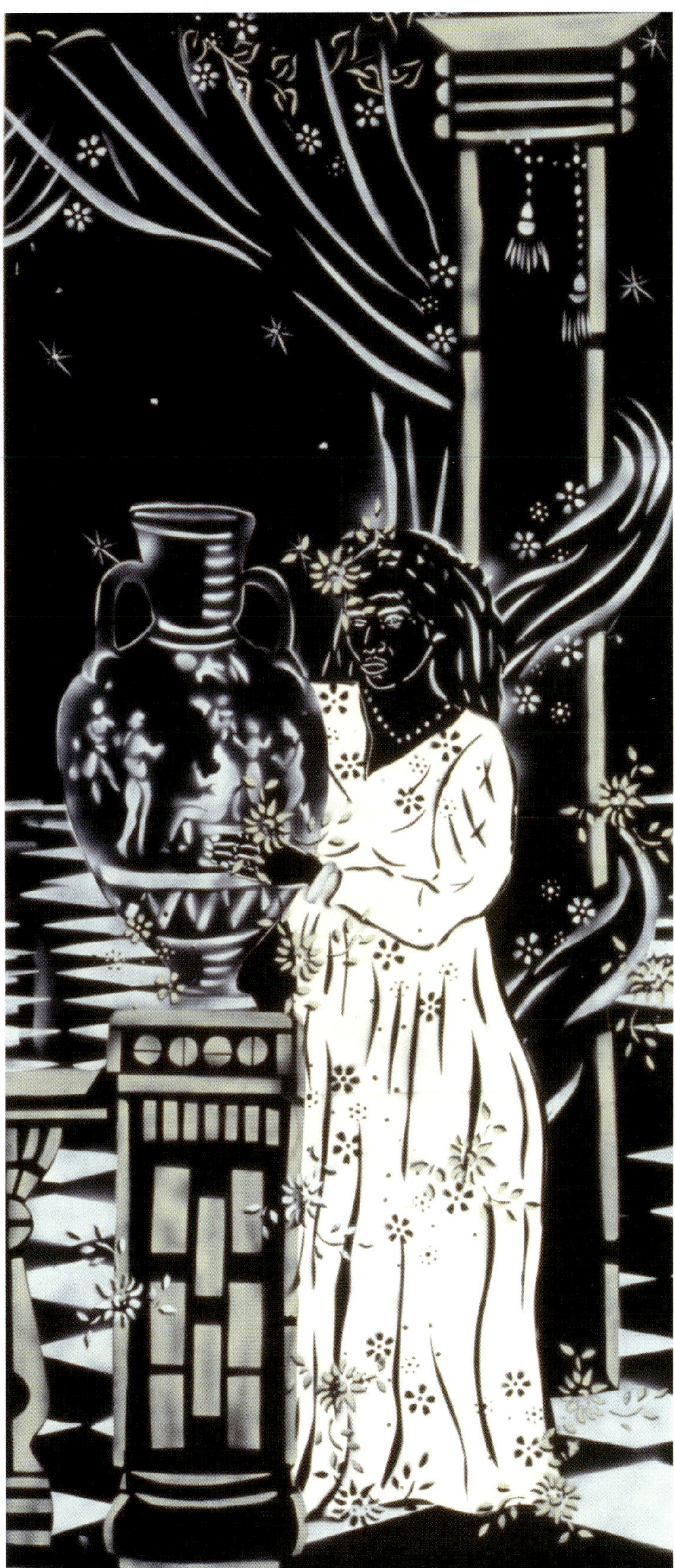

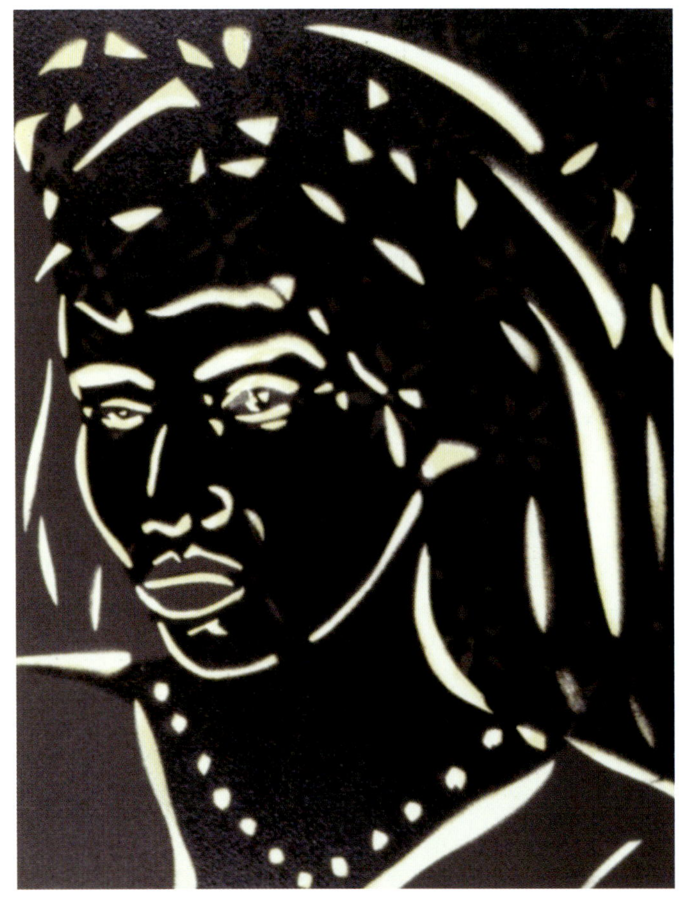

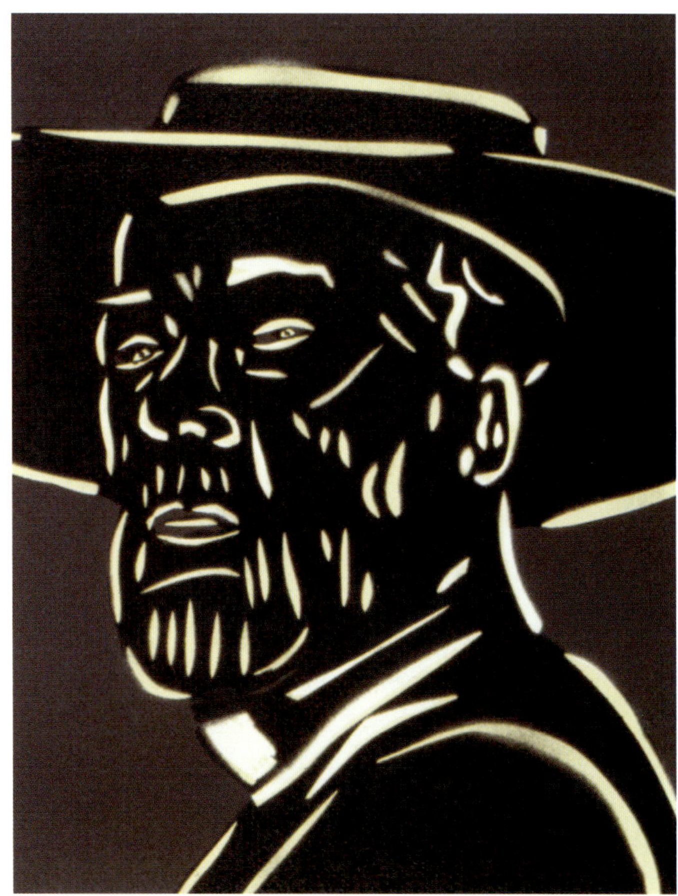

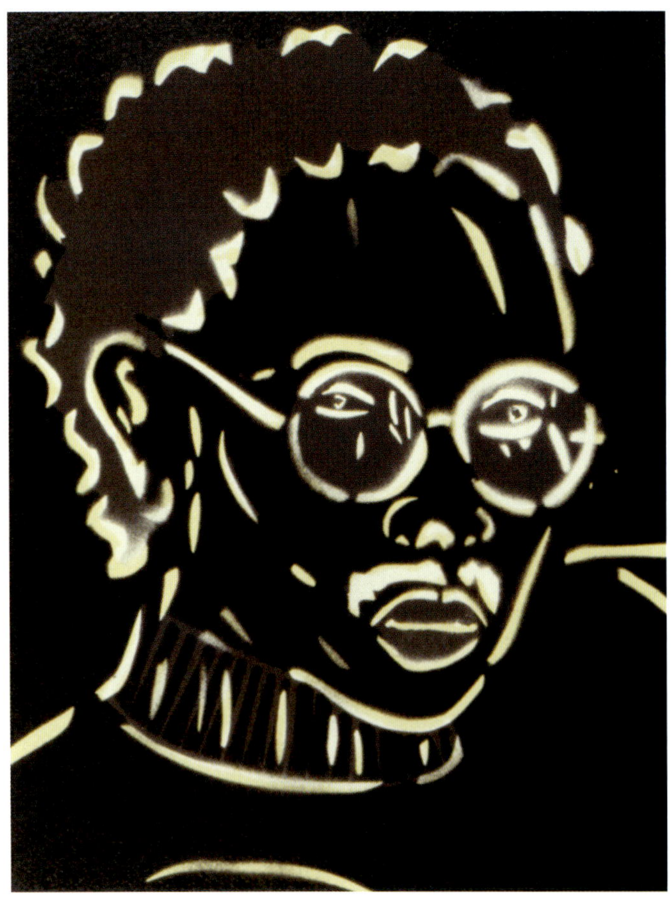

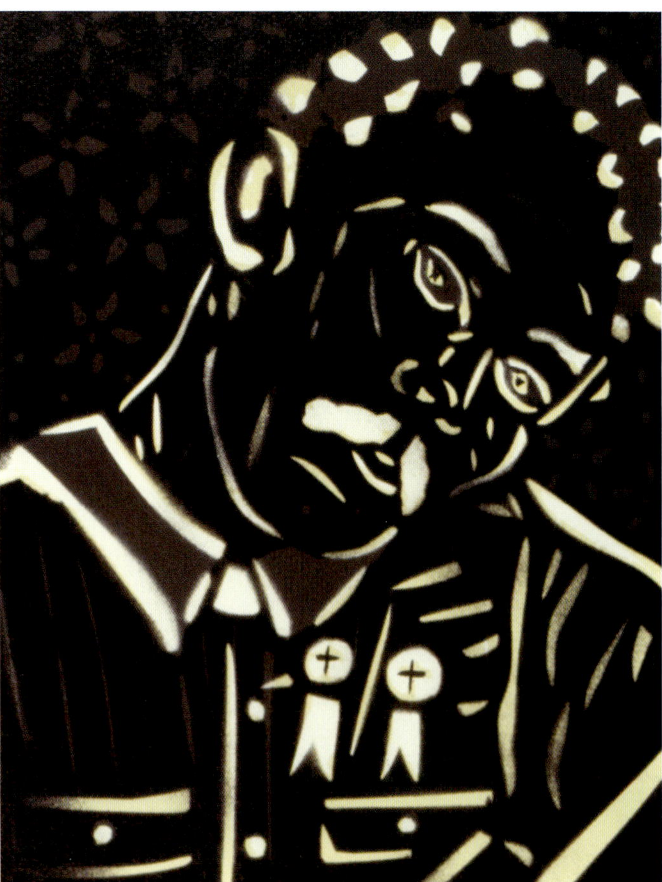

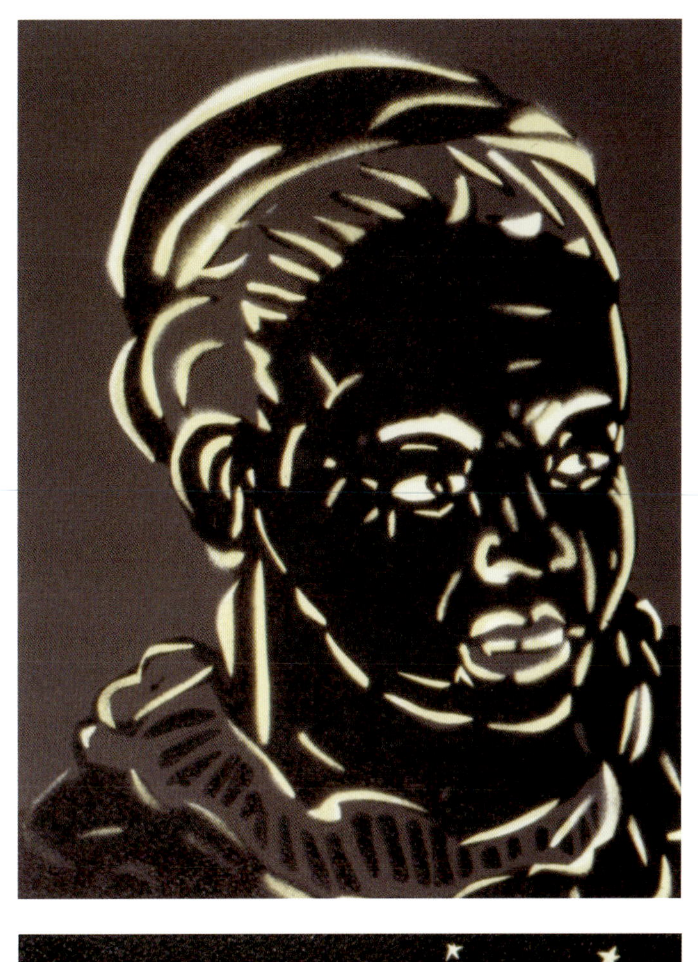

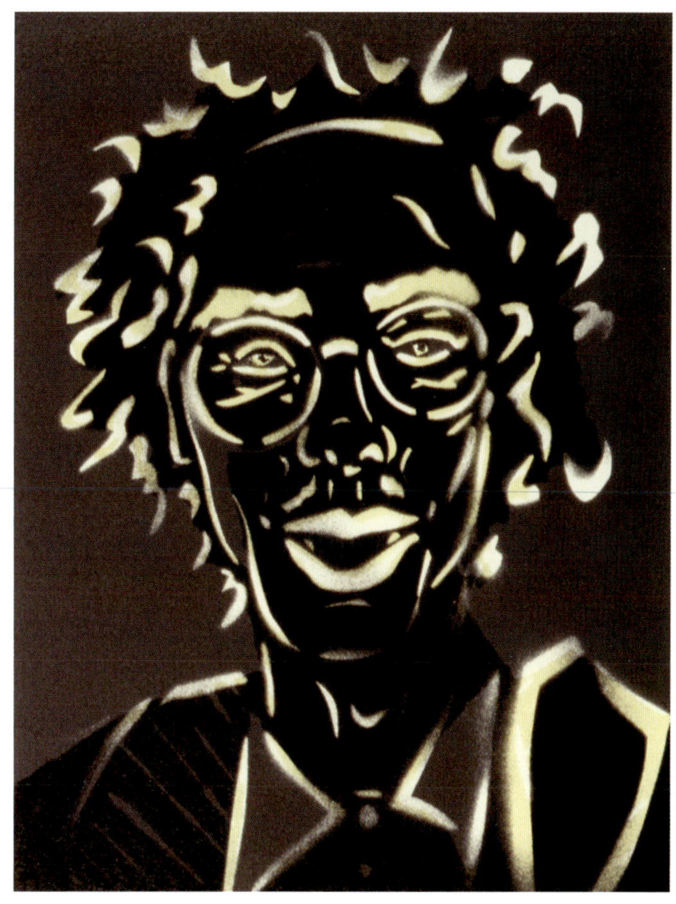

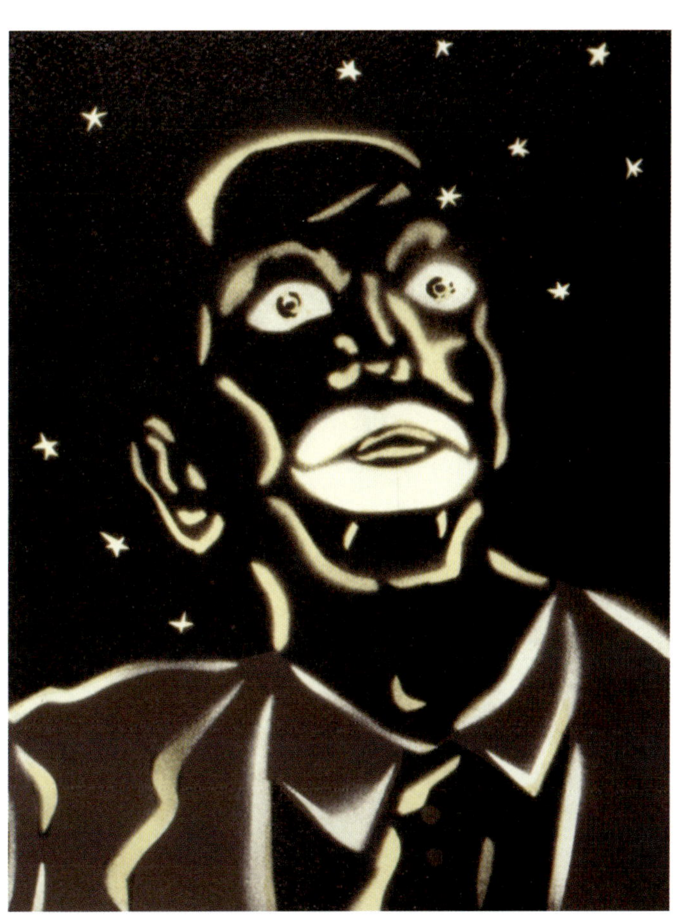

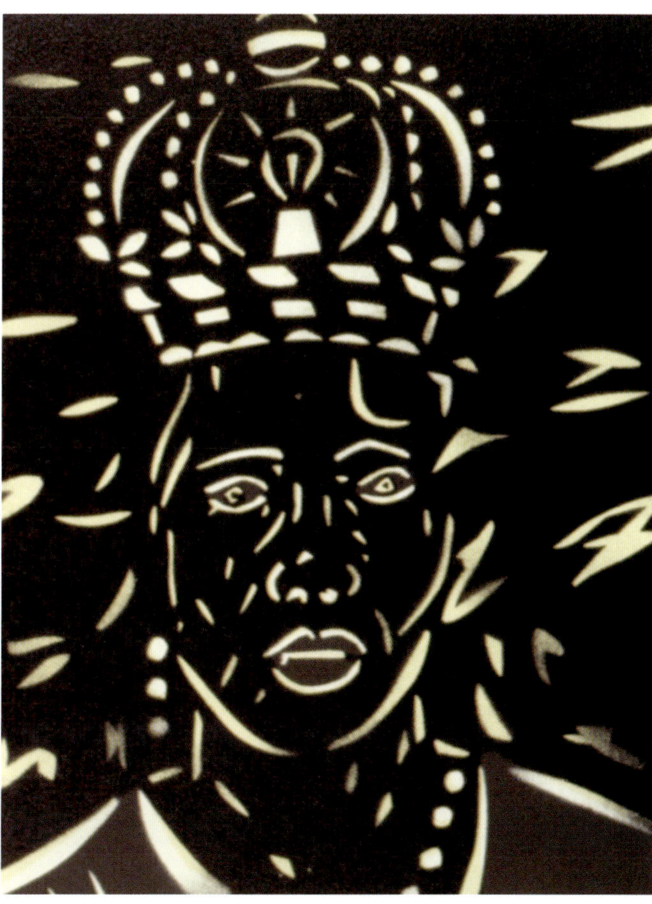

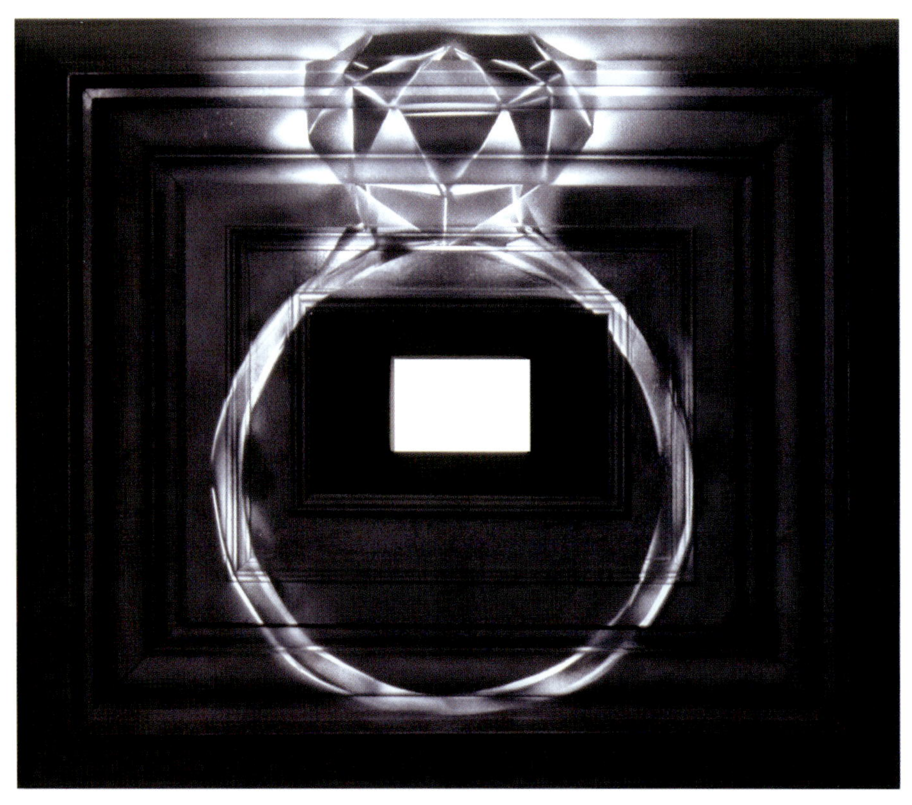

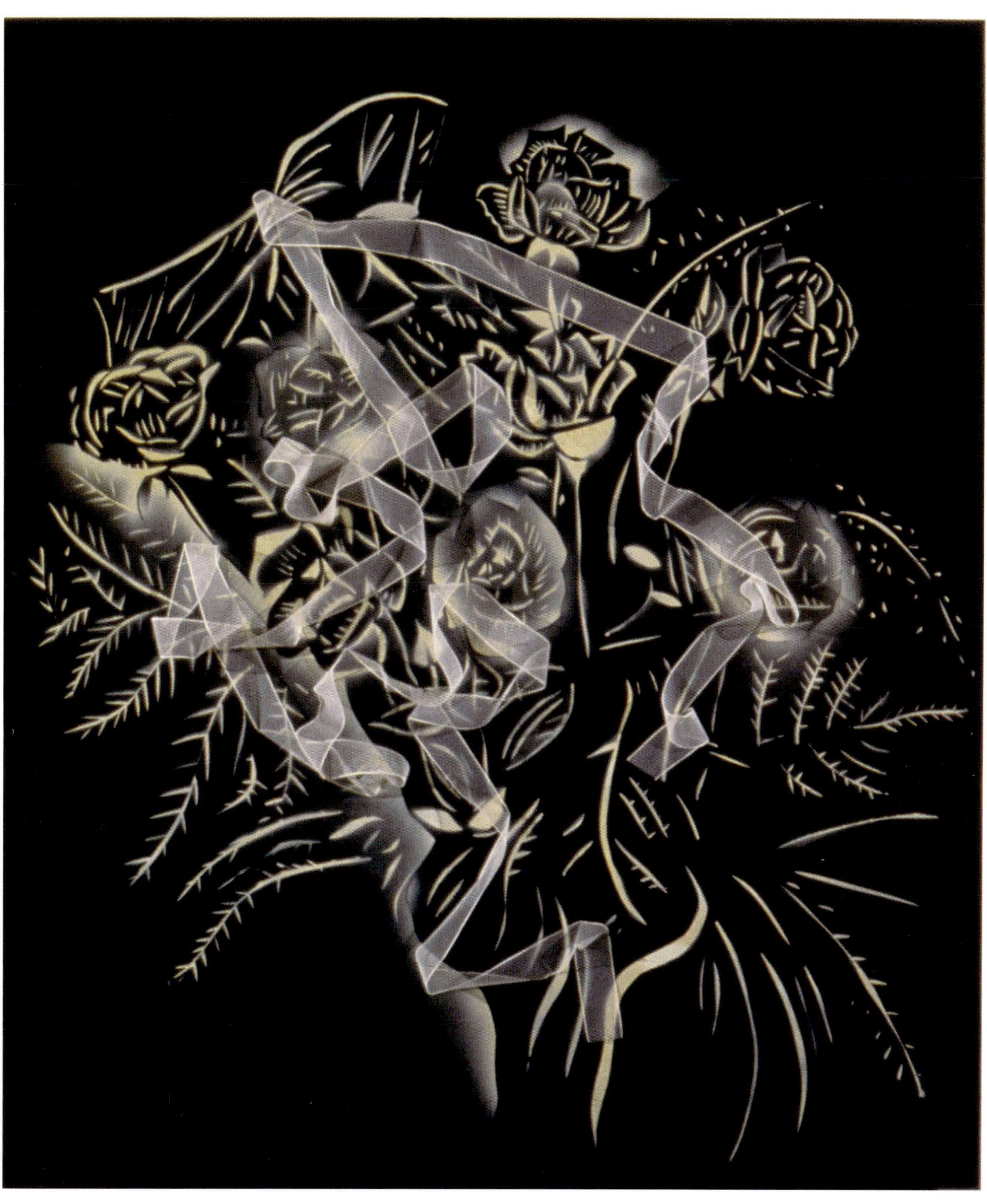

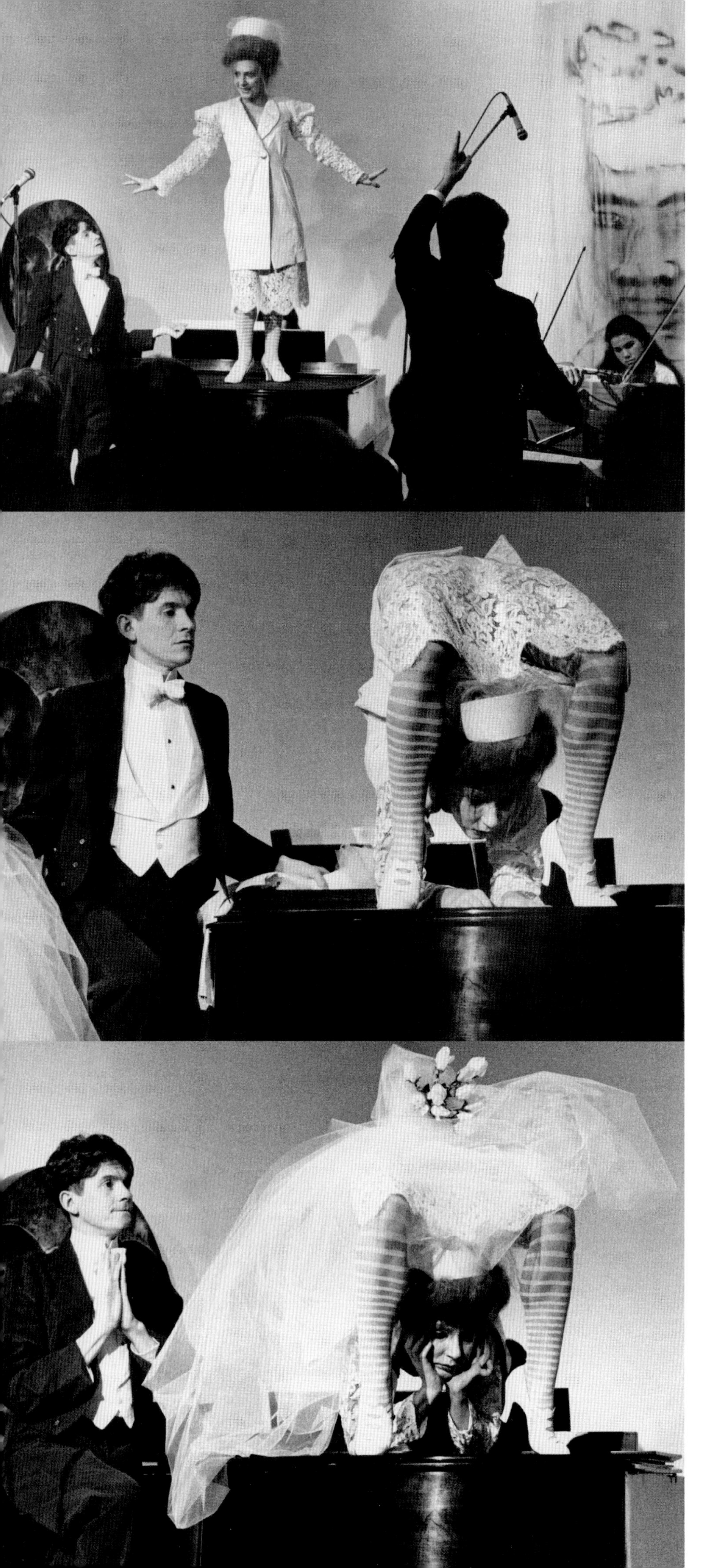

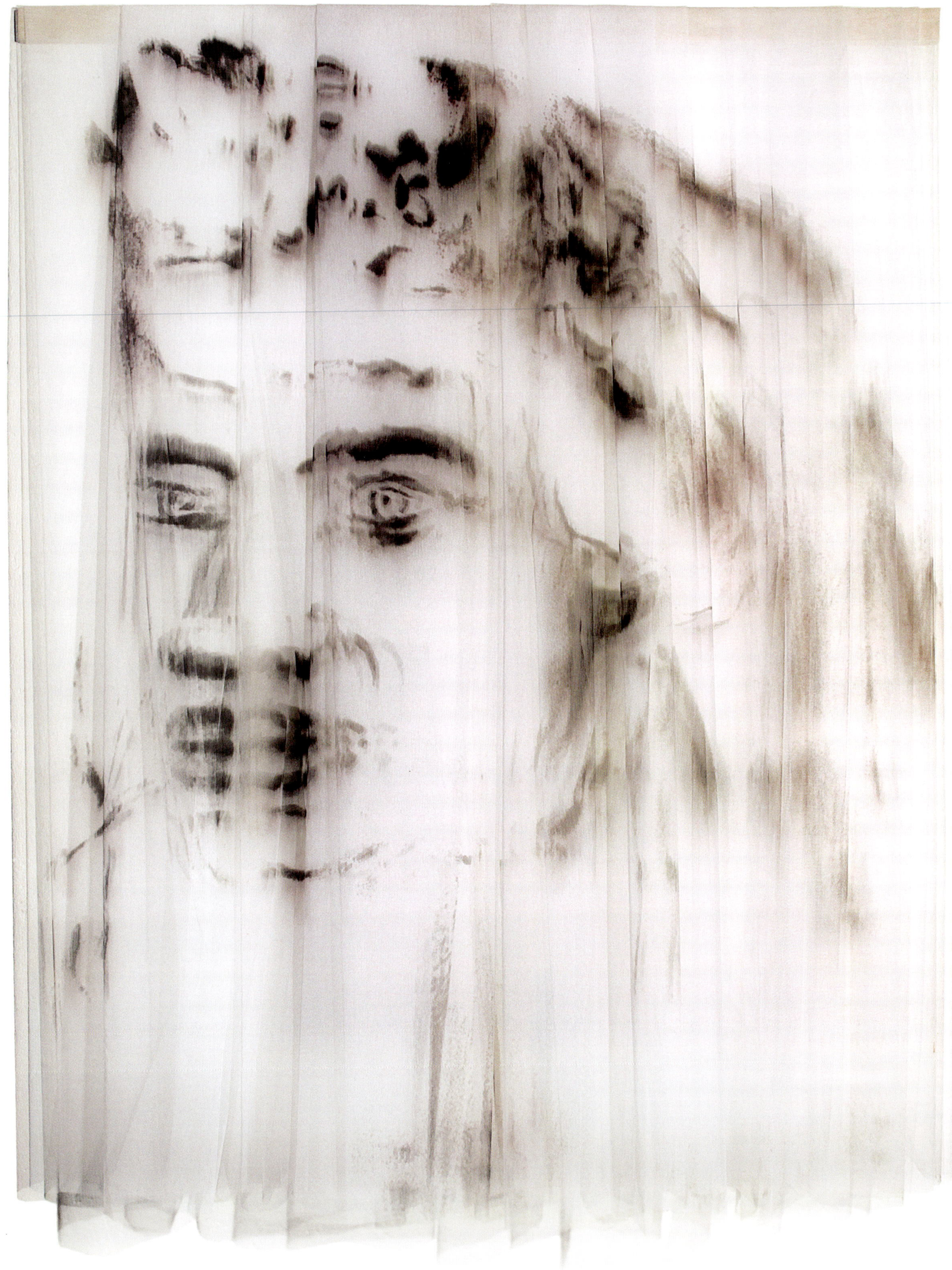

A Surreal Encounter: Izhar Patkin, Arie Aroch,

In his foreword to the catalog for Izhar Patkin's 2003 show at the Tel Aviv Museum, "Host Culture, Homage to Arie Aroch," Moti Omer wrote: "In the early '90s, I visited Patkin's studio in New York, where I saw a series of paintings based on Asian rugs, 'Gardens for the Global City.' The encounter with those paintings reminded me of a 1928 rug that was made in honor of Sir Herbert Samuel by Zionist Iraqi Jews. Sir Herbert Samuel was the first High Commissioner of Palestine during the British Mandate. That rug was the inspiration for one of the most celebrated paintings by Arie Aroch: 'The High Commissioner,' 1966."[1]

Patkin's homage to Aroch yielded six paintings collectively titled *Host Culture* (pages 142–43), which became part of his *Gardens for the Global City* series (1991–present, pages 144–49). In that context, the host culture was traditional Persian and Iraqi rug culture, as it accommodated the weaving of a carpet for Zionist Jews with the image of their fêted Jewish British high commissioner. But Patkin's use of the concept "host culture" is more far-reaching.

I would like to review the Patkin and Aroch "encounter" in the context of two other imaginary artistic rendezvous—the association of each with Marcel Duchamp. Aroch, who arrived from Kharkov to Mandatory Palestine as a young man, probably didn't hear of Duchamp until the 1960s and definitely never heard of Patkin, who was nineteen when Aroch passed away in 1974. It was then that Patkin learned about him, from the sculptor Yitzhak Danziger, but Patkin only specifically addressed Aroch's work in the 1990s as a response to Omer's proposal regarding the connection between the *High Commissioner* painting and the *Gardens for the Global City* paintings. Duchamp died in 1968, and Patkin was only introduced to his work in the 1970s. Proposing a surreal encounter between the three in the pages of this essay may seem capricious, but Surrealism was not a foreign concept to Duchamp or Aroch, nor has it been to Patkin.

In the late 1970s Patkin arrived in the United States to study and, soon afterward, to practice his art. A superficial glance at the early days of his career in the New York art scene might suggest that his ascendance was meteoric, but, his naturalization aside, Patkin's work never lost its intense awareness of or commitment to conveying the question of *otherness* in his own Jewish and Israeli identity, or as a guest who hosts other artists. He opens up his work to host other "guests" of American culture, artists of other diasporas: the Iranian Shirin Neshat, the Korean Nam June Paik (pages 196–97), and Agha Shahid Ali from Kashmir.

The almost total lack of acknowledgment of the connections between Patkin's work and that of Marcel Duchamp, the "premier" guest of American visual art of the first half of the twentieth century, is a curious omission in writings about Patkin's art. The United States embraced Duchamp more openly than did his birth country. He, in turn, brought the flag of Modernism, or even post-Modernism, first with his painting *Nude Descending a Staircase* (1912), and then more symbolically with *50 cc of Paris Air* (1919). In the 1990 catalog for Patkin's Stedelijk Museum show, one can find three illustrations that refer to Duchamp. One is a photographic portrait of Duchamp peering between the panels of a parted curtain.[2] Undoubtedly, this image appears in the catalog in relation to Patkin's deep fascination with theatricality, which Michael Fried posited as representing all that opposes the purity of Modernism, in "Art and Objecthood."[3] Below this photo is a reproduction of *The Large Glass* with its full name: *The Bride Stripped Bare by Her Bachelors, Even* (1915–22). This illustration was meant to evoke links to other aspects of Patkin's work, primarily the concept of "the Bride" and the fact that the glass was painted on its backside like Patkin's "reverse paintings" on screens, which he invented in the early 1980s. In the "reverse paintings" the paint literally passes through the wire-mesh canvas to the front of the painting, while in Duchamp's work it is the light that delivers the colors from back to front, through the transparent glass.

Elsewhere in the catalog is an illustration of Duchamp's *Monte Carlo Bond* (1924), Man Ray's notorious portrait of Duchamp with shaving foam in his hair that is sculpted like horns. Recalling the other image, Duchamp appears before a curtainlike background.[4] The shaving-foam image, which gives Duchamp a playfully demonic face, is reproduced next to a 1958 photo of the American actress Sandra Gillis stepping out of a bathtub wearing nothing but a frothy soap-bubble dress. Both of these images are juxtaposed with images of Patkin's series *Presidential Wax* (1985–86), in which his 1980s drippy wax sculptures act as the deformed stand-in models for the portrait re-creations of George and Martha Washington.

But strangely, while the Stedelijk catalog explicitly makes a visual connection between Patkin's work and that of Duchamp, Duchamp's name is never mentioned in the any of the texts. (In his essay "The Dream Corps," on page 136 of this volume, Itamar Levy proposes the high/low duality of Duchamp's readymades as a mirror to Patkin's secular treatment of sacred Jewish objects.)

Duchamp had a weighty presence in the American avant-garde from the moment he presented *Nude Descending a Staircase* until his death in 1968. In the following decade, critics and young artists alike were deeply engaged with his contribution to the fledgling Conceptual art phenomenon, and his influence extended beyond the United States. But one should remember that in those days only a very particular segment of the avant-garde did not subscribe to mainstream postwar abstraction or to Greenbergian views of Modernism. This polarizing distinction did not exist before the war, and afterward the artists who for a brief moment were referred to as "neo-Dada" forged a strong affinity to Duchamp's legacy. They were the new generation of transmedia and interdisciplinary artists. Robert Rauschenberg, Jasper Johns, John Cage, and Merce Cunningham made fresh use of time-based arts, stage-sets, narrative, and texts. Rauschenberg illustrated Dante's *Inferno* and Johns illustrated Beckett's prose.

The links between Patkin's work and that of Duchamp are much more diverse and unpredictable than these general references or the hints in the Stedelijk catalog. We can discover deeper layers and even more profound connections when we recognize the presence of Duchamp's influential signature in Aroch's work and the parallels between all three cultural guests: French-American, Israeli-American, Russian-Israeli. These connections can be found not only in the many motifs their work has in common, or in the winks and clues Patkin embeds in his work, but later in his *Host Culture* homage to Aroch.

In 1981 Patkin had his first New York solo show, at The Kitchen, which is known for supporting new video, performance, and interdisciplinary art. The Kitchen provided two archetypal "generic" art spaces: a white gallery and a black-box theater. The fusion of paintings, theater, and black-and-white has remained characteristic of Patkin's work throughout his career. In 1983, two years after the Kitchen exhibition, his show "The Meta Bride" opened at the gallery of Holly Solomon, a former actress who remained his devoted dealer for the rest of her life. In this show Patkin debuted his white (ink) on black (rubber) technique, which became a prominent thematic device in *The Black Paintings* (1985–86; pages 212–17). Also reappearing in *The Black Paintings* is the "meta-bride" (page 225). This time she is cast as the lead character, Stephanie Virtue Secret-Rose Diop (pages 217, 219–20).

The 1983 show was rich with references to Duchampian motifs—first, through nuptials as an allegory for an alchemical process of uniting disparate elements, and, second, through the bride title. "The Meta Bride" was both the show's title and the title of the painting of the black bride on white tulle, which was based on an image of a black bride from a discarded photograph Patkin found on a New York sidewalk. There was also the *Bridesmaid's Dream* (1982), a bridal rose bouquet called *Savtah Shoshana* (*Grand Mother Rose*, later changed to *Santa Shoshana*) (1982; page 223), and *My Parents, '53* (1983; page 37), based on a wedding photo of the artists' parents. The painting *Staircase* (1983) refers to Duchamp's staircase, but rather than the single nude, it depicts multiple identical brides descending the staircase. A *Mile of Screen* (1982) is a direct nod to Duchamp's *Mile of String* (1942), and *Tie & knot* (1982), painted on an ironing board, recalls Duchamp's obsession with articles of clothing as well as his famous readymade proposal to use a Rembrandt as an ironing board.

The "Meta Bride" show also included an Easter Sunday concert featuring a contortionist bride and a fifteen-piece orchestra (page 224). Theatricality has been a mainstay in Patkin's oeuvre from his early works to date. His use of a curtain or a screen (tulle, rubber, wire mesh, or scrim), not as a mere canvas for painting but as an inseparable part of the painting itself, demonstrates how integrated painting and theatricality are for him. The paintings hang as curtains; they veil and unveil, hide and seek. The narrative quality of the paintings and his adaptations of prose and historical events are also part of that engagement. The characters in the paintings often operate as personas in a play. They are actors, devices, and themselves all at once. Patkin painted himself in the role of Velásquez in *The Maids of Honor* (1988; pages 190–91), but as a magician peering from behind a curtain.

At the entrance to the 1986 show "The Black Paintings," a large banner declared: "Based on The Blacks: A Clown Show by Jean Genet." Patkin drew viewers into the white ink and black rubber room and led them into the color black, the text, and all its political implications. Black and white were prominent colors in Duchamp's works: in his chessboard, in his photography, in the dark lead of the *Large Glass,* and in *Fresh Widow* (1920) (see the reference to *Fresh Widow* in Patkin's *My Promise Can't Be Broken,* 1981; page 28), and so on.

Just as Patkin built an entire show based on a Genet play, Duchamp credited Raymond Roussel's 1910 play *Impressions from Africa* with being perhaps his most significant source of inspiration. "I owe him everything," he said about Roussel (the two never met). Roussel's play, too, was colored by colonialism in Africa.

Duchamp's works were a theater of identities: in *Wanted, $2,000 Reward* (1922), as Rrose Sélavy (1921), and in the photographs of the thirty-five-year-old Marcel Duchamp photographed as an eighty-five-year-old. Duchamp participated in theatrical performances such as the live tableau of "Adam and Eve" in 1924 that was probably a single performance for *Ciné-Sketch,* Francis Picabia's journal. Duchamp appeared naked, as Adam standing next to Eve as they are depicted in Lucas Cranach's sixteenth-century painting (see Patkin's painting *The Fall,* 2000; pages 198–99). In 1985 Patkin presented *Before the Law Stands a Doorkeeper* (1984–85; pages 232–33). The title alludes to Kafka's story of the same name, but the object, a large wooden barn door, refers to Duchamp's *Étant donnés* (1946–66).

The dialogue with Duchamp illuminates Patkin's seemingly inadvertent relationship with Aroch's work. Aroch's late works have many affinities with Duchamp. On the entrance banner to his own show at the Israel Museum in 1968, Aroch added in his own handwriting: "Today we received notice of the death of Marcel Duchamp." He painted *Coat Hanger* (1972) after Duchamp's *Hat Rack* (1917) and even built himself a replica of the bicycle wheel, as seen in a 1974 Ariella Schweid photo of him with his wife.

The unexpected connection between the three artists—two Israelis and one French father figure—runs deep. Duchamp's mythical couplings of Adam and Eve in Eden or the King and Queen surrounded by Swift Nudes are not unlike the double figure of the high commissioner in Aroch's painting. The high commissioner is both representative of and a substitute for the king. David Ginton argued in a 2000 article titled "The High Commissioner-ess"[5] that the high commissioner painting is an extension of the bride of *The Large Glass.*

Patkin painted his versions of high commissioners long before he made the explicit reference to Aroch and the Persian rug. He based his *Presidential Wax* series on Gilbert Stuart's iconic 1795 portrait of George Washington—a naive painting by European standards, but undoubtedly high in status, and featuring the same blue, red, and white regalia. Patkin showed the series at the Holly Solomon gallery in 1992. When Omer wrote about Patkin's paintings of the high commissioner, he neglected to mention that Patkin had produced a series about another high commissioner ten years earlier.

Duchamp also created a portrait of George Washington, entitled *Genre Allegory* (1943). Made out of iodine-soaked gauze, it unites the profile of the first American president's face with the geographical border of the United States. As T. J. Demos writes:

> it also suggests a wounded body where its material resembles bloody bandages and where its several gold stars are seen to be brutally attached with long nails. Further, a series of oppositions tear its surface between collectivity and individuality, between national symbols (of the flag, the nation, the president) and their metonymic dispersion (as part objects). The sordidness of the portrait, not surprisingly rejected by *Vogue* magazine, which commissioned it in the first place, is that it pierces the boundaries of national identity and dissolves its subject and community. It suggests the violence hidden behind the homogenization and essentialism of national identity. There the desire for collective unity turns into a symptom of bloody fragmentation.[6]

The 1992 presidential portraits show, called "Icons," also included works that reflected on the early-twentieth-century Russian avant-garde. Naturally, Aroch dedicated works to that subject as well. *Chuckfar* (1961–66), for example, resembles a combination of oval portrait frames and an abstracted image of a boot, which Aroch recalled as a Russian shoemaker's sign. One may wonder whether the references these artists make to authority are tied to the fact that all three painted images of their own biological fathers. Duchamp included a portrait of his father in *Box in a Valise* (1935–41), Aroch painted an oval-shaped portrait of his father, and Patkin painted a posthumous portrait of his father on a large veil (pages 38–41).

It seems to me, however, that the most profound linkage between the three artists, especially in a contemporary reading, is to what Demos concludes is "the complexity of what could be called a 'homeless aesthetic.'"[7] He interprets Duchamp's seminal piece *Box in a Valise*, which the artist created after he escaped the Nazi occupation and became a refugee, first from Paris to the South of France and then to America: "For the suitcase's central concerns of collection, reproduction, and portable storage address the needs of exile, defined by the loss of possessions, homesickness, and unending mobility. Further, the suitcase offers the means to combat the fragmenting effects of exile through the reconstruction of a kind of portable home."[8]

Aroch's work is pregnant with motifs of wandering, going back in time, and longing for home. He lived many years outside of Israel in various diplomatic posts in Russia, Sweden, and Brazil. From abroad he scribbled this line inside his painting *Red House* (1960): "What's new what's new at home what is the peace of [=how are] the people there how are they doing [?]." Many of his paintings go back to his childhood in Kharkov and the early years in

Bezalel. In his late works he devoted special attention to *Ulysses*, written by James Joyce, the expatriate Irishman, about Homer's *Odyssey.*

Exile is a vital motif in Patkin's collaboration with the late Kashmiri-American poet Agha Shahid Ali (1949–2011). That elegiac project includes *The Veil Suite* painting (2007; pages 68–75), based on Shahid's own requiem, and the painting *Evening* (2006; pages 176–85), which draws on a poem by the late Palestinian poet Mahmoud Darwish (1941–2008), who lived in exile. In these collaborations with masters of language who lived outside their native languages and homes, and whose poetry is rich with memories and lament, Patkin positions loss and home in the center of his work—which is perhaps the best place to file one's longing.

Ellen Ginton

NOTES

1
Mordechai Omer, foreword to *Izhar Patkin: Host Culture, Homage to Arie Aroch* (Tel Aviv: Tel Aviv Museum of Art, 2003), 78.

2
Izhar Patkin: Four-Piece Suit (Amsterdam: Stedelijk Museum, 1990), 17.

3
Michael Fried, "Art and Objecthood," *Artforum* 5 (June 1967): 12–23.

4
Izhar Patkin: Four-Piece Suit, 33.

5
David Ginton, "The High Commissioner-ess," *Hamidrasha* periodical (Beit Berl College, May 2000), 200–234.

6
T. J. Demos, "Duchamp's Boîte-en-valise: Between Institutional Acculturation and Geopolitical Displacement," *Grey Room* 8 (MIT Press, Summer 2002): 29.

7
Demos, 12.

8
Demos, 10.

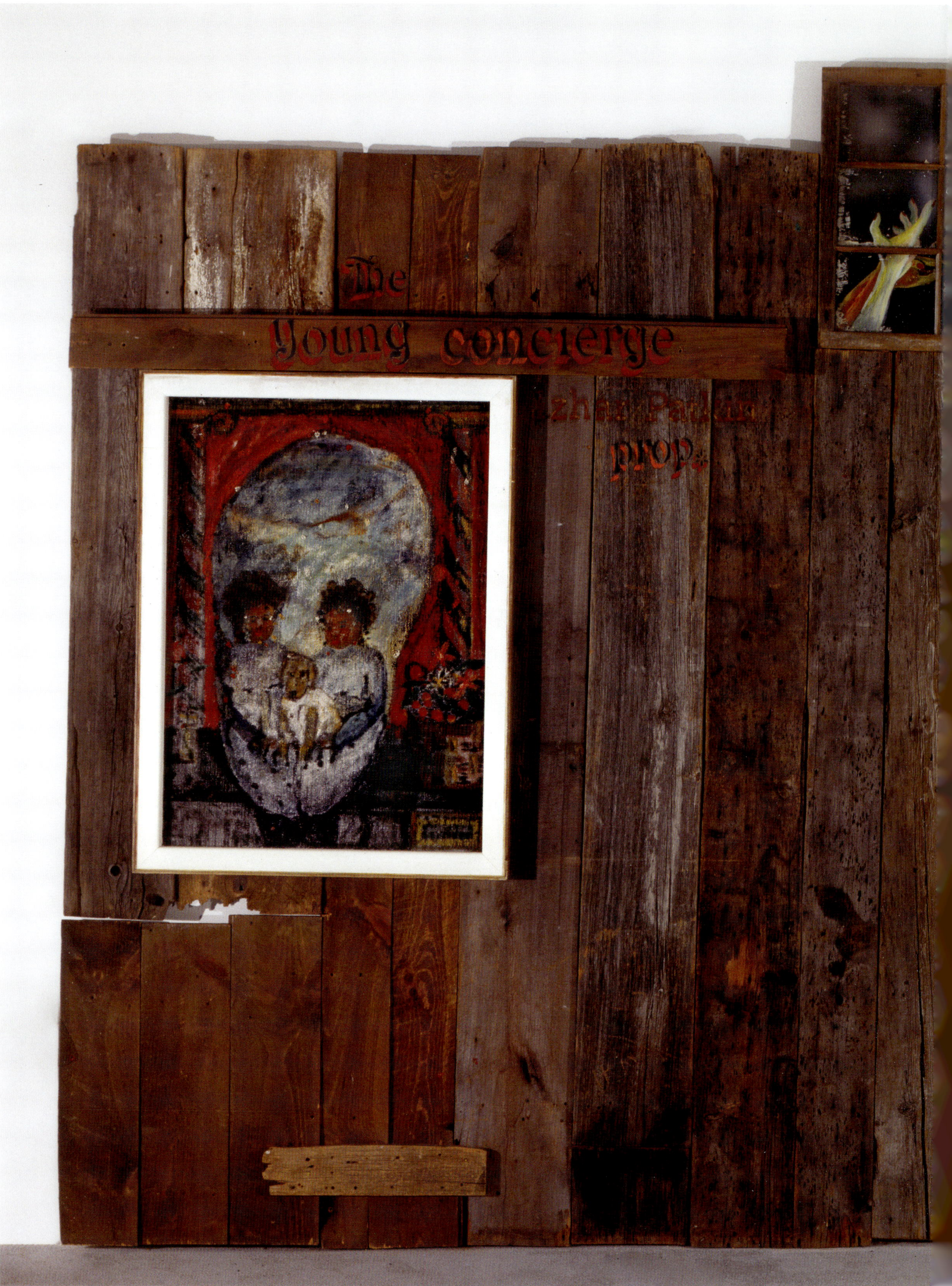
The
young concierge
zhan Paulin
prop.

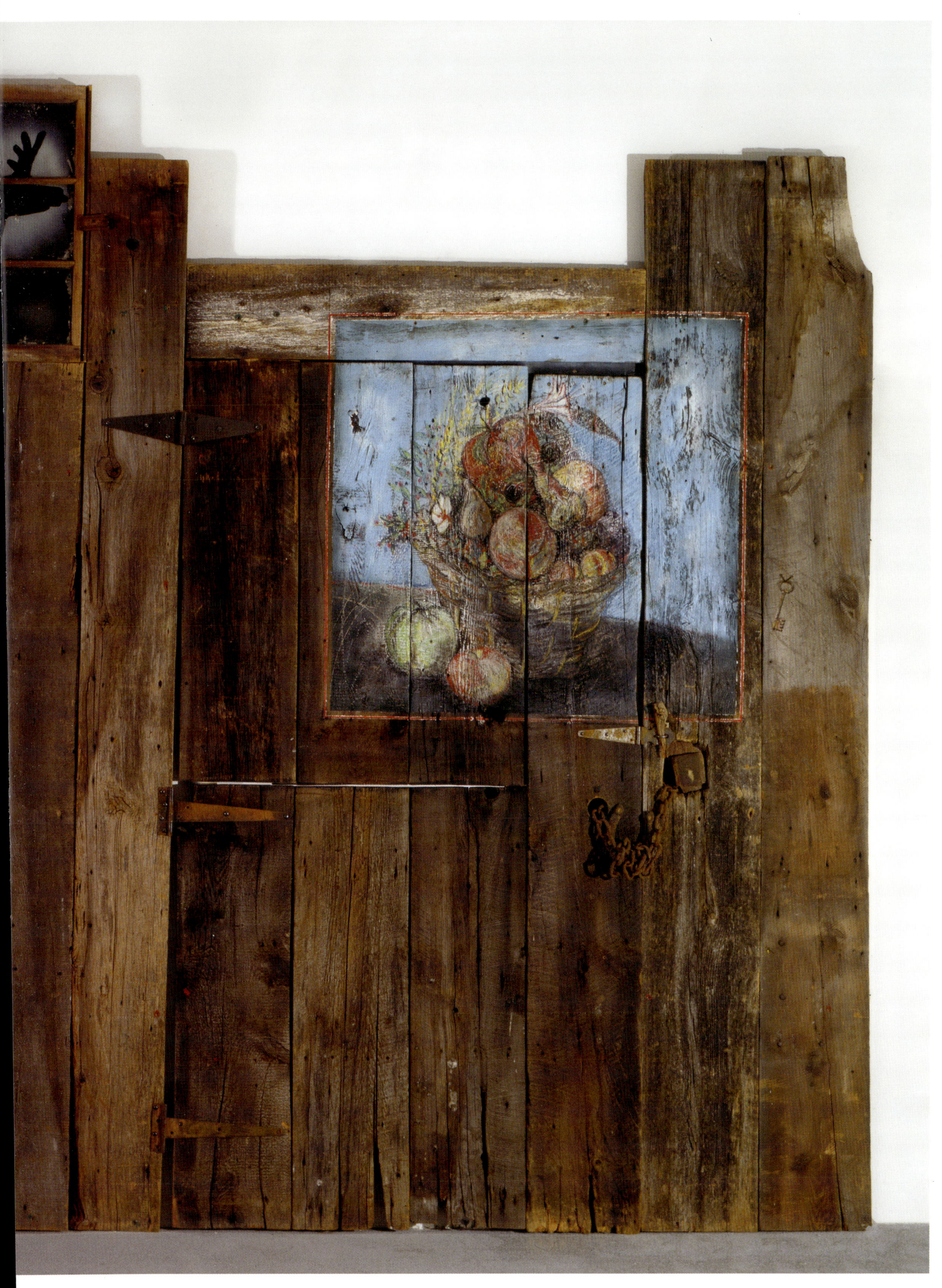

List of Works

THE NAME AND THE FATHER

FRONT ENDPAPER
The Encounter (part 2) (detail), 1987

FRONT INSIDE ENDPAPER
The Dead Are Here (detail), 2009

PAGE II
You Can't Escape the Body, 1981
Enamel, rubber gloves, 17 x 12 x 4½"
(43.18 x 30.48 x 11.43 cm)
Collection Brooklyn Museum

PAGE 28
Gloomy Gallery (My Promise Can't Be Broken), 1981
Ink, neoprene, stained wood, magnets, Plexiglas,
80 x 62" (203.2 x 157.48 cm)

PAGE 30
Izhar Patkin 1934–52, 2012
Oil, wire mesh, 35 x 27" (88.9 x 68.58 cm)

PAGE 31
Ghost Chair, 1978
Pencil, photograph, 11 x 8½" (27.94 x 21.59 cm)

PAGE 32
Funnels and Trumpets: Portrait of the Self as a Breather, 1986
Enamel, perforated Kromekote paper and
photographs, 82 x 53¾" (208.3 x 136.5 cm)
Collection Brooklyn Museum

PAGE 33
Self-Portrait (Samaritana), 1980–81
Neoprene, satin, spray paint, 112 x 74"
(284.48 x 187.96 cm)
Collection Brooklyn Museum

PAGES 34–35
Untitled, 1980–81
Perforated Kromekote paper and photographs,
26 x 35¼" (66.4 x 89.5 cm)
Collection Brooklyn Museum

PAGE 36
Souvenir for Arik Patkin, 2002
Lithograph, 22 x 30" (55.88 x 76.2 cm)
Collection Tel Aviv Museum of Art

PAGE 37
My Parents '53, 1983
Enamel, undeveloped black-and-white photo paper,
80 x 62" (203.2 x 157.48 cm)

PAGES 38–39
The artist in his studio with *Arik Patkin WTC*, 2006
Ink, pleated illusion (tulle),
160 x 192" (406.4 x 487.68 cm)
Collection Tel Aviv Museum of Art

PAGES 40–41
Arik Patkin WTC (detail), 2006
Ink, pleated illusion (tulle), 160 x 192"
(406.4 x 487.68 cm)
Collection Tel Aviv Museum of Art

PICTURES ARE NETS

PAGES 52–53
Violins, 2006
Installation at CCJ, São Paulo, Brazil,
September 2010
Ink, pleated illusion (tulle), painting for four walls,
14 x 24 x 25' (426.72 x 731.52 x 762 cm)

PAGES 54–55
Violins (detail), 2006
Installation at CCJ, São Paulo, Brazil,
September 2010
Ink, pleated illusion (tulle), painting for four walls,
14 x 24 x 25' (426.72 x 731.52 x 762 cm)

PAGE 56
Violins (detail), 2006
Ink, pleated illusion (tulle), painting for four walls,
14 x 24 x 25' (426.72 x 731.52 x 762 cm)

PAGE 57
Violins (detail), 2006
Ink, pleated illusion (tulle), painting for four walls,
14 x 24 x 25' (426.72 x 731.52 x 762 cm)

PAGE 58
Violins (detail), 2006
Ink, pleated illusion (tulle), painting for four walls,
14 x 24 x 25' (426.72 x 731.52 x 762 cm)

PAGE 59
Violins (detail), 2006
Ink, pleated illusion (tulle), painting for four walls,
14 x 24 x 25' (426.72 x 731.52 x 762 cm)

PAGES 60–61
Violins (detail), 2006
Installation at CCJ, São Paulo, Brazil,
September 2010
Ink, pleated illusion (tulle), painting for four walls,
14 x 24 x 25' (426.72 x 731.52 x 762 cm)

PAGES 62–63
Recital of Agha Shahid Ali's *Violins*
Caetano Veloso, vocals, and Jaques Morelenbaum, cello
Installation at CCJ, São Paulo, Brazil,
September 2010

PAGE 66
Studio view with *The Veil Suite* in progress, 2007
Ink, pleated illusion (tulle), painting for four walls,
14 x 22 x 25' (426.72 x 670.56 x 762 cm)

PAGES 68–69
The Veil Suite (detail), 2007
Ink, pleated illusion (tulle), painting for four walls,
14 x 22 x 25' (426.72 x 670.56 x 762 cm)

PAGES 70–71
The Veil Suite (detail), 2007
Ink, pleated illusion (tulle), painting for four walls,
14 x 22 x 25' (426.72 x 670.56 x 762 cm)

PAGES 72–73
The Veil Suite (detail), 2007
Ink, pleated illusion (tulle), painting for four walls,
14 x 22 x 25' (426.72 x 670.56 x 762 cm)

PAGE 74
The Veil Suite (detail), 2007
Ink, pleated illusion (tulle), painting for four walls,
14 x 22 x 25' (426.72 x 670.56 x 762 cm)

PAGE 75
The Veil Suite (detail), 2007
Ink, pleated illusion (tulle), painting for four walls,
14 x 22 x 25' (426.72 x 670.56 x 762 cm)

PAGE 76
Time Clipping the Wings of Love, 2005–11
Sèvres porcelain, pâte nouvelle,
30 11⁄16 x 17 5⁄16 x 12 3⁄16" (78 cm x 44 cm x 31 cm)
Private collection, New York

PAGE 77
Time Clipping the Wings of Love, 2005–11
Sèvres porcelain, pâte nouvelle,
30 11⁄16 x 17 5⁄16 x 12 3⁄16" (78 cm x 44 cm x 31 cm)
Private collection, New York

ENDANGERED SPECIES

PAGE 86
Madonna and Child (Ophrah) (detail), 1998
From the *Madonna and Child* series
Oil, wire mesh, 68 x 44" (172.72 x 111.76 cm)

PAGE 87
Madonna and Child (Ophrah), 1998
From the *Madonna and Child* series
Oil, wire mesh, 68 x 44" (172.72 x 111.76 cm)

PAGE 88
Sèvres atelier with *Madonna and Child* in progress, 2007
Plaster

PAGE 89
Sèvres atelier with *Madonna and Child* in progress
(detail), 2007
Plaster

PAGES 90–91
Sèvres atelier with *Madonna and Child* and
Time Clipping the Wings of Love in progress, 2011
Plaster

PAGE 92
Confirmation, 1988
From *The Perfect Existence in the Rose Garden* series
Oil, gold leaf, wire mesh, lamé, 64 x 40"
(162.56 x 101.6 cm)
Private collection, New York

PAGE 93
Madonna and Child (Lisa), 1998
From the *Madonna and Child* series
Oil, wire mesh, 68 x 44" (172.72 x 111.76 cm)

PAGE 94
Tradition, 1988
From *The Perfect Existence in the Rose Garden* series
Oil, gold leaf, wire mesh, lamé, 64 x 40"
(162.56 x 101.6 cm)
Private collection, New York

PAGE 95
Felix Mendelssohn, 1998
From the *Judenporzellan* series
Enamel, Kromekote paper, 109 13⁄16 x 66 ⅛"
(279 x 168 cm)

PAGE 96
Vase (from the Black Paintings' stencils), 1986-98
Enamel, Kromekote paper, 24 ⅞ x 15 ¾"
(63 x 40 cm)

PAGE 97
Fanny Mendelssohn, 1998–2002
From the *Judenporzellan* series
Enamel, Kromekote paper, 77 15⁄16 x 59 ⅞"
(198 x 152 cm)

PAGE 98
Eight, 1998–2002
From the *Judenporzellan* series
Enamel, Kromekote paper, 59 x 59"
(150 x 150 cm)

PAGE 99
Left to right:
Orphan's Spout, 1998-2002
From the *Judenporzellan* series
Enamel, Kromekote paper, 49 ¼ x 25 15⁄16"
(125 x 66 cm);
Orphan's Beak and Snout, 1998-2002
From the *Judenporzellan* series
Enamel, Kromekote paper, 72 ⅞ x 25 15⁄16"
(185 x 66 cm);
Orphan's Nose, 1998-2002
From the *Judenporzellan* series
Enamel, Kromekote paper, 49 ¼ x 25 15⁄16"
(125 x 66 cm)

PAGE 100
Sèvres atelier with the series
Time Clipping the Wings of Love in progress, 2008
Sèvres porcelain

PAGE 101
Time Clipping the Wings of Love (eggcups), 2005-11
Sèvres porcelain, pâte tendre, sizes variable
(according to the extinct birds' eggs)

PAGE 102
Time Clipping the Wings of Love (plate), 2005-10
Sèvres porcelain, pâte tendre, 9 ⅜" dia. (24 cm)

PAGE 103
Time Clipping the Wings of Love (plate), 2005-10
Sèvres porcelain, pâte tendre, 9 ⅜" dia. (24 cm)

PAGE 104
The Emperor's Platter, 2005-10
Sèvres porcelain, pâte tendre,
18 2⁄16 x 15 5⁄16" (46 x 39 cm)

PAGE 105
Cannibal Vase, 2005-10
Sèvres porcelain, pâte tendre, 8 13⁄16 x 11 ⅜ x 8 ⅝"
(22.5 x 29 x 22 cm)

A COMPLICATED LANDSCAPE

PAGES 110-11
You Tell Us What to Do (detail), 2010
Ink, pleated illusion (tulle), painting for four walls,
14 x 22 x 25' (426.72 x 670.56 x 762 cm)

PAGES 112-13
You Tell Us What to Do (detail), 2010
Ink, pleated illusion (tulle), painting for four walls,
14 x 22 x 25' (426.72 x 670.56 x 762 cm)

PAGE 114
You Tell Us What to Do (detail), 2010
Ink, pleated illusion (tulle), painting for four walls,
14 x 22 x 25' (426.72 x 670.56 x 762 cm)

PAGE 115
You Tell Us What to Do (detail), 2010
Ink, pleated illusion (tulle), painting for four walls,
14 x 22 x 25' (426.72 x 670.56 x 762 cm)

PAGE 116
You Tell Us What to Do (detail), 2010
Ink, pleated illusion (tulle), painting for four walls,
14 x 22 x 25' (426.72 x 670.56 x 762 cm)

PAGE 117
You Tell Us What to Do (detail), 2010
Ink, pleated illusion (tulle), painting for four walls,
14 x 22 x 25' (426.72 x 670.56 x 762 cm)

PAGES 118-19
You Tell Us What to Do (detail), 2010
Ink, pleated illusion (tulle), painting for four walls,
14 x 22 x 25' (426.72 x 670.56 x 762 cm)

PAGE 120
The Messiah's glAss, 2003-07
Glass, steel 124 x 85 x 43"
(314.96 x 215.9 x 109.22 cm)

PAGE 121
The Messiah's glAss (detail), 2003-07
Glass, steel 124 x 85 x 43"
(314.96 x 215.9 x 109.22 cm)

PAGES 128-29
Et in Arcadia Ego, 2012
Ink, pleated illusion (tulle), 13 x 62 ⅜' (3.96 x 19.03 m)

PAGES 130-31
Et in Arcadia Ego (detail), 2012
Ink, pleated illusion (tulle), 13 x 62 ⅜' (3.96 x 19.03 m)

PAGES 134-35
Et in Arcadia Ego (detail), 2012
Ink, pleated illusion (tulle), 13 x 62 ⅜' (3.96 x 19.03 m)

PAGE 142
Eshkach Yemini (Let my right hand wither)
(detail, painting in progress), 2001
From the *Host Culture* series
Oil, wire mesh, 72 x 48" (182.88 x 121.92 cm)
Collection Tel Aviv Museum of Art

PAGE 143
Eshkach Yemini (Let my right hand wither), 2001
From the *Host Culture* series
Oil, wire mesh, 72 x 48" (182.88 x 121.92 cm)
Collection Tel Aviv Museum of Art

PAGE 144
Gardens for the Global City, 1991 (series)
Oil, wire mesh, velvet, 72 x 48" (182.88 x 121.92 cm)
Collection Whitney Museum of American Art

PAGE 145
Gardens for the Global City, 1991 (series)
Oil, wire mesh, velvet, 72 x 48" (182.88 x 121.92 cm)
Collection Guggenheim Museum

PAGE 146
Gardens for the Global City, 1991 (series)
Oil, wire mesh, velvet, 72 x 48" (182.88 x 121.92 cm)
Private collection, Los Angeles

PAGE 147
Gardens for the Global City, 1991 (series)
Oil, wire mesh, velvet, 72 x 48" (182.88 x 121.92 cm)
Private collection, Basel

PAGE 148
Gardens for the Global City, 1991 (series)
Oil, wire mesh, velvet, 72 x 48" (182.88 x 121.92 cm)
Collection Whitney Museum of American Art

PAGE 149
Gardens for the Global City, 1991 (series)
Oil, wire mesh, velvet, 72 x 48" (182.88 x 121.92 cm)
Collection Whitney Museum of American Art

WHERE EACH IS BOTH

PAGES 154-55
The Dead Are Here (detail), 2009
Installation at the Shoshana Wayne Gallery,
Los Angeles, January 2012
Ink, pleated illusion (tulle), painting for four walls,
14 x 22 x 25' (426.72 x 670.56 x 762 cm)

PAGE 156
The Dead Are Here (detail), 2009
Ink, pleated illusion (tulle), painting for four walls,
14 x 22 x 25' (426.72 x 670.56 x 762 cm)

PAGE 157
The Dead Are Here (detail), 2009
Ink, pleated illusion (tulle), painting for four walls,
14 x 22 x 25' (426.72 x 670.56 x 762 cm)

PAGES 158-59
The Dead Are Here (detail), 2009
Installation at Shoshana Wayne Gallery,
Los Angeles, January 2012
Ink, pleated illusion (tulle), painting for four walls,
14 x 22 x 25' (426.72 x 670.56 x 762 cm)

PAGES 160-61
The Dead Are Here (detail), 2009
Ink, pleated illusion (tulle), painting for four walls,
14 x 22 x 25' (426.72 x 670.56 x 762 cm)

PAGE 162
The Dead Are Here (detail), 2009
Ink, pleated illusion (tulle), painting for four walls,
14 x 22 x 25' (426.72 x 670.56 x 762 cm)

PAGE 163
The Dead Are Here (detail), 2009
Ink, pleated illusion (tulle), painting for four walls,
14 x 22 x 25' (426.72 x 670.56 x 762 cm)

PAGES 164-65
The Dead Are Here (detail), 2009
Ink, pleated illusion (tulle), painting for four walls,
14 x 22 x 25' (426.72 x 670.56 x 762 cm)

PAGE 166
Palagonia, 1990
Wax, gold leaf, wood, and mixed-media,
72 x 108 x 52" (182.88 x 274.32 x 132.08 cm)

PAGE 167
Palagonia (details), 1990
Wax, gold leaf, wood, and mixed-media,
72 x 108 x 52" (182.88 x 274.32 x 132.08 cm)

PAGES 168-69
Left to right:
St. Therese's Tambourine, 1990;
Putto and Bow, 1990;
Sphinx and Violin, 1990;
Buddha, 1990
From the *Palagonia* paper veils
Perforated C prints, each 63 x 50"
(160.02 x 127 cm)

PAGE 170
Buddha (detail), 1990
From the *Palagonia* paper veils
Perforated C print, 63 x 50" (160.02 x 127 cm)

PAGE 171
Buddha (detail), 1990
From the *Palagonia* paper veils
Perforated C print, 63 x 50" (160.02 x 127 cm)

PAGE 172
The artist in his studio with *Evening* in progress, 2008
Ink on pleated illusion (tulle curtains), painting for four walls, 14 x 22 x 25' (426.72 x 670.56 x 762 cm)

PAGES 176–77
Evening (detail), 2008
Ink, pleated illusion (tulle), painting for four walls, 14 x 22 x 25' (426.72 x 670.56 x 762 cm)

PAGE 178
Evening (detail), 2008
Ink, pleated illusion (tulle), painting for four walls, 14 x 22 x 25' (426.72 x 670.56 x 762 cm)

PAGE 179
Evening (detail), 2008
Ink, pleated illusion (tulle), painting for four walls, 14 x 22 x 25' (426.72 x 670.56 x 762 cm)

PAGE 180
Evening (detail), 2008
Ink, pleated illusion (tulle), painting for four walls, 14 x 22 x 25' (426.72 x 670.56 x 762 cm)

PAGE 181
Evening (detail), 2008
Ink, pleated illusion (tulle), painting for four walls, 14 x 22 x 25' (426.72 x 670.56 x 762 cm)

PAGES 182–83
Evening (detail), 2008
Ink, pleated illusion (tulle), painting for four walls, 14 x 22 x 25' (426.72 x 670.56 x 762 cm)

PAGES 184–85
Evening (detail), 2008
Ink, pleated illusion (tulle), painting for four walls, 14 x 22 x 25' (426.72 x 670.56 x 762 cm)

PAGES 186–87
Don Quijote Segunda Parte, 1987
Installation at The John and Mable Ringling Museum of Art, Sarasota, Florida, December 1989
Anodized cast aluminum, 92 x 75 x 40" (233.68 x 190.5 x 101.6 cm)
Collection The John and Mable Ringling Museum of Art

PAGE 188
Don Quijote Segunda Parte (details), 1987
Anodized cast aluminum, 92 x 75 x 40" (233.68 x 190.5 x 101.6 cm)
Collection Los Angeles Museum of Contemporary Art; private collection, Tampa; private collection, New York

PAGE 189
Don Quijote Segunda Parte, 1987
Anodized cast aluminum, 92 x 75 x 40" (233.68 x 190.5 x 101.6 cm)
Collection Guggenheim Museum

PAGES 190–91
The Maids of Honor, 1988
Ink, pleated neoprene, 123 x 197" (312.42 x 500.38 cm)
Private collection, New York

PAGE 192
Gardens for the Global City, 1991 (series)
Oil, wire mesh, velvet, 72 x 48" (182.88 x 121.92 cm)

PAGE 193
The Bath, 1987
From the *Five-Piece Suit* series
Oil, wire mesh, leaf, 72 x 48" (182.88 x 121.92 cm)

PAGE 194
Panels #1 & #3 (pentaptych), 1989
From the *Chinese Whispers* series
Oil, wire mesh, leaf, silver lamé, 60 x 40" (152.4 x 101.6 cm)
Collection Marie-Claude Stobart, Geneva

PAGE 195
Panels #4 & #5 (pentaptych), 1989
From the *Chinese Whispers* series
Oil, wire mesh, leaf, silver lamé, 60 x 40" (152.4 x 101.6 cm)
Collection Marie-Claude Stobart, Geneva

PAGE 196
Ghost Money (details), 1991
Collaboration with Nam June Paik
Mirrored Plexiglas vitrine filled with joss paper sculptures, steel, enamel, TV monitors, light bulbs, wood, wax, plaster, video, 88 x 104 x 44" (223.52 x 264.16 x 111.76 cm)

PAGE 197
Ghost Money, 1991
Collaboration with Nam June Paik
Mirrored Plexiglas vitrine filled with joss paper sculptures, steel, enamel, TV monitors, light bulbs, wood, wax, plaster, video, 88 x 104 x 44" (223.52 x 264.16 x 111.76 cm)

PAGES 198–99
The Fall, 2000
Ink, pleated neoprene, 10 x 17' (304.8 x 533 cm)
Private collection, Winterthur

PAGE 200
Where Each Is Both (details), 1994
Blown glass, steel, wood, 168 x 84 x 84" (426.72 x 213.36 x 213.36 cm)
Collection Guggenheim Museum

PAGE 201
Where Each Is Both, 1994
Blown glass, steel, wood, 168 x 84 x 84" (426.72 x 213.36 x 213.36 cm)
Collection Guggenheim Museum

BLACK SHADOWS WHITE GHOSTS

PAGE 208
Secret-Rrose Angel Out, 1980–83
From the *Tatting* series
Photostat, scrim, lights, embroidery, wood frame, 84 x 65 x 6" (213.36 x 165.1 x 15.24 cm)
Private collection, Vicenza

PAGE 209
Secret-Rrose Angel In, 1980–83
From the *Tatting* series
Photostat, scrim, lights, embroidery, wood frame, 84 x 65 x 6" (213.36 x 165.1 x 15.24 cm)

PAGES 212–13
The Black Paintings (Black Rolls), 1985–86
Ink, neoprene, painting for four walls, 14 x 22 x 28' (426.72 x 670.56 x 853.44 cm)
Collection Museum of Modern Art

PAGES 214–15
The Black Paintings (White Ghost), 1985–86
Ink, neoprene, painting for four walls, 14 x 22 x 28' (426.72 x 670.56 x 853.44 cm)
Collection Museum of Modern Art

PAGES 216–17
The Black Paintings (Dawn), 1985–86
Ink, neoprene, painting for four walls, 14 x 22 x 28' (426.72 x 670.56 x 853.44 cm)
Collection Museum of Modern Art

PAGE 218
The Black Paintings Cast (Diouf), 1986
Enamel, Kromekote paper, 93 x 42" (236.22 x 106.68 cm)
The Black Paintings Cast (Augusta Snow), 1986
Enamel, Kromekote paper, 93 x 42" (236.22 x 106.68 cm)

PAGE 219
The Black Paintings Cast (Deodatus Village), 1986
Enamel, Kromekote paper, 93 x 42" (236.22 x 106.68 cm)
The Black Paintings Cast (Stephanie Virtue Secret-Rose Diop), 1986
Enamel, Kromekote paper, 93 x 42" (236.22 x 106.68 cm)

PAGE 220
The Black Paintings: Cast of Characters Portfolio, 1988
Lithographs, 21 x 17" (53.34 x 43.18 cm)
Clockwise: *Stephanie Virtue Secret-Rose Diop, Missionary, Governor, Archibald Absalom Wellington*

PAGE 221
The Black Paintings: Cast of Characters Portfolio, 1988
Lithographs, 21 x 17" (53.34 x 43.18 cm)
Clockwise: *Augusta Snow, Edgar Alas Newport News, Queen, Valet*

PAGE 222
Master Frame, 1982
Enamel, wood, velvet, glass, 33 x 37" (83.82 x 93.98 cm)
Collection Rivka Saker and Uzi Zucker, Tel Aviv

PAGE 223
Santa Shoshanah, 1982
Enamel, ink, neoprene, lace, wood, 55 x 48" (139.7 x 121.92 cm)

PAGE 224
The Meta Bride
Concert at Holly Solomon Gallery, Easter Sunday, 1983
With David McDermott, Ula, Jeff Bruner, Diane Pernet, Sally Beers, Kristian Hoffman, and John Patrick

PAGE 225
The Meta Bride (She's Flesh and Blood Just Like Her Man), 1982
Enamel, pleated illusion (tulle), 9 x 8' (274.32 x 243.84 cm)
Collection Whitney Museum

PAGES 232–33
Before the Law Stands a Doorkeeper, 1984–85
Oil, chalk, barn wood, wire mesh, glass, window track, nails, metal chain, hinges; size variable, approx. 133 x 176" (337.82 x 447.04 cm)

BACK INSIDE ENDPAPER
The Encounter (part 2), 1987
Oil, wire mesh, velvet, 34 x 28" (86.36 x 71.12 cm)

BACK ENDPAPER
The Encounter (part 2) (detail), 1987

Selected Monographs and Catalogs

Cuperman, Pedro. *American Baroque*. New York: Holly Solomon Gallery, 1988.

Cuperman, Pedro, and Izhar Patkin. *Go East by Going West*. Milan: Carla Sozzani, 1990.

deAk, Edit, ed. *Izhar Patkin: The Black Paintings*. Essay by Herbert Muschamp. Kyoto: Kyoto Shoin International, 1989.

Izhar Patkin: Four-Piece Suit (Vierdelig Grijs). Essays by Marja Bloem, Pedro Cuperman, Donna De Salvo, Susan Martin, and Herbert Muschamp. Amsterdam: Stedelijk Museum, 1990.

Izhar Patkin: Host Culture: Homage to Arie Aroch. Essays by Daniel Ben-Simon and Mordechai Omer. Tel Aviv: Tel Aviv Museum of Art, 2003.

Izhar Patkin: Icons. Essay by Donald Kuspit. New York: Holly Solomon Gallery, 1992.

Izhar Patkin: Palagonia. Essays by Edit deAk, Izhar Patkin, and Paola Serra Zanetti. Florence: M Galleria d'arte, 1989.

Izhar Patkin: The Perfect Existence in the Rose Garden. Essay by Pedro Cuperman. San Francisco: Rena Bransten Gallery, 1988.

Judenporzellan. Essay by Mark Daniel Cohen. Tefen: Open Museum, 2008.

Patkin, Izhar. *Mistresses and Wives, Husbands and Other Lives*. Essay by Jean Nathan. New York: Malo, 1998.

Patkin, Izhar, and Agha Shahid Ali. *The Veil Suite*. Conversation with Ariana Reines. San Francisco: Artspace Books, 2007.

Acknowledgments

This show and catalog would not have been possible without the generous support of BFAMI / British Friends of the Art Museums of Israel; Marie-Claude Stobart, Blancpain Art Contemporain; Suzy and Elihu Rose; Wendy Fisher; Dafna Schmerin; Anne Marie MacDonald; Melissa and Robert Soros; Ilana and Martin Moshal; Sandy Tabatznik; Irit Strauss; Artis; and Rivka Saker and Uzi Zucker. Thanks to Ellen and Harvey Sanders, and Thomas Rom. Very special thanks to Carmel Mulvany and Lawrence Deurloo, for their endless support and time. We are also grateful to the individuals who lent works to the exhibition.

We were fortunate to have a rich array of writers contribute stimulating essays to the catalog: David Ross, Itamar Levy, Sefi Rachlevsky, Shlomzion Kenan, and Shimon Adaf. We are also very grateful to Michael Stout at the Herbert Muschamp Estate and to Agha Iqbal Ali at the Agha Shahid Ali Literary Estate.

We extend special thanks to Kristin Johnson for her graceful and intelligent book design. We are also grateful to Kfir Malka for print production and for the Hebrew graphics, to Orna Yehudaioff for editing the texts in Hebrew and to Einat Adi for translations, and to our English editors, Kristin Jones and Ariana Reines.

We offer special thanks to the team that brought the glass sculpture to life, led by Françoise Guichon at the Centre International de Recherche sur le Verre et les Arts Plastiques (CIRVA): Pierre Hessmann, Christelle Notelet, David Veis, Matteo Gonet, Raphaël Véloso, Yann Oulevay, Arnauld le Calvé, Nuno Galvao de Almeida, Olivier Fonderflick, Samuel Sauques, Roberto Avila, Fernando Torre, Stéphane Pelletier, Jean Buchmuller, Huguette Epinat, and Isabelle Reiher.

We would also like to express our appreciation to the team that produced the porcelain works at the legendary Manufacture nationale de Sèvres: David Cameo, René-Jacques Mayer, Valérie Jonca, Bruno Ecault, Michel Maillot, Dominqie Combot, Nadine Préteux, Joëlle Secly, François Combot, and Ombeline d'Arche.

Special thanks to Jacob Lee for his help and dedication in engineering the unique printing technology for the veil paintings.

We owe very special thanks to Stef Wertheimer and Lynn Holstein for their unceasing collaboration with The Open Museum, Tefen Industrial Park, and to Shuli Kislev, acting director of the Tel Aviv Museum of Art.

Thank you to the assistants to the curator at The Open Museum, Dana Gross and Yasimín Kunz, to The Open Museum's registrar, Rachel Lazar, and to Anat Danon-Sivan, associate curator at the Tel Aviv Museum. We also thank the team at the Tel Aviv Museum: Dina Papo, director of public relations; Orit Aderet, the museum's spokesperson; Yael Shavit at Tikshoret Public Relations; Pnina Karpin, administrative coordinator; the registrars Shraga Edelsburg, Alisa Friedman-Padovano, Shoshana Frankel, and Hadar Oren; the conservators Dr. Doron J. Lurie, Maya Dresner, Hasia Rimon, Noga Schusterman, and Klara Karlova; Yaakov Nahum, maintenance; and the lighting team of Naor Agayan, Lior Gaba, Asaf Menachem, and Haim Beracha.

Special thanks for the installation production to Tucan Ltd. at the Tel Aviv Museum; to Sami Sisso and Issac Elmakias at The Open Museum, Tefen; and to Dante Birch, John McAlister, Richard Criddle, Paulette Wein, and Art McConnell at MASS MoCA.

Thank you to the people who helped with the production of the videos that accompany this show: Caetano Veloso, Jaques Morelenbaum, David Horowitz, Kathy Brew and Roberto Guerra, Jacki Lyden, Fred Wasser, Monique Gardenberg, Fernando Grostein Andrade, Paula Lavigne, Yael Steiner, John Solomon, Thorbjorn Hansson, Ivan Orkeny, Susan Martin, Rona Kenan and Noam Enbar.

And finally, we extend our deepest gratitude to the artist, Izhar Patkin, for allowing us the privilege of entering into his rich and fascinating world.

Ellen Ginton
Ruthi Ofek
Joseph Thompson

About the Poets

Agha Shahid Ali (1949-2001), who began collaborating with Izhar Patkin in 1999 on the artist's veil rooms, was an American poet of Kashmiri ancestry and upbringing. He wrote his last poem, "The Veiled Suite," for one of Patkin's rooms, and it provided the title for a posthumously published anthology of his poetry. Ali's poetry collections also include *The Half-Inch Himalayas, A Nostalgist's Map of America, The Country Without a Post Office, Rooms Are Never Finished* (finalist for the National Book Award, 2001), and *Call Me Ishmael Tonight,* a selection of English *ghazals.* Ali was also a translator of the work of Faiz Ahmed Faiz (*The Rebel's Silhouette: Selected Poems*) and an editor (*Ravishing DisUnities: Real Ghazals in English*). He was widely credited with helping to popularize the *ghazal* form in the United States.

Mahmoud Darwish (1941–2008) was a Palestinian poet and author and was regarded as the Palestinian national poet.

Faiz Ahmad Faiz (1911–1984) was one of the most influential poets of the Urdu language.

About the Authors

Shimon Adaf has published three poetry books and five novels.

Ellen Ginton is senior curator at Tel Aviv Museum of Art.

Shlomzion Kenan is a literary critic and scholar. She currently hosts a radio show on IDF radio.

Itamar Levy is a psychoanalyst and an art critic.

Herbert Muschamp (1947-2007) was an American architecture critic.

Ruthi Ofek is chief curator at The Open Museums, Israel.

Sefi Rachlevsky is an author, a scholar of Jewish theology, and a *Ha'aretz* columnist.

David A. Ross, former director of SFMOMA and the Whitney Museum of American Art, is chair of the MFA Art Practice program at the School of Visual Arts in New York City.

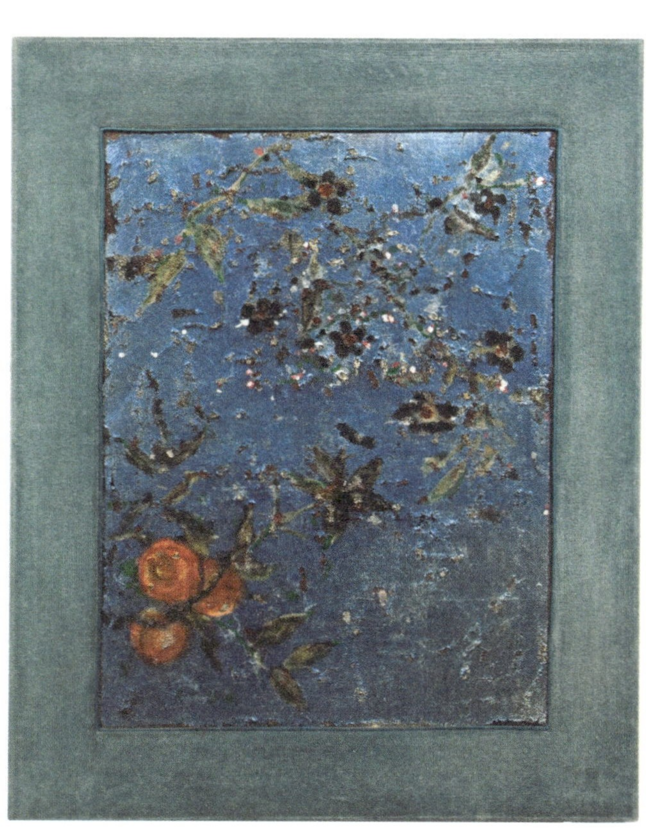

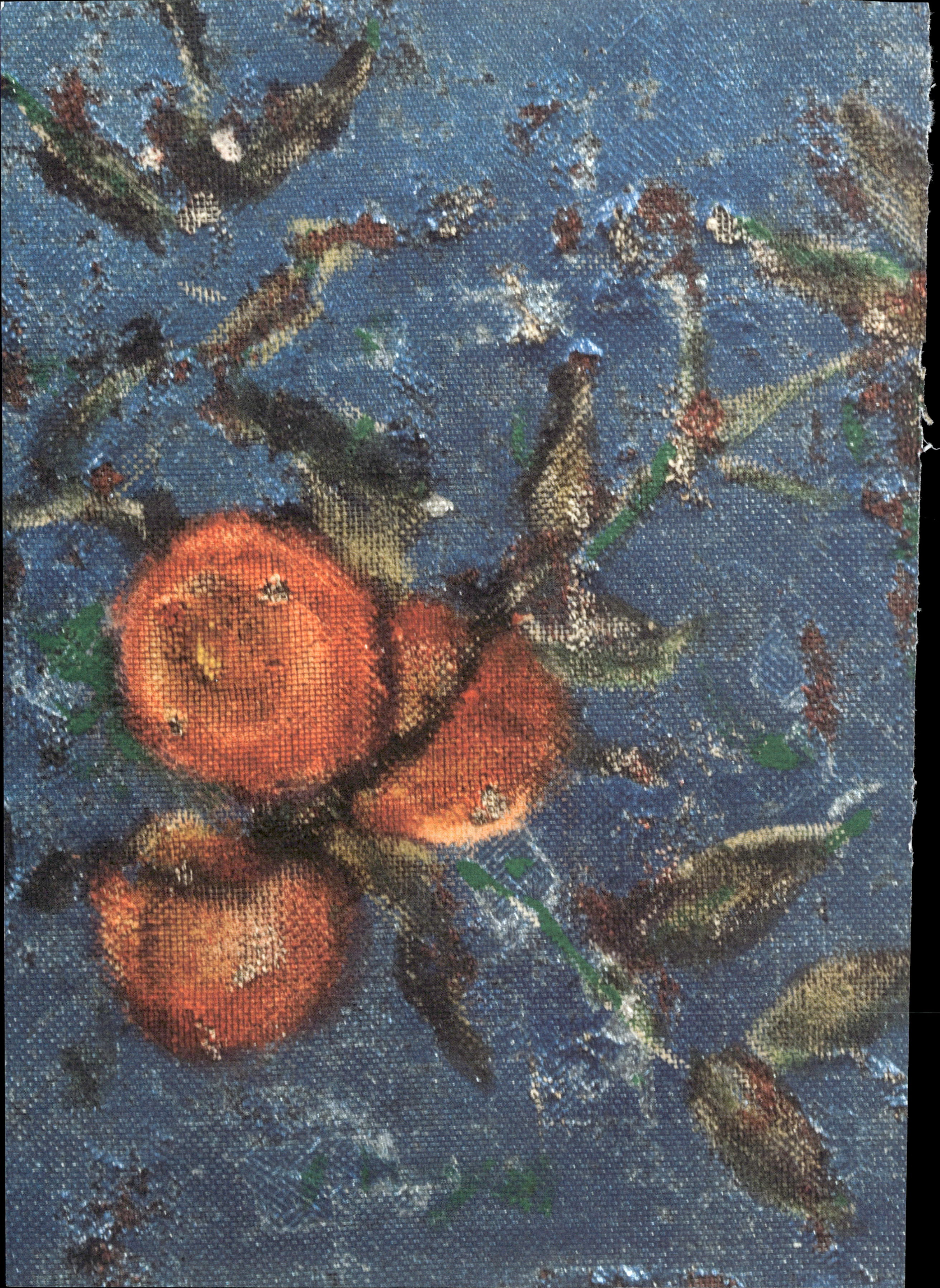